INSHORE CRAFT

Inshore Craft

Traditional Working Vessels of the British Isles

Consultant Editor: Dr Basil Greenhill
Editor: Julian Mannering

Seaforth PUBLISHING

*Half title illustration: Deal sprat boat
(NMM, Oke, neg no PAI7507)*

*Frontispiece: Scottish fishing craft off Great
Yarmouth (NMM, neg no P75443)*

Copyright © Chatham Publishing 1997

This edition first published in Great Britain
2013 by Seaforth Publishing,
Pen & Sword Books Ltd,
47 Church Street,
Barnsley S70 2AS
First published under the title
The Chatham Directory of Inshore Craft in 1997

British Library Cataloguing in Publication Data
A catalogue record for this book is available
from the British Library

ISBN 978-1-84832-167-0

Typeset and designed by Tony Hart
Printed in China through Printworks International Ltd.

Editor

JULIAN MANNERING

Consultant Editor

DR BASIL GREENHILL

Contributors

ALISON GRANT
North Devon salmon boat

DR BASIL GREENHILL
Boats and Boatmen and their Study
Barges of Devon and Cornwall,
Clovelly picarooner
Peggy of Castletown

MICHAEL MCCAUGHAN
Planked craft of Ireland

DAVID R MACGREGOR
Emsworth oyster dredger

ADRIAN OSLER
Craft of Scotland

TONY PAWLYN
Fishing craft of Devon and
Cornwall

OWAIN ROBERTS
Craft of Wales

ROBERT SIMPER
Craft of the Thames Estuary and
Wash, and the South Coast

MICHAEL STAMMERS
Craft of Northwest England

PETER STUCKEY
Bristol Channel pilot cutters

DESMOND TOAL
Irish curraghs

GLORIA WILSON
Craft of Northeast England

Contents

Introduction and Acknowledgments

AT THE beginning of this century our coasts and ports were the home of an extraordinary array of craft from Achill yawls to zulus, as diverse in form, function and name as the Parrett flatner and the Brixham mumble-bee: they are no longer. The traditional fishing boats have all but disappeared; the coastal craft which traded under sail have long ago been superseded by the lorry, the container and the motor ship; and the thousands among our population who gained a living from the sea, precarious as it was, have been succeeded by descendants most of whom work on land. We are no longer a maritime nation in the strictest sense, but an abiding interest in the lost world of traditional working craft remains and, indeed, is growing.

The intention of this book is to list, define and describe, and illustrate those distinct types which once fished and traded in home waters; its structure as a gazetteer is self evident. There have, of course, been a number of notable predecessors. Edgar J March's *Inshore Craft of Britain in the Days of Sail and Oar* and Eric McKee's *Working Boats of Britain* particularly stand out but they are by no means inclusive of the huge range of types – McKee's work was not intended to be so, of course – and while it would be presumptuous to pretend that this work is 'all-inclusive' it is hoped that it contains the majority of identifiable types.

The criteria for inclusion were easy enough to establish though more difficult to apply; we have tried to include all those craft which were built for a particular task in a particular locality or region, during an era when fishing and trading under sail and oar were at their zenith. This is the period when the country's population was growing fast with industrialisation and when there was an ever increasing need for food which fish went a long way to meet; and when that industrialisation, in tandem with the expansion of empire, led to a huge increase in coastal trade. This really is the period roughly 1820 to 1920. By the latter date the motor was changing the face of our coasts and country. So the English herring buss is excluded for being too early: the many coastal schooners, ketches and barquentines left out because they were not built for any particular locality – though they were often easily recognisable as having come from a particular yard.

The initial inspiration for the book came from sifting through the wonderful collection of plans and photographs at the National Maritime Museum at Greenwich. In the 1930s The Society for Nautical Research had the foresight to commission the recording of our indigenous craft. Philip Oke travelled the country taking off lines of craft and models and measuring and reconstructing sail plans. Oliver Hill took hundreds of photographs of the same. Indeed, he continued to do so throughout his life and until as late as the 1960s. By this time a great number of the craft were in a poor state and many of the photographs in this book tell the story of sad decline. William Maxwell-Blake, a naval architect who amongst other activities involved himself with the design of small yachts, also recorded a number of vessels which he then drew up and described in *Yachting Monthly*, also in the 1930s. Many of the lines plans which have been included have appeared before in diverse publications, but not before at a scale at which so much of the detail can be as-

similated. Many of the Oliver Hill photographs have not seen the light of day before, and certainly this is the first time that so many illustrations of all these craft have been assembled together. The accompanying texts are intended to introduce the types – they are not definitive texts – and point the reader to further sources. In that sense this is a first step book for those with a real enthusiasm who may be well acquainted – even highly knowledgeable – with one or more types but who want the broader picture in a single volume.

While we may mourn the passing of the age of sail and oar we can enjoy our present prosperity to look back on the men and the boats of a harder world and learn more about their skills and their tools. The accurate restoration of the few remaining craft, the building and sailing of authentic replicas, the development of maritime museums, and the increase of interest in local history will all further our knowledge. In Ireland, for instance, their regional craft are just now being researched by local enthusiasts with the backing of the French traditional boat magazine *Chasse Marée*. Though most of the vessels and the men who sailed them have now disappeared there is still much we can learn. We hope that this book will encourage and further promote the enthusiasm.

Acknowledgments

This book would not have been possible without the help of a large number of people whom the publishers would like to thank. First, Basil Greenhill and all the contributors applied themselves with an enthusiasm which knew no bounds and, on top of their textural responsibilities, helped with the sorting of the illustrations and filled many gaps from their own collections. The great majority of the illustration comes from the archives of the National Maritime Museum, particularly the Coastal Craft Collection and the Oliver Hill Collection, and thanks are due to a number of staff members there. Pieter van de Merwe quickly recognised the potential of the project and lent encouragement during the early stages. David Hodge was unfailingly helpful with the picture research and pointed me to many corners of the Museum's collection which were, indeed, dark in their obscurity. Chris Gray, Head of Picture Research, ensured that all the material we needed could be made available and David Taylor lent every assistance to ensure that the illustrations were processed when they were needed.

Many others offered great support in the search and reproduction of pictures. Frances Matheson kindly lent the Maxwell-Blake drawings so that they could be copied for publication. True's Yard, King's Lynn, searched through their archives for what are rare images of Wash smacks; the Ulster Folk and Transport Museum lent generously from their collections; and Roger Hadley of the Royal Exchange Art Gallery provided the dust jacket painting. Many other individuals and museums, credited throughout the book, were all, unfailingly, helpful and efficient. My thanks to them all.

JULIAN MANNERING
October 1997

Boats and Boatmen and their Study

OFTEN IN pre-industrial societies those who, for one reason or another, cannot hold their own on land are pushed by economic and social forces to the sea. Here, on the marginal land of the coast, not fertile enough to prosper by farming alone, the more enterprising take to seafaring in order to survive. Sometimes the results are brilliantly successful, as with the Scandinavians during their Iron Age – the Viking period. In New England and Atlantic Canada deep sea fishing was the genesis of settlement and, in due course, seafaring proved, for a while, a highly prosperous and prestigious occupation for the lucky, the entrepreneurially venturesome, and the hard-working.

But more often the men of the sea were despised by the more prosperous people of the land and the two groups became alienated, suspicious and fearful of one another. The seafaring places were often physically separated from the nucleus of the farming communities which were perhaps around the parish churches. You can see this clearly today in a number of places in Britain. Appledore in north Devon, although enormously changed since the days before the mid-twentieth century when it was the last home of merchant schooners in Britain, is still quite distinct from its former parent parish, the settlement of Northam. Lyme Regis has its former seafaring settlement around the rootes of the Cobh, quite separate from the old town. Sidmouth had its 'lower town' of fishermen, so well

described by Stephen Reynolds, notably in his book *A Poor Man's House*. In Staithes in north Yorkshire one can today feel strongly the hardness and poverty of the life in these small coastal communities in earlier periods.

As the late T C Lethbridge, the archaeologist, pointed out in his book *Boats and Boatmen* agricultural and seafaring communities, in the days when people earned their living with sailing boats, really faced opposite ways. They stood back to back rather than face to face, the one regarding the sea, the other the land. Relatively few people moved into fishing villages. These communities had a highly specialised way of life and you had to be born to it to cope with it. A man had to marry a woman who knew the life and who could be his true partner in it if they were to survive. Even the class structures of the two types of community tended to be different.

The communities that prospered were usually on the shores of reasonably deep and sheltered water which enabled them to enter the carrying trade – transporting cargoes, often between ports in other countries, coastwise and across deep water. In due course, this kind of trade could result in the slow growth of capital, and eventually to real prosperity. A well documented case of this kind of development took place in the Åland Islands of Finland where, in the course of little more than a century, marginal farmers and inshore fishermen were transformed through merchant shipping (and in favourable political circumstance) into a highly successful economic community. Successful merchant seamen could and did become very prosperous, some very rich indeed.

But such opportunity rarely came the way of most fishermen and boatmen. Unlike the farmers and the merchant seamen of the coastal communities, the fishermen had almost no chance of building up capital and they were destined to a very hard, poor life with no escape. It was in the big fishing ports, employing large sailing vessels – Brixham, Hull, Grimsby in Britain; Lunenburg in Nova Scotia; and Gloucester in Massachusetts – that a man might find opportunity to break out of poverty. Stephen Reynolds, writing of the beach fishermen of Sidmouth in Devon with whom he lived and worked, described the reality of the life in the early twentieth century before the first motors became available. He wrote of what poverty and disease and hunger meant in an existence of watching and waiting for fish, which, when at last they came, did so often enough in such numbers that the prices to the fishermen could become almost derisory. Of one night's fishing he wrote:

> . . . let me describe . . . the last night I was herring drifting . . .
> There was no wind. We had to row ten miles to the ground with
> heavy, warped sweeps that twisted one's wrist at every stroke . . .
> For three hours we rocked at the sweeps, crawling to the ground . . .
> Just before dark we shot out nets, put on oilskins against the cold,
> ate thick sandwiches, drank oily tea heated up over a paraffin flare,

Stephen Reynolds photographed (foreground) with fishermen and their lugger drawn up on the beach at Sidmouth. Reynolds, who had a comfortable upbringing, moved to Sidmouth as a young man before the First World War and there lived among the fishermen and their families and recorded his experiences in *A Poor Man's House* and *Alongshore*. His was an early interest from the outside in the more hermetic world of fishing communities. *(Basil Greenhill Collection)*

looked at the nets, and settled down for an hour's sleep. But we didn't catch off. It was too cold . . . The night wore on. We hauled in our nets, picked out a thousand or so of herrings, and shot again. We finished our food and our tea, squatted down, and with coats over our heads we tried very hard to sleep. All our old clothes were damp; the bowsheets on which we lay, were soaking with water and fish slime, and underneath them some dirty bilge water, which we had had no time to clean out, stank like drains. I jammed myself under the cutty, in the warm; but oilskins over damp clothes, making one itch like forty thousand fleas, turned me out again into the cold. We all sat up, shivering and dithering, while the moon, muffled in clouds, spread a dull cold light over the water. One thought of feather beds, of clean warm night clothes, and, curiously enough, not of hot grub but of cooling drinks.

The early hours were a long-drawn nightmare of discomforts. About three o'clock we started hauling in for another thousand of fish, and by four o'clock we were ready to take the ebb tide homeward. There was nothing to eat aboard, nothing to drink, and very little tobacco. We had drifted a dozen miles from home and had scarcely wind enough to fill the sail. We took perforce to the sweeps. The boat had no life in her . . . Until nearly eight in the morning we rocked at the sweeps. Finally, as if to mock us, after rowing all that way, a breeze sprang up from the south-east, and we sailed the short mile home.'

We have to allow for the fact that Reynolds was a writer and not born to the life. His companions would have been far less sensitive to the hardships than he was, and they certainly would not have thought of feather beds. Nevertheless, this is a fine picture to convey the realities of the life to a modern reader.

The men who sailed working boats had to do everything they possibly could in fitting out, maintaining and repairing their boats themselves. Their gear had to be simple and cheap; their boats had to be roomy and stable and able to look after themselves while the crew fished, or the pilot was away in a ship, or the men simply recovered from the strain of a period of bad weather or hard work. Many boats, built of poor timber, held together only because so much timber went into them that extensive rot was not fatal. To appreciate a boat one must be aware of the factors that gave rise to her building, the timber available, the general environment, the building traditions of the society which produced her and, above all, the purpose for which she was built and the environment in which she operated.

The basic question to ask about a working boat is, 'Is she fitted for her purpose in relation to broad local circumstances?'. You can judge a boat only in the light of the requirements for which she was built and the resources of the society that built her. Boats should never be judged by a comparison with other boats built for different purposes, of different materials, in different circumstances and in different societies. A working boat's shape, as McKee has so clearly shown, is governed by her purpose, the circumstances in which she will operate, and the materials and resources available for her construction. For operation from a harbour offering deep water, at least on the tide, up to wharves or moorings, a boat can be of deep draft with a marked deadrise, even though she may have to rest on legs on the

ebb. Such vessels tend to be suitable, within the limits of size, for operation in deep water and wild weather, dragging trawls or dredging for shellfish. At extremes of size of this type of boat were the big sailing trawlers of Plymouth and Brixham, the North Sea and the Irish Sea ports, and the oyster dredgers of Emsworth in Hampshire in the biggest class; and at the other extreme the oystermen of the Fal in Cornwall which represented the smallest class.

Some of the latter boats in the 1940s and '50s were still vessels which had been built for the general inshore fisheries of Cornwall, operating from small tidal harbours often with granite breakwaters and originally rigged with a dipping lug and a mizzen. Also rigged in this way, but different in detail of their rigging, were the Beer luggers operating in the same kind of inshore fishery but from the open beaches of south Devon where they had frequently to be brought ashore after use. They were of necessity of working environment, beamy, relatively shallow, clinker built boats with little rise of floor, transom sterned and very roomy to carry drift nets, able to be pulled as well as sailed as the extract from Reynolds' account of fishing with a boat of this type has shown. While writing this introduction I visited Beer, still a lively centre of a beach fishery, and was interested to find among the powerful motor vessels (which show their local ancestry in their hull form) a reconstruction of a 17ft lugger, complete with iron work and other details of early twentieth-century form.

Very many complex factors played their part in determining what McKee called 'boatshape' and these included local cultural traditions. The entries in this Directory show the extent and great variety of shapes which developed in Britain. McKee deals exhaustively with the matter of hull form, with numerous drawings and examples, especially in Chapters 6 and 7 of *Working Boats of Britain*.

Meanwhile, north European influence is very clear in some of the boats of northern Scotland, though international cross fertilisation otherwise appears rarely. Similar problems, however, tend to produce similar solutions. The sheltered shallow waters of the Fleet and Poole Harbour in Dorset call for shallow draft, flat bottoms, stability and load carrying capacity. These conditions have produced the Fleet trow, with these marked characteristics. Similar conditions on the southern coast of the Swedish island of Gotland have lead to the development of the *flatäska*, a very similar type, but there is most unlikely to have been any cultural exchange.

The complexity and variety of British boat types has produced one of Europe's richest fields for their study. Though some boat forms, like the coble, with her bold sheer, sharp bows and flat floored stern with transom, have become associated with a long stretch of coastline, no type has become nationally – much less internationally – ascendant in the same way that the long, lean, sharp bowed, Cape Islander/Jonesporter boats, with their (nowadays) broad sterns and flat floors aft over a deep skeg, have established themselves on the northeast coast of North America all the way from Connecticut down east to Prince Edward Island and the Magdalenes. These boats bear some resemblance to cobles in form. They represent perhaps the most successful regional working boat type ever developed anywhere.

Similar conditions can produce similar solutions despite wide cultural differences. Two types of craft of remarkable similarity evolved in the shallow, sheltered waters of the Fleet in southern England and along the coast of Gotland in Sweden: the Fleet trow photographed here at Park Wall on the Fleet (above) and the Swedish *flatäska* seen here at Kovik, Gotland (left). Both photographs were taken in 1995 and demonstrate how a few vernacular types have retained their usefullness even at the end of this century. *(Basil Greenhill Collection)*

Until comparatively recently most boats have been the products, not of an organised industry with full time craftsmen specialised in their trades, but of the work, perhaps part-time work, of men who had learned local building traditions as part of their preparation for life. It was in such circumstances that the oldest elements in local traditions lasted longest.

A working boat showed the scars and bruises of a hard life in a community which we would now consider to be economically and socially deprived. She was dirty. She smelled of Stockholm tar, fish and linseed oil. This is a very long way from sailing for pleasure even in replicas or restored working boats, and there is an unbridgable gulf between the life around working boats before the introduction of power and sailing for recreation as it is done now. It is the case, as the annual Wooden Boat Show at Greenwich clearly shows, that very expensive 'reconstructions' of working boats have become ever shinier and glossier and quite remote in appearance and feeling from the boats by which hard men scraped a living by labour at the beginning of this century.

The boat as man's tool and toy has had a very special significance in many societies. She has been extremely important in the ascent of man and, occasionally, as with the Vikings in Europe and the Polynesians in the Pacific, boats have represented not only the supreme technical achievement of a society, but perhaps its principal aesthetic and, in its ownership and manning, an important social achievement as well. Not only have boats been essential to mankind's encounter with water, especially with the sea, but they have also been so fundamental that, despite the low status in many societies of their professional users and the alienation of these men from their fellows, boats have acquired aesthetic, religious and sexual significance beyond their great utilitarian importance. Perhaps an extreme example of this may be seen in the beautiful inshore Oseberg ship of around AD 820 excavated in southern Norway and now on display at Bygdøy, Oslo. She is elaborately decorated and her contents comprise the greatest single find of Viking art.

The boat on which the boatman was dependant for his very life and livelihood could acquire very special significance. In Swedish, as Dr David Papp the Swedish ethnographer pointed out in an oral communication, a boat could be referred to simply by her name 'Swan', in Swedish 'Svan'. But sometimes she would be referred to as 'Svanen' (the swan) or 'Svanan' (the female swan). This terminology indicated the special relationship of the speaker to the boat or vessel, and its use revealed that she was thought of, at least subconsciously, as animate, perhaps almost as a human companion.

It is not perhaps surprising, therefore, that boats became the objects of serious attention at quite an early date in the evolution of ethnographic studies in Europe. This process began in Scandinavia, and especially in Norway. Here, the relics of the past could be seen by ordinary people to be directly relevant to the contemporary society of the early twentieth century. Norway was a poor country, its wealth, such as it was, could be seen to be drawn largely from the sea, and, especially in the north, whole regions were dependant on open boat fishing conducted from isolated communities. Bernhard Faerøyvik was born into a farming and fishing family in western Norway and grew up in an economy dominated by oar and sail. A teacher by profession, he recognised in the early 1920s that, with the introduction of cheap reliable motors, the world of the fishing communities would rapidly change, as would their boats, and that the study of the surviving local boats could be part of the broader movement then developing to investigate and record rural culture in Norway. Boats could tell something of the origins of the 'national heritage', to use a modern term. At his death in 1950 Faerøyvik left a magnificent, if regionally uneven, collection of drawings, notes and photographs, together with actual boats now on display in museums, notably at Bygdøy near Oslo. His work set a standard which has never been bettered and which had great influence on subsequent developments in a number of countries. Moreover, the element of nationalism which was in his work has tended to be a feature of ethnographic and archeological studies of boats ever since. Faerøyvik's work has not been fully published in English but is available in an abbreviated form in *Inshore Craft of Norway*.

Faerøyvik identified a field of study which was to be tilled by many other Scandinavians. To mention one or two, Professor Arne Emil Christensen in Norway has published many books and papers, some in English, including the excellent little study *Boats of the North*. Albert Eskeröd in Sweden, and David Papp and Birger Törnroos in Åland, Finland, all writing in Swedish, have published excellent accounts of indigenous boats. Jerzy Litwin, publishing in Polish, is an outstanding exponent of late twentieth-century study and recording of working boats.

There was pioneering work in Britain in the early twentieth century which tended to be international in its scope rather than concentrating on British boats. Waterington-Smyth's *Mast and Sail in Europe and Asia* was first published in 1906. Sir Alan Moore's *Last Days of Mast and Sail – An Essay in Nautical Comparative Anatomy*, concerned mainly with the rigging of small craft, is as informative as it is delightful. The outstanding work of James Hornell, which was to culminate in the compilation *Water Transport*, was well under way with publications, now collectors' pieces, in Calcutta before the First World War.

In the 1930s the Society for Nautical Research in Britain, partly at least as the result of the enthusiasm and work of the late Commander H Oliver Hill RN, established a Coastal and River Craft Subcommittee to encourage Scandinavian-type recording of indigenous craft in this country. A grant from the Pilgrim Trust made possible the employment of the late Philip Oke who, Oliver Hill told me, toured the coasts of Britain on a motorcycle (he was eventually killed in a motorcycle accident) measuring and drawing boats and builders' models and talking with the men who handled the boats.

But the wide interest in the material artifacts of earlier cultures, so evident at the end of the twentieth century, is a luxury resulting from the development of the most prosperous societies, in western Europe and North America, that the world has ever known. In the 1940s and '50s Oliver Hill and I found it impossible to revive interest in the work of the Coastal and River Craft Subcommittee, or to get Oke's work published comprehensively. This situation gradually changed. The late Edgar March's *Spritsail Barges of the Thames and Medway*, *Sailing Drifters* and *Sailing Trawlers* all became in time established classics. Gradually, more books and papers began to be published and the study of boats and boatmen, the construction of boats, their handling and operation and the economic and social backgrounds of their operation became academically respectable and more common. Eric McKee in his great *Working Boats of Britain*,

This Cape Islander/Jonesporter fishing boat, *Sea Foam*, was photographed off Maine in 1989. Seen here tending lobster traps, she represents one of the most successful fishing types to have evolved into the diesel age. *(Basil Greenhill Collection)*

the culmination of a life's work, described many types of sailing and oared craft to be found around the coasts and in the rivers of Britain but the book is not a catalogue of British small craft. It begins with an analysis of the factors that determine the shape of a boat and of how these factors influence boat builders and result in great variations in design. The second part of the book deals with the techniques of boatbuilding and includes a survey of distribution patterns. McKee's work set new standards internationally in the study of inshore and river craft and their backgrounds. Such a landmark was it that in this field of study in Britain work can virtually be divided into pre-McKee and post-McKee periods. McKee's book is essential reading for anyone whose interest in British working boats extends beyond the superficial.

Meanwhile, developments were taking place in North America which were to have a profound effect on British interest in indigenous craft in the last decades of the twentieth century. Howard I

Chappelle, a naval architecture historian, recorded in various books and articles the results of assiduous travel up and down the east coast of the North American continent from Florida to Newfoundland. He had a great flair for producing naval architect's drawings which were both attractive and accurate, and, working very fast, he was enormously productive. Moreover, the east coast of North America has a great variety of attractive small boats, many of which are suitable for leisure use, and even for development into forms which lend themselves to construction with modern materials. By a great fluke of good fortune Chappelle was appointed Keeper of the National Watercraft Collection in what was then the Museum of History and Technology, now the National Museum of American History, part of the Smithsonian Institution in Washington DC. He used his position, quite correctly, to present the history of naval architecture and particularly the study of eastern American working boats. He can be criticised for his concentration, as quite distinct from McKee, on the boats themselves, largely ignoring their geomorphalogical, climatic and economic environments, and the societies from which they emerged. Most of Chappelle's output was the result of original field work. Where it was not he often did not indicate his sources and he was inclined to decorate his drawings with charming detail for which there was not always authority. But to a degree it was these decorations which made the drawings very at-

The working lives of some fishing boat types were extended by the adoption of the engine for auxiliary power. This Selsey crabber, *Gwendolen* LI49, was photographed at Littlehampton in 1944. She still has all her gear which is in good working order, but just visible amidships is the engine casing. Types with broad beam and plenty of buoyancy aft were most suited to the installation of motors. *(NMM, Oliver Hill Collection, neg no P75411)*

tractive and they played their part in converting many a layman into a boat buff, or something more serious. At the end of his working life Chappelle confounded the critics by producing *American Fishing Schooners*, his most scholarly and probably his best work which contains 371 pages of notes and source material in a book of 683 pages and has become the standard work on the subject. It is unlikely ever to be improved on.

I knew Howard Chappelle well in the 1950s and '60s. He was intolerant then of some aspects of American, as we might now say Western, life, as they were developing at the period. But he would have been surprised at the extent to which his work was taken up on the grounds that it provided an escape from such developments. His St Paul was John Gardner, a practical boat builder who in the 1960s began writing for a regional monthly trade newspaper called *The Maine Coast Fisherman*, later *The National Fisherman*, and Gardner became the high priest of a kind of revivalist movement of interest in wooden boat building generally, and the construction of replicas of American working boats of the early years of this century in particular. John Gardner's work in *The National Fisherman* was aided by such factors as the studiously accurate and very attractive drawings of Sam Manning, and it really took off. A minor industry of building and promoting wooden boats, selling wooden boats and writing about wooden boats developed, centred initially in the State of Maine.

This movement developed to a point at which it could support the American journal *WoodenBoat*, now with a circulation of over 100,000 copies an issue. Started by Jon Wilson as something of a personal crusade, *WoodenBoat* blossomed into an influential commercial success. Interest in indigenous craft began to change its nature. Jon Wilson told me in the early 1980s that the success of *WoodenBoat* grew from a market of readers many of whom would never own one.

What had begun in Europe as a very specialised ethnographic study became in North America something of a cult with at times social and almost religious overtones. In a less extreme form this cult approach spread to Britain and Europe in the 1980s and early '90s, and interest in varying degrees of seriousness in 'classic boats' is now widespread internationally. But this book is in the ethnographic tradition. It deals with British boats and often their physical, social and economic backgrounds. It is broadly of the school of McKee and may be regarded as a companion volume to *Working Boats of Britain* providing descriptions of many boats that McKee was unable to cover.

It may also possibly be the last book in the old ethnographic tradition. An essential part of this study was, of course, the gathering and assessment of the recollections and oral traditions of the men who worked with the boats as well as the boats themselves, and almost none of the former and few of the latter now survive. The future development of this study will probably rest with, for example, the serious experimental study of the handling and abilities of the old working boats, and particularly their rigs and sails, using reconstructions or rebuilt original boats. First-class work of this kind has already been done, notably in Denmark and Sweden with the single square sail, and in Britain with the dipping lug.

At the end of the twentieth century it is very important to remember that the working boat is not a shining product of high class

The fate of thousands of local craft was one of simple, slow decay after a life of uneventful work and many of the photographs taken by Oliver Hill, as the era of sail and oar drew to a close, depict vessels in this sort of condition. This deck view of a Polperro gaffer, well past her working days, was taken in September 1935. *(NMM, Oliver Hill Collection, neg no P74335)*

craftsmanship, and certainly not a fetish, but an ordinary job built as cheaply as possibly for her work, maintained by men who were dependant on her for livelihood and living, as well as they could afford the time and skill to do so. She was the tool of societies incredibly poor by the standards which we enjoy on the eve of the second millennium and the hardships involved in getting a living with her are almost unimaginable now. Unless the economy was a rapidly expanding one (as happened at times in the history of North America) it was for most of its members a life, whether they recognised it or not, without hope. There was nothing romantic or morally absolutely good about it.

The boatmen and his family were sustained in their situation because people all around them were in the same situation and they conceived of nothing else. Prosperity for them was unattainable, riches impossibly remote. In the history of getting a living on the water this is how most boatmen have lived. This is the gulf between sailing for a living and sailing for pleasure. He who sails for a living ceases, often only to die.

Scotland

TOPOGRAPHICALLY, the sea margins of Scotland exhibit a wide range of coastal features – from tombola sandspits to the highest sea cliffs in Britain – but they are constrained by an underlying geology which is largely confined to older strata, the hard rocks of which break through with forbidding frequency. Although smaller in land area than 'mainland' England and Wales, Scotland has a lengthy and often convoluted coastline, a position which lies more directly in the path of Atlantic cyclones, and northern extremities which create a barrier to the oceanic tidal streams. All these factors combined in the past to produce operating conditions

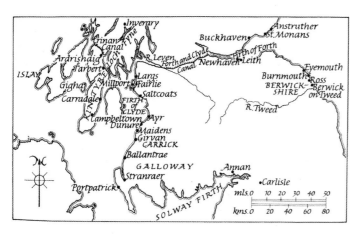

for coastal working craft which at least equalled, and often exceeded, the demands placed on boats and men further south.

The cold was worse at all seasons, and wind-chill and wet weather exposure took their physiological toll on crews. True, the almost unbroken mid-summer daylight allowed extended trips to sea, but conversely the short days of winter heightened the risk of being 'caught out'. When hauling boats ashore the boundaries of human strength were reached too, and contemporary commentators noted that chronic back injuries and ruptures were endemic in the men of the beach fishing stations.

Without the historical imperatives of subsistence needs and economic pressures, it is difficult to imagine that the people of the coastal communities – within what was often a sparsely populated landscape – would have ventured much to sea, and without such pressures they probably would not have developed the diverse and numerous coastal craft which came to characterise the Scottish coastal scene. For, if it was local sea conditions which eventually shaped the intentions of those who evolved a particular kind of boat, it was an underlying double hunger which provided the principal incentives to develop it in the first place: the hunger in the bellies of subsistence-level fishers and crofters for fish to eat and, increasingly, the indirect 'hunger' of landowners, merchants and tenants to turn surplus fish into cash and escape their low-earning economies. Fortunately, until the coming of the steam-powered fishing vessel, the biologically rich environment of Scotland's cool northern waters, flanked by the incoming warmth of the Gulf Stream, provided plentiful – if fluctuating – high quality supplies of bottom-living and surface-feeding fish, whilst the disposition of the surrounding continental shelf provided ample opportunity to extend the fisheries out to the biggest and best of stocks, provided some seagoing risks were taken.

Although within the last two centuries Scotland's coastal boat users were dominated by the call of the fisheries – and thus had fewer of the specialised, non-fisheries, kinds of craft evolved in the more populous maritime areas of England – they did of course participate in all kinds of occupational opportunities, including: pilotage for the (few) major ports and the (many) small harbours, often using accredited local fishermen and fisherboats at the latter; regional passenger services, since local inhabitants and visiting dignitaries alike depended on reliable (if spartan) ferry crossings and inter-island passages by boat; localised transport of goods and materials, for such needs as carrying crofting products to a town, or bringing in winter fuel from the peat-diggings; and the nationally famous (or infamous) garnering of natural windfalls, 'caa'in' whales, smuggled goods and wrecks amongst them. Trading smacks and sloops were found in abundance, but differed little from their English contemporaries.

The Scottish boat user has perhaps been regarded by some as

Scottish fishing craft, based on the inhospitable west coast, rarely found time for reflection in still waters. Here, in the Lochranza anchorage in the Isle of Arran, three Lochfyne skiffs from nearby Carradale in Kintyre lie alongside a smack. *(NMM, neg no N29759)*

relatively isolated from outside influences, and moreover slow in acceptance of the new, but there seems little evidence of either. For example, if the Scottish east coast herring fisherman seems to have been slow to take up the adoption of the, apparently, safer decked boat in place of his open boat in the mid-nineteenth century, there was a complex interplay of reasoning which underlay his reluctance to change: the nature of boat ownership or tenure; familiarity of handling when using seasonal, part-time crew; the need to work the (staple) winter line fishery with another kind of boat; understanding of the restrictions of space and tidal access in local havens; the desire to accumulate capital and become an outright owner of boats and property; and the vested interests of those who produced hundreds of cheaply-built, open boats. The matter was certainly not a clear cut one. However, when change came it came swiftly and in a spirit of unparalleled innovation, for the decked Scot's luggers quickly became the driving force in Britain's east coast herring fleet.

As to the technology, form and structure of Scottish boats themselves, they long seem to have embraced outside influences. Most significant perhaps were the influences which came out of the Irish Sea through the Gaelic provinces of the west, together with those which came more directly from the north. These latter were principally Norwegian in origin and – whether from the hands of early Norse Jarls, or, from the timber stocks of later Norwegian merchants – they proved seminal in many areas. Such Norwegian products not only dominated the boat usage of Shetland but penetrated the Western Isles and the Irish Sea coasts too, whilst east coast imports of 'boats boards' were made as far south as Montrose (and no doubt beyond). Indeed, through its seaborne contacts, Scotland was always very much a maritime European nation. Internally, the rapid diffusion of fishery practices was aided by seasonal migratory working, including passages through the Caledonian Canal (1822).

At regional and local levels, practical issues of boat evolution revolved around the immediate coastal topography, available human and natural resources, and local sea state. These factors were to the fore in determining a locality's boat shape and usage. Community attitudes and personal skills might play a defining role too, for few areas were without a boat-using community or an individual boat builder who was accredited with the origin or perfection of a type, whether it be the Lewismen of 'Ness' (Niseach) with their sgoths, or the Shetlanders of 'Ness' (Dunrossness) with their yoals – built by a McLeod or a Eunson respectively.

Scotland's east coast contains the country's longest uninterrupted stretches of coastline. Running broadly north-south for 200 miles, and broken only by the 80-mile dog-leg of the Moray shore together with the penetrations of the 'firths' of Forth, Tay, Moray, Cromarty and Dornoch – which provided varying levels of navigation and shelter – it is characterised by moderate cliff lines and occasional high 'heads', generally interleaved with small, natural havens and beaches sufficient both for accommodating boats and providing the shore-side foothold required by fisher communities.

East coast seagoing hazards were largely confined to the inshore zone, where local knowledge might even turn them to advantage, and shallows and tidal races were relatively few. In its southern sector especially, river estuaries such as those of the Tweed at Berwick, the South Esk at Montrose, and the Dee at Aberdeen, provided limited natural harbourage (and salmon), though always with an intervening bar and the prospect of shifting channels. Though never less than demanding, this coast proved to offer great scope for development. Good line fishing grounds were readily accessible, herring was eventually ascertained to be plentiful, and nineteenth-century developments in land transport opened up inland markets. Incentives to innovate and expand new fishing technologies – including boats – were often great, and the east coast's regions could at times support huge numbers (thousands) of boats.

Elsewhere, the situation was less favourable. At the opposite extreme perhaps was an area such as West Sutherland which, despite its unpromising westward-facing (lee shore) and high, rocky coastline, was provided with fine, but limited, natural shelter within its sea lochs. However, although it adjoined productive fishing areas much exploited by 'stranger' boats, indigenous boat usage evolved little beyond subsistence activity. Large-scale crofting 'clearances' from the interior to fishing tenures on a now overcrowded coast, together with a lack of accessible markets, all played a part in limiting fishery development. What return on the fishing there was resulted largely from the purchase of secondhand open boats, and supplying summer crewmen to the Caithness herring fishings. Consequently, the West Sutherland region did not develop an identifiable boat culture of its own.

Paradoxically, many of the isolated outer islands – which were exposed to the Atlantic's full oceanic fetch and its fast-moving weather systems – were able to develop their fisheries and associated boat types to a still-remembered peak, though not without cost to men's lives. For example, at 60° N (the same latitude as southern Greenland) Shetland is a microcosm of British coastal typology, from the routeways of its submerged-valleys, the 'voes' and 'sounds', to the open shingle beaches so necessary for drying the prime white fish caught at the 'far haaf'. Even closer inshore the hazards were turned to profit, with its specialised yoal crews traversing the very edges of the breaking tide races to take the big, exportable saithe.

Indeed, tide and wind could make or take profits and lives alike. Everywhere, the direction and speed of the coastal tidal stream was of great significance to the line and net fisherman, or the coastal car-

rier, alike. On the east coast the streams were generally moderate, rarely more than 2 knots, but at its northern tip, in the funnelled entrance to the Pentland Firth, ill-timed crossings from Orkney or Stroma might face an incredible 12-15 knots of eddying current, accompanied by seas which could swamp a steamship. Tidal range was important too; on the east coast at some 15ft (springs) it combined with the coastal features to produce a multiplicity of 'half-tide', drying harbours, impossible of entry for twelve hours of every day. Even in the later nineteenth century, every stretch of this coast, from Berwick to Wick, desperately required improvements in order to provide protected, 'full-tide', fishing harbours – but few townships achieved that.

As to wind, in relation to the prevailing southwesterlies then large stretches of the Scottish coastline, especially in the east, are nominally 'weather' or sheltered shores. But such designations must be observed with great caution. For example, the seemingly safe, east-facing (weather) shore at Wick, actually lies in a local regime where southeasterlies predominate. And it was a severe, if short-lived, southeasterly summer gale which caused the tragic loss of life there – and at similarly exposed Peterhead – in 1848, whilst the neighbouring Moray coast formed a lee shore to which all of its crews came in safety. At the very extremes of wind exposure lie ports such as Stornoway in Lewis, with its 21 per cent frequency of strong or gale force winds.

But our survey of Scottish coastal craft begins in the relatively sheltered waters of one of the southwest coast's characteristic sea lochs, Lochfyne.

A pair of Lochfyne skiffs, almost dried out at Catacol Bay in northern Arran, reveal their straight stems. 317RO displays the type's characteristic layout of the half deck, open fish hold, pump beam and sternsheets compartment. *(NMM, neg no N29755)*

Lochfyne Herring Boats

CAMPBELTOWN AND LOCHFYNE SMACKS

Small half decked, gaff rigged smacks used for drift net fishing in and around the Firth of Clyde. The appearance, in the 1840s, of this smack rigged 'superior description of boat', helped mark a resurgence in the rich, drift net herring fisheries of Lochfyne, the lower Clyde and east Kintyre. Soon, four classes of boat were in operation, ranging from 17ft to 19ft on the keel, and all but the smallest sported 'smack' (gaff cutter or sloop) rig, and might be fitted with 'half decks'. In the 1850s, the resultant 'Campbeltown smacks', crewed by four to six men, ranged from the Minches to the Isle of Man.

These mid-century changes in rig and hull were concurrent: from two masted, gaff sailed 'wherry' rigs on open hulls (characterised by relatively bluff bows and narrow sterns) to weatherly, single masted 'smacks' with half decks, fine bows and broad transom sterns. Clench build, with a broad beam across the open hold, was universal. For economy of purchase and turning ability, keels were kept unusually short in relation to an LOA of 27ft and 7 (ballasted) tons. Later smacks also remained as part deckers, and size remained moderate – only a few reaching 35ft to 36ft on the keel. Smack building continued on in the same communities too, including Campbeltown, Carradale, Fairlie and Rothesay.

A smack's drift nets could be shot either under sail or oar, and in open water its full train might amount to 2000 yards in length. Characteristically, individual smacks might also be used during the summer as the floating base for a couple of Lochfyne skiffs (see below) – providing accommodation, storage, and fish carriage. The smack fishery's heyday was in the 1860s and 1870s. A single spring day of 1862 saw over forty passing through the Crinan Canal towards Lewis and, in 1876, thirty-one sailed for Howth. Briefly, during this latter decade, they

were accompanied to the Irish herring and mackerel fishings by Campbeltown's expanded fleet of decked, Cornish-style luggers.

However, competition from boats employing 'trawls', together with the appearance of the half decked Lochfyne skiffs (*qv*), sent the smacks and luggers into rapid decline. By the turn of the century, the region's drift net fishery had become uneconomic, and the days of smack and lugger were over. The influence of their design, however, may have lived on – in the hulls of surviving Lochfyne skiffs.

LOCHFYNE SKIFF
(Zulu skiff)

The Lochfyne skiff was the ubiquitous fishing craft of southwest Scottish waters in the late nineteenth century. Its use was synonomous with the locally-pioneered technique of ring-netting for herring.

The skiff's raked, zulu-style stern, straight stem, and hollow-floored 'V'

sections, together with the marked drag of keel, made for an efficient and manoeuvrable craft. A relatively lofty rig, characterised by a high peaked, standing lug sail, set from a well-raked mast right forward, was equally distinctive. In layout, the late nineteenth-century skiffs were marked out from earlier (entirely open) types by the introduction of a half deck forward, giving their four-man crews the bare facilities – stove, bunks and storage – which were needed in order to extend their range as unsupported fishing units.

There was remarkably little change in the Lochfyne skiff's design between the introduction of the half deck, in 1882, and the end of the sail era. They were invariably divided into three sections: the decked forecastle or 'den' (occupying about one-third of the vessel's length) forward, was enclosed inboard by a bulkhead at the 'forward beam'; the open fish hold, amidships, terminated at the 'pump-beam'; the well-rounded stern sheets, aft, provided a sizeable compartment

for stowing and shooting the ring-net, and a 'taft' for the helmsman. Though such 2nd class skiffs ranged from 18ft to 30ft on the keel, they popularly ran out at 32ft to 37ft overall. A typical boat of the 1890s might be some 32ft 6in overall, just over 9ft beam, with 5ft 6in of draft, measuring around 7 net tons. Developed for use in relatively sheltered waters, Lochfyne skiffs had recognised limitations for open sea and coarse weather work.

Construction, though, was not overly light. Typically, a 35ft to 36ft carvel built skiff would be planked with twenty planks a side of 1in pitch-pine and larch, fastened onto substantial oak timbers (at just over 1ft spacings) and tied with heavy floors forward of each alternate frame; keels were of elm, with a well built-up deadwood for the overhung stern. The half deck, of 1¼in pine, was pierced by a stoutly-built box housing a mast of some 8in maximum diameter. Mast length approximated that of the skiff itself, and steps in the keel-mounted mast chock

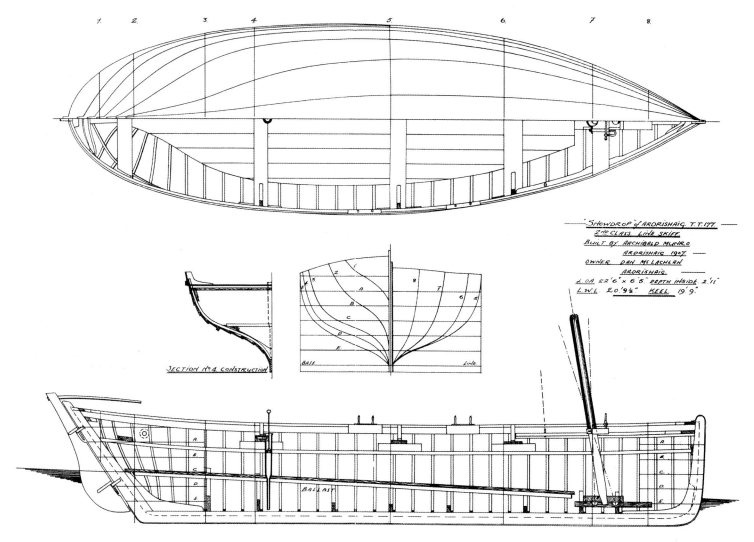

"SNOWDROP of ARDRISHAIG. T.T.177.
2ND CLASS LINE SKIFF
BUILT BY ARCHIBALD MUNRO
ARDRISHAIG 1907
OWNER DAN McLACHLAN
ARDRISHAIG.
L.OA 22'6" x 6'5" DEPTH INSIDE. 2'11"
L.W.L. 20'9½" KEEL 19'9"

SECTION Nº 4 CONSTRUCTION

BASE LINE

BALLAST

might allow the changes in mast rake appropriate for heavy and light winds. Around 2 tons of selected, dense, ballast stones were packed carefully below the hold 'platform' (sole). Secondary ballast, comprising a dozen or two sand bags, was stowed athwartships in the hold where it could be trimmed, shifted or lightened.

The standing lug sail was always hoisted to starboard, so two fixed stays were set up on that ('back') side. A single stay, supplemented by the wire halyard tie and its tackle, sufficed to port. Secondary characteristics of the rig were an iron horse, positioned just forward of the mast, for the tack (providing an efficient airflow over the luff), and a continuous sheet system for the clew. Early skiffs had no bowsprits (or permanent forestays) but, later, short bowsprits were fitted to carry headsails for steadying and steerage. Eventually, long running-bowsprits were installed, but they were used for little more than

passage-making, light weather sailing, or annual regattas. However, a pair of 25ft sweeps allied to an 18ft oar were essential; 20- to 30-mile pulls were not unknown.

Builders of these eponymous boats lived mainly in the Gaelic-speaking townships of Lochfyne itself, especially in the west shore fishing communities such as Ardrishaig and Tarbert (which had no less than five builders). But the popularity of the skiffs was such that their building ranged over a 60-mile length of coast, from Inveraray, at the northern head of the loch, to the principal fishing port of Campbeltown in southern Kintyre. Sites on the Clyde and adjacent coasts featured too. A very few talented individuals transferred from fishing to boatbuilding, but most skiffs were built at small established yards, typically employing just a few craftsmen or an owner and sons (these included members of the well known yacht-

building Fyfe family). Normally, each builder's production was small, but overall demand was high. For example, in 1902, seventeen skiffs of 18ft to 30ft on the keel (averaging nearly £100 each) were built in the Inverary district alone – the greatest output of that size of boat in any Scottish fishery district.

The Lochfyne skiff's primary use was in the shoal-encircling practice of ring-netting for herring. Crews worked in co-operative pairs, with their two skiffs setting, then closing, and finally hauling the loosely hung, rectangular 'ring-net' (some 200 yards in length by 50 yards depth) and its long sweep lines between them. Shoals were skilfully located by the crews' observance of natural phenomena – the 'flash' of phosphorescence, or a gannet's angle of dive – after which a skiff's speed and manoeuvrability played a vital part in the encirclement.

The ring-net's prototype was the beach-based seine, known as a 'trawl',

This small, 22ft, 2nd class, open line skiff *Snowdrop* TT177, of Ardrishaig, encompasses, in a small and shallower form, many of the features of her larger, ring netting sisters, noticeably the straight stem, sharply raked stern and steep rise aft. Note the three positions for stepping the mast. (*NMM, Oke, Coastal Craft Collection*)

which originated on Lochfyne in the mid-1830s. 'Trawling' proved vastly superior to established drift netting, and was soon transferred from the beach fisheries out into inshore waters. Its extraordinary success caused bitter and violent controversy at sea, together with administrative and legal confusion on land. Indeed, questions as to its legality and practice were not finally resolved until the late 1860s. But the way was then clear to develop a carrier-supported fishery whose exponents could range not only over the waters of Lochfyne and its neighbouring coasts, but up into the Minches, the Hebrides and the northwestern sea lochs too.

Though the ring-net fishery continued to be prosecuted until the 1960s, the successful introduction of motor-power, in 1907, led to the introduction of larger (canoe and cruiser-sterned) boats after World War I, resulting in the disappearance of the 'thousand strong' sailing fleet. But the Lochfyne skiffs' legacy as cultural signifiers has remained strong, a tribute to the makers and users of these handsome and almost too-efficient craft.

LOCHFYNE TRAWL-SKIFF

This was the original type of boat employed in the beach-based 'trawl' fisheries (1830-60) on Lochfyne. Four oared, lightly built, entirely open and with a relatively narrow beam (of around 6ft on overall lengths of 20ft to 25ft), it was fast and manoeuvrable when setting the net and light for pulling ashore to haul it. These same characteristics helped trawl-skiff crews evade fishery officers and naval boats in periods when the use of 'trawls' was prohibited.

Early boats were unballasted, and not all carried sail, though both ballast and sail had become commonplace features by the 1860s. Incomers from Ayrshire were credited with introducing '. . . a good style of skiff with a single lugsail' around 1840, and this may have been the progenitor of the later distinctive rig. The direct relationship, if any, between the trawl-skiffs and the Lochfyne skiffs (*qv*) which superseded them is uncertain.

Sources
Fortunately, the surviving oral, documentary and pictorial legacy of the Lochfyne-based fishery was recognised by a former fisherman of the region, Angus Martin, whose timely researches resulted in *The Ring-Net Fishermen* (Edinburgh 1981). Arguably, this work stands as the most sympathetic and comprehensive history of any British regional fishery.

As always, Capt J Washington's respondents in *Fishing Boats (Scotland)* (1849), give tantalising early accounts, whilst for later periods March's *Sailing Drifters*, and his *Inshore Craft*, contain short, usefully illustrated descriptions. East coast-based Peter F Anson's references were brief in the extreme, but his few drawings of skiffs in *Fishing Boats and Fisher Folk on the East Coast of Scotland* (London 1930), are a delight. Mckee's *Working Boats of Britain* clearly explains the 'tack horse'.

Mike Smylie (owner of the Lochfyne motor skiff *Perseverance*) has further popularised the subject through articles such as 'The Ring-Netters of Loch Fyne', *The Boatman*, No 9 (1993).

Boats of the Firth of Clyde, Ayrshire, Galloway and Solway

GABBART

Gabbarts comprised a variety of craft used for lighterage and carrying purposes on the coastal waters and inland navigations of southern Scotland. Coastal sailing gabbarts were round-bilged, decked, capacious double enders of some 75 tons (cargo capacity) at around 60ft length by 13ft 6in beam, and drawing 5ft to 6ft (laden). Characteristically, they exhibited a long narrow central hatchway, under-deck crew accommodation for two to three men aft, low rails or bulwarks, large outside rudder, and a plain gaff sloop rig set on a lowering mast – with decorated masthead and windvane.

Largely Clyde-built, their heyday was the first half of the nineteenth century, when they prominently traversed the Forth & Clyde Canal (built 1790) and its estuaries, whilst 30 to 40 tonners worked up the Leven. Around the coast, they ranged to the inner

Hebrides, eventually giving way to coastal smacks and ketches, also termed gabbarts, and steam 'puffers'.

LARGS LINE SKIFF

The typical fishing boats of the lower Firth of Clyde were 18ft to 19ft, beach-based skiffs. Shallow, double ended, and of fairly light build (pine-planked), with a lean wedge of a bow merging to a markedly fuller stern, they were round-sectioned and reputedly fast sailers under a single square-headed standing lug, needing shifting ballast. Several of their line-fishing crew members – from Saltcoats, Millport and Largs – achieved fame both in local regattas and as racing yacht skippers.

AYSHIRE SKIFFS

A generic grouping of open craft used from the tidal fishing havens – including Ayr, Dunure, Maidens, Girvan and

Ballantrae – of Ayrshire's three districts. In the mid-nineteenth century these skiffs, sometimes called 'nabbies', appear to have been larger – 25ft long by 8ft beam – forerunners of those later found around Largs (*qv*). Carrying a lug sail and jib they were reported to be, 'handsome, and work and sail well'. This form was reflected in a 27ft boat for the prolific Ballantrae Banks (herring, cod and turbot) in the 1870s too, though a slightly later and larger, 35ft vessel indicates adoption of Loch Fyne skiff characteristics – Ballantrae town's own lack of harbourage seemingly restricted its skiffs to 22ft.

Though slightly smaller, and with differences in rigging, this gabbart at Hunter's quay c1883, appears little different from a sailing flat on the Mersey, emphasising the commonality of hull form and function which could be found around the Irish Sea. (*NMM, neg no 3697*)

Right: An 18ft Largs line skiff, built by Boag of Fairlie c1890. The rowlocks, rather than the more usual tholes, suggests some outside influence. The shallow, round sections which made these craft quick, are clearly seen. *(NMM, Oke, Coastal Craft Collection)*

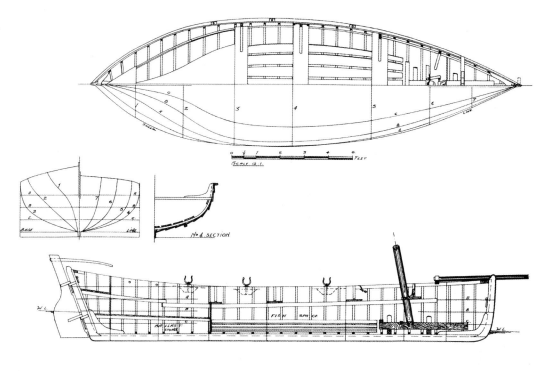

Below: An Ayrshire skiff, the 22ft *Maggie Campbell* of Girvan, built c1890. The body plan emphasises the deepish sections. The mast would be raked further back in strengthening winds. *(NMM, Oke, Coastal Craft Collection)*

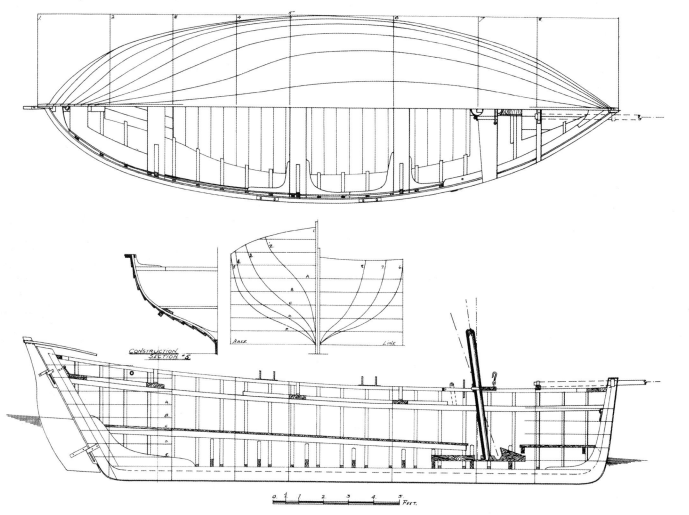

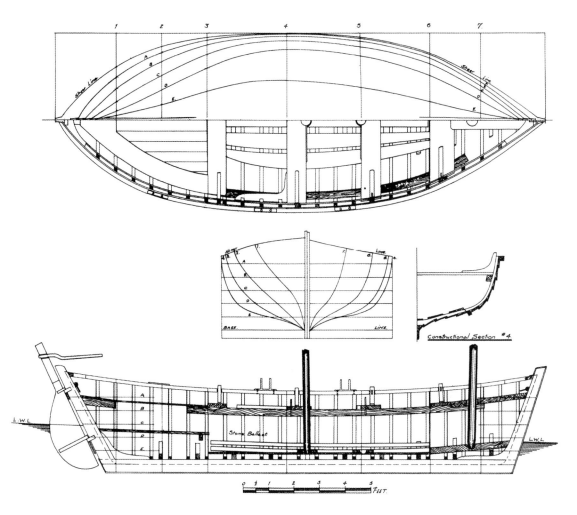

Left: The Portpatrick line boat *Brothers* BA318, built in 1898. These beamy, long keeled craft were fast and weatherly. *(NMM, Oke, Coastal Craft Collection)*

Below: The Portpatrick line boat *Brothers* BA318 is rowed home in light airs. The usual powerful rig is here replaced with a rather makeshift affair. *(NMM, Oliver Hill Collection, neg no P75436)*

Right: Two shrimpers at Annan in 1936. Though they have the characteristic fine, yacht-like hulls of the Morcambe Bay prawner from which they derived, they are nonetheless plain workmanlike craft. *(NMM, Oliver Hill Collection, neg no P75435)*

Below: This Annan whammel net boat, 19ft 3in overall, was built on the Annan waterfront in 1900. This example, like most, had watertight compartments under the side decks and iron ballast. *(NMM, Oke, Coastal Craft Collection)*

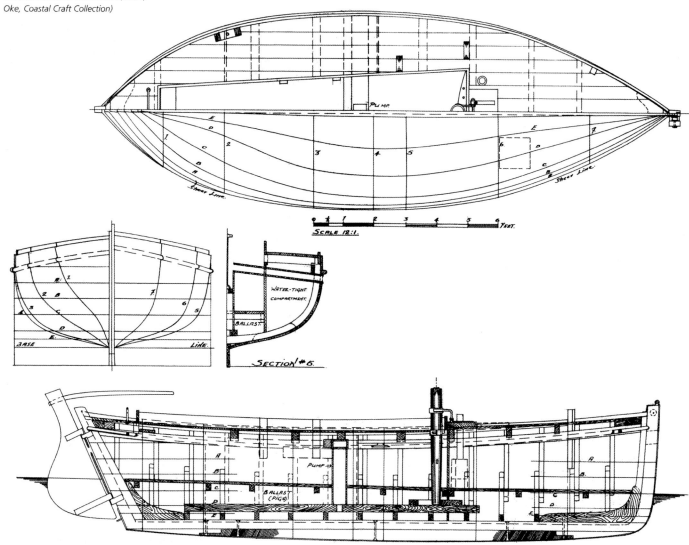

An Annan whammel net boat, believed to be the *Dora*, being poled into shore. These shallow craft were well adapted to their estuarine environment. *(NMM, Oliver Hill Collection, neg no P72616)*

Towards the end of the century Ayrshire's open skiffs, though reputedly finally built up to 45ft, largely gave way to 32ft to 36ft half decked types (narrower and squarer-sterned in Carrick than the upper Firth).

The Carrick coast also supported several coble-based salmon fisheries in the late eighteenth and early nineteenth centuries, but stake nets later replaced boat fishing.

STRANRAER YAWL

A little-mentioned type of the latter half of the nineteenth century, with a strongly raked stern and mast reminiscent of the 'Zulu skiff' (*qv*).

PORTPATRICK LINE BOAT

A slightly hollow floored, open skiff, of around 15ft to 16ft on the keel, with slightly raked straight stem, fullish bow and quarters, and fair beam. Unusually, it was 'lug schooner' rigged, with dipping foresail and standing (midships) main, perhaps betraying Irish Sea 'wherry' connections.

ANNAN TRAWL SMACK

The local Scottish inhabitants of the Solway shore had a poor reputation for fishing, and this was an incomer type, arriving around 1865 with Morecambe Bay (English) shrimpers and flatfishers. They initially used their 'home' builders to produce familiar square

sterned, part decked, clench built trawlers. And, after the turn of the century, their 36ft to 39ft, two man trawlers continued to follow closely the light (carvel planked), yacht-like build and gaff cutter rig of the English

'nobbies' (*qv*), even though now built locally on the Solway.

SOLWAY FIRTH (ANNAN), WHAMMEL NET BOAT

A robustly carvel built, full sectioned, double ender, capable of taking the ground and used for salmon 'hang-netting' in the upper Solway. Developed from earlier, smaller, clench built and sprit rigged open boats, the later whammel boats were locally built half deckers of up to 19ft in length, carrying lug and jib rigs on lowering masts. Despite their iron ballast and buoyancy tanks they were essentially river and estuarine craft. Their building ceased (but motorisation commenced) between the wars.

Sources

As one of Scotland's lesser fishery districts, the boat types of the Clyde to Solway coast have been little described. This is doubly unfortunate, for the area contains a major commercial estuary and is at a confluence of the Scottish, Irish and English fisheries. P J Oke's fine, prewar, series of drawings and E J March's *Inshore Craft* Vol 2 remain the only readily available sources. Such deficiencies might still be remedied, as Catherine L Czerkawska's excellent *Fisherfolk of Carrick* (Glasgow 1975), showed, though it says little on sailing era boats.

Boats of the Northwest

SGOTH

A large, unique, open, line fishing boat, with markedly raked sternpost, the famed 'sgoth Niseach' – Ness (Lewis) skiff – was renowned for its seakeeping abilities in truly exposed waters. The double ended sgoth's strikingly raked sternpost was surmounted by a full, bowl-shaped stern above the water. A curved and moderately raked forestem led to fine underwater sections forward, though again, the flare and fullness above gave a bluffly purposeful appearance afloat. Deep, powerful mid-sections, together with the reserve buoyancy in its ends, helped equip the sgoth to work on the region's oceanic waters to the west, in the irregular seas and tides of the

This full size, 33ft overall sgoth *Sulaire* (Gannet) SY465 was built by the third generation Lewis boatbuilder John Murdo Mcleod, along with one assistant, in 1995. The powerful, short luffed, dipping lug sail is set on an unstayed, 30ft mast with the halyard belayed to windward. *(Eolas Productions Ltd, Stornoway)*

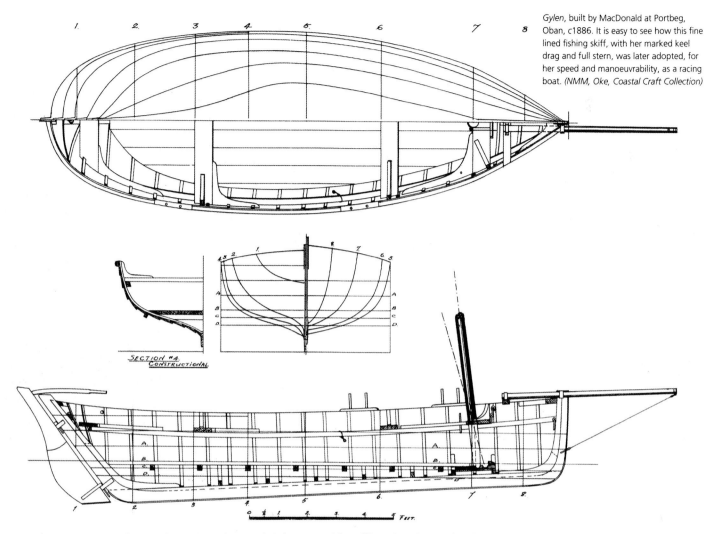

Gylen, built by MacDonald at Portbeg, Oban, c1886. It is easy to see how this fine lined fishing skiff, with her marked keel drag and full stern, was later adopted, for her speed and manoeuvrability, as a racing boat. *(NMM, Oke, Coastal Craft Collection)*

Minch, and through the surf zones of its home shore. Few boats of its era can have been asked to meet such demanding diversity (throughout all seasons) but, as a beachable boat, it became comparatively big and heavy.

The clench built hull comprised some dozen planks each side. The bottom strake had a tapered section and fitted direct to the rabbetless keel. Together with the second and third planks it comprised the standing strakes which shaped the hollow sections so necessary for weatherly sailing. In building, no frames were inserted until the turn of the bilge was reached and then, as the topsides were completed, sgoth construction showed its true character. A complex, closely-spaced system of sawn and joggled frames was inserted into the boat's mid-section '. . . since all the work of the boat will be carried out there'. This was further strengthened by heavy risings and shelves below load-bearing thwarts. Cant frames firmed up the

ends, and an angled frame ('squit') tied in the bow planks. Typically, such sgoths were 30ft to 31ft overall at 21ft keel, with a good 11ft beam and 4ft 6in of depth inside. Builders included the three generations of those MacLeod's still so ably represented by John Murdo McLeod; in 1884, another Ness-based McLeod told visiting Royal Commissioners that he built six sgoths a year.

Set on a mast slightly shorter than the boat's length, the sgoth's low-profiled dipping lug had plentiful reefs and a rather short luff which tacked (to weather) to hooks on each bow. Ballast was up to a ton of rock or sand. Unusually, the mast was raised from forward, its heel pivoting in a shaped step until it could be secured in the thwart clasp and stayed with the halyard tackle. The six-man crew worked oars in double tholes. When beach landing, unnecessary ballast might be dumped and the remainder shifted aft to keep the rudder well immersed.

Then, the skipper waited for a smooth spell and endeavoured to run in on the back of a sea, with four men rowing hard until the bowman could time his leap ashore. Hauling up over wooden 'lunnan' was work 'sufficient to make an old man of one while he is yet young', and it shortened the boat's life too (to around five years).

Though six- and eight-oared line fishing boats were common in late eighteenth-century Lewis, the sgoth's origins are generally dated to the (often unsuccessful) pier and harbour works commenced in the mid-1830s. In truth, the only current certainty about the sgoth's origins are its uncertainties: a treasured enigma of western Gaeldom's confluence with the Norse and Scots east. Sadly, the cod and ling fishing Lewisman's needs and aspirations could not always match the turbulence of the elements and the marketplace. The later nineteenth century was marred by fishing tragedies, and dominated by the herring fishery.

Such factors, together with World War I, saw the disappearance of the sgoth as a working tool.

Sources
Significant sources for the sgoth can be summed up in one name, John Murdo MacLeod, whose writings, communications, skill and experience (and the desire to pass them on) are encapsulated in the building of *Sulaire* 'on camera': video, *An Sgoth*, Eolas Productions (Stornoway, Lewis, 1995). For the boat's technology, *Working Boats of Britain* gives an excellent exposition in text and illustration, whilst Donald McDonald's, *Lewis: a history of the island* (1978), provides much readable and informative background.

CROFTERS' BOATS

A diverse group of smallish boats, employed throughout the more sheltered waters of the northwest mainland and Outer Isles. Older boats, working a few nets close inshore for herring and lobstering (to supply well-smacks), were of two-man, double ended 'skiff' form, some 14ft on the keel (1845), with west coast characteristics: raked stems, bowl-shaped stern, oars on single tholes, and single standing lug sail. Later additions were disparate and included east coast skiffs, Scandinavian prams, locally-built (Scottish) cobles, and Loch Broom's 15ft transom-sterned 'postboat' amongst them.

OBAN SKIFF

The west coast's semi-circular stern is seen here in almost exaggerated form, on a shallow, rather flat floored, 18ft hull. Characteristically, the standing lug has its tack set to a sliding hook.

ISLAY SMACK

A 20ft to 25ft keel variant of the east coast fifie (*qv*), with the more manoeuvrable smack rig. Relatively small numbers of these were built in Buckie in the early years of the century specifically as 'Islay Boats', for the fishermen of the inner Hebridean island of Islay, replacing earlier luggers.

GREENCASTLE SKIFFS
(*Greenies*)

Distinctive, Norwegian-derived, open, double enders, imported directly across the Irish Sea from builders in Antrim (Greencastle yawl) (*qv*) in the late nineteenth and early twentieth centuries, and used at Islay, Gigha, Campbeltown and Dalintober.

With relatively upright stems they measured little longer than their 22ft to 26ft on the keel, but were shallow and narrow. For example; a skiff 25.8ft overall and 24ft on the keel, had a beam of only 6.5ft, and 2.5ft depth. Rather tender, but fast, they stepped two masts with low profile sails (variously gaff, sprit or dipping lug), and worked under four oars.

A few migratory Islay fishermen hand lined for saithe and cod from skiffs alongside similarly equipped Kintyre men in the notorious tideway off the Mull after the turn of the century. Long lining was carried out from skiffs off Gigha and Kintyre, the latter supporting a few dozen such boats before the age of motorisation.

Sources
There is no definitive work on the diverse small boats of this region, though pointers can be found in *Working Boats of Britain* and Angus Martin's *The Ring-net Fishermen* (Edinburgh 1981) together with his fascinating, 'The Mull of Kintyre Hand-line Fishery', in *Northern Studies* Vol 20 (1983). Michael McCaughan, 'Ulster Boat Types in Old Photographs', *Ulster Folklife*, Vol 28 (1982) amplifies the Irish end of the story.

This small pulling boat, photographed in 1959, is typical of Oban; the beautiful rounded stern, so clearly delineated in this photograph, could be found all round the west coast. *(NMM, Oliver Hill Collection, neg no P75439)*

Shetland

SHETLAND MODEL

The term 'Shetland model' originated both in Shetland and Norway in the nineteenth century, and has been applied throughout the island group to any boat which is recognisably of Shetland build and character.

Externally, all such boats are distinguished by double ended hulls with raked, strongly curved stems. They have straight, narrow-sided keels of small depth; parallel-sided garboards; a bold sheer, often emphasised by broad strakes; and have rounded to quite slack bilged mid sections, giving rather shallow, open forms. Until recently, all Shetland models were of shell clinker construction, with inherited Norwegian structural elements, including a 'T' section keel with the garboards through-fastened to its flanges; vertical keel-to-stem scarphs; strake ends fastened directly to the sides of 'V' section (non-rebated) stems; light, sawn frames lacking direct connection to the keel, and positioned primarily by (rowing) 'room' space; and an inclined

'Like butterflies on the water...', a trio of small Shetland fourerns lie becalmed off Symbister on the Isle of Walsay in 1904. Unlike dipping lugs, it can be clearly seen that their Shetland square sails are set outside rather than inside the shrouds. *(NMM, Oliver Hill Collection, neg no P75441)*

A near contemporary model of a late nineteenth-century, five-plank Fair Isle yoal. She has a true square sail which could be quickly swung 'tack for tack' whether the craft was turning through the wind or wearing round. *(Trustees of the National Museums and Galleries on Merseyside)*

This beautiful, classically proportioned Ness yoal is the *Roodeport* LK103, built in about 1920 by George Johnson. While ideally adapted for handling in the confused tide races in which they worked, they were not suited to bigger offshore seas. *(A G Osler)*

frame ('stamron') in each stem end. Though size might range from 9ft to 27ft on the keel, the hull proportions of most types lay within a defined range. For example, keel length rarely varied much from seven-tenths of overall length. Distinctive features of the nineteenth- and early twentieth-century boats were the single masted, asymmetric square sail (not dipping lug) rig, and great reliance upon square-loomed, non-feathering oars worked against removable wooden 'kabes' (tholes) within restraining 'humlabands' (grommets), whilst their rudders were secured by a bolt-like upper fastening for ease of shipping.

The Shetland model's origins lie in the import of complete and dismantled boats from Norway. From the sixteenth to early nineteenth century this trade, which was based in Sunnhordaland and the port of Bergen, provided fully for (treeless) Shetland's needs. Initially, Shetlanders simply used, or adapted, the fjord-based Norwegian types supplied. Later, the participating merchants furnished craft modified for Shetland usage. Finally, in the early nineteenth century, economic incentives and improved craft skills saw the development of island-built types designed solely for local needs and conditions.

FAIR ISLE YOAL

Found only in Shetland's southernmost outlier, the Fair Isle, this was a light and extremely shallow three-man 'Shetland model', carrying a true square sail rig. Until the third quarter

of the nineteenth century the yoals of Fair Isle were markedly Norwegian in design, with a short rockered keel merged into well raked stems, slack bilges, three rowing positions, and flexible, five-strake a side hulls. Later yoals were often larger, with four rowing positions, longer keels and more upright stems. Mostly of six strakes a side, such boats were rather flat sheered but still remarkably shallow, only 1ft 6in amidships for a typical 17ft keel (22ft overall) yoal of 6ft beam. The lightly stayed mast was stepped amidships, carrying a square headed sail of low profile that was flown outside the shrouds (and was worked tack for tack). This was not replaced by the asymmetric square sail until the 1930s, and sail did not entirely give way to (outboard) motor till after the War.

An island population which averaged only forty families required no more then a couple of dozen yoals, but these were vital in maintaining the community's viability. So yoal building – using selected driftwood – was an occasional activity, led by men with recognised skills. In experienced hands these characterful boats were valued for their responsiveness in rough water, and their true running qualities under sail. Historically, they were used for great line fishing, then later for hand lining saithe along the island's 'roosts' (tide races), and finally for haddock and halibut. Yoal crews also maintained the dangerous 22-mile link to mainland Shetland (or Orkney) and 'went off', opportunistically, to trade for supplies from passing ships.

NESS YOAL

A light, elegantly sheered, three-man boat of restricted form, used exclusively from the fishing stations of the south Mainland (Shetland) parish of Dunrossness. Narrow and fine lined, yoals carried their maximum beam well forward and had long, buoyant foreheads. Their rounded mid-sections were purposely slack bilged, ensuring quick reaction in rough water. For lightness, the planking of their six-strake hulls was of larch below and whitewood above, with slender 'red fir' or oak keel and larch framing. Flexibility was greatly valued. In practice, yoals ranged from 14ft to 15ft 6in on the keel, but to gain the ascription 'Ness' yoal, boats had to conform to dimensions of 15ft on the keel, 22ft 6in 'between stems', 5ft 6in beam, and 1ft 9in depth amidships.

Rowing three men, single banked, and using finely made oars, yoals were

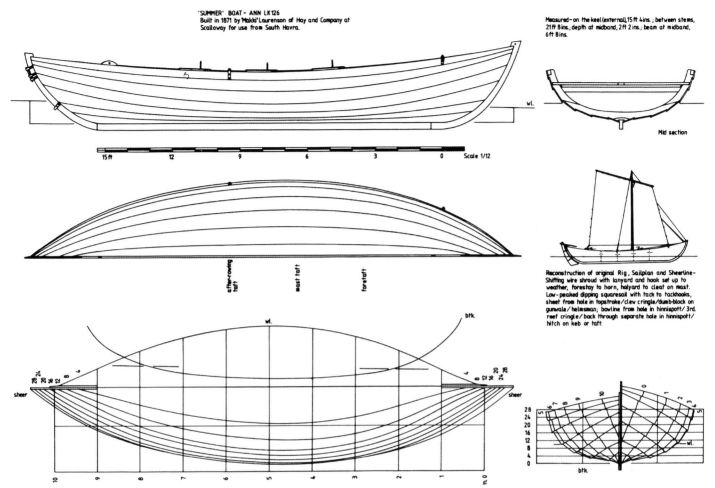

'SUMMER' BOAT – ANN LK126
Built in 1871 by 'Makki' Laurenson of Hay and Company at
Scalloway for use from South Havra.

Measured – on the keel (external), 15 ft 4 ins.; between stems,
21 ft 8 ins.; depth at midband, 2 ft 2 ins.; beam at midband,
6 ft 8 ins.

15 ft   12   9   6   3   0   Scale 1/12

after-rowing taft   mast taft   foretaft

wl.

btk.

sheer   sheer

Mid section

Reconstruction of original Rig, Sailplan and Sheerline-
Shifting wire shroud with lanyard and hook set up to
weather, forestay to horn, halyard to cleat on mast.
Low-peaked dipping squaresail with tack to tackhooks,
sheet from hole in topstroke/clew cringle/dumb-block on
gunwale/helmsman; bowline from hole in hinnispott/3rd.
reef cringle/back through separate hole in hinnispott/
hitch on keb or taft.

This typical 'Shetland Model' is the 'summer boat' Ann LK126, one of the diverse and extensive family of fourerns and haddock boats. She was 15ft on the keel and was built in Scalloway in about 1870. She worked long lines until World War I and survivied in general use until the 1960s. *(A G Osler)*

acknowledged as the fastest boats in the islands. In skilled hands, the low peaked, asymmetric square sail with its bowlines and adjustable tack position allowed for very fast and efficient sailing .

Such specialised craft demanded dedicated local builders, amongst whom George Eunson and George Johnson were best known at the turn of the century; each was capable of turning out a dozen boats a year. Up until the 1920s, the yoals' use was synonomous with the summer saithe fishery, their crews boldly, and safely, hand lining up to a ton of fish from the margins of the 'roosts' (tide races) during each tidal trip. Though often held to be a continuance of the original Norwegian imports, the Ness yoal is better regarded as a sophisticated and most successful adaptation, developed in response to specific local needs – a testament to Shetland's nineteenth-century fishers and craftsmen. Today, there has been a revival in yoal usage, for competitive leisure rowing.

FOURERN AND HADDOCK BOAT

Nominally rowing four oars, the fourern was a versatile type found throughout much of Shetland from the seventeenth century until quite recent times; it was represented by many variants, including the open haddock boat. Though owing their origins to the three-strake Norwegian faering, the hundreds of later nineteenth-century fourerns and 'whillies' (*qv*) of the island group had well-established Shetland model features. Beamier, deeper, and of greater displacement than yoals, the fourern's well rounded sections generally showed a shallow rise of floor consonant with good rowing qualities. Construction materials varied, but larch and whitewood were preferred for planking, with larch for frames too, whilst keel and inwales were often of red fir. Good driftwood, however, was never cast aside. Of 14ft to 17ft on the keel, a typical six-strake fourern might measure some 22ft 6in

'between stems', at 15ft on the keel, with a beam of some 6ft 6in at the midband, and a depth of just over 2ft. Builders of fourerns were widespread, and ranged from professionals like the Laurenson brothers (at Hay's large yard in Scalloway), through trained, self-established men like Walter Duncan Senior of Burra, to untaught occasional builders.

Though nominally rowing four oars, fourern crews might row up to six oars in a variety of single and double banked configurations. In rig, the low peaked asymmetric square sail gave way in the 1890s to a more weatherly high peaked sail, with local variation in bowline and tack arrangements. Mast heights now exceeded length of keel, and boats carried loose (expendable) stone ballast in strengthened 'ballast rooms'.

The fourern's principal use in the late nineteenth century was in the nearshore white fisheries, with crews working 'small lines' – comprising over forty, 50-fathom 'baukts' (lines) – on a daily basis. In Burra, Aith and Voe, the

self-owned 14ft keel 'haddock boat' was much favoured, and in some localities the rather larger, seven-strake 'codling boats' would also work the winter through. Elsewhere, fourerns might be deployed for fishing as 'summer boats' only, but everywhere they played another important role in the crofting economy, as major tools of transport.

SIXERN

The sixern was the largest open Shetland model, developed solely for use in the 'far haaf' (deep sea) fishery, reaching an apogee of use and performance during the third quarter of the nineteenth century. The sixern's

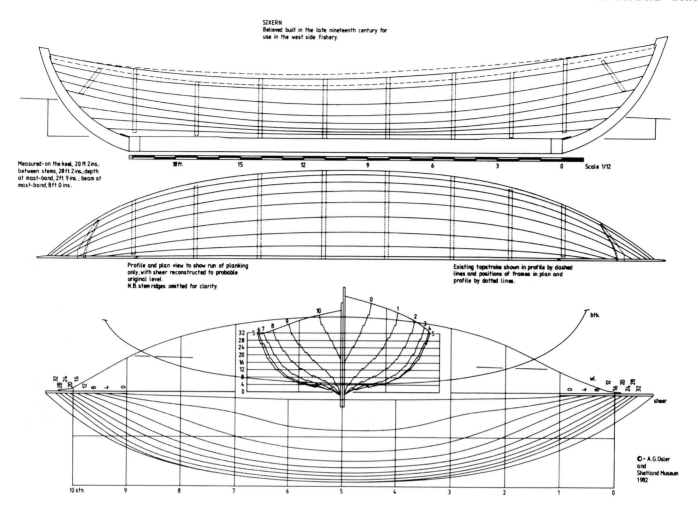

SIXERN
Believed built in the late nineteenth century for
use in the west side fishery.

Measured-on the keel, 20 ft. 2 ins.;
between stems, 28 ft 2 ins.; depth
at mast-band, 2 ft. 9 ins.; beam at
mast-band, 8 ft. 0 ins.

18 ft.   15   12   9   6   3   0   Scale 1/12

Profile and plan view to show run of planking
only, with sheer reconstructed to probable
original level.
N.B. stem ridges omitted for clarity.

Existing topstroke shown in profile by dashed
lines and positions of frames in plan and
profile by dotted lines.

© - A.G.Osler
and
Shetland Museum
1982

10 stn.   9   8   7   6   5   4   3   2   1   0

ancestry lay in the eighteenth-century six-oared boats, specifically imported from Norway for nearshore use. After the Napoleonic Wars ended larger, 18ft (keel) boats were imported, and significant island-based advances appear to have been made in developing the form, rig (and consequent range) of these larger 'Norway yawls'. Self-building commenced and by the latter part of the nineteenth century, the resultant 'sixerns' had become most impressive open boats, designed with great regard for seaworthiness and speed in oceanic waters.

Of full, well rounded bilge, it was more or less hollow in the garboards according to localised needs for best performance under sail or oars. The underwater hull was closely balanced fore and aft, but there were powerful shoulders and the maximum beam was carried well forward. A roomy 'fore-head' and high sheered bow provided reserve buoyancy there too. To provide liveliness afloat, and ease of handling ashore, lightness of construction was paramount. On a working dis-

placement of 3 tons, the stripped out ¾in planked hull might beach at under a ton.

In earlier days 'Norway deals' (fir) were the prime building material, but after the mid-nineteenth century, tre-nail and iron-fastened Scottish larch and oak came to predominate. However, the sixern's gradually increasing size, from some 15ft to 20ft on the keel, necessitated some changes in construction, the introduction of part rabbetted stems and additional frames amongst them. A typical sixern of the 1880s measured some 30ft overall at 20ft on the keel, with a maximum beam of 8ft, and internal midships depth of only 2ft 6in. Their specialised, widely spread constructors are largely unrecorded, but at the very end of the era included such well regarded boatbuilders as Harald Nicolson at Unst, and Hay and Co's John Shewan at Lerwick and 'Makki' Laurenson at Scalloway.

Though a seven-man crew rowed the descriptive six, double banked oars, large sixerns actually possessed four rowing positions, the foremost for

use when working lines. A solid mast, some 6in diameter at the base, had a length equal to the keel's, and 'haaf' sixerns invariably hoisted a low peaked, asymmetric square sail that, in earlier times, often carried a horizontal reef at the head for reducing it to square headed form. Complex bowlines and three position tacks aided all round sailing efficiency. Their light weight and fine lines, combined with experienced handling, gives no cause to doubt anecdotal evidences that hard-pressed sixerns reached over 9 knots, surfing breaking swells and having to be restrained from the dangerous business of planing.

From the mid-eighteenth century onwards sixern crews fished the 'haaf', with their descendants working five to six miles of 'great lines' to catch ling and tusk on the edge of the continental shelf, up to 40 miles offshore. A bounden activity of the tenant crofter, the 'haaf' fishery was based at outlying beaches from May to August, with boats making trips of up to 36 hours duration twice or even more a week. At

The lines of a surviving Shetland sixern. She was built in 1891 to carry the mail to the island of Foula. She shows powerful, sea kindly lines on a 20ft keel, and would originally have carried a trapezoidal Shetland square sail on a 26ft mast. *(A G Osler, courtesy the Shetland County Museum)*

its peak in the late 1850s, over 600 boats fished out of some 55, often remote, curing stations. Thirty years later, a rapid terminal decline began which involved diminishing markets, occupational competition, the onset of trawling and – not least of all – the impact of the disaster of 1881 in which fifty-eight men were lost. Even the best of open boats, and the best of island men, might not match the worst of summer weather.

EELA *(Whilly boat)*

Present in great variety of form and size, this small ubiquitous 'Shetland model' fulfilled general purpose functions throughout the island group. Named in dialect after its former principal subsistence use, the nearshore

The high peaked square sail, taut bowline and full crew suggest that this Shetland eela may be engaged in one of the popular summer regattas. Its oars are retained in the 'humlibands', a practice which added a little freeboard too. *(NMM, neg no 5345)*

The handiness of the Shetland smack, with its long boomed cutter rig on a fifie hull, is emphasised here as a clutch of boats work the light winds along the narrow, rock edged waters. *(NMM, Oliver Hill Collection, neg no P75421)*

'eela' fly-fishery for immature saithe, the eela boat's form and usage over-lapped that of the fourern (*qv*). Boats of 8ft 6in on the keel, simply rowing one pair of single banked oars, were the smallest regular size, whilst boats of 10ft to 12ft on the keel were perhaps the most popular and versatile. These last might carry sail and ballast, and with sufficient crew might row double banked, an advantage if making long inshore passages. Duties ranged from carrying sheep to off-lying islets or crews to herring boats, to cash econo-my shell fishing. Moderate of size and outlay, a professional builder might put together several in a winter, on the common understanding of a cheap boat 'light to haul up and easy to row'.

However, the 'whilly' proved adapt-able and enduring, and was the prog-enitor both of a successful range of small, motorised working craft from the 1920s onward, together with the racing boats which have excited Shet-land's summer scene for over a centu-ry. The rating rules for these last at-tempted to preserve the 'Shetland model', whilst always encouraging modernity, so epoxy-ply construction and bendy rigs now enhance a fiercely competitive tradition.

Decked Fishing Boats in Shetland

HALF DECKED HERRING BOAT

An obscure type of part decked craft which owed its inspiration to Scottish mainland practices, and was success-fully deployed in Shetland waters from 1820 to 1840. Though two part-decked boats had been brought in from the Firth of Forth in 1820, the major pur-chases later in the decade were from Caithness and, perhaps, Moray. Un-usually for the period these boats had half decks forward, and probably ranged from 20ft to 30ft on the keel. Later, the main merchant house in-volved, Hay and Ogilvy of Lerwick, commenced building half deckers themselves.

Of the 500 boats employed for Shetland herring fishing in the 1830s well over 200 were half deckers, with the remainder sixerns (*qv*). However, in the early 1840s the half decker fleet was irrevocably laid up, a result of loss-es during the gale of 1840, declining catches, and banking failures in 1842.

SHETLAND SMACKS

Decked, line and herring boats, mostly purchased secondhand out of the Scottish east coast fisheries from the mid-1870s onwards and rerigged as gaff cutters or ketches. Between 1876 and 1885, the desire to reinvigorate the herring fishery, together with aspirations to copy the recent success of Banffshire fishermen in working 'great lines' under sail in Shetland waters, caused local merchants and fishermen to steadily purchase Scottish luggers 30ft to 40ft on the keel. In some areas these were known, despite their fifie build, as 'Buckie boats', though for safe handling on Shetland's intricate coastline they were generally converted to sturdy 'lang boomer' (gaff cutter) rig, one already familiar in the islands' trading ketch and cod fleets. Some smacks were also built locally, with Hay's constructing over 30 and, by 1885, the fleet of such boats totalled 350.

From 1885 to 1905, they were followed by major acquisitions of Scots fifies and zulus (*qv*). Of 40ft to 60ft on the keel, these large boats were generally rerigged as finely proportioned 'smacks' – gaff ketches – with lowering mainmasts. Relatively few were newly built or Shetland built, though the latter buildings culminated in Hay & Co's 67ft fifie smack, *Swan*, of 1901.

At the peak of its herring sail fishery, in 1905, Shetland possessed some 400 such craft, though they were far outnumbered by the 1,300 visitor boats. Market changes, the Great War, and competition from steam drifters, saw the Shetland owned sailing fleet decline to a dozen by the early 1930s, and disappear altogether in 1937.

Below: A sketch plan of a ketch rigged Faroe cod smack. Quite bluff bowed and with a wide, square counter, her depth seems almost eighteenth-century. *(NMM, Coastal Craft Collection)*

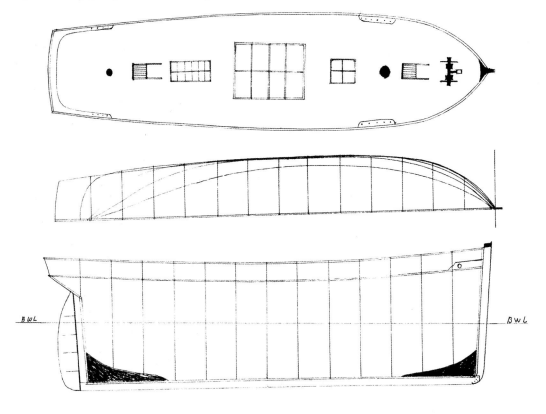

SHETLAND COD SLOOPS AND 'FAROE' SMACKS

Though distinct in size, range and period of operation, these sloops and smacks used Shetland as a base throughout the nineteenth century for exploiting the cod fisheries of the northern seas. Several dozen small, fore-and-aft rigged 'sloops', each crewed by six to twelve men, worked the cod grounds off west Shetland with hand lines during the early nineteenth century. These decked sloops, of 6 tons to 40 tons (burden), were bought in from northeastern Britain or built in Shetland. However, a variety of pressures saw larger vessels employed for trial trips in the 1830s and 1840s to the Davis Straits, Rockall, Iceland and, closest and most successful, Faroe.

Between 1855 and 1865 there was profitable exploitation of the Faroese cod banks, and needs for increased seaworthiness (together with increased concentration of ownership) saw the acquisition of a mixed group of powerful, ketch rigged, 'Faroe smacks' of over 50 tons and 60ft to 80ft length. By the early 1860s more than a hundred such smacks, employing a thousand crew, made three or four trips per season, with each smack's twelve- to fifteen-man crew landing catches of up to 10,000 fish.

Such success was shortlived for, despite the introduction of welled smacks in the 1870s, there was now real competition from the Faroese, and potentially greater profits to be made in Shetland's rejuvenated herring trade. The smack fleet dwindled rapidly, falling to a couple of dozen by the 1890s and, finally, to a single survivor in the smacks' last year, 1908.

Sources for all Shetland vessels
Deepened by a Shetlander's insight, Hance D Smith's definitive *Shetland Life and Trade, 1550-1914* (Edinburgh 1984), provides an economic and historical context within which to place Shetland's fishing and trading craft. Alexander Fenton's equally valuable folklife study, *The Northern Isles: Orkney and Shetland* (Edinburgh 1978), supplies a detailed overview of everyday life, together with a masterly demonstration of how early evidences and comparative terminology can help elucidate boat developments.

Atle Thowsen's fine *Sjøfartshistorisk Årbok (Bergen)* article of 1969, supplies the essential Norwegian link, whilst Adrian Osler's monograph, *Open Boats of Shetland: South Mainland and Fair Isle* (London 1983) provides in-depth information on some important resultant types.

J R Nicolson, *Shetland's Fishing Vessels* (Lerwick 1981) is a succinctly pictorial account and, of earlier texts, Captain A Halcrow's *Sail Fishermen of Shetland* (Shetland 1950) makes an enjoyably informative read, whilst Charles Sandison, *Shetland Sixareen and Her Racing Descendants* (Lerwick 1950) is an absolute must. To his son, Duncan Sandison, and the Shetland County Museum, goes great credit for preserving examples of historic open boat types, and the smacks are now represented too through the worthy efforts of those who have restored the *Swan*. Fortunately, the building of Shetland model boats has lived on.

The Boats of Orkney and Pentland

ORKNEY YOLE

Open, double ended boats that, although generally less than 20ft in length, incorporated sufficient carrying capacity for inter-island transport or subsistence activities, and which, characteristically, were worked under easily handled, two masted rigs.

Typified by their substantial beam and ample internal volume, Orkney yoles were once found throughout the entire island group, whilst the finer lined skiff was restricted to the northern isles only. Both types were of shell clinker construction but, compared to their Shetland counterparts, they had far more strakes and were stiffened by a closer-spaced framing system (with discontinuous elements). Original imports of Norwegian boat timber declined in the nineteenth century and Scottish materials became dominant. Oak was used for keels, stems, aprons and frames, with Norwegian white pine or Scottish larch for planking; spars remained of pine. Copper fastenings and steamed timbers were largely twentieth-century introductions.

Building was largely carried out by several recognised part-time, family based boatbuilders. Builders in the North Isles included Miller of Westray and Omond of Sanday, whilst in the South Isles several generations of the Duncans of Burray were prominent, as was Nicolson of Flotta. There were significant contributions from the shipyards and yard-trained workers (such as Baikie) of Stromness and Kirkwall too. Boats of the largest class ran from 12ft to 12ft 9in on the keel with over 7ft beam, whilst the smaller class were around 11ft on the keel. The larger boats sported distinctive two masted rigs, with mainmasts positioned amidships and their, slightly taller, foremasts well forward; smaller boats were single masted. Oars, worked between double tholes, were definitely considered an auxiliary to sail, for calms, and helping cross tidal streams.

Documentary, early pictorial, and comparative evidences point to these boats' origins in pre nineteenth-century imports of 'Norroway' boats. But the significant changes in hull design and building technology which followed suggest some acculturation from mainland practices, although the major

The Orkney yole *Lizzie* seen here off her native island in the 1950s. She was built around 1870, at Burness in the north Orkney island of Sanday. Here, the smaller yoles generally set only a single dipping lug. *(Orkney Library Collection)*

This drawing, based on Holdsworth, represents a North Isles yole with its two masted, standing lug sail rig. By the date of this drawing only the main is recorded as having had a boom. *(NMM, Oke, neg no PAI7530)*

thrusts of development seem to have remained Orkney ones. The origins of the distinctive two masted Orkney rigs remains speculative. Already well developed in the mid-nineteenth century, it seems that their appearance may date from the late-eighteenth when, as a longstanding 'maritime crossroads', Orkney's seafarers had been exposed to a wide variety of boat-using experiences, including naval small craft, Dutch busses, Irish wherries, Greenland whaleboats, and service in the Navy and the Hudson's Bay Company.

Yole usage was centred around crofting, inter-island transport, and subsistence rather than cash crop fishing. The latter did feature from time to time, though only the fisherman of North Ronaldsay, the northernmost isle, had a high reputation. Inevitably, activites such as pilotage, lifesaving and, sometimes lucrative, salvage work featured too. Today, though not of yole design, the modern Orkney creel boat is well regarded, with its users continuing what began as a successful late eighteenth-century fishery.

NORTH ISLES YOLE

Though apparently similar to the South Isles yole of the early twentieth century, the North Isles yole which survived it was built with more widely spaced frames and had slightly more upright stems and greater beam. This marked beam, some 7ft 6in on 17ft overall length, helped make a dry boat of considerable capacity, capable of

carrying 1-2 tons of farm produce (including livestock). But the hull form still provided the shallow draft needed for manual handling at the home 'boat noust', or for working loads at open landings. However, a deepish keel surmounted by vertical garboards provided good grip on the water when sailing.

The standing lug sails of the two masted rig were loose footed, but the main was extended along a (gooseneck pivoted) boom by a clew traveller. The two lugs, together with a jib on a bowsprit, made for an effective and manageable sail plan. Smaller yoles carried a single dipping lug sail and, compared to their South Isles equivalents, had more upright stems and less flare in the ends. No examples of the large yoles are thought to survive, though one or two of the smaller types remain.

WESTRAY SKIFF
(North Isles skiff)

Though occurring in the same areas as the North Isles yole, the skiff was of narrower hull form, with slacker bilges and finer ends (especially aft). It provided a more easily driven and weatherly hull, though it had less carrying capacity and was wetter. Large skiffs, which measured up to 19ft 6in overall by 6ft 4in beam, carried a standing lug sail and a jib set to a bowsprit. The smaller skiffs, around 14ft 9in by 5ft 10in, set a dipping lug only.

Although sometimes linked to the yoals of Shetland (*qv*), the straight

stemmed Westray skiff does not really evidence their extremes of hull form, and appears unrelated. However, its potential performance did see it survive into the modern regatta era, albeit with part decking and a stayed, bermudan sloop, dinghy rig.

SOUTH ISLES YOLE

As the working counterparts of the yoles of the North Isles, these South Isles yoles appeared similar in many respects, but exhibited a few significant differences. Typically of tenstrake a side construction, their frame spacing was rather narrow, with continuous (gunwale-to-gunwale) frames and floors alternated with paired ('floating') frames, these latter running from the gunwale to the garboard stroke top only. Typically, a large yole was around 18ft length overall, by 7ft 2in beam, at a keel length of some 12ft to 12ft 8in.

Famously, they set a two sailed spritsail rig, using unstayed, keel stepped masts supported by thwarts. Mast length was around four-fifths of overall boat length, with the foremast slightly higher than the main, and each was positioned one-sixth and one-half of the boat's length from the fore stemhead respectively. The foresail was loose footed whilst the main was rigged to a boom (especially when racing or sometimes a short club was set outboard to improve sheeting). The spritsails were cut with some peak, a rope cringle in the head receiving the

With their loose footed, boomed mainsails and jibs, these Westray skiffs are living up to their reputation for speed by giving their regatta crews a fast reach across Pierowall Bay, Westray. *(Orkney Library Collection)*

tip of the sprit whilst the heel was slung in a 'shangie' (a rope grommet, bighted round the mast, which provided a simply-adjusted support). The smaller yoles, of around 11ft on the keel (15ft overall, by 6ft 4in beam), used a single mast positioned about one-quarter of the boat's length inboard, setting a single, loose footed, boomless spritsail with accompanying jib and bowsprit.

Though motors were fitted from early in the century, by the 1950s the large yoles survived as pleasure and racing craft only, usually re-sparred with a stayed mast and bowsprit, setting a gunter main and jib.

STROMA YOLE

Though bearing Orkney yole characteristics, this distinctive double ender was used exclusively from the Caithness island of Stroma off the southern shore of the Pentland Firth. To cope with the extreme tidal streams and seas which their users might encounter, these large yoles were more barrel chested above the waterline than their Orkney counterparts and carried two extra topside strakes for greater freeboard. Underwater, they exhibited the characteristic standing

A pair of South Isles yoles drawn up on the beach at St Mary's, Holm (on mainland Orkney). Here they show their characteristic fullness of form and nine or ten plank-a-side construction. A herring fifie is laid up beyond. *(Orkney Library Collection)*

strakes and relatively fine ends flared above. Strongly constructed by shell clinker methods, their internal framing (which was not commenced until half a dozen strakes were raised) alternated continuous and discontinuous elements, with floors bolted to the keel. Later boats at least had larch planking, and larger motorised ones might bear decking.

They were built to 12ft, 14ft and even 18ft on the keel and were typically, and respectively, used for inshore lobstering, working the tidal streams when hand lining for cod, and crossing with cattle to the mainland, and bringing fuel and goods home. Sailing rig was Orkney style, with two spritsails and a jib for boats under 15 ft of keel, and two lug sails and a jib for larger ones. Island families might possess one or two boats of different sizes, kept in 'geos' (narrow inlets) or hauled ashore.

Stroma-based boatbuilding is believed to have stemmed from one Donald Smith, who learnt yole building from John Duncan of South

Ronaldsay (Orkney) early in the nineteenth century. Smith is said to have incorporated features from a Norwegian boat washed ashore on Stroma in his eventual design, and his apprentices, Simpson and Banks, continued his work. The former commenced building on Stroma in 1845 and, amazingly, built the last boat there in 1913. Stroma's later carpenter boatbuilders also included Donald Smith senior and junior, and Donald Banks. Though the island was largely de-populated by the late 1950s, the reputation of Stroma's yoles was such that many survived in nearby mainland use until modern times, and copies have also been built.

Sources
Much previously published material on Orkney boats is rather superficial and repetitive, so that this contributor has been privileged indeed to have been allowed to draw upon the insight and unpublished research material generously provided by the Orkney-born naval architect, Dennis Davidson.

Elsewhere, Michael Marshall, *Fishing, the Coastal Tradition* (London 1987), contains some evocative and informative material on Stroma and its yoles, whilst *Working Boats of Britain* illustrates their hull form and typology with great clarity. Much incidental information and sourcework is contained in Alexander Fenton, *The Northern Isles: Orkney and Shetland* (Edinburgh 1987) whilst *Deep Sea Fishing and Fishing Boats* has a classic illustration and description of the Orkney yole.

Herring and Line-fishing Boats of the Northeast

OPEN HERRING BOATS OF ABERDEENSHIRE AND CAITHNESS

Beamy, double ended, open boats, with straight keels, whose crews worked in the herring and line fisheries out of the exposed stations of the Aberdeenshire, East Sutherland and Caithness coasts.

Though locally varied, these mid nineteenth-century boats shared many characteristics in common: long, straight and relatively shallow keels; stems of slight rake with little, or only moderate, curvature; slackly rounded bilges above slightly hollowed, standing strake, garboards; a maximum beam of around one-third overall length, carried slightly aft of amidships; slight hollowing of entry and run; and, for ease of rowing and net handling, low topsides with modest sheer. All were of relatively light clench build, which, for boats which were typically 26ft to 30ft on the keel (34ft to 40ft overall), resulted in beachable hulls of only 3-5 tons weight (5-7 tons ballasted). However, this hull form still provided the burthen, up to 15 tons, and volume needed in the herring fishery. The sheer numbers in use and the

short boat life of around seven years necessitated series building practices.

An equi-sailed, two masted, dipping lug rig was universal. Cheap and versatile, it left the afterbody of the boat clear for the bulky drift nets and catch, whilst the relatively short masts could be handled by the five-man crew when at sea. In port, the masts and gear could be stowed within the boat, a vital consideration in the region's small, overcrowded harbours. Sadly, in adverse sea conditions, with a tired or inexperienced crew, the limitations of both boats and rig could become tragically apparent.

In the early nineteenth century, the successes and potential profits of the 'boat fishery' for herring had led to significant increases in size of boat. In the first decade, boats of 15ft to 16ft on the keel carrying eight to ten nets were the norm, but in the second, these figures rose to 18ft to 24ft keel and over eighteen nets; by 1840, 30ft boats, with twenty to thirty nets, were commonplace. Numbers rose dramatically too, from a couple of hundred in the 1790s, through some eight hundred (local and 'visitor' boats) after the Napoleonic Wars, to more than 1000-plus in the 1820s. This thousand-plus figure was

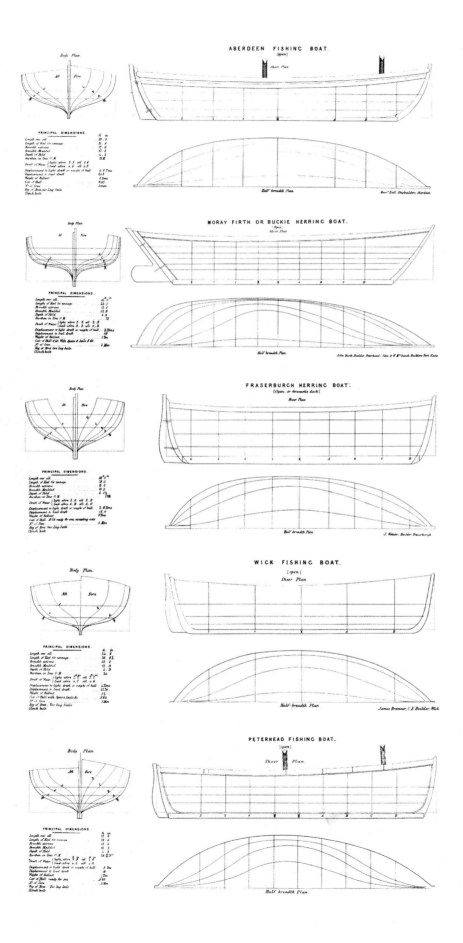

ABERDEEN FISHING BOAT.
[open]

MORAY FIRTH OR BUCKIE HERRING BOAT.
[open]

FRASERBURGH HERRING BOAT.
[Open, or forecastle deck]

WICK FISHING BOAT.
[open]

PETERHEAD FISHING BOAT.
[open]

These five plans were derived from various measured sources, and published in the Washington Report of 1849. The characteristics of the boats depicted are described and discussed in the main text, but the reader should remember that these few plans, allied to sparse contemporary comment, represent the hundreds of boats then found herring fishing along the 200 miles of coast. *(NMM, Coastal Craft Collection)*

then maintained for another 30 years when, at the open boats' peak, in 1855, there were 1500 working from Caithness stations alone.

Many large herring boats were built solely for the 10 to 12 weeks of a region's summer herring fishery and were drawn ashore for the rest of the year. But full time fishers voyaged far (from Lewis to the Forth) and long, whilst, seasonally, continuing to operate boats of similar type – but smaller – in their local white fisheries too. Indeed, it seems likely that the herring boats' ancestry lay directly in the smaller open boats of the region's ancient, staple, line fisheries. The consistent nature of the mid-century boats' characteristics suggests formative Scandinavian influences, by derivation or direct import; for instance, the hull of Washington's Aberdeen Boat, 1849, closely parallels the contemporary Shetland sixern (*qv*).

OPEN HERRING BOAT OF THE MORAY FIRTH
(Buckie boat, scaffa, scaith, scaffie)

A distinctive, light and handy, open double ender, with heavily raked stems and marked hollow to the floors, favoured by crews from the numerous fishertowns and villages of the south Moray coast.

An apparently quite uniform type whose overhanging, equally-raked stems (together) totalled a quarter of the boat's length, resulting in a proportionately shortened keel. The body sections were similarly characteristic, with very firm bilges above flat floors, and well hollowed standing strake garboards – sections said to damp rolling when lying to nets. The entry was hollowed and fine but flared above, and the maximum beam, of less than one-third overall length, was carried well past amidships; aft, reserve buoyancy was created by a full, well rounded stern. As with other open herring boats, the loaded draft approximated internal depth (thwart-to-floor), with less than 2ft of freeboard remaining when laden.

Clench build, and the reduction of plank weight in the extremities effected by the overhanging stems, resulted in lightness for length – only 3 tons for a boat 41ft overall (33ft on the keel) – whilst the deep, hollow midship sections produced righting power with as little as 1 ton of ballast. Significantly, scaffies could be constructed of '... larch fir or other description of pine wood found in the locality ... and built cheap', so many of Moray's coastal villages and townships had building capacity, including the several shipyards at Kingston, or, more typically, the three masterbuilders and their twenty-two employees of Cullen, who produced fourty-four boats in a year (1842). Similarly, the Mcintoshes of Portessie had a high reputation whilst, outside the immediate area, Peterhead's builders constructed their scaffie-influenced Peterhead herring boats and true scaffies too. The average boat life was short, from five to ten years.

By mid-century the prevalent rig was the ubiquitous equi-sailed, two masted, dipping lug, but earlier scaffies sometimes bore a full three masted rig, with the fore and main lugs supplemented by a small mizzen whose clew was extended by a boom (outrigger). The ancient technique of hardening the fore and main luffs for weatherliness by use of a 'wand' (pole) long survived, whilst their keel drag, cutaway stems, and large rudders were conducive to manoeuvrability.

In the late eighteenth century Moray shared in the opportunities created by the withdrawal of government subsidy from the large, inefficiently-operated, drift netting 'busses'. There was rapid increase in boat size, numbers and area of operation, especially since the peoples of Moray's numerous coastal villages (both old and new) were long term, line fishing fisherfolk, rather than crofters with recently developed fishing interests. Their early move from rental to self-ownership of boats (1815-20) is indicative of this, as is the level of boat usage. For instance, in 1830 the eighty fishing families of Boddam owned fifty-seven boats:

Right: This photograph shows so clearly the hollow floors and the sharp turn to the bilges of the now well known scaffie yawl *Gratitude* BCK252. She is photographed at Portnockie on the Moray coast c1936. *(NMM, Oliver Hill Collection, neg no P75448)*

Below: The herring season at Aberdeen. INS2092 and ISN34 display their unmistakeable scaffie profiles. In the light airs shown here, with sweeps to hand and their lofty lug sails tacked down, there is only a hint of their sailing powers. *(NMM, neg no D4456)*

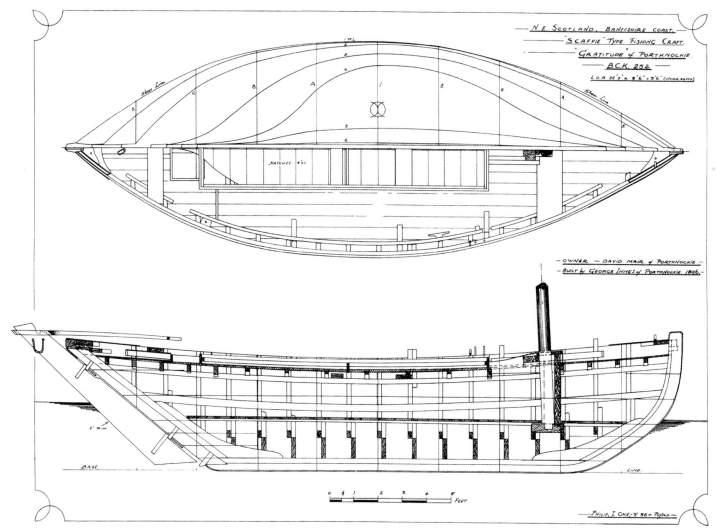

The lines and constuction plan, together with sections, of the small scaffie yawl *Gratitude*. The original can now be visualised through the medium of a recently built replica, as well as through these plans and photographs. *(NMM, Oke, Coastal Craft Collection)*

twenty-three large herring boats; twenty-two small yawls for summer 'small lining' of haddock inshore; and twelve large yawls (cod boats) for setting and hauling 'deep lines' in winter over 30 miles off. Typically, the boat length and crewing of these would have been: over 30ft, five or more men; under 20ft, four men and a boy; and, around 25ft, six men.

The scaffie's ancestry seems to lie in the early line fishing boats of the region, exampled perhaps by Pitsligo's 'six man' boats of 1681. These 'scaiths' represented a small, but locally important, division within that great commonwealth of Scandinavian-influenced boats which dominated the east coast's shore fisheries, from Shetland's Skerries to Humberside's Holderness.

DECKED SCAFFIE
(Skaffie)

A decked (or part decked) double ender, with heavily raked afterstem and characteristically curved forestem, which became the preferred boat of many of the Moray harbour crews who prosecuted the British herring fisheries. Though directly evolved from the mid-century open boats of Moray, scaffies built in the 1870s and 1880s showed three significant modifications: a re-shaped bow, the introduction of decking, and the adoption of a distinctive foresail-with-mizzen rig. The replacement of the long, raked forestem by a snubbier one (having a rounded forefoot and upright stem above) made for bluffer bows but,

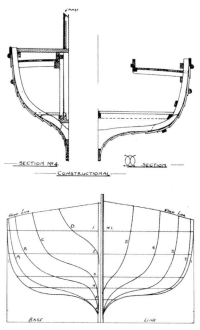

importantly, it constrained overall length on the same length of keel and also helped if boats overrode floating nets. The decking of scaffies (as with fifies (*qv*)) remained a controversial issue until the 1870s, and its uneven introduction owed at least as much to factors involving personal investment and potential gain as to perceptions of safety.

A literal shift of the sails – with enlargement of the dipping lug foresail, elimination of the mainsail, and a new role for the mizzen – saw the evolution of a distinctively high-peaked profile in which both masts were fore-raked and the relatively small, standing lug mizzen's luff paralleled the big foresail's leech; a short running bowsprit with jib generally came to complete the sail plan. The scaffie's cutaway forefoot, allied to a relatively short keel with slight drag, made it manoeuvrable and especially handy when turning to windward. However, though reckoned to 'stand up' well overall, they lacked directional stability in running or quartering conditions.

More conservatively, and perhaps more economically, scaffie builders retained clench build with inserted frames until the end of the boat's era, when size had risen to as much as 60ft overall on a 36ft keel, with 17ft 6in of beam, and 7ft depth of hold, this last, reflecting ongoing improvements in harbourage. Scaffies of more modest size were perhaps more typical, less than 50ft overall, on keels of around 32ft. The few recorded builders reflect the scaffies' unique provenance, and include McIntosh of Buckie, Gardiner of Cullen, and Slater of Portessie.

As with their other Scottish contemporaries and competitors – the fifies and zulus (*qv*) – the scaffies ranged far and wide, with their crews benefiting from the greatly increased catching power conferred by cotton nets.

Scaffie Yawl (*Yawl*)

A small, commonplace boat of scaffie hull form, decked, but with a long central hatch, rigged with a single dipping lug sail (with jib) placed forward, and employed in the inshore fisheries of the Moray coast.

Known principally through records of the *Gratitude* BCK252, built around 1896, such boats seem to have been around 25ft overall, 16ft on the keel, a proportion close to that of the large contemporary scaffies (ie the keel equal to two-thirds overall length). Beam approximated one-third boat length, whilst the fir mast's length equalled it, an inside depth of only 3ft 6in assured easy draft and beaching.

Clench built, of around a dozen ¾in larch planks, the shell was well stiffened by oak frames and stringers, with the regular floors and their overlapping frames bolstered by intermediate floors.

Zulu

An innovative hybrid which coupled the raked sternpost of the scaffie (*qv*) with the straight stem of the fifie (*qv*) to produce a unique, and highly successful, class of big, fore and mizzen rigged luggers during the last decades of the herring sail fishery. Anecdotally, a domestic compromise between a fisherman ('Dad' Campbell of Lossie-mouth) and his wife, the zulu (so-named after the contemporary conflict of 1879) exploited a practical combination of fifie and scaffie features. Compared to the pure scaffie, its straight stem was simpler and cheaper to construct, whilst also improving weatherliness through the increased forefoot and length of keel. However, the raked scaffie-style stern was retained for its virtues of its simplicity of build, provision of deck area aft, and protection of the rudder in overcrowded harbours. The scaffie's distinctive body sections seem to have been modified in the zulu to a more fifie like form, though with comparative depth of body and well 'V'd floors. All told,

A fifie and two zulus (right) being towed out of Great Yarmouth from where some of these Scottish vessels worked the great autumn North Sea herring fishery. These massively built vessels employed steam to haul the heavier gear. In the background is a steam drifter, a vessel which was eventually to spell their demise. *(NMM, neg no P39536)*

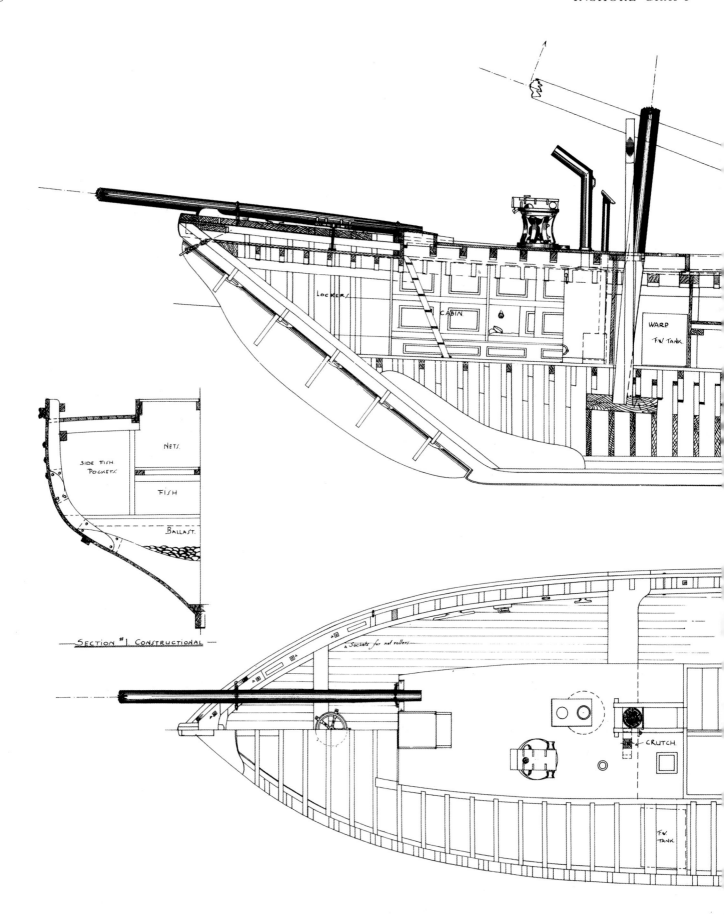

LOCKERS

CABIN

WARP
F.W. TANK

NETS.

SIDE FISH
POCKETS.

FISH

BALLAST.

SECTION #1. CONSTRUCTIONAL

Sockets for net rollers

CRUTCH.

F.W
TANK

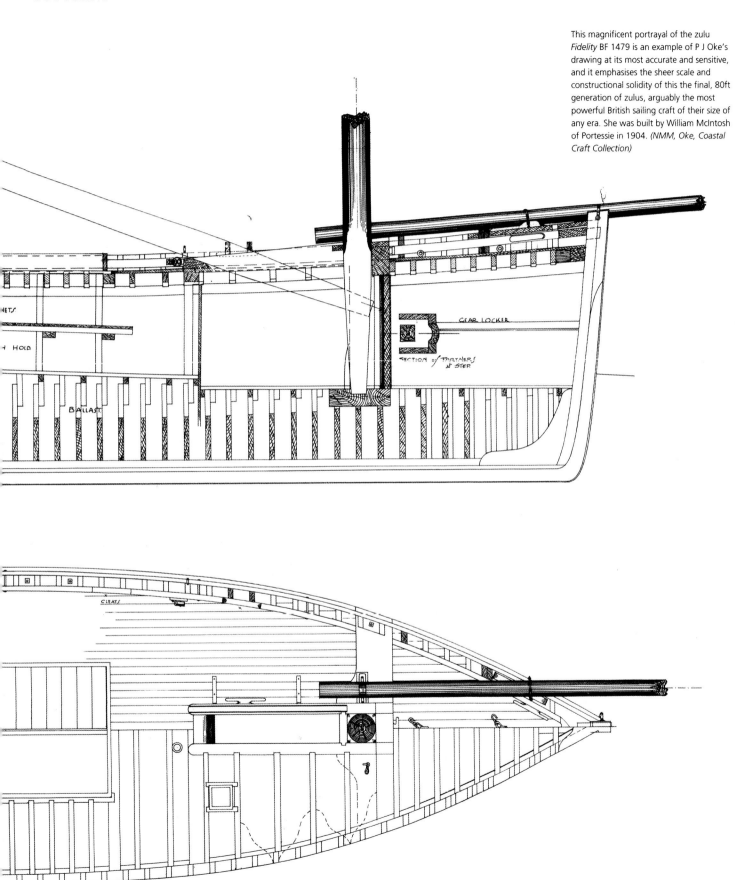

This magnificent portrayal of the zulu *Fidelity* BF 1479 is an example of P J Oke's drawing at its most accurate and sensitive, and it emphasises the sheer scale and constructional solidity of this the final, 80ft generation of zulus, arguably the most powerful British sailing craft of their size of any era. She was built by William McIntosh of Portessie in 1904. *(NMM, Oke, Coastal Craft Collection)*

GEAR LOCKER

SECTION of PARTNERS & STEP

NETS

H HOLD

BALLAST

CLEATS

the design produced the most powerful, economically built, boat possible
within a given overall length, thus sat-
isfying the late nineteenth-century
herring industry's criteria for afford-
able boats of increased size, range,
speed and catching power. The zulu's
rapid advance as a type is well indicated by the 480 listed on the Buckie register in 1900.

Until the mid 1880s, clench build
persisted, and was used to construct
boats of up to 40ft on the keel. A
change to carvel construction, along
with the introduction of steam capstans
afloat (for hauling nets and hoisting
gear), then allowed for a significant
growth in size. Boats of up to 60ft on
the keel (75ft to 80ft overall) and of
70-80 tons carrying capacity became
commonplace. Beam to length ratios
increased to nearly one in four, and
greater sternpost rake gave even longer
overhangs and waterline lengths, with
potential for yet higher speeds. Built
typically on a backbone of a beech keel
strengthened by a 7in deep keelson
with stem and sternpost of oak, the 2in
larch hull planking was fastened using
4¼in galvanised spikes on 4in sided
floors and frames, with the deck planking (also 2in larch) supported by Scots
fir beams. The frames were carried
through the decking to form 'timberheads' inside the low, 12in to 14in, bulwarks, a characteristic of all Scottish
built types. Layout followed that
established by the earlier decked fifies
and scaffies, with boats later fitting
their steam capstan and its (below
deck) boiler immediately aft of the
mizzen mast. Rudder size, and the
need to save space, saw tillers give way
to wheel steering (through a worm
screw gear), but the massive rudders
were still removed when lying to nets.

In the 1890s the zulu's (and fifie's)
dipping lug rig reached the technolog-
ical boundaries of wood and cordage,
fully stretching the professional resources of eight-man crews. Vast
(1500sq ft) and aerodynamically efficient, the stemhead fitted fore lug
came to dominate its sail plan, and
boats were often handled under this
alone. Neither this sail's massive, keel
length mast – up to 2ft diameter at
deck level – nor the mizzen carried any
standing rigging, each relying for support entirely upon its sail halyard and a
burton stay tackle set up to windward.
Any failure was catastrophic. For stability, the stiffness of hull form was
supplemented by 30 tons of stone ballast, some of which might be 'shifted'
if need be. Speeds of some 10 knots
were reached.

During the three decades of its
working pride, 'south' Moray remained the big zulu's stronghold, but its
spiritual home was the wide herring-
shoaling sea. Sadly, steam drifting
brought about its rapid disappearance,
for the zulu's hull proved poorly
shaped for power.

ZULU SKIFF

Though generally lacking a complete
deck, and exhibiting a greater diversity
of rig, the zulu skiff was a smaller variant of the same provenance and characteristics as its larger namesake. Early
boats retained clench build and sometimes carried a two masted, standing
lug rig with jib. These were supplanted
by carvel built skiffs, and the characteristic rig became a high peaked standing
lug. Set from an aft raked, lowering
mast, stepped well forward, the sail
tack was secured to a short iron horse.
Most zulu skiffs bore only a short fore-

castle, accommodating three or four
men, but later examples exhibited full
decking with a long central hatchway.

Skiffs of around 30ft on the keel
(42ft overall) proved popular for inshore fishing, and at a size of 12 to 15
tons proved adaptable to motor power.

Sources
These effectively parallel those for the fifie
(*qv*), with the Scottish Fisheries Museum's
zulu *Research* (ex *Heather Bell*) standing in
place of the *Reaper*. Portsoy has recently
built a copy of the Scaffie Yawl, *Gratitude*.
Peter F Anson's later work, *Scots Fisherfolk*
(Banff 1950), has a few details not in his earlier work, whilst Matthew Tanner's recent,
Scottish Fishing Boats (Princes Risborough
1996), provides (as for the fifie) intimacy
and technical comment via skilfully selected photographs.

The East Coast Fifies

THE EARLY FIFIE
(Newhaven Boat, Yawl)

A beamy, double ended, entirely open
boat with upright stems and straight
keel, worked initially from the beaches
and shallow harbours of southeast
Scotland in the herring and line fisheries. Boats of the mid nineteenth century had good rise of floor with slackish
bilges and a slightly concave garboard.
Though full ended at the sheer, and
carrying a substantial (nearly one-third
overall length) beam amidships, the
underwater hull was well hollowed forward, reckoned 'long in the floor', and
provided good bearing aft. It earnt a
reputation for weatherliness amongst
its contemporaries. A simple, two mast-

ed rig was the norm, comprising fore
and main dipping lug sails of similar
size, carried on masts approximating
the boat's length, with the foremast
right forward and the main near amidships. Their five-man crews reckoned
them 'light and easy to row', an essential attribute when entering harbour,
passage-making (in light conditions),
and working long lines.

These mid-century boats were typically around 27ft on the keel (36ft
overall) and of 7 tons (light-ballasted)
displacement, although the indications
are that boats up to 33ft on the keel
(38ft overall) were in use where deeper harbours were available. Beam remained fairly constant in boats of these
sizes at around 13ft, with internal
depth (thwart-to-floor) optimised at
4ft for rowing and net-handling.
However, a great virtue of the fifie design was its ability to accept variation
in size without the loss of its characteristics, with crews working the large
boats in the summer herring and autumn line fisheries, then transferring
to their smaller 'fifie yawls' for inshore
haddock lining in winter and spring.

Builders were concentrated in the
coastal townships of the Forth, Fife
and Borders, and in particular at Leith.
For cheapness (£80 to £90 complete)
the preferred method was clench build
using 'local larch and pine'. Expanding
herring fisheries provided high demand in the second quarter of the century, with principal builders having
production levels of a dozen to a score

The plan of this early fifie was published in
the 1849 Washington Report and shows a
very beamy and shallow drafted vessel
which was buoyant and light for rowing
(*NMM, Coastal Craft Collection*)

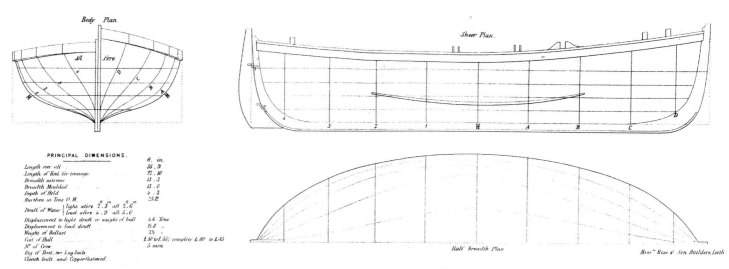

PRINCIPAL DIMENSIONS.

Length over all . . . . 36 . 9
Length of Keel for tonnage . . . . 27 . 10
Breadth extreme . . . . 13 . 5
Breadth Moulded . . . . 13 . 0
Depth of Hold . . . . 4 . 3
Burthen in Tons O.M. 25.22
Draft of Water { light afore 2.3 aft 2.6 / load afore 4.9 aft 5.0
Displacement to light draft or weight of hull . 5.6 Tons
Displacement to load draft 21.8
Weight of Ballast 2½
Cost of Hull . . . . £ 50 to £ 55; complete £ 80 to £ 85
Nº of Crew . . . . 5 men
Rig of Boat, two Lug Sails
Clench built and Copperfastened.

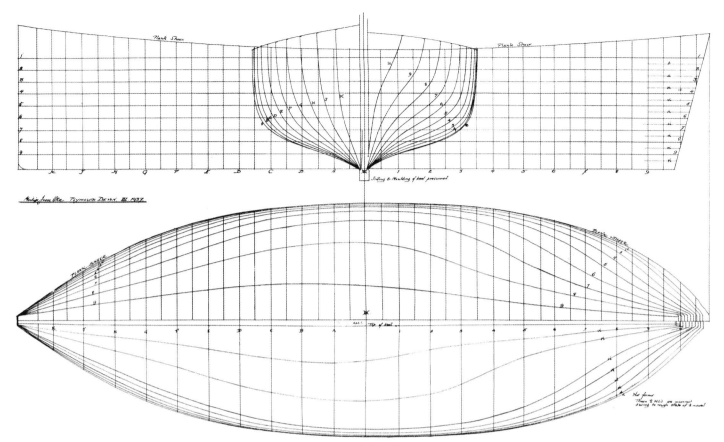

Above: The sketch lines plan of a small fifie hulled boat – probably a baldie – taken from a half model by the famous fifie builders, Miller & Sons, of St Monance in Fifeshire. *(NMM, Oke, Coastal Craft Collection)*

Right: A pair of baldies lie with masts lowered at Pittenween in 1936. These boats readily adopted auxiliary engines. *(NMM, Oliver Hill Collection, neg no P73263)*

of 1st (over 30ft) and 2nd class boats, together with numerous 'yawls', in a year.

The type's predecessors seem to date to at least the eighteenth century, and contemporary comment described them as '[having] been used for centuries'.

SKIFF AND BALDIE

Small and medium sized boats of fifie hull form, open or part decked, carrying a single (or main and mizzen) dipping lug sail rig, and employed primarily in the line and herring fisheries along the length of Scotland's east coast. During the second half of the nineteenth century such boats

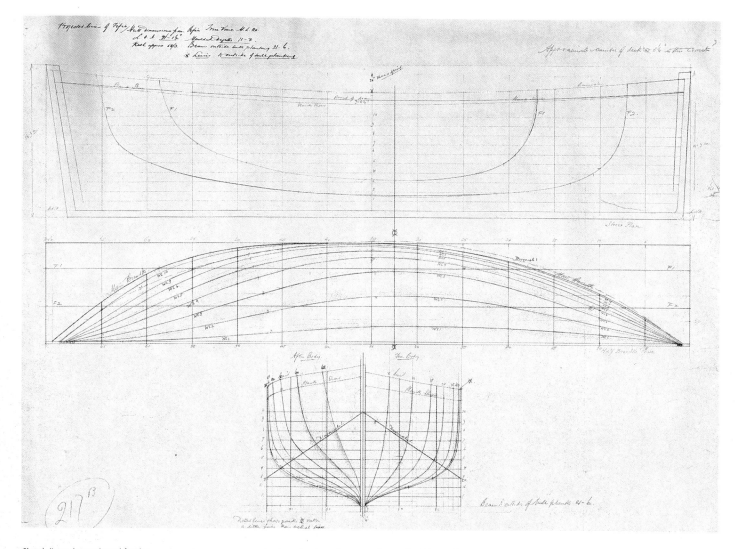

Sketch lines plan projected for the dimensions of the big sailing fifie, the 71ft *True Vine* ML 20.
(NMM, Oke, Coastal Craft Collection)

exhibited considerable variation in size, rig and attitude to deck structure and, though maintaining the basic fifie hull form, there was a general trend to hollower sections, and a move to carvel construction in the later, decked, types.

However, the mid-century fishermen strongly opposed the introduction of decked boats, on sound grounds of increased cost and the difficulties of operation. So, small open skiffs, that could be worked locally or seasonally by small crews (or even 'a man and boy') under a single dipping lug and oars, remained an important component in many communities' fleets from the late eighteenth to early twentieth centuries.

However, official and economic pressures saw the introduction of part decked boats in the upper Forth in the early 1860s. Initially, these kept the universal two masted dipping lug rig, but had a full deck built on from the bow to mainmast, whilst, aft of amidships, a section of open hull was retained for handling the nets, all terminated by a short afterdeck with steering well. This hybrid was quickly rationalised into a design with foredeck cuddy, dipping lug main, and smaller, standing lug, mizzen. The town of Leith, and the then popular Italian radical, Garibaldi, were the derivation of the eponymous '(Leith) Baldie'. Baldies, of 23ft to 30ft on the keel, and a crew of five, soon became a popular and enduring type.

FIFIE

A large, fully decked, straight stemmed and sharp bowed vessel, carrying a powerful rig of lofty dipping lug sail forward, with smaller standing lug aft. The fifie was a characteristic fishing boat type of Britain's great, late nineteenth-century, east coast herring fisheries.

This was the ultimate development of the sailing fifie. Whilst maintaining its original features, increasing length (up to 70ft overall) eventually allowed for a proportionate rise in beam-to-length ratio, with beam now carried aft of amidships. Its sharp, slightly hollowed entrance, fair run, great waterline length (almost equalling overall length) and span of straight keel below hollowed garboards, made for a fast, easily driven, and weatherly hull without resort to excessive depth or rise of floor. Even though the first fully decked boat had been built at Eyemouth in 1856, and part decking was formally promoted in the 1860s (*qv* baldie), the change to fully decked boats with secure hatchways was halting and uneven, with some places, in-

cluding the important Fifeshire community of Buckhaven, resisting change till the 1880s.

The 1870s seems to have been a period of major experimentation, resulting in a mix of part decked and part hatchway craft, together with cheaply converted and lengthened open fifies. Hull design and construction became more varied too, and the building of larger fifies by carvel, not clinker, methods was commenced. Rigs, though, often still approximated to the early, equi-sailed, forms, with a foremast (marginally longer than the boat's length) right forward, and the fore lug only slightly larger than the main amidships. But this trend was accelerated by increasing the size of the foresail at the expense of the main, which was moved aft of the boat's working area to become a standing, auxiliary sail. Higher peaked lugs, and a headsail on a running bowsprit, made for gains in windward and light weather performance. In adverse or light weather conditions, crews used the oar power of their 20ft sweeps, or paddle tug towage, to clear or make harbour.

Crail on the Fife coast, basking in the peace of a summer's day in 1913, is a reminder of the east coast's prolific inshore fleet and the compact nature of its havens. Some two dozen, fifie hulled yawls are crammed ashore and afloat. *(NMM, neg no N30276)*

In the 1880s the largest class of fifie reached 55ft on the keel (exceptionally 60ft) and, at the turn of the century, when they reached their apogee, were commonly 66ft to 68ft on the keel, giving over 70ft overall. From fore to aft they were invariably divided into the foreroom with mast tabernacle, the fish hold (accessed by a long narrow hatchway), and the cabin. The deck edge was marked by a bulwark only 12in high. Construction, which took three to four months, involved heavily-fastened components of large scantling, for example: keel, of oak or beech, 12in by 8in with ⅞in iron bolts; floors, 2ft 4in moulded by 5in sided at 12in apart; frames, of oak, 4½in by 8in, at 12in apart; and 2in planking with 4½in galvanised nails. The lowering foremast, whose length equalled the keel, was a single stick of Norwegian pine (or pitch-pine), over 20in diameter at the deck, and weighed some 3 tons. The fore lug itself had a 40ft luff and, together with its 30ft yard, could only be hoisted through use of triple and double blocked tackles allied to the steam capstan. It had to be lowered and dipped aft of the mast when tacking. Total sail area could reach 3650sq ft, counterbalanced by many tons of stone ballast. By the end of the century the building of such large, high-capital boats had become concentrated in specialist 'fifie' yards, of which those at St Monance (Miller's, established there since 1779) and Anstruther were perhaps best known. Elsewhere, local

A Scottish coble, showing the type's characteristic flat bottom, plumb square stern and high bow. This large 'bay boat' type, used for working salmon stake nets at St Cyrus, derived its power from hauling out along an anchor line rather than the elderly Seagull outboard shown here. *(A G Osler)*

builders, such as James Weatherhead at Eyemouth, met smaller markets.

From the the mid-1880s onwards the fifie became a supreme herring catching and sailing machine, capable of taking dozens of tons of fish in its 2000 yards of (seventy-eight) drift nets in a night and, in favourable conditions, delivering them fresh to market at speeds approaching 10 knots. Geographically, fifie crews ranged from the Irish Sea, north-about through the Western and Northern Isles and down south to the coasts of East Anglia. Seasonally, they might work almost throughout the year, seeking the shoals in the winter days of Caithness and the west, then under the short summer darkness of the far north, and on into the fading autumn of the south. But, such dominance under sail was shortlived. Few sailing drifters were built after 1903, for steam drifters were rapidly outfishing sail and, though the fifie design proved adaptable for motor, both converted and new-built motor fifies were outmoded by the early 1930s.

FIFIE SMACK

A smack rigged variant of the fifie which, in mainland Scotland, proved of limited success and spread. During the developmental period of the 1870s, gaff cutter and ketch 'smack' rigs were introduced on fifie built boats along the

Aberdeenshire and Banff coasts (from Fraserburgh to Macduff). The rig was acknowledged as handy and economical of maintenance, but was discarded in the area in the 1880s for the (now much-improved) lug rig, a decision attributed partly to local sailmakers' inexperience in cutting gaff sails. Decked, but with an open fish hold and fore hatch (for mast lowering), the smacks' narrow decks provided precarious working space for a five -man crew.

Sources
The scarcity of surviving material remains, and the passing of those with first hand memories, ensures that March's *Sailing Drifters* endures as the single definitive source on such Scottish sailing vessels of the late nineteenth century. However, care must be exercised as, for example, his restricted remit downplayed the long-term role and importance of such boats in the line fisheries. Careful reading of two definitive works: Malcolm Gray's *Fishing Industries of Scotland* (Oxford 1978), and J R Coull, *Sea Fisheries of Scotland* (Edinburgh 1996), can help redress that balance though, other than as recorded in official statistics, both are weak in descriptions of the boats themselves. Fortunately, Capt John Washington's *Fishing Boats (Scotland)* (1849), is unexpectedly strong on the Forth area, and, pictorially, the work of northern mid-Victorian artists can repay attention.

Peter F Anson, *Fishing Boats and Fisher Folk on the East Coast of Scotland* (London 1930), still provides by far the best evocation of associated people and places.

SCOTTISH COBLE

A very distinctive open boat, marked out by its keel-less flat bottom, square stern and generally upswept bow, once found in estuarine and beach based fisheries along the entire Scottish east coast. In place of a conventional keel the coble is built up from a heavy, central, flat plank (the ram). Typically, two or three clench-fastened strakes on each side of this form the boat's flat bottom aft, and these rise and twist forward to join a slightly curved and raked stem. Outside each outer bottom plank, a descriptively-named 'rising strake' turns the bilge, leading to the three or four strakes which produce somewhat flared topsides. A plumb, flat, square stern terminates the boat aft. Transverse strength is increased by regularly spaced, three-piece sawn frames, together with thwarts (on risings) and a sheer-level net platform right aft. Simplicity, economy of build, and ease of maintenance, were Scottish coble attributes. Building was often in the hands of long established families who supplied the dominant salmon companies, for example, the Eastons for J Johnstone & Sons (Montrose), and six generations of Lees at Berwick.

The coble's boxy after sections, combined with the smooth entry and lift of the bow, provided good load carrying capacity (for wet nets or pots) at

relatively small size, whilst maintaining the static stability, shallow draught and buoyancy needed when launching and landing through moderate surf. Size ranged from 12ft up to 30ft of overall length and, in some localities, as along the Tweed at Berwick, different sizes might be employed for up-river (14ft), mid-river (18ft) and river-mouth (21ft) fishings. With few exceptions, cobles were propelled by crews of one to three men, each working a pair of captive, non-feathering oars on single, wooden tholes.

From the Tweed at Berwick to the Findhorn in Moray (and even into Caithness), the Scottish coble was synonymous with the profitable river and shore based seine and stake net salmon fishings of the early modern period. Large seining stations supported two or three dozen cobles, with crews of seven or eight men each working a pair of boats and some 40 fathoms of net. Cobles were also widely used for nearshore shellfishing, small lining and subsistence activities, as for example at the Berwickshire havens of Ross and Burnmouth, and they might act as estuarine transports too. Some larger Scottish cobles proved adaptable for motorisation but, overall, the fleets have declined drastically owing to the recent closure of the net fisheries, a move designed to enhance rod fishing stocks.

Though termed the 'Scottish coble', this square-sterned type actually overlaps the 'English' raked-stern variety, and was formerly found at least as far south as the Tyne. It may well be a relict type, representative of incoming, seminal Irish influences, for throughout its range the coble often seems to be associated with sites of early Christianity and the salmon.

Sources
Working Boats of Britain provides by far the most recent and informative material on the boats themselves, whilst several of the salmon fisheries are covered in specialised publications, for example, Bruce Walker's 'The Salmon Industry', in *The Port of Montrose* (Ed G Jackson) (1993).

The English North Sea Coast

SEAFARING ACTIVITY along the coast of northeast England from Berwick to the Humber has been extremely varied owing largely to the exploitation of natural resources in its hinterland such as coal and iron ore, the nearness to rich fishing grounds, and the presence of great rivers which gave rise to vast maritime trade and port development.

The coast borders a varied hinterland and therefore shows numerous different features. The broad estuaries of the Tyne, Wear, Tees and Humber provided advantageous conditions for shipping, but elsewhere the many dangerous cliffs and rocks have confined port activities to a few favoured locations.

Taking a survey from north to south, the northernmost strip of Northumberland, better known for the scenic splendours of Holy Island and the Farne Islands, is largely inhospitable. Further south

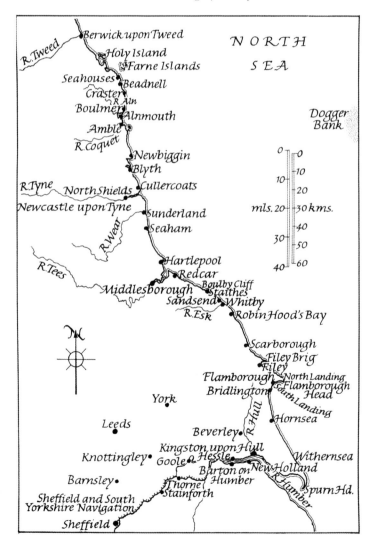

in the county ships and boats have found opportunities in the lesser river estuaries including those of the Aln, Coquet and Blyth and also in small indentations in the coastline. Southwards, beyond the Tyne, Wear and Tees, and beyond the Durham coast defaced by coalmining activity, is the coast of Yorkshire with spectacular cliffs, bays and inlets, steep ravines and perilous shelving rocks, and picturesque villages and ports. Here, port sites range in size and variety from river mouths such as the Esk at Whitby and the smaller beck at Staithes, to places largely protected by considerable headlands, such as Filey, Scarborough and Bridlington. There are smaller landing places in bays providing partial shelter such as Runswick Bay, Robin Hood's Bay and the Flamborough Landings, or on wide stretches of beach as at Redcar. Last, the eroding lowland coast of east Yorkshire ends at Spurn Head and the Humber estuary.

Although prevailing winds are southwesterly and can be gusty when coming off high ground, dominant easterly gales turn the coast into a treacherous lee shore with heavy breakers and surf sometimes well out to sea, preventing safe entry to many harbours. Sailing boats had to be weatherly enough to reach shore in offshore winds, and in onshore gales needed to be capable of beaching or else weathering the storm. Countless craft have foundered on the perilous scaurs and rocks and at the foot of precipitous cliffs.

Bridlington Bay was a well known anchorage, sheltered by the land and the off-lying Smithic Sands from all but easterly gales. Even in good conditions fishermen must take care to locate the exact approach to a landing such as the difficult channels through Redcar scaurs; and a thick sea mist or 'roke' is also a particular hazard of northeast England.

Along this stretch of coast the tide rise travels north to south but tidal streams can be rapid and irregular in estuaries and shallow water and around rocks and headlands. These problems are worsened in the Humber where shifting silt makes it one of the most treacherous tidal waters in Britain.

The North Sea is amongst the richest fishing grounds of all continental shelves. Herring, white fish such as cod, haddock, ling and plaice, and also lobster, brown crab and salmon have been fished extensively. There were numerous fishing ports. For example, in 1817 the small river port of Staithes with seventy cobles and some seventeen five-man boats was the largest fishing station along the English east coast north of the Wash. The northeast supplied fish to inland towns and exported locally cured dried fish to Catholic countries. Towards the end of the nineteenth century the emergence of steam trawlers able to fish more distant grounds led to the growth of ports such as Hull and North Shields and many smaller fishing communities declined. A later change occurred when non-European Union countries imposed territorial limits in the 1970s causing the dwindling of distant water fleets and a revival in inshore fisheries.

The coalfields of Northumberland and Durham gave unique opportunities for coastal trade in coal to London and the southeast. This was once the biggest coasting trade in Britain, there being some 400 colliers even by the early seventeenth century. Many ports were improved primarily for shipping coal. More sailing colliers were built at Whitby and Scarborough than near the coalfields. Whitby in 1792-93 was the second largest builder in England for tonnage of shipping produced. Captain James Cook's vessels of exploration *Endeavour* and *Resolution* were converted Whitby-built colliers chosen for their sturdiness and beaching properties. Whitby also exported locally quarried and processed alum to London in the seventeenth and eighteenth centuries and took part in the Greenland whale fishery in the late eighteenth and early nineteenth centuries.

Industrial activity in the nineteenth and early twentieth centuries was colossal. The Tyne, Wear and Tees with their nearness to coal

The coble was the dominant beach boat of the North Sea coast. Here a little salmon coble pushes off into a calm sea at Scarborough while Scarborough yawls lie at anchor. Cobles were remarkable boats and would sometimes put out to sea off an open beach when the weather forced bigger boats to seek shelter. *(NMM, Oliver Hill Collection, neg no P75444)*

and iron ore and other requirements developed variously into iron and steel, shipbuilding and engineering and chemical processing centres of worldwide significance. There have also been imports of timber from Scandinavia and much coastwise and international trade in general cargoes. Exchange of goods between seagoing vessels and river craft was important in the Humber estuary with its huge inland waterway connections to much of eastern England. For years a variety of specialised small craft have provided all manner of assistance to shipping and industry along the coast and in the ports and rivers of northeast England, offering lighterage and pilotage for instance, or handling mooring ropes. Some were themselves coastal traders such as the billyboys and Humber sloops. Plenty of illicit trade took place as well. For instance, 200 years ago whole populations were involved in profitable smuggling of dutiable goods such as spirits, tea, tobacco, lace and silk. Fishing was not always the sole pursuit of cobles and five-man boats.

In the late twentieth century, links to North Sea oil and gas fields support the huge oil refineries and petro-chemical industries in the Northeast. Tourism is everywhere and yacht marinas occupy some former commercial docks though many places still support inshore fishing fleets, known for the quality and freshness of their catches.

A Tyne foyboat leaving the river to 'seek' for ships at sea, sometime in the 1920s. The wooden fender blocks are visible on the sheerstrake. *(Photograph by the late E G Hails)*

TYNE FOYBOAT

The Tyne foyboat in the late nineteenth and early twentieth centuries was a stalwart, manoeuvrable, two manned rowing, sculling and sailing boat employed in mooring and unmooring ships, chiefly steam colliers, at staiths and buoys in the busy river Tyne. She was designed to tow alongside ships at sea and withstand work in the congested river, while having good rowing, sculling and inshore seakeeping capabilities.

A typical foyboat was around 16ft long with a length/beam ratio of just over 3:1. The hull was straight keeled and vertical stemmed, with flat floors and rounded bilge amidships which, despite full lines carried well forward, produced an easy waterline with lean entry and fine run. The transom was wineglass shaped and sheerline strong with tumblehome on the top strake. The rig consisted of a single dipping lug sail on a lowering mast.

Foyboats were clinker planked of larch on oak and were heavily strengthened and protected against tow rope and hawser abrasion and the inevitable knocks of mooring work. Wooden fender blocks on the sheerstrake would pull off rather than jeop-

ardise the boat herself if they snagged on an obstruction. The steam bent timbers were supplemented by three sawn and joggled frames. Large knees reinforced the mast thwart against longitudinal stress during towing. Foymen preferred firwood oars, made from the heartwood for strength and stiffness.

A towing rope was clipped to a suitable projection on the ship by means of a hook on a 16ft pole, and an off-centre lead for the tow rope prevented the foyboat from yawing towards the ship when towed alongside. The tow rope passed to the mast thwart through a thimble on the outer end of the short 'snotter' rope hitched to the stem ringbolt.

Foying was dangerous. Ships rarely slackened speed when accepting the tow rope; boatmen sometimes fell off mooring buoys when handling hawsers; and there was always the risk of having an anchor dropped on them in error.

Foyboats sailed far to sea to 'seek' incoming ships, until 1933 when competitive 'seeking' was abolished and foyboats were employed on a rota basis.

Principal builders between the Wars were Mitchelson and Campbell of

South Shields and Clarkson of North Shields, and several dozen boats were in use.

Foying most probably developed along with the coal trade and some 500 men are thought to have worked as pilots and foymen in the early nineteenth century. At that time foyboats towed or kedge-hauled the sailing ships along in calms or unfavourable winds and were probably longer and narrower than the later boats.

A replica sailing foyboat, *Bonny Tyne*, was built in 1977 by F McNulty and Sons, South Shields, for Tyne and Wear Museums. A few diesel powered foyboats, of modern design, built by Robsons (Boatbuilders) Ltd at South Shields, are still active today.

Sources
My account is based largely on a paper and further research (in publication) by Adrian Osler.

TYNE KEEL

The Tyne keel was a beamy double ended, shallow rowing, sailing and poling lighter used until the nineteenth century for transhipping coal from riverside loading points to seagoing colliers lying in deeper water further downstream.

Carrying capacity was a 21 tons 'keel' of coal, fixed for five centuries by law to prevent avoidance of coal taxes by the use of oversize craft. Coal was carried almost at deck level, keeping the difference in working levels between the keel and collier to a minimum. Unlike other river trading craft, which stowed cargo below deck, the Tyne keel could therefore have round sections and finer ends.

Surviving illustrations, writings and models suggest keels were 42ft long on a 16ft or 17ft beam, with round slack bilges, wedge shaped entry, raked curved stem, broad cutwater forefoot, vertical stern, slightly hollow run, no bulwarks and completely flat sheer. The hold floor or 'shuts' was only 1ft 6in below deck level and the heaped coal was contained on three sides by vertical boards named 'jells'.

Early keels set a single square sail but in the nineteenth century many changed to fore-and-aft rig with a spritsail and jib. They could further be propelled by two oars and steered by a huge oar or 'swape'. A rudder and tiller later replaced the steering oar. In shallow water 30ft punting poles called 'puoys' were worked from the side decks.

Keels had to work with the tides and

the five-man crew needed good local knowledge. Conditions on the river included shifting shoals, and heavy freshets which could override the flood tide.

Keels were carvel built with broad oak or elm planks on close spaced oak frames, and trenail and copper fastened. A hatch in the afterdeck gave access to the crew's quarters.

The Tyne keel was a strictly localised type but numbers were estimated to have reached some 800 in the early nineteenth century. As a type the Tyne keels seem to have retained their medieval characteristics for five centuries: even eighteenth-century writers note their seeming antiquity and unaltering character. Use of keels declined rapidly in the nineteenth century when colliers could navigate the now deepened river and load direct from the newly introduced coal drops.

Sources
Roger Finch, *Coals from Newcastle* (Lavenham 1973) tells the story of the Northeast coal trade in the days of sail and devotes a chapter to Tyne keels. My account also draws on a paper read by Adrian Osler at 'Medieval Europe '92' (York 1992), and on model keels in the Newcastle Discovery Museum, Newcastle-upon-Tyne.

TYNE WHERRY

The Tyne wherry was a beamy, capacious, double ended sailing, rowing, poling and later dumb, and then steam or motor powered river boat, related to the Tyne keel but larger and more versatile to meet the cargo carrying needs of the expanding manufacturing and shipbuilding industries in the nineteenth century.

A typical wherry was 50ft long and 20ft in the beam, with fairly full round bilges, bilge keels, flat sheer, wedge entry, straight raked stem, virtually flat curved floors, straight keel and slightly fuller at the quarters than forward. The hold was the full depth of the hull, and short decks at bow and stern were linked by narrow sidedecks alongside the large open cargo hatch.

Early wherries were propelled by tides, oars and punting poles or by square sail, and later a spritsail and jib. Groups of dumb wherries were towed by steam paddle tugs. In the late nineteenth century many wherries were fitted with steam engines and screw propellers and carried a small hand-operated crane forward.

Wherries were extremely heavily constructed to survive groundings and

Above: The Tyne wherry *Elswick No 2*, photographed when she was still a dumb barge. She is, typically, clinker planked while the open cargo hatch has had its sides built up in order to increase her load. A rudder and tiller are fitted, not common features on a dumb barge. *(NMM, Oliver Hill Collection, neg no P73926)*

Below: This sketch of a Tyne wherry shows her full quarters and the rounded sections, quite unlike the London River barges *(qv)* with their flat bottoms and sharp chines. She measures 47ft overall and 18ft 9in on the beam. *(NMM, Coastal Craft Collection)*

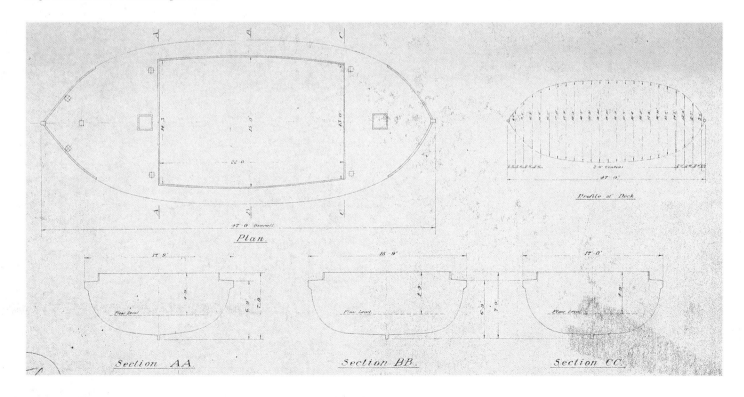

collisions, and being crushed in the busy river environment, but unlike keels they were clinker planked.

Wherries supplied visiting seagoing vessels with provisions and bunker coal, and carried raw materials and manufactured goods between riverside sites or to and from shipping. By 1900 over two dozen companies and individuals operated wherries on the Tyne and some major industries including lead refiners and chemical manufacturers ran their own fleets.

Elswick No 2 belonged to the Vicker's Scotswood factory and conveyed huge pieces of machinery manufactured there downstream for shipment. She was nearly 55ft long and over 23ft in the beam, was the last

Tyne wherry to work on the river and one of the last to be built, in the 1930s. Bought by N Keedy and Sons after World War II, she undertook similar tasks such as ferrying steel sections between shipyard locations. She was saved by the Maritime Trust and later gifted to Tyne and Wear Museums.

Some wherries remained in use after the War but numbers had begun to decline following the 1914-18 War owing to the loss of river trade and competition from road transport.

Sources
My account is based largely on research by Adrian Osler and a model of a wherry in the Newcastle Discovery Museum, Newcastle-upon-Tyne.

Cobles

ENGLISH SQUARE STERNED COBLE

The English square sterned coble in the nineteenth and early twentieth centuries was a very distinctive clinker planked rowing and sailing boat used for fishing, piloting and foying, and on occasion as a pleasure and racing boat along the northeast coast of England. She was designed for launch and recovery stern to shore through heavy breaking surf yet could go to sea for long distances, sail unusually close to the wind, and in the hands of experienced men she could survive a gale.

The hull form was curious and complex. She had pronounced forward sheer with high slightly curved forward-raking stem and deep rounded forefoot. Her entry was fine, with lean,

Square sterned cobles moored in the river at Staithes in Yorkshire, in 1926. In the middle of the last century some 400 men were employed here in the fisheries. The broad planking and sharp tumblehome are clearly shown as is the common practice in the northeast of painting the planking in contrasting bands of light and dark colours. *(NMM, neg no G3427)*

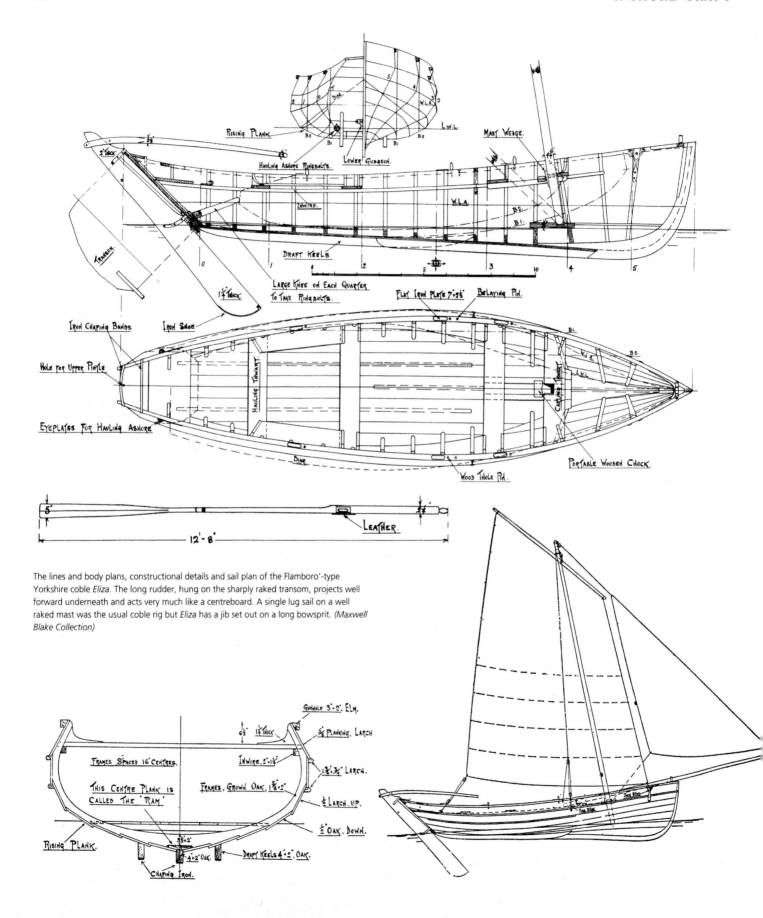

The lines and body plans, constructional details and sail plan of the Flamboro'-type Yorkshire coble *Eliza*. The long rudder, hung on the sharply raked transom, projects well forward underneath and acts very much like a centreboard. A single lug sail on a well raked mast was the usual coble rig but *Eliza* has a jib set out on a long bowsprit. *(Maxwell Blake Collection)*

hollow lines below the waterline and considerable flare above. Forming a continuation of the forefoot, the part-keel ended just abaft amidships. Her afterbody was shallow with flat floors and hard bilges. Two side keels or 'drafts' extended from just forward of amidships to the stern. Strakes were uncommonly wide and for much of its length the sheerstrake had a generous tumblehome. The sheerline curved up sharply aft and the horseshoe shaped square stern was half the maximum beam and half the height of the stem and raked aft at 45 degrees.

The forward flare gave lift in heavy seas and buoyancy when heeling. Along with the high bow it prevented water breaking inboard when she was putting to sea or making a landing.

The abnormally deep forefoot, fine entry and hollow underwater lines helped keep her head to the sea at the water's edge and also gripped the seas for windward sailing.

The tumblehome increased the degree to which she could heel before water came inboard, and the drafts facilitated beaching, prevented her after end from digging into the sand, and held her upright when ashore.

Cobles came in all lengths from 10ft to 40ft and even larger. A length/beam ratio of 4:1 was usual for a medium sized sailing coble. *Toiler of the Sea*, built at Whitby in 1895 for Staithes, measured 33.9ft long with 7.9ft beam and carried a lug sail and jib. Although details of rig could vary, cobles normally carried a single large dipping lug sail with several rows of reef points, hoisted by a single heavy rope halyard. A bight was given a turn around the sailing pin which pointed downwards from the outside gunwale. The fall was jammed between the gunwale and the standing part of the rope so a quick pull would release it and allow the lug to fall rapidly in squalls. Set up on the weather bow the tack was held by a hook on the gunwale or on a tack rope secured athwartships. A bowline kept the luff taut and helped the coble to point well up into the wind. The mainsheet was never made fast but was taken around the inwire abaft the after thwart and held by the helmsman. Big cobles sometimes set a jib on a bowsprit.

This fine photograph of the square sterned, Filey coble *Joan and Robin* was taken in 1955. The lug sail has five rows of reef points, a blunt testimony to the sorts of weather that a coble was intended to stand up to, and the high clew is typical. *(NMM, Oliver Hill Collection, neg no P75445)*

A very long rudder descended a good way under the hull and also functioned as a keel to reduce leeways drift. The long tiller was shaped to slope into the coble and be within quick and easy reach of the helmsman. Coble oars had an iron ring on one side of the loom which fitted over a thole pin in the sheer so that they should not be lost should the rower let go. Ballast, maybe sand, stones or pig iron, was carried.

Having no full length keel the coble was constructed around a centreline plank called the ram. Stout sawn floors and timbers were joggled to fit against the broad clinker strakes. The stern was usually planked after the drafts were in place and the part-keel was fitted last. Each builder had his own method of shaping a coble. One of the last coble builders, Tony Goodall at Sandsend, near Whitby, who retired in 1995, used a predetermined set of plank widths and angles of bevel for the lands at various stations along the boat's length. Larch and oak were favoured materials and planks were fastened with copper nails rivetted over roves.

Principal builders active at the turn of the nineteenth and twentieth centuries included Hopwood at Flamborough and Cambridge Brothers at Hartlepool. Founded in 1870, J and J Harrison at Amble was still building cobles in the 1980s. After World War II, Whitby had more coble builders than anywhere else.

The coble's main occupation was fishing. According to season they worked drift nets for herring, pots for crab and lobster, drift or fixed nets for salmon and trout, and long lines for cod, halibut, ling, haddock and skate. Larger cobles worked trawls, and small cobles were carried aboard Yorkshire yawls and five-man boats and launched and used for long lining on the Dogger Bank.

Procedures for hauling cobles up the beach varied. At Filey horses hauled them up on wheels, while a steam powered hauling engine was used on the steep North Landing at Flamborough.

Typically, a 30ft coble carried a three-man crew but four worked the larger herring cobles. High standards of seamanship were called for; a coble could be dangerous when running, for instance, as the forefoot could gripe and cause her to broach and capsize.

Cobles worked from some thirty beaches, harbours and creeks between the Tweed and Humber and were numerous in the late nineteenth century. In the years 1869 to 1879 around 120 were registered at Whitby as belonging to Staithes alone.

Sailing cobles had reached their purest form by this time. It has been suggested that they developed from Celtic skin boats, yet much of their build indicates Dutch or Norse ancestry and the terms used for her components derive from various languages. *The Oxford English Dictionary* quotes use of the word coble in various spellings from as early as about AD 950 but no known writings prior to the nineteenth century describe the boat in any detail.

By the 1940s most cobles had an engine, positioned forward of amidships to keep the shaft angle low and retain the boat's shallowness aft; and the propeller was housed between the drafts to shield it from damage.

In Northumberland the drop-drive

The two double ended cobles *Rock of Ages* and *Caroline*. The hollow run aft is clearly seen. There were also larger, double ended, decked boats but they were not true cobles – they had a full length keel. *(NMM, neg no P1163)*

was favoured. The outboard section of stern gear was lifted by means of a draw bar to lie close to the coble's bottom when she was ashore. Yorkshire cobles preferred the 'raised ram tunnel', originated in the 1930s in Whitby by bending the bottom planking into a wave-like concavity.

Cobles are still preferred by many inshore fishermen. The modern coble is three beams long and has fuller and deeper lines to provide buoyancy for carrying the diesel engine, wheelhouse, hydraulic haulers and more fishing gear. Scantlings are heavier to

withstand forces exerted by the engine. A heavier coble needs more powerful aids to beaching such as a tractor-driven trailer with pneumatic tyres.

Tony Goodall produced more than thirty cobles between 1953 and 1992. *Winnie S*, built in 1985, is typical with a length of 32ft and a beam of 10ft 4½in. Strakes are ¾in thick on frames 2¼in by 3½in thick and spaced on 14in centres. Based in Whitby she works pots for crab and lobster and trammel nets for white fish and is powered by a 46.25hp Lister air cooled diesel engine.

DOUBLE ENDED COBLE
(Mule Coble or Coble Mule)

The double ended coble had the appearance of the transom sterned type except for her after end which differed

remarkably in shape. In place of the square stern she had a part-keel aft, pointed stern and raked sternpost. The strakes had a hollow run and the drafts ended well short of the stern. For much of its length the sheerstrake tumbled home but twisted back at its after end to meet the sternpost.

A double ended coble could run more safely in a big following sea than the square sterned type but, lacking buoyancy aft and the steadying effect of drafts, she could be more difficult to beach. She was favoured by pilots and some fishermen working from rivers and harbours or fairly flat beaches.

TWO MASTED COBLE

Some larger fishing cobles set a small lug mizzen sail to provide greater sail area and hence more power for towing

a trawl net. It also kept the coble's head to the wind when riding at herring drift nets with the mainmast lowered.

A bumpkin extended the mizzen sheet aft. A mizzen was sometimes set by pilot cobles or those taking part in regattas to obtain a bit more speed.

Sources
Cobles are well documented. *The English Coble*, National Maritime Museum Monographs and Reports, No 30 (1978) is the standard work, edited by Commander J E G McKee and based on the journals of Commander H Oliver Hill. N C A Bradley, 'North East Coast Sailing Cobles', *Model Shipwright*, Nos 26 and 28, has much detail and contains an extensive bibliography.

Robin Gates 'The Coble', *Classic Boat* (April 1990), and Gloria Wilson 'Yorkshire's Beamy Cobles', *Classic Boat* (July 1993) describe modern cobles.

Yorkshire Luggers

FIVE-MAN BOAT
(Yorkshire lugger or farm)

The five-man boat, so named because five shareholders were involved and usually sailed in her, was a robust three masted, lug rigged herring drifter and line fishing vessel used primarily by Yorkshire fishermen during the years spanning the turn of the eighteenth and nineteenth centuries.

A splendid model dated *c*1800 in the Science Museum in London represents a large Yorkshire lugger 61ft between perpendiculars on a 19ft 6in beam and 7ft 6in draft, clinker built and fully decked, with bluff bows, curved stem, straight keel, fine run, round bilges and slightly hollow floors, short bilge keels and lute stern. The model carries large, fairly low peaked dipping lug sails on main- and foremast and a smaller topsail on the mainmast. The small standing lug mizzen is more sharply peaked and its sheet rove through a sheave at the end of an outrigger. There is no bowsprit though topmasts are a distinctive feature. A capstan for hauling drift nets stands abaft the mainmast.

Nineteenth-century drawings in a private collection show these luggers full in the head for carrying herring and some have a bowsprit. A drawing 'Five-man Boats 1843' by J W Carmichael, in the Laing Gallery in Newcastle-upon-Tyne, shows elaborate scrolling on the lute sterns.

Many five-man boats were built in Scarborough and Whitby. A late, relatively fine lined example was *York*, constructed in 1848 by Robert Skelton of Scarborough, 63ft 6in long with 17ft 3in beam and planked with 1in wainscot and copper fastened to the waterline. Frames were fastened with fir trenails through every plank.

From March to September five-man boats went line fishing primarily for large cod, ling, haddock and turbot on the edge of the Dogger Bank or even further afield, usually sailing on Monday and returning on Friday. In the autumn the five-man boats took part in the Yarmouth herring fishery and were then laid up for the winter. They might carry seven crewmen when lining but eight or more for working drift nets. Fishing was done from two square sterned cobles which the bigger boat had carried to sea on deck. Fine seamanship was called for for waves broke dangerously on the Dogger Bank, and these vessels could lie in heavy weather without running for shelter.

Smuggling was rife and customs officers kept an eye on these luggers for their rig made them speedy and able to outrun the revenue vessels. At least one five-man boat had a false bulkhead behind which contraband could be hidden.

About forty five-man boats belonged to Staithes, Runswick Bay, Robin Hood's Bay, Scarborough, Filey and Flamborough in 1825, with Staithes owning the most at seventeen. Fish prices were high following the Napoleonic Wars and about twenty five-man boats were built, many by Skelton of Scarborough, in the five years ending 1820.

E W White in *British Fishing Boats and Coastal Craft* says the five-man boats 'succeeded the square-rigged buss in the North Sea herring fisheries but it is not known exactly when the change occurred'.

SCARBOROUGH YAWL

The Scarborough yawl was a two masted, fully decked sailing craft around 45ft to 60ft long, used primarily for line and herring drift net fishing in exposed waters off the Yorkshire coast in the mid to late nineteenth century. Seakeeping qualities were paramount and yawls could weather all but the harshest conditions.

Generally of finer hull form than the five-man boats and cheaper to build and requiring a smaller crew, they had a broad lute stern, fine run, round bilges and fairly steep slightly hollow floors and were full and high at the shoulder to meet the seas. *Hope*, built by Robert Skelton at Scarborough in 1840, measured 47ft 2in long with a 15ft 4in beam. *Amelia*, built by Skelton in 1857 was 60ft long.

Yawls initially carried a dipping lug foresail, standing lug mizzen sheeted to an outrigger, and a jib on a bowsprit. Around 1870 they changed to a handier ketch rig with gaff mainsail, gaff and boom mizzen and one or two jibs. Topsails could be set above mizzen and mainsail.

They were clinker built with joggled frames and floors. Bulwarks were carvel planked with a gate to facilitate the launch and retrieval of the coble used for line fishing. Other yawl builders in Scarborough included Edmond (at one time foreman to Skelton), Smith, Clark and Walker.

Often staying at sea for several days, yawls worked the outside herring grounds more than 30 miles offshore.

The model of the five-man boat from the Science Museum, London. The very square-headed lug sails are quite distinct and are a sign of the type's eighteenth-century derivation, and its origins in the English herring buss. *(Science Museum, London)*

The warp was hauled by a capstan whose bars were usually turned by four men. This was gruelling work and wooden treads nailed to the deck helped them keep their footing.

More than one hundred yawls were owned on the Yorkshire coast in the 1860s, the majority at Filey and Scarborough, and many of these were built in the 1850s. Indeed, the Yorkshire herring fisheries were the most profitable in Britain from the 1850s to the 1870s.

Evolution of the Scarborough yawl needs further study. Writing in 1849, John Edmond, foreman to Robert Skelton, said the type was introduced when his employer built the 34ft 1in *Integrity* in 1833, the idea being derived from boats which came in the herring seasons from 'Cromer, Cley and surrounding places'.

Herring drifting by yawls declined towards the end of the nineteenth century owing to competition from faster

Scarborough yawls lying aground. These yawls concentrated on fishing with lines and herring drift nets, though a number were converted to smack rig and were used for trawling. (*North Yorkshire County Library*)

Scottish zulus and fifties which could reach market first. The offshore line fisheries gave way to steam trawling. One or two yawls continued line fishing up to 1918.

Sources
Letters from John Edmond, in the *Washington Report on Fishing Vessels* (1849) describe five-man boats and Scarborough yawls. March describes the Science Museum lugger model in detail in *Sailing Drifters*. Rob Robinson, *The History of the Yorkshire Coast Fishing Industry 1780-1914* (Hull 1987) is an excellent study of the county's fisheries. Ernest Dade, *Sail and Oar* (1933, reprinted Ipswich 1988) and 'The Old Yorkshire Yawls', *The Mariner's Mirror*, 91 (1933) draws and describes these vessels.

Humber Keels and Sloops

HUMBER KEEL

A sailing barge used for carrying freight on the river Humber and inland waterways which survived into the twentieth century under single masted, square sail rig. The craft's design was dictated by the size of locks on the navigations and the need for maximum cargo space.

She was a double ender with flat bottom, hard round bilges, long straight vertical sides and easy sheerline. Her bow was uncommonly bluff but the stern slightly more rounded with a hollow run. Short decks at bow and stern were connected by narrow gangways flanking the long cargo hatch which usually had cambered covers. A typical keel was the Sheffield-size, carvel planked *Guidance*, 61ft 6in long with a 15ft 6in beam and depth amidships of about 7ft, built by Worfolk and Co at Stainforth in 1905. One of the largest types was the Barnsley-size, 70ft long with a 14ft 4in beam.

Keels set a square mainsail and short topsail, carried leeboards and could sail surprisingly close to the wind. A slab line lifted the mainsail foot to spill wind, or avoid obstructions on the narrow waterways. Nine winches, known as 'rollers', handled the running rigging, anchor and leeboards and enabled her to be worked by captain and mate. The mast was lowered for passing under bridges.

Keels were very solidly built to handle cargoes, take the ground, and withstand crushing in crowded docks. Oak and elm were often used. Typically, planks were 2in sided at topsides and 3in on the bilge and bottom. Frames and floors, spaced at 9in centres, generally measured 4in by 4in but were thicker at the bilge and doubled where necessary. Because of the bluff bow the first few frames were set at right-angles to the side frames. Before about 1860 most were clinker planked. Keels continued to be built of wood until the 1920s but from the late nineteenth century many were of iron and later steel construction.

Among more than thirty well known builders were Clapson of Barton on Humber, Richard Dunston of Thorne, Scarr of Hessle and Staniland of Thorne.

Sail was used where possible but keels were also towed by steam tugs, poled along by stowers, hauled by horses or crew members, or simply made headway with the tide. Keelmen were skilled navigators able to cope with strong currents, eddies and shifting sandbanks in the estuary, and bridges, locks and restricted areas on the navigations.

Cargoes were varied including coal, grain, fertilisers, bricks and tiles, mineral ores, foodstuffs, hides and paper, and they traded as far inland as Leeds, Sheffield and York. Many imported goods were loaded from ships in Hull.

Before World War I many keelmen and their families lived on board for part of the year, the wife often acting as mate. Accommodation was located at both the bow and stern.

Keels were documented as a distinct class as long ago as the fourteenth century and much of the rigging, including the pear shaped deadeyes, resembled that of Elizabethan craft. Sail remained in use until around the mid-twentieth century, though many keels were motorised during World War II. Economic changes and increasing competition from road transport brought about the keel's decline and many were scrapped or sold for houseboats.

The Sheffield-size steel keel *Comrade* built by Warren at New Holland in 1923 and still active in the early 1970s under Captain Fred Schofield is now owned and restored to sail by the Humber Keel and Sloop Preservation Society.

HUMBER SLOOP

The Humber sloop was similar in hull form and construction to the keel but was fore-and-aft rigged with mainsail

and headsail, serviceable enough for her to make coastal voyages as far afield as the Tyne and Thames and continental ports. The majority of sloops remained within the Humber, however, often conveying goods and raw materials such as farm produce, coal, bricks and tiles, sand and gravel, cement and chalk-stone between the estuary ports.

Larger sloops were 68ft long with a 17ft beam although many were built to size restrictions for occasional canal work.

Halyard rollers, or winches, were placed alongside the mast. Sloops performed less well than keels before the wind but the high peaked gaff and boom mainsail was more effective for beating and close hauled sailing in the shoal-bedevilled estuary.

Clapson of Barton on Humber was a prominent builder of wooden sloops. In the twentieth century perhaps more sloops than keels were built of steel, suitable for carrying bulk cargoes.

Sloops carried a captain and mate but employed an extra man for coastal trips so that watches could be kept.

The Sheffield-size steel sloop *Amy Howson*, 61ft 6in long and of 15ft 6in beam, built as a keel in 1914 by Joseph Scarr of Beverley now belongs to the Humber Keel and Sloop Preservation Society.

Sources
Fred Schofield, *Humber Keels and Keelmen* (Lavenham 1988) is the standard work on the keel and also has a chapter on the sloop. Michael E Ulyatt, *Flying Sail* (Hull 1974, revised and republished Howden 1995), gives a lively account of keels and sloops and their activities.

BILLYBOY

The billyboy was a small, slow, capacious double ended, bluff bowed and sterned, stoutly built, fore-and-aft rigged coaster built and owned in the Humber and Wash areas which traded along the English south and east coasts until the early twentieth century.

She was similar in hull form to the Humber keel (*qv*) with long, straight vertical sides and a flat bottom for maximum cargo carrying capacity, but she was beamier, with a pronounced sheer, deep bulwarks and slightly more rounded bow and bilges to give her seagoing capabilities.

Some billyboys were 60ft to 70ft long and 17ft to 18ft in the beam. Many had wheel steering and a clipper shaped cutwater. Leeboards were usual. A number of billyboys were narrower in

The lines and body plan and sail plan of a Sheffield-size Humber keel. Her dimensions are given as 61ft 6in overall with a beam of 15ft 6in. The keels, which went as far as York, sometimes carried a topgallant which helped to catch the wind above the trees. *(Humber Keel and Sloop Preservation Society)*

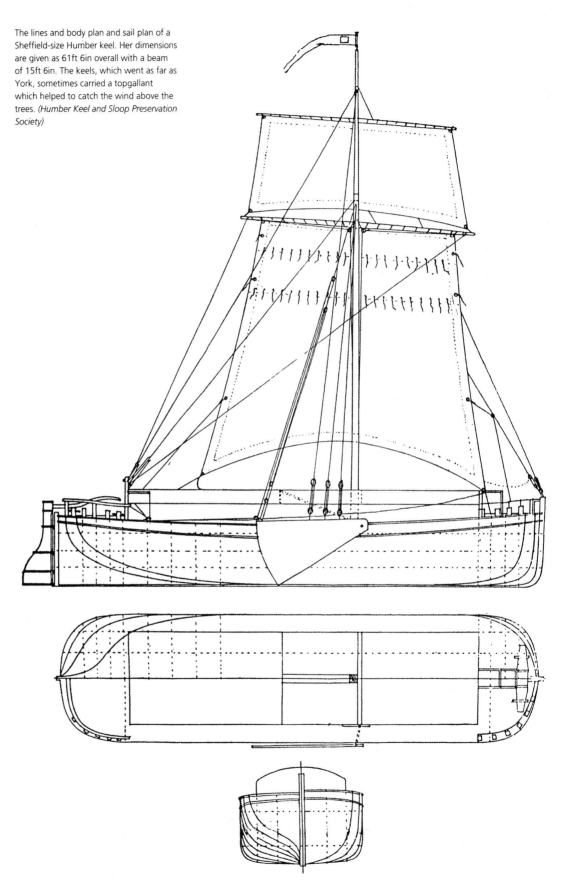

Keels at Thorne on the Stainforth and Keadby Canal. This photograph was taken around 1900 and shows a number of the older clinker built keels. Their pole masts were stepped in a tabernacle and could be lowered when going under bridges. (NMM, neg no P75413)

order to negotiate the navigations and trade inland but as a consequence behaved badly at sea in rough weather.

Billyboys, generally, were often sluggish and abnormally slow but considered to be safe. In *The Nautical Magazine* Philip Kershaw says the billyboys *Jehovah Jireh* and *Joshua* were reputed to have been the slowest coasters in the trade; at least once they took three weeks on passage from Hull to Yarmouth and were cheered by stevedores when they finally arrived.

Early examples carried sloop rig with one or two headsails but by the late nineteenth century many were ketch rigged to provide more sail area for longer voyages. In addition, they often set a square topsail and topgallant in following winds. The bowsprit was well steeved up and carried several jibs. Sails were handled by winches, called 'rollers', grouped near the foremast between the two cargo hatches.

One of the best known billyboys was the wooden carvel planked *Aimwell* built by Routh and Waddingham at Winteringham in North Lincolnshire in 1883 and owned at Barton on Humber and able to carry 100 tons of cargo. She was 64ft long with a 17.5ft beam, some 2ft beamier than, say a 61ft Sheffield-size Humber keel.

Early billyboys were clinker built but by the 1870s were usually carvel planked. Many were built in Hull and neighbouring towns including Beverley, Goole, Knottingley and Thorne. From the 1890s several were built of iron or steel with lines based on the wooden hulls. The 71.8ft by 17.8ft *Mavis*, built of iron at Beverley in 1896, survived into the 1960s as a motor barge.

Cargoes included coal, fertilisers, oil-cake, grain, bricks and tiles and cement, with voyages to the Tyne and East Anglia and south to the Channel ports, with the occasional crossing to

Four Humber sloops, one light and three loaded. While sloops, with their high peaked gaff mainsails, were handier for windward work than the keels, the lowering of their masts was a more complex task as it involved taking off the mast hoops and parrel beads. (NMM, neg no P73847)

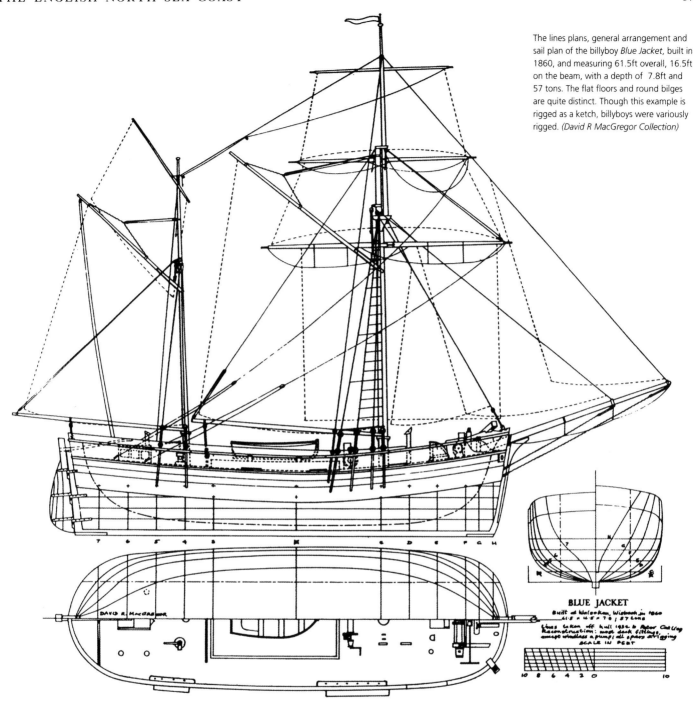

The lines plans, general arrangement and sail plan of the billyboy *Blue Jacket*, built in 1860, and measuring 61.5ft overall, 16.5ft on the beam, with a depth of 7.8ft and 57 tons. The flat floors and round bilges are quite distinct. Though this example is rigged as a ketch, billyboys were variously rigged. *(David R MacGregor Collection)*

BLUE JACKET

the Continent. Three or four crew might be carried and some billyboys were family-crewed. By the turn of the century they were unable to compete with powered coasters and the faster sailing craft such as spritsail barges *(qv)* and so became obsolete shortly after World War I.

Some historians ascribe Dutch origins for the billyboy with the name derived from that of the 'bijlander' used in the Low Countries. Others consider the name to have come from an eigh-

teenth-century expression for a Hull sailor, a 'billyboy'. In fact, the billyboy's hull resembles that of the bluff ended English herring buss, hinting that both these craft and the Humber keel derived from a common type of small English sailing vessel with their vertical sides rather than the Dutch tumblehome.

Sources
Fred Schofield, *Humber Keels and Keelmen* (Lavenham 1988), Appendix 3, gives an ac-

count of billyboys. Philip Kershaw, 'Yorkshire Billyboys', *The Nautical Magazine*, (Dec 1964) and Ian Johnson in 'Billy Boy', *Yachts and Yachting* (May 1970), give useful summaries.

Brief accounts are also given in the *Humber Yawl Club Journal* (1916 and 1935).

HULL DUSTER
(Hull gold duster or Humber gold duster)

The Hull duster was a fast open rowing and sailing boat used in the rapid

and breezy tideway of the Humber and its approaches to attend on ships visiting the docks or lying in Hull Roads.

Although some varied in lines and dimensions an average duster at the start of the twentieth century was 18ft long on a 5ft 6in beam with full flat floored midships section, hollow entry and run, fine bow, plumb stem, easy sheer, wineglass stern, slightly rockered keel, thole pins, four thwarts and a stern bench. She was schooner rigged with two spritsails of similar height and area, though sometimes in strong winds only the forward sprit was used, with some assistance from an oar to help her go about.

Dusters were strongly built for going alongside ships, with typically ½in larch or oak clinker planking on steamed elm timbers spaced 6in apart. Thwarts had hanging and lodging knees for reinforcement against longitudinal strain when the boat was under tow and stout rope fenders were carried.

Competition was fierce and the first duster to reach an incoming ship procured her boating work, such as handling mooring hawsers. An iron hook on a 12ft pole, often bamboo, with a tow rope attached was used to hook onto the ship and the duster was towed along until needed to carry out her duties. The two boatmen needed courage and skill as ships rarely slackened speed when accepting the tow rope.

Earlier Hull dusters were larger and deeper drafted with wineglass sections but by the early twentieth century these had given way to the smaller, more easily rowed type. By 1905 only six or so Hull dusters remained in use. In 1997 a very late example, the *Grampus*, built by Richard Dunston at Thorne *c*1930, was under restoration by the Hull Town Docks Museum.

Sources
George F Holmes in the *Humber Yawl Club Yearbook* (1905) describes the Hull duster and shows drawings.

BLOBBER *(Blobbing boat)*

The blobber was a sculling or sailing boat used for various purposes including fishing for eels on the river Hull or racing under sail on the Humber. She

Above: The *H H* of Goole. Most of the billyboys came from either Goole or Hull but many traded as far afield as down Channel for clay, and this photograph is thought to have been taken at Shoreham. She is sloop rigged with a topsail. Her bold sheer, round stern and 'out of doors' rudder' are all shown to good effect. (NMM, neg no P73852)

Right: Hull dusters taking part in the Hull City Regatta. These were fast and powerful boats which, like the Tyne foyboats *(qv)* and the Falmouth Quay punts *(qv)* , raced to sea 'seeking' ships to render assistance. (NMM, Oliver Hill Collection, neg no P75423)

was usually an old sailing or steam trawler's boat, rejected for sea work but still sound enough for river use.

Typically she was full bodied and 17ft to 18ft long on a 6ft 6in or 7ft beam, with bluff bow, wineglass stern, easy sheer, full round bilges, flat floors amidships, plumb stem, straight keel and four thwarts. She was clinker planked with close spaced steamed timbers. Depending on her intended function her new owner might fit a flush deck or a cabin for living space.

Blobbers used for sailing and racing were given a rudder and tiller and a rockered false keel and carried cutter rig with large gaff and boomed mainsail and sometimes a mizzen. Those used on the upper Hull had no rig but maybe carried a sculling oar, an eel spear, and some rods from which to hang the eel 'blob', a baited lure of rags or string in which fish got caught by their teeth. Writing in 1902 George F Holmes suggested there were maybe a hundred blobbers on the river Hull and in the creeks and dock basins.

Sources
George F Holmes in 'The Blobber', *Humber Yawl Club Yearbook* (1902), describes the blobber and shows a lines and sail plan

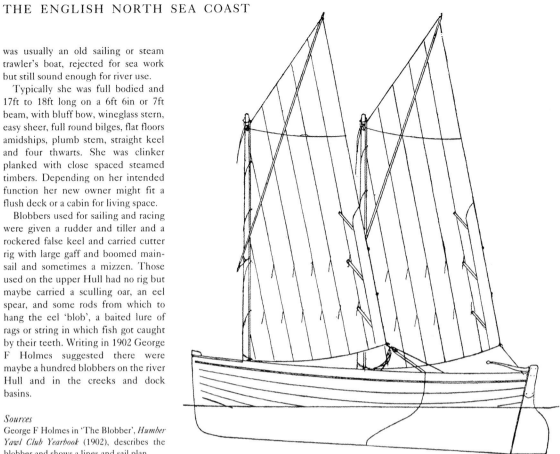

Left: The sail plan of a Hull duster. The masts were short enough to be stowed inside the length of the boat, while the sprit rig and brails allowed sail to be taken in quickly and easily when the duster came alongside a ship or was under tow. *(From Dixon Kemp)*

Below: Blobbing boats, with their low cabins, at North Ferriby on the Humber. The Hull dockers and lightermen who lived on these vessels used them for shrimping and eel 'blobbing' and not infrequently for raiding local orchards and chicken sheds, thus the colourful tag 'cock and hen boats' by which they were sometimes known. A story relates of how a farmer's wife discovered her chicken shed nearly empty one morning and a note explaining:
'We've robbed the rich to feed the poor,
We've left a pair to breed some more.'
(NMM, Oliver Hill Collection, neg no P75424)

The Wash and Thames Estuary

THE THAMES estuary stretches from the North Foreland in Kent across to Orfordness, a lonely shingle headland on the Suffolk coast. This estuary is a maze of channels between shifting banks. The Wash is a smaller version, but even more dangerous because once caught in here there is no real harbour for ships to seek shelter – just miles of hard sand. The River Thames was the centre of activity when traditionally rigged sailing vessels carried the trade and commerce on the east coast of England, and London was the main market for most of the catch landed in the east coast ports.

The tidal River Thames was originally a wide shallow estuary with vast areas of saltings on either side which were pierced with numerous creeks. From the early medieval times the saltings were gradually walled off which confined the channel. In the nineteenth century dredging took place transforming the river into a deep narrow channel which could be navigated by the largest ships of the day. It was the construction of the network of docks in London that sucked in both coastal and worldwide trade. Craft anchored at the mouth of the Thames below Gravesend and then went up to London on the flood tide so that at times the whole tideway was a mass of sails. The ebb tide saw another fleet coming back down to sail to ports all over Europe and the world.

The Thames, or the London River as it was known to men who worked on it, was by far the largest of a whole series of tidal estuaries which cut into the eastern side of England but only the Medway, flanked by vast areas of ooze and saltings, came anywhere near rivalling it in size. All the rivers provided a highway into the heart of the countryside. The Fen rivers ran right up into the centre of England and into western Norfolk. On the eastern side of that county the tidal rivers of the Yare, Bure, Ant and Waverney link many inland towns with the sea. Further south, the Blackwater, Colne and Orwell, which are about ten miles long, and many smaller ones like the Deben and Blyth, connected the eastern counties to the London River. Some, like the Butley River, Roach and Swale were not really tidal estuaries but just channels through marsh islands.

Both the Thames, and the ports on the rivers leading into its huge estuary, had wharves which dried out at low tide. The craft used, such as Thames barges, had to be flat bottomed to carry cargoes to these ports, and sit on the mud beside the wharves without straining their hulls. The fishing craft, such as the Colchester oyster smacks, which worked these rivers were not intended to take cargoes on the mud, and had relatively deep keels so that they could beat up the narrow channels.

On the open coast Harwich was the only real place of shelter, but before dredging even this great harbour had to be entered through a narrow shifting channel. There were harbours at Yarmouth, Lowestoft and Southwold, but these had narrow entrances with shallow shingle bars across them. The coastal sailing ships did not expect to make port for shelter but anchored in the open roads off the towns.

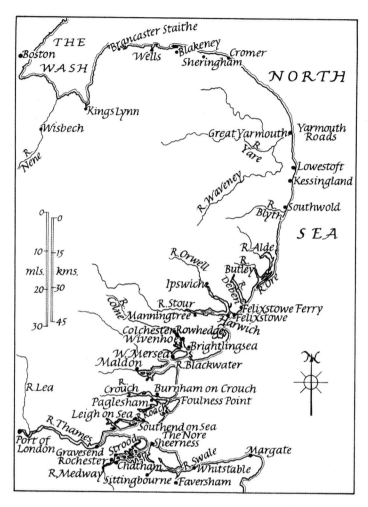

Hollesley Bay and the roads off Southwold, Lowestoft and Yarmouth often had several hundred ships lying at anchor in bad southwesterly weather. If the wind changed direction then these sheltered roads became vulnerable and exposed and ships might break their cables and be driven ashore. Sometimes, vessels caught like this on a lee shore attempted to sail to the safety of the open sea, but many ended by pounding to pieces on some hard sand bank amidst boiling surf.

This was a coast which was hard on sailing ships and men. Just getting into the rivers under sail called for great skill and not an inconsiderable amount of luck. The smaller rivers, for instance, with their shallow bars and fierce tides at the entrances were particularly difficult places to enter. The early seafarers on this coast used the beaches almost as much as the rivers and by the nineteenth century there were hundreds of men working open boats – fishing, salvaging and piloting from the beach landings. This has steadily declined in the twentieth century and by the 1990s there were only about 150 men working fishing boats off the East Anglian beaches.

In the nineteenth century by far the largest fishery on the east coast of England was the great autumn herring fishery or, as it was know more simply in Lowestoft, the home fishery. Huge shoals of herring gathered in the southern North Sea, usually in the Smith's Knoll area, and a vast fleet of East Anglian and Scottish luggers sailed out to take this harvest from the sea. All around the coast smaller versions of the autumn herring fishery took place as the smaller shoals moved along the shore. The other great autumn fishery was the sprat fishery. This mostly took place from Southwold down to the River Blackwater.

In the winter when the inshore waters were colder the cod came close to the coast and the longshore fishermen took them with long lines, miles of line on the surface with baited hooks spread below. There was also an inshore fishery, particularly in the Wash, landing shellfish which were sold to the long line fishermen as bait. The other important winter fishery was oyster dredging. The cultivation of oysters went on all the year round. In the Wash there was a considerable mussel fishery in the winter and then in the summer the boats went after cockles.

Off the North Norfolk coast the crab fishery was regular summer work, while boats from Harwich and some Suffolk beach landings worked lobster pots wherever there was a rocky sea bed. Boats from the Wash ports, Yarmouth, Lowestoft, Harwich, Leigh and Gravesend would go after shrimp with a fine mesh trawl. The other inshore summer fishery was trawling for flat fish on the seabed.

In the early nineteenth century the Nore, off the mouth of the River Thames, was an anchorage for warships as well as merchant ships, the former associated with the naval dockyards at Sheerness and Chatham, while the latter anchored there awaiting suitable conditions to make their way up the Thames. Once steam tugs were introduced they were towed straight up the Thames. Gravesend became the place where the emigration ships anchored to take on stores before being towed down to the English Channel for voyages to North America, Australia and New Zealand.

The River Medway and the Swale channel behind the Isle of Sheppey were a smaller version of the Thames, but traffic here was mainly local trade. By the 1890s there was a considerable fleet of sailing barges carrying cement and bricks from the Medway and the Kentish brick fields up the Thames to meet the huge housing demand of a fast growing population. They made their way to the hundreds of wharves on the river front, up shallow creeks which could only be navigated at high water and even further inland on the many canals leading off the Thames. Places like Chelsea Dock and the Great Western Dock at Brentford were used to tranship goods such as timber, bricks and coal which were then taken inland by rail and canal narrow boats.

The industry on the Medway and Swale caused pollution which destroyed the oyster fisheries there, but the oyster fishery on the flats off Whitstable was expanded in the late nineteenth century. Whitstable has a tiny harbour on the open coast and this was the last place on the east coast where barquentines, brigantines and schooners operated in the coal trade from the north of England. This was because the sailing colliers could sail right into the harbour here and did not need to hire a tug as they had to at Dover and Shoreham. This small advantage kept the Whitstable colliers sailing until as late as the 1920s.

There are harbours, just short piers built out over the sands, at Margate and round the North Foreland at Broadstairs, both of which had barge traffic. However, the north Kent coast consisted mostly of small beach landings with boats which worked running trips for holidaymakers in the summer and fished in the winter.

The Wash, at the northernmost point in our area, is both smaller and far shallower than the Thames estuary and capable of kicking up particularly short, steep seas. Once it was a vast marsh with tidal water almost reaching Cambridge. The Romans built earth banks to keep back the sea and the Anglo-Saxons had more banks built before 1086 reclaiming most of the Fens. Because of silting and bank building the sea has slowly receded leaving the modern Wash as a great shallow bay between Norfolk and Lincolnshire. There are two main channels into the Wash, the Boston Deep and the Lynn Deep, but the channels and banks are constantly moving. One of the main medieval Norfolk ports was Castle Rising, but the river here has completely silted up, and the nearby harbour at Heacham also silted up and was closed early this century. Dredging has kept open the main rivers to King's Lynn and Boston and the smaller rivers Welland and Nene remain open and navigable.

The coast between the estuaries of the Thames and the Wash is made up of the long beaches of Suffolk and Norfolk and there are few ports. The beach yawls which were based there were to East Anglian shores what the luggers and galleys were to Deal and the Downs. *(NMM, neg no A1985)*

Fen Barge *(Fen lighter)*

A long, narrow, flat bottomed, clinker or carvel barge with a curved stem which was evolved to be sailed or towed on the rivers and waterways of the Fens. The hull was nearly all oak with some elm deck planking. The outside of the hull was left bare wood and then coated with 'charlico', a mixture of coal tar and horse dung, for preservation. The bow and stern were sometimes decked. However, some Fen barges were completely open. The large barges were up to 47ft long and loaded 20 tons while there were smaller versions of about 27ft long.

At the beginning of the nineteenth century they had a curved stempost making a rather attractive bow, but in their hey day around 1850 this had conformed to the Victorian fashion and

This fen lighter is shown loading sugar beet at Nordelph in 1933. Though well down by the bow the distinct curved stem and the wide clinker planks are clearly visible. *(Lilian Ream Exhibition Gallery)*

become much straighter. From earliest times the Fen barges were moved around in 'gangs' of about five or six barges. Each barge had a wooden arm with a chain on its bow which extended over the stern of the barge in front to which the chain was fixed. The gangs were pulled by men for short distances or more often by three horses. The gang also took with it a 'horse boat' for moving the horses from one 'haling way' (tow path) to the next. The leading barge in a gang was called the 'forebarge' and loaded up to 30 tons. In some cases they had a short mast to set a square sail for use when there was a fair wind. The sails and horses were replaced by steam tugs in the late Victorian period. After this the wooden barges were replaced by steel barges towed by diesel tugs and were used for transporting sugar beet until after the World War II.

Fen Boat

Flat bottomed boat, usually poled but could be rowed on the rivers and

meres of the Fens. All around the Fens there were small boats and punts which had the same curved bow as the barges and were again double ended. The 'Fen boat' or 'Fen butt' was a very heavily built boat of about 20ft long and they were towed in gangs of three along the smaller waterways. There were also 'turf boats' which carried about 4 tons and in the 1880s were still using spritsails. These also carried wheel barrows and planks so that they could be taken to load turf from the bog to the villages and towns for use as fire fuel. By contrast, the Fen punt, used for eel fishing, was 18ft long, with a beam of 5ft, and was quanted with a 12ft pole. The shallow clinker hull was double ended and had a curved bow.

Sources
Most information on the Fen barges and boats is contained in 'Fenland Lighters and their Heyday *c*1700-1850', by H J K Jenkins in *The Mariner's Mirror*, 79 (1993).

Wash Smacks

Decked, tiller steered, single masted, gaff rigged smacks with straight stems and counter sterns used mainly for shell fishing in the Wash and off the north Norfolk coast. They sailed out of Boston, Wisbech and Lynn and went trawling for shell fish in the summer and drift net fishing for herring and sprat in the winter.

The Wash smacks can be generally divided into three sorts. The smallest was the shrimper which was half decked and pole masted and trawled for brown shrimps in the estuary, and was around 35ft long, with a beam of 12ft and a draft of 5ft. They usually carried a copper for boiling the shrimps. The prawner was much the same as a shrimper but was decked and a little longer at around 40ft long, 14ft beam and 6ft draft. They trawled further out for pink shrimps and prawns. The big whelkers could be up to around 60ft overall, with a beam of 16ft to 17ft, and a draft of 8ft. They

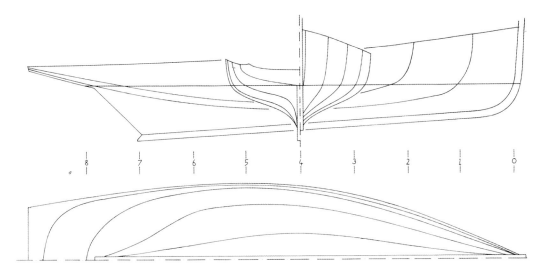

Lines plans of the Boston prawner *Albert*. They show well the characteristics of the Wash smacks with their wide, square counter sterns and fine lines forward. She is 44ft overall, 13ft 1in on the beam with a draft of 4ft 9in. These lines were taken off the starboard side during the vessel's restoration in 1997 and it should be noted that the bulwarks are not shown.
(Ian Dunmore)

mostly fished off Brancaster and were often away from Monday to Friday. They caught whelks in round pots baited with crabs, carried a topmast and had a cabin aft.

BOSTON SMACKS

Because they spent most of their time sailing in narrow channels the Wash fishermen developed a smack of around 50ft which would sail close to the wind. These smacks had a high bow for the short Wash seas and a bowsprit mounted over the top of the rail. For their size they were rather narrow and very fine forward of the mast. The 53ft *Telegraph*, with a 14ft beam and drawing 7ft, was built by Gostelow

The Lynn whelker *The Affiance* LN 82, from a painting by a local artist, George Laidman. A characteristic of the big whelkers, some of which were up to 60ft, was the separate topmast. Most of the prawners and all the shrimpers had a simple pole mast. They fished for whelks off Brancaster which they caught in round pots baited with crabs and which were mostly sold for bait for long line fishing. They died out after the introduction of engined vessels working out of Wells.
(True's Yard, King's Lynn)

at Boston in 1906; she has a square counter stern and can be rather tender in a fresh breeze.

Fishermen said these powerful gaff cutter smacks could 'go to windward like a knife'; but in fact they did not sail much closer to the wind than the other Victorian cutter smacks, though they did come round through the eye of the wind very quickly. When tacking the foresail on these smacks was always aback to pull them round and when in the narrow 7-mile Haven a hand had to stand by with an oar just in case the head did not come round.

Some smacks were bought in, mostly from Essex, and these may have influenced the local builders Charles Thompson, Alexander Gostelow and

William Keightley. Several books repeat the legend that Boston smacks had a rockered keel, copied from a prize-winning yacht, but none of the surviving smacks show any sign of this. The Boston builders favoured a low, rather square counter stern, although in 1928 Gostelow built the smack *Witham* with an elliptical counter stern and followed this with some smack yachts with the same stern. Most of the smacks started to have engines fitted in the late 1920s, and nearly all the fleet of wooden smacks survived as motor craft until after World War II. The last ones fishing were *Majestic* and the 52ft *Pam* until the early 1980s.

It appears that early in the nineteenth century the Boston men were

using open, double ended clinker boats with two short masts on which they set spritsails, a rig which was popular on the east coast in the eighteenth century where there were narrow channels.

WISBECH SMACK

A smaller version of the Boston smack, more suitable for the narrow Nene river. Often clinker built, they had powerful windlasses to enable them to anchor in the fierce tides. In 1980 two motor smacks were working from Sutton Bridge sealing in the Wash, but protesters came down and set light to them. Only the *Mermaid* survived which is 36ft on the deck, with a 10.5ft beam. and 4.5ft draft. She was built by Worfolk in 1904 and was fitted with her first engine in 1935.

LYNN SMACK

A Lynn smack was carvel built, decked, usually about 50ft long on the deck and had a gaff cutter rig with a topmast. Typical of the larger smacks built at King's Lynn was the *Freda & Norah* built by Worfolk in 1912 and sold to owners at Boston. She is 54ft long with a 15ft beam and a draft of 5.6ft. The beam was slightly more than most smacks of her size and in a blow she could carry more sail and lead the Boston fleet home. Before 1899, when Thomas Worfolk opened a boatyard near Fisher Fleet, most of the craft appear to have been bought from Great Yarmouth. Worfolk developed the el-

Lynn shrimpers in the Fisher Fleet sometime at the turn of the centruy. The two boats on the right of the photograph are double ended. *(True's Yard, King's Lynn)*

This Lynn shrimper, *Witham* LN 103, was originally built as a fisheries protection craft, though she was designed along the lines of a Lynn shrimper. Here, photographed in 1959, she still retains her pole mast and her mainsail, but she has an auxiliary engine fitted. These craft were very narrow forward which helped them in the short, steep seas of the Wash. The Lynn shrimpers were among the last traditional fishing boats to work off the east coast but *Witham* was finally broken up in 1996. *(NNM, Oliver Hill Collection, neg no P75425)*

liptical or round stern which took longer to build but was popular with fishermen because they thought it looked smarter.

Most Lynn smacks went out on short daily trips but those which went whelking were away all week working near the Dudgeon lightship off the north Norfolk coast. The whelkers towed 18ft open boats which were used to row around and pick up the whelk pots. There were several occasions when the boats were separated from the smacks and it took the fishermen several days to row to Yarmouth or Grimsby. The whelks were sent by rail to ports where they were used as bait on long lines for cod.

In the 1870s there were about twelve 30-ton Lynn smacks oyster dredging near the Dudgeon. Another Wash fishery which required a large smack was stow netting for sprat. This required anchoring in the channel and lowering a huge, cumbersome net down over the bow. However, Wash fishermen gave up stow netting in about 1912 but continued fishing for sprat. In 1924 the *Freda & Norah* caught 21 tons of sprat and returned with decks awash. The 58ft whelker *Britannia* built in 1913 was the largest smack built at Lynn. Later these lst class smacks were fitted with engines and went shrimp trawling.

LYNN SHRIMPER

The Edwardian Lynn shrimper was another of the Worfolk developments. These were carvel built, counter stern gaff cutters about 36ft in length with a pole mast, but unlike the smacks they did not have a windlass and instead of being completely decked they had a long open well aft of the mast. When handling the nets the men could stand up, making it less back breaking than on a small decked smack. The shrimpers had a small hand capstan for hauling the net and a boiler for cooking the brown shrimp on the way back to port so that they could be sold as soon as they were landed. They trawled for shrimp in the summer and went after cockles during the winter.

In the 1870s there were over one hundred shrimpers at Lynn and nearly as many at Boston. The Lynn fishermen, like the Boston men, were keen on their annual smack race. The course was over some 21 miles and was usually timed to finish at Fisher Fleet in the afternoon so that people could watch the end. In 1912 Worfolk built the *Queen Alexandra* intending her to be the fastest smack. She had a long canoe stern instead of the more normal

counter. The Lynn fishermen went on having sailing shrimpers built until the mid 1920s. One of the last ones which Bill and Gerald Worfolk built was the 41ft *John & Rebecca* in 1924 which was later worked under power as the *Rob-Pete*. The last sailing smack that worked from Lynn was the *Lily May*, until about 1938. Most of fleet were then fitted with engines and because they operated in sheltered waters they went on working far longer than other English smacks. The last former Lynn sailing shrimper, *Queen Alexandra*, finished about 1995. Like many of the other former smacks her canoe stern had been sawn off to reduce harbour bills and save maintenance.

LYNN YOLL

Clinker, double ended boat used for transporting cockles. Lynn fishermen gathered cockles by running out at high tide and anchoring on the banks where they hand raked the cockles out of the sand and loaded them into the hold of the smack. To speed up the operation a heavy clinker boat, which had no thwarts amidships, was taken out, loaded up with cockles and these were transferred to the smack anchored off.

Because it took a whole tide to go 'sand topping' for cockles the fishermen were always looking for a faster way. About 1890 some Lynn men bought an old north Norfolk crab boat and fitted it out with gaff sails. This proved very successful, not least because the clinker hull was more flexible and did not leak as much as the carvel boats when pounding on the sands. William Worfolk's first order for a new boat was to build a double ended, carvel cockler and, using the crab boat as a basic design, he built the 33ft, 11.10ft beam *Baden Powell* in 1900. After this came other similar cocklers with a cuddy forward of the mast. Because of their origin these boats were also sometimes called 'luggers' or yolls. The word yoll, often written down as yawl, is a norse word meaning boat which was still used by fishermen in the nineteenth century to mean any open boat, while a decked gaff boat was termed a smack.

Sources
Robert Simper, *British Sail* (Newton Abbott 1977) has some material on the Wash smacks, while Hervey Benham and Roger Finch, *Sailing Craft of East Anglia* (Lavenham 1987) also covers them. Colin Swindale has written in the Sailing Smack Association's journal *The Smack* (December 1993) about Boston smacks.

Norfolk Beach Boats

NORTH NORFOLK CRAB BOAT
(Sheringham crab boat)

Clinker, double ended, open boat, with very shallow draft and a wide beam to give stability, used in the crab fishery off the northeast Norfolk coast. A typical sail and row crab boat was 18ft overall, 6.8ft beam and 3ft depth, and was built with an oak keel, oak planks and English elm sheerstrake and joggled frames. The crab boat had oar holes or 'orruck holes' similar to some Viking longships and the fishermen put oars through these to carry them down the long beach; they had no gunwales for tholes. These boats set a single dipping lug sail 100 to 120sq ft on a short mast, and the rudder went down below the hull to act as a centreboard. Like all East Anglian beach boats they carried shingle ballast to sea in bags. These were moved around the hull to improve the trim for sailing and if they got a good catch the ballast was simply shot overboard.

A 'bitt' across the inside of the bow for making the anchor rope fast is exactly the same fitting as a Danish smakkejolle has, and, indeed, the Norfolk crab boat appears to be very similar to the Danish open boats, but their origin is pure speculation as before 1750 there is no real clue to their ancestry.

The crab boats retained their ancient hull shape and were well suited to the conditions met with on the open beaches between Bacton and Weybourne. Here the beaches are very shallow, necessitating a long passage through breaking water before safety was reached. The hull shape was evolved solely for the few brief, but highly dangerous moments coming off and on the sandy beaches in a mass of boiling white water. The shallow hull lifted as soon as a wave hit it, while, on landing, the pointed stern parted the waves roaring up behind; at the last moment the boat was easily carried sideways up the beach. The normal work was crabbing in the summer and long lining for cod in the early winter. The main fleet was at Cromer and Sheringham, and in 1905 there were around 110 crab boats each working some 70 pots. The last sailing crab boat, *Little Swallow*, was built by Billy May, who built most of the last wooden boats, at Potter Heigham in 1959.

The first engine was fitted in a crab boat in 1915 and the other boats were

soon fitted with them. A larger type of motor crab boat was built on the same lines as the old rowing and sailing ones, except that they have a straight sternpost to accommodate a prop instead of a curved one. These boats are taken down to the water on trailers towed by tractors.

HOVELLER

At Cromer and Sheringham they had lug rigged 'hovellers', larger versions, around 25ft overall, of the crab boat which had a movable deck over the bow. They were used for salvage work and attending passing shipping, but they also went drift netting for herring and mackerel. The hovellers made voyages around the coast as far south as Southwold and the last of these gave up in the early 1930s.

WELLS WHELKER

The sailing whelkers of Wells-Next-the-Sea were often old Sheringham crab boats or naval whalers. Just after World War II the crab boat builders produced double ended, motor clinker whelkers, 22ft overall, with a beam of 9ft. These were open apart from a cuddy forward and later a wheelhouse, and on the starboard side a pot-hauling capstan was fitted. In 1997 most of Well's twenty-two fishing hulls were GRP, transom sterned, but three of the wooden whelkers were based at nearby Thornham.

BRANCASTER FLATTY
(Blakeney mussel canoe)

A flat bottomed, carvel, open punt with small transom, and either sprit or gunter rigged, used in the shell fisheries in the north Norfolk harbours. At Cley the 'canoes' were painted white and were from 13ft to 16ft with a beam of between 4ft 10in and 5ft 9in. They had flat, but slightly rockered bottoms built of elm, deal sides and oak knees. They were cheaply built and fastened with galvanised nails. The canoes made a very stable working platform and were usually worked under oar. For sailing they were steered with an oar over the stern, but they were a bit cranky under sail although generally they handled better when partly loaded. Musseling began to die out at Cley and Blakeney in about 1939 but the last canoes were still lying around at Blakeney in 1981.

Sheringham crabbers massed together on the beach. The 'orruck holes' and the bitt across the inside of the bow can be clearly seen. They fished for crabs and lobsters between March and September and for cod, much further out to sea, from October until Christmas. In the middle distance is a hoveller, the bigger version of the crab boat which was partly decked and used for herring fishing as well as hovelling. All these boats, including the ones which worked off the beaches at Cromer, were built at Sheringham. *(NMM, Oliver Hill Collection, neg no P75427)*

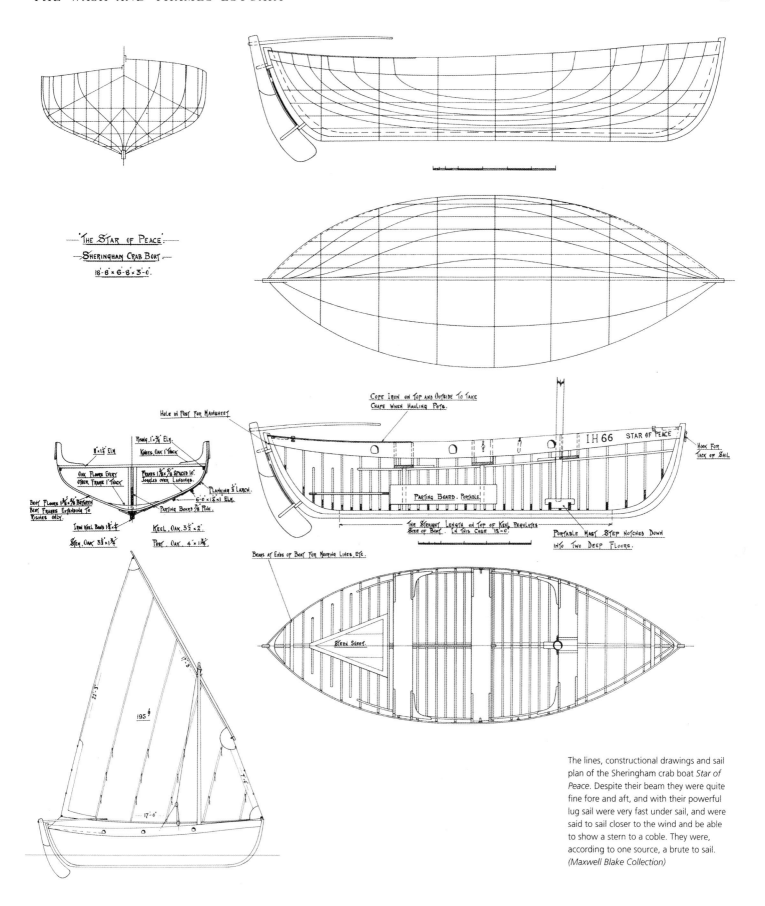

'The Star of Peace'. Sheringham Crab Boat 18'-8" × 6'-8" × 3'-0".

The lines, constructional drawings and sail plan of the Sheringham crab boat *Star of Peace*. Despite their beam they were quite fine fore and aft, and with their powerful lug sail were very fast under sail, and were said to sail closer to the wind and be able to show a stern to a coble. They were, according to one source, a brute to sail. (*Maxwell Blake Collection*)

Whelk boats alongside at Wells-next-the-Sea, photographed in 1929. Although they worked from a tidal harbour they were developed from the north Norfolk crab boat and the beamy shallow hulls were well suited to crossing the Wells bar in bad weather. *(NMM, neg no G3489)*

The 'flats' built for shell fishing at Wells were very similar to the canoes, but had a heart shaped transom. By 1996 only the Brancaster flats were still in use. These had mostly been built by Worfolk and had higher sides than the canoes and were sometimes clinker planked.

NORFOLK BEACH PUNT

Clinker, double ended boat used for inshore fishing north of Yarmouth to Haisbro' (Happisburgh). The punt was around 18ft long, had rather a deep hull and a single lug sail. These craft were really a cross between the Norfolk crab boats (*qv*) and the Suffolk beach boats (*qv*).

Sources
P Stibbons, K Lee, M Warren, *Crabs and Shannocks* (Norwich 1983) is the main source while *Inshore Craft of Great Britain*, Vol I, gives good coverage of their construction and employment.

Top left: The sail plan of a 30ft whelk boat, built at Friars Boatyard, King's Lynn. *(NMM, Coastal Craft Collection)*

Lower left: A Blakeney mussel boat could carry up to 6cwt of mussels and having brought in eatable mussels they would then transport the same quantity of small ones back to the beds. This 'canoe' was photographed in 1960. *(NMM, Oliver Hill Collection, neg no P72732)*

Norfolk Keel and Wherry

NORFOLK KEEL

Clinker hull with a straight stem and small transom stern, an open hatch and single square sail, used to carry cargoes in the east Norfolk rivers until about 1880. The Anglo-Saxon word *ceolae* meant a seagoing boat and these early medieval boats were shallow draft, clinker built, double ended, open boats. This was the starting point for the Norfolk keel which was an inland craft carrying cargoes on the rivers of east Norfolk and northern Suffolk. Like its Anglo-Saxon predecessor, the Norfolk keel had a single square sail. These ancient vessels had been working for 800 years on the Norfolk rivers before the last one, the 55ft, 13ft 8in beam, 4ft draft *Dee Dar*, ceased its task of carrying logs up to Norwich in the 1880s.

NORFOLK WHERRY

Doubled ended, clinker hulled cargo carrier of the Norfolk Broads and rivers, propelled by a single, loose footed gaff sail on a mast stepped in the bow which could be lowered to go under bridges. The wherry was built of oak with each plank overlapping 2in; there were fourteen planks to a side. The 40ft mast was originally English larch, a heavy wood, but in the late nineteenth century imported pitchpine was used. The counter balance at the foot of the mast was around 1½ tons of lead or cast iron. The gaff was 40ft long and the single black sail of some 1200sq ft. The wherries trading between Norwich and Yarmouth carried about 40 tons, while the wherries trading up the North River to parish staithes on shallow dykes and the canals to North Walsham and Aylsham often only loaded about 15 tons.

The Norfolk wherry appears to have originated from the fast passenger row-

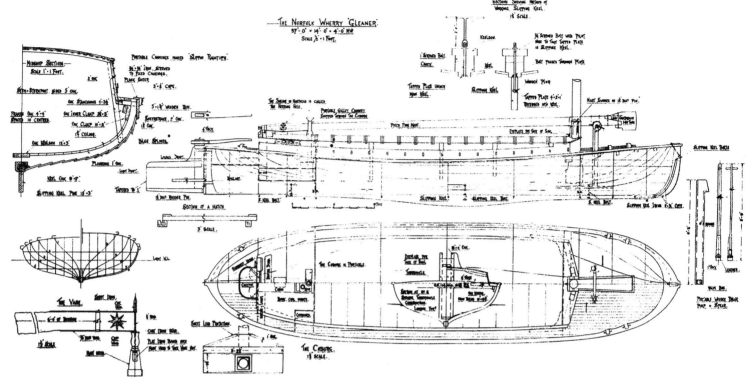

Lines plans, constructional drawing and sail plan of the Norfolk wherry *Gleaner*. For ease of raising and lowering the mainsail, it was hoisted by an ingeniously designed, single halyard for both the throat and the peak, but this in turn caused the gaff to fall away to leeward when being lowered which could make the big mainsail difficult to handle. *(Maxwell Blake Collection)*

ing boat which was remarkably similar to the Thames wherry *(qv)*. Since the wherry hull form was faster than the Norfolk keel a slightly larger wherry hull for carrying cargoes evolved. The great advantage of a Norfolk wherry was that the mast, stepped very far forward in the bow, enabled them to sail very close to the wind.

Before the arrival of the railways most of the trade for the city of Norwich came up by water from Great Yarmouth and trade to villages continued by wherry after this. In the Victorian period the growing holiday trade created the need for pleasure wherries with cabins and then carvel wherry yachts with counter sterns were built on the North River. The last pleasure wherry built was the 59ft *White Moth*, by Ernest Collins at Wroxham in 1915. In 1996 the only former trading wherries left afloat were the Norfolk Wherry Trust's 58ft, 15ft beam, 4ft 6in draft *Albion*, the only carvel wherry built; and the clink-

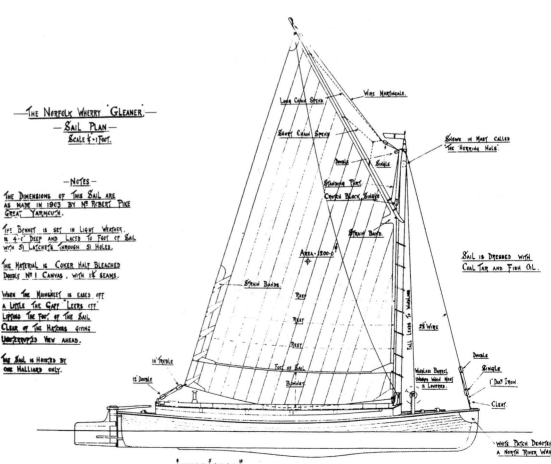

er built 60ft *Maud,* originally built in 1899 and now completely restored.

REED LIGHTER
(Load boat)

A beamy, shallow draft, open, clinker, double ended boat which could be rowed or quanted from either end and was mainly used on the northern wa-

ters of the Norfolk Broads for transporting hay, 'marsh litter' (sedge) and reed for thatching, which was cut out on the marshes and then taken back to the staithes. The 20ft lighter, or 'load boat', could carry 600 'shoofs' (sheaves) of reed. For smaller loads and shallower dykes there were 'half load' and 'quarter load' boats while those used just for runabouts appear to have been

called punts. The load boats were taken up very shallow dykes and were loaded about 6ft high and because they were double ended could be moved out without turning round. After World War I the practice of cutting the marshes by hand with scythes was no longer economic. As the reed lighter had a pointed stern it was difficult to fit an outboard so they dropped

This scene of utter tranquility belies the burdonsome life of the wherry crew who spent almost as much time quanting their craft as sailing them, even though the huge gaff enabled a good amount of sail to be carried high up. The black sail was dressed with coal tar and fish oil. *(NMM, neg no P27496)*

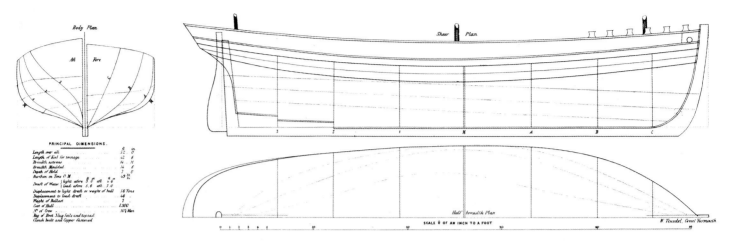

Body Plan

Aft *Fore*

Sheer Plan

Half breadth Plan

SCALE ⅜ OF AN INCH TO A FOOT

W. Teasdel, Great Yarmouth

PRINCIPAL DIMENSIONS.

This Yarmouth fishing lugger appeared in the Washington Report of 1849, shortly before the fishermen began to remove the mainmast for ease of handling the capstan. She has little rise of floor, indicating her origins as a beach craft. In the bows can be seen the different positions from which the drift net could be led, while the stern boasts a very vertical rudder, reminiscent of the eighteenth century. *(NMM, Coastal Craft Collection)*

out of use. Three new reed lighters, however, have been built for the conservation work at How Hill, Hickling and Ranworth.

Sources
Roy Clark, *Black Sail Traders* (London 1961) is regarded as the basis of knowledge about the wherries. Other sources are Robert Malster, *Wherries and Waterways* (Lavenham 1971) and Robert Simper, *Norfolk Rivers and Harbours* (Ramsholt 1996) .

YARMOUTH AND LOWESTOFT LUGGERS AND DANDIES

Ketch rigged, decked fishing smacks, with straight stems, short counter sterns and steered by tiller, employed for herring and mackerel drifting. During the summer they worked the

Westcountry fisheries: in winter they returned to their home grounds in the southern North Sea.

Before Yarmouth and Lowestoft harbours were improved many of the lute sterned, three masted luggers worked off the beaches. Even when the Yarmouth boats started working from the harbour they were still built with the 'Yarmouth hump', a slight reverse sheerline forward which seems to have originated in the beach craft and was presumably meant to keep the water off the bow as they pushed through the first wave. Around 1850 the North Sea herring fishermen start-

ed to take out the mainmast, which was in the way for working the hand capstan, of the three masted luggers and sailed them as two masters. In the two masted lugger the forward mast is called the foremast. Then, since drift netting for herring was only an autumn

This lines drawing is captioned 'The last sailing drifter built by Richards of Lowestoft'. This dandy rigged drifter is a markedly different ship to her predecessor, the lugger. With a more rounded forefoot, a steeply raked sternpost and a finer run aft she would have made a more weatherly sea boat. *(Maxwell Blake Collection)*

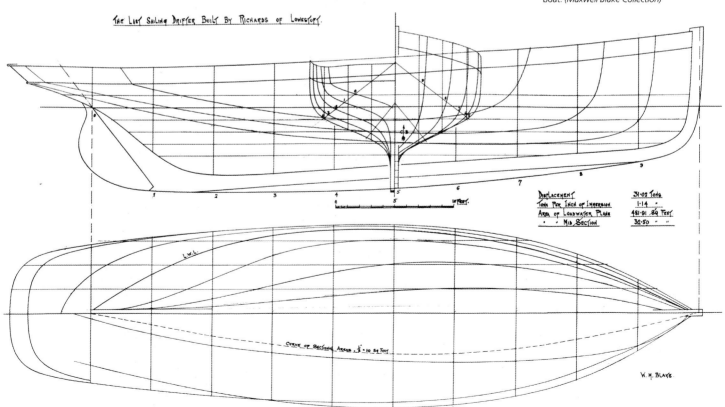

THE LAST SAILING DRIFTER BUILT BY RICHARDS OF LOWESTOFT.

L.W.L.

CURVE OF SECTIONAL AREAS ½" - 10 SQ FEET

DISPLACEMENT	31·02 TONS
TONS PER INCH OF IMMERSION	1·14
AREA OF LOADWATER PLANE	481·91 SQ FEET
MID SECTION	32·50

W. M. BLAKE.

and winter fishery, the Yarmouth and Lowestoft men removed the lug foresail in the summer and fitted gaff sails so that these smacks could go trawling. These 'converter' smacks could always be spotted because their foremast was stepped so far forward. The next step was the dandy rig which incorporated a permanent loose footed gaff sail on a short foremast and a large jackyard topsail. The mizzen was raked forward and had a gaff and boom sail with a large jackyard topsail set above it to give a good light weather sail area. A dandy was around 65ft long with an 18ft beam and had a short foremast which was lowered at sea while drifting to the nets. Although gaff rigged, the fishermen at Lowestoft always called the dandy a 'lugger'.

CROMER AND WALBERSWICK BOATS

There was a fleet of forty decked, lute sterned, two masted luggers, known in their home towns as the 'great boats', which sailed from Cromer and Sheringham. They worked from Yarmouth in the autumn herring fishery and returned home to be hauled up on the beaches for the summer. Another small fleet of dandies with loose footed gaff mainsails were owned in Walberswick and Southwold. Around 1870 these were clinker built with lute sterns and smaller than the Lowestoft boats. The end of the dandy smacks came very quickly once steam drifters were introduced in 1897. The high profits from the North Sea herring fishery gave owners the incentive to build steam drifters and by 1905 the luggers were abandoned.

Sources

Edgar March, *Sailing Drifters* is the book most people draw on for information about drifters, and also David Butcher, *The Driftermen* (Reading 1979).

YARMOUTH, LOWESTOFT AND RAMSGATE SMACKS AND TOSHERS

Ketch rigged, deep draft sailing smacks with straight stems, counter sterns, and tiller steered with a steam capstan for hauling in the nets. They were employed for trawling in the southern North Sea.

In the mid-nineteenth century when new trawling grounds were being discoverd in the North Sea 45-ton cutter smacks, known as 'long boomers', were used, but these were not very manageable trawling in a big sea. The introduction of steam capstans for hauling the trawl allowed larger ketch rigged smacks to be used and all the trawling ports had their own versions. The Lowestoft smack favoured an elliptical counter stern and a mizzen raked well forward; the Yarmouth smack had a small mizzen and square counter stern. On a Lowestoft smack all the sheets and halyards led to the capstan so that once at sea the sails could be handled by the skipper while the mate and two hands worked the nets and sorted the fish, and the boy did the cooking. The sailing smacks moved slowly over the ground and did not damage the fish in the way that later steam trawlers did. The capstan fire was kept alight in port, usually by an older fisherman, so that the capstan could be used to set sail as soon as they left port. The 60-ton, 70ft ketch was a most manageable vessel because the mizzen and headsails could be used to balance the smack and make her go sideways over the ground while the big mainsail and topsail pulled her forwards. The North

The Yarmouth drifter *Harry* YH856, built in 1882. The skipper sports a bowler hat which was, at that time, fashionable wear for fishermen and coasting men. Cast-offs, they were given a coat or two of varnish to make them weatherproof. *(NMM, neg no P39511)*

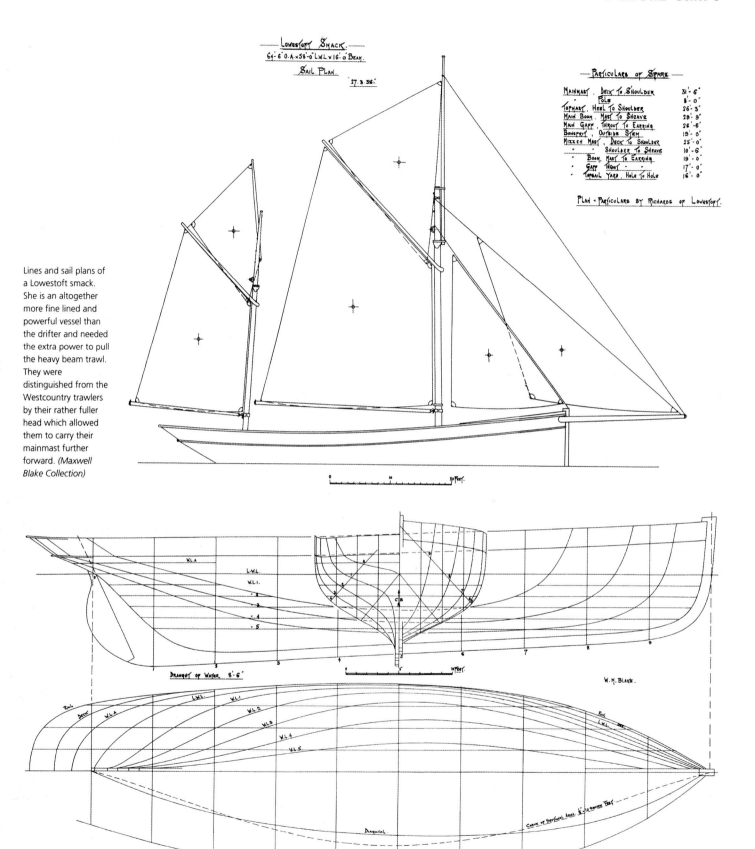

Lowestoft Smack.
64'-6" O.A. × 58'-0" L.W.L. × 16'-0" Beam.
Sail Plan.

27.3.36.

Particulars of Spars

Mainmast, Deck to Shoulder	31'-6"
" Pole	8'-0"
Topmast, Heel to Shoulder	26'-3"
Main Boom, Mast to Sheave	28'-9"
Main Gaff, Throat to Earring	26'-6"
Bowsprit, Outside Stem	19'-0"
Mizzen Mast, Deck to Shoulder	25'-0"
" Shoulder to Sheave	10'-6"
" Boom, Mast to Earring	19'-0"
" Gaff Throat	17'-0"
" Topsail Yard, Hole to Hole	16'-0"

Plan & Particulars by Richards of Lowestoft.

Lines and sail plans of a Lowestoft smack. She is an altogether more fine lined and powerful vessel than the drifter and needed the extra power to pull the heavy beam trawl. They were distinguished from the Westcountry trawlers by their rather fuller head which allowed them to carry their mainmast further forward. *(Maxwell Blake Collection)*

W.L.A.
L.W.L.
W.L.1.

Draught of Water 8'-6"   W.H. Blake.

Rail
Deck
W.L.A.   L.W.L.   W.L.1
                   W.L.2
                   W.L.3
                   W.L.4
                   W.L.5

Diagonal.

Diagonal.

Curve of Sectional Areas. ½" = 10 Square Feet.

Sea smack had a rather full bow which supported the mainmast stepped well forward, when plunging into short, steep seas. Just before World War I around two thousand of these smacks were trawling in the North Sea. These were big craft and the building of each required over one hundred winter cut oak trees.

After 1894 smack masters had to have certificates, and to get around this rule a smaller 52ft smack of under 25 tons, known as a 'tosher', was built for uncertificated men to sail. Lowestoft and Ramsgate smacks remained mainly skipper owned, or owned by small groups. Many Ramsgate smacks were lost by enemy action during World War I and the port never recovered as a trawling centre; Lowestoft also lost a number, but in the 1920s the owners started to build replacements. Until about as late as 1938 there was still a limited market for the prime fish land-ed by the few remaining Lowestoft smacks, but by then most of the fleet had been laid up.

Some of the smacks that were in good order were bought by the Norwegians and taken back to be converted into inter-island cargo traders. In the 1950s two of these former 'English trawlers' were sold to a sail training organisation in Gothenburg, Sweden, and converted back to sail. They were so impressed with these smacks as being good seaboats that in 1981 they had a new one, the 86ft *Atlantica*, built. Many Swedish owners went to Norway and bought old smacks and there are now more of them afloat and sailing in the Stockholm area than in Great Britain. The 77ft *Excelsior*, built by Chambers at Lowestoft in 1921 to replace a smack of the same name lost in World War I, was found by John Wylson in the early 1970s carrying cargoes in a Norwegian fjord and he brought her back to Lowestoft for restoration. She was authentically rebuilt and restored, complete with steam capstan.

COD BANGER

Ketch rigged, well smacks of 50ft to 60ft which sailed to the North Sea and Icelandic waters long lining for cod. The cod came back alive in the well, a watertight section amidships, and were then taken out and killed with a short stick, a 'cod banger', just before sale. Barking, on the Thames, had a large fleet of well smacks, which supplied the demand for fresh cod in London until the 1880s and after this a small fleet of Harwich- and Aldeburgh-owned well smacks operated from Harwich Harbour. The Aldeburgh 'cod bangers' were sometimes yawl rigged and the last well smack, *Gypsy*, sailed from Aldeburgh in 1914.

Sources
Sailing Trawlers is the original source of material on the sailing trawlers, but there is also some good material on the Lowestoft boats in David Butcher, *The Trawlermen* (Reading 1980), while Clive Powell, *A History of the Ramsgate Fishing Industry 1850-1920* (Ramsgate 1988) covers the Kent port. There is a good general summing up of the trawling industry by John Dyson in *Business in Great Waters* (London 1977).

YARMOUTH AND LOWESTOFT SHRIMPERS

Half decked, clinker built fishing boat with a straight stem and transom stern

A Yarmouth shrimper with its shrimp trawl. The boom required no clew outhaul and the foot of the sail was set up by heaving the spar aft; reefing was likewise simplified with no bee blocks being necessary. *(NMM, neg no P25570)*

The Lowestoft shrimping boat *Pride of the West*. A number of craft with lug and mizzen rig went shrimping out of Lowestoft and were based on the local beach boats. This vessel, recorded in 1929, has an engine fitted. *(Maxwell Blake Collection)*

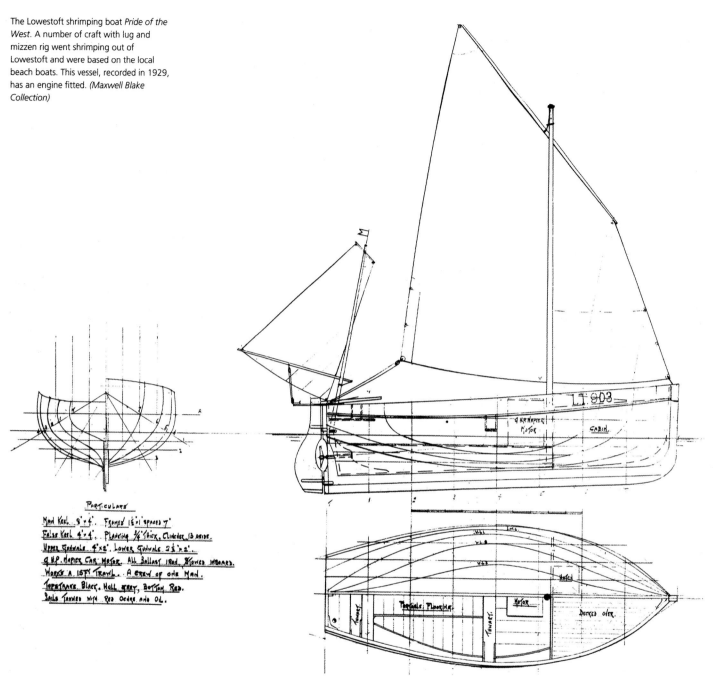

and single mast with a gaff sail and jib, and employed in day shrimping. The mid nineteenth-century shrimpers were rowing boats, worked from the beach, but by the 1890s they were gaff rigged and single masted and working from the harbours. However, their hulls were in effect clinker beach boats with fairly deep keels. The largest were about 22ft long, 9ft on the beam and 3.6ft draft, with a single headsail on a bowsprit, similar to those used by the yachts on the nearby Norfolk Broads, and since some of the shrimpers had to

beat around two miles down the long narrow Yarmouth harbour the single headsail made handling considerably easier. The most unusual part of the Yarmouth shrimper's rig was the loose footed mainsail which was stowed by letting go the peak halyard while the throat halyard remained fast. This allowed the gaff to fold down against the mast where it was made fast with a gasket. When the sail was hoisted a pole which extended forward of the mast was set up to act as a boom. This arrangement made it very easy to spill

the wind and control the boat's speed when trawling with two small nets. The shrimpers at Lowestoft had a boom on their mainsails and were very much more lightly built, clearly betraying their beach boat origin.

There were sixty-five shrimpers sailing daily from Yarmouth in 1900, and when Fred Symonds started with his father in 1926 they once counted fifty-six boats shrimping. This fleet seems to have been hit very hard by the Depression and in 1931 there were only thirty-one boats, of which all bar

four had engines. The Symonds survived the Depression by buying a smaller boat, the 19ft *Horace & Hannah*. Fred worked this boat until 1957 when he had the 22ft *Crangon* built (bought and restored by Jonathan Simper in 1996). In 1996, Chris Moore's *Boy Frank*, the *Crangon*'s sistership, remained at Yarmouth fitted out for shrimping.

Sources
'Shrimps for Tea', by John Mellor and Robert Simper in *Classic Boat* (March 1995).

Norfolk and Suffolk Beach Yawls

Long and narrow, double ended, clinker built, open boats with a two masted lug rig used for salvage. The men who worked the beach yawls actually referred to them as 'yolls'. To operate the yawls the fishermen grouped together into a co-operative known as a 'beach company'. The yawls were from 45ft to 70ft long and had to be fast and able to go to sea in any weather. The clinker hull had to be flexible and twist when sailed hard in a heavy

The Southwold yawl Bittern, built in 1892. These fine, fast vessels were used mainly for carrying out passengers and pilots and for salvage work on the offshore banks. The fine shape of the forefoot and the sternpost compensated for the lack of a centreboard or deep keel, as did the rudder which projected down below the line of the keel. (Maxwell Blake Collection)

sea and come back into shape like a basket when landed on the beach. They suffered enormous strain and none have survived.

The yawl was kept on the beach ready to put to sea at any time there was a possibility of salvage work. Any member of a beach company who assisted in the launch, crewed in the yawl or was a share holder took a percentage of the money earnt. The centres of the beach companies were Yarmouth, Lowestoft and Southwold where huge fleets of sailing ships anchored in the Roads for shelter in bad weather. The 'bullocks', heavy double enders, were for taking out spare anchors while a gig was used for taking out pilots and passengers. At the beginning of the nineteenth century the beach yawl was a three master, but by their heyday in the 1880s the yawl had become a two-master.

A large crew of fifteen or even more was needed to shift the fore lug, move the bags of ballast, and row in calm weather. There were companies in the

coastal villages from Mundesley in north Norfolk down to Felixstowe Ferry in Suffolk. The Aldeburgh companies were mainly involved in putting pilots on to ships bound into the Thames Estuary. South of Orfordness there were small companies at Orford, Shingle Street, Bawdsey and Felixstowe Ferry which did not get much work. Here they used a dual purpose double ender known as a 'great galley' which could do salvage or carrying work.

Sailing a yawl called for considerable skill because if, as sometimes happened, the sails were caught aback, it could capsize and sink. The mizzen was set on a long outrigger which, because the Norfolk men could not pronounce their r's, was known as an 'outlinger'. The mizzen was used as much as the rudder to steer. When tacking in heavy weather the fore lug was lowered and manhandled round the mast while some men rowed the head round. The plan of a yawl shows a

downhaul to the lower end of the yard which was used in light weather to pull the yard upright, pass the sail round behind the foremast, and take it forward again to the iron bumkin on the bow and then haul the sail up tight again with a burton tackle on the halyard. With a skilled crew this method of tacking was just as fast as tacking in a gaff rigged craft.

Pleasure Yoll

Clinker, double ended, gaff sloop with bowsprit and a single big headsail like the Lowestoft and Yarmouth shrimpers (qv), employed in taking holiday makers for short trips. Every summer the railways brought thousands of holidaymakers to Yarmouth and here the beachmen devised a type of yoll to run trips, crammed with people, off the beach. One of these yolls to have survived is the 37ft Amity, built in 1912, but damaged when German warships shelled the Lowestoft beach during

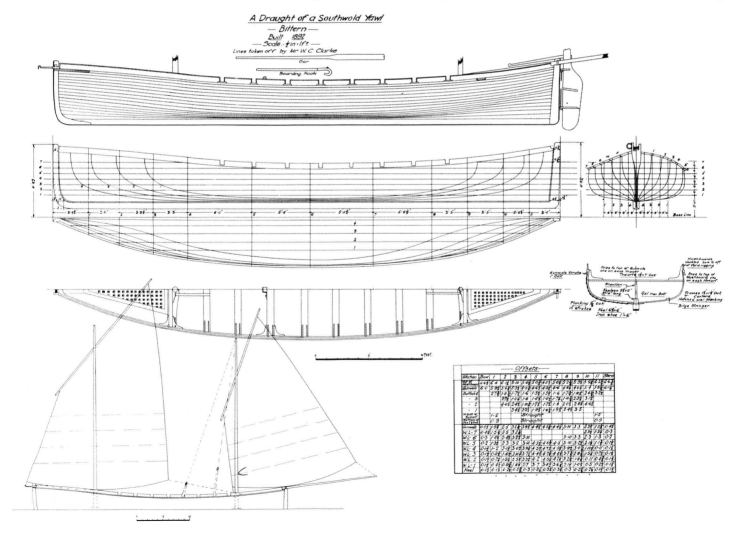

Baden Powell is an example of the rather beamier version of the Southwold beach yawl which was used mainly for carrying out spare ground tackle and stores to ships offshore. Speed was less of a consideration than carrying capacity. *(Maxwell Blake Collection)*

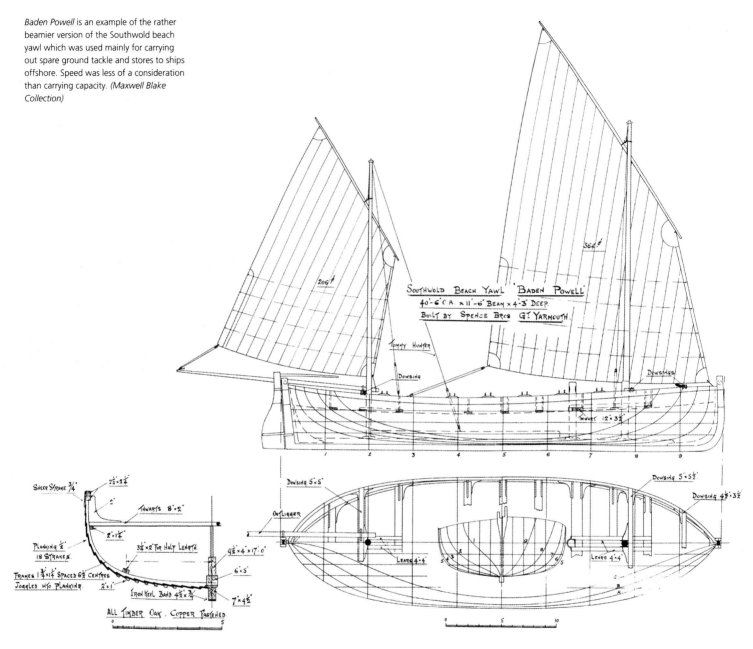

World War I. She was bought by William Loose of Brancaster in 1916 and sailed round to the Worfolk yard at King's Lynn to be converted for cockle and mussel gathering.

NORFOLK AND SUFFOLK LIFEBOAT

Open, double ended, clinker rowing and sailing lifeboat, with a small, two mast lug rig. They also carried oars and some had centreboards. When lifeboats were first introduced to the eastern Norfolk and Suffolk coasts the men who were used to working beach yawls insisted on having a lifeboat which

could be sailed. The Norfolk and Suffolk type was designed for safety, not speed. It appears that the practice was to have lifeboats stationed all along the coast and the boat furthest to windward was called out. Some of these wooden sailing lifeboats have survived. The 47ft Gorleston Volunteer Lifeboat Association's *Elizabeth Simpson*, built by Beeching Brothers at Yarmouth in 1889, became a tripper boat, although in 1996 she was laid up at Potter Heigham. Another of the Norfolk and Suffolk type is the 44ft *Alfred Corry* which was built at Lowestoft in 1893 and presented by John Cragie to a trust at Southwold for preservation.

However, the oldest boat afloat in Norfolk at that time was the former 43ft wooden lifeboat *Friend of All Nations*, built by James Critten at Southtown, Yarmouth, for the Young Fliers beach company in 1863. The last RNLI double ended lifeboat, a steel motor craft, on the East Anglian coast was withdrawn from Aldeburgh in 1994

Sources

A man who sailed with lifeboats and beachmen was Southwold's town clerk E R Cooper who wrote a series of articles and books dealing with beach yawls, notably *Storm Warriors of the Suffolk Coast* (London

1937) and an article in *The Mariner's Mirror*, 13 (1927). On Norfolk, David Higgins, *The Beachmen* (Lavenham 1987) covers the background of the beach companies and their yawls.

SUFFOLK BEACH BOAT
(Southwold punt, Aldeburgh boat)

Open, clinker, transom sterned, two masted lugger, without a centreboard, used for longshore fishing. Because the clinker beach boat was almost flat bottomed it was called a 'punt' at Southwold and was about 18ft long. Larger boats were tried, up to 22ft, but they do not appear to have been economic. Built entirely with local oak and joggled timbers for strength, the fishermen claimed that an 18ft boat was able to load 3½ tons of herring. To achieve this they did not worry too much about their sailing qualities but liked a fairly beamy hull. If the catch was good they loaded the boats down to within a few inches of the gunwale and rowed home.

Early nineteenth-century prints and paintings of the Suffolk coast between Pakefield and Aldeburgh usually show double ended, clinker fishing boats hauled up on the beach. These appear

The Caister-on-Sea lifeboat in 1893. They carried the same rig as the beach yawls whose lines they also replicated, and were originally crewed by the yawl men who had to be fine seamen to handle such powerful open boats. If the yawl began to take in green water over the lee gunwale the coxwain would call 'leggo' to the sheet man who eased the mainsail – split-second reactions were essential. *(NMM, neg no G3652)*

to have been rather like the Yarmouth punts, but with a two masted lug rig. Around 1820 this all changed and paintings show a clinker, two masted lugger with a transom stern. In around 1900 there were about 300 of these boats working off the beaches between Pakefield and Aldeburgh. A larger version of the Suffolk boat worked out of Lowestoft harbour.

The Suffolk beach boat was a sailing and rowing boat, and often, because of the difficulties of dipping the fore lug, the men rowed to windward. In calm weather or in the summer races they 'swung the lug' right round forward of the mast. In a fresh wind the sail had to be lowered and passed aft of the mast. The foremast was raked aft to keep the luff of the foresail tight and to help the boat sail closer to the wind. The mizzen was always cut very flat so that it would help push the bows around when tacking.

The 17ft *Lassie*, built for Shingle Street in 1924, appears to have been the first Suffolk motor beach boat. These early motor sailers had low pow-

ered engines; the 18ft *Bonnie*, built for Aldeburgh fisherman Hector Burrell by Everson in 1937, had only a 4hp petrol engine. With these engines they still carried and used oars and sails. In the 1960s Frank Knight's yard at Woodbridge was regularly building 18ft boats to work off Aldeburgh beach with 8hp diesel engines. By the 1970s a new type of Suffolk boat was produced with a wide 'bulldog' bow and a more powerful engine. In 1994, the *Three Sisters*, 18.5ft long, 7.1ft on the beam and 1.8ft draft, originally built at Thorpeness in 1896, probably by Denny , was restored to a dipping lugger and is sailed for pleasure by Robert Simper.

FELIXSTOWE FERRY LOBSTER BOAT

Open, 15ft clinker boat, rowed or sailed with a very square lug sail. The Felixstowe Ferry lobster boat appears to have been in use at the beginning of the nineteenth century and since they were built at Woodbridge their use

spread to Bawdsey and Shingle Street. The lobster boats had a mast stepped almost amidships on the main thwart and the square cut lug sail went to a hook inside the bow. To dip the lug the sail was lowered, the mast lifted up and the sail pushed across to the other side; the mast was then restepped and the sail hoisted on the new tack. The bow was sometimes helped around with an oar.

During World War I the Royal Navy ordered most of the Felixstowe Ferry lobster boats to be taken off the beach near the ferry landing and put in the dykes behind the river wall. Most of them rotted away here, but in about 1954 'Jockey' Hunt was still rowing a weatherbeaten lobster boat out to his hoops near the Cutler Sand. The last boat of this type was *Gem*, built by Everson in about 1935 for the Shingle Street pilot Eric Andrews.

Sources
Beach Boats of Britain and *Rivers Alde, Ore and Blyth*, also by Robert Simper (Ramsholt 1994), cover the Suffolk beach boats.

The Southwold luggers LT769 and LT792, photographed in 1904, are typical of the beach boats, or punts as they were known locally, which could be found all along the coast at Dunwich, Aldeburgh and Kessingland. They were generally painted white above the waterline, tarred below it, and given a splash of colour along the planksheer. *(NMM, Oliver Hill Collection, neg no P75428)*

DUCK PUNT

A low, narrow punt, double ended, and usually partly decked which was rowed or sailed in pursuit of wildfowl around Brancaster, Woodbridge, Manningtree and Maldon. The Buckel family at Maldon claimed to have invented the gun punt in about 1820. The punt gun, often 9.6ft long with a 1½in bore, was mounted on the bow and the punt gunner lay down behind the gun and used hand paddles to move quietly up to a flock of wildfowl and then fire into the middle to take the largest possible number. The bottom of the punt was flat so that it could manoeuvre in very shallow water, but the bottom was always curved, or 'rockered', to avoid the danger of suction holding it down in the mud. Each wildfowling centre had

A Felixtowe Ferry lobster boat was an open pulling and sailing boat which could cross the notorious Deben Bar to make the short two-mile trip to the lobster grounds. *(Robert Simper collection)*

its own version of the gun punt, most of them were open in the 1880s, but by 1920 were partly decked. They were from 16ft to 20ft length overall with a beam of 2ft 6in to 3ft.

The sail, usually a high peaked spritsail, was used mainly for the summer races rather than while wildfowling. The Manningtree punts, which are still keenly raced, are fast, but difficult to sail and can easily be turned over. They are steered by an oar over the lee stern which acts as both rudder and centreboard.

On the Norfolk Broads the duck punts used on Breydon Water had a round bottom while those used on Hickling Broad were flat bottomed and were very fast when sailed with sprit or lug sails. Punt racing started on Hickling in 1923 and three years later the Norfolk Punt Club was formed to foster racing. The length of the Norfolk punt was standardised to 22ft and every year Herbert Woods, one of the Club's founders and a talented boatbuilder and designer, produced a new punt and they evolved into high performance racing boats. After World War II David Wyche's punt *Scoter* became the prototype for the plywood racing punts. Then in 1976 Colin

McDougall used the plywood *Shoveller* as the plug of a mould for GRP punts of which the *Golden Jubilee* was the first. There are thought to be about forty-five punts in Britain, but because of the conservation lobby, the wildfowlers are very secretive about their activities.

Sources
John Lewis, *Vintage Boats* (Newton Abbott 1975) records how to built a traditional Manningtree duck punt while in *Classic Boat* magazine (January 1997) Richard Johnson-Bryden updates the racing scene and describes the building of his 15ft racing punt.

The narrow, flat bottomed duck punt was designed to be paddled as close as possible to its prey as they either rested or fed in the estuaries and shallow creeks of the east coast. The barrel of the gun rested aft of the foredeck. *(Robert Simper Collection)*

Essex Smacks

Deep draft, gaff cutters, with long bowsprits, straight stems, low counter sterns, and tiller steered, used for oyster dredging and stowboating. Some of the large, 1st class smacks had a hand capstan, but the nets were usually hauled by hand.

COLCHESTER SMACK

The term Colchester smack is a little misleading because none of these smacks ever sailed from or were connected with the port apart from carrying the letters CK as their fishing registration. The larger, 1st class Essex smack was 65ft long, 15ft on the beam, and 8.6ft draft; they were built with an elm keel, pine keelson, oak frames, deck beams and wale, and pine planking.

From the end of the eighteenth century until 1914 there were far more smacks owned in Essex than the local waters could support and the 1st class smacks roamed all round the British Isles looking for deep water oysters, venturing as far afield as the Solway Firth and the Channel Islands where they dredged oysters from Gorey, off Jersey. Others, the 'skillingers', went dredging deep water oysters in the North Sea off the Dutch island of Terschelling. These smacks were cutter rigged until five were lost in the gales of the early 1880s. Because the booms were such a liability, banging around in heavy weather, about half the fleet of around twenty-five were converted to ketch or dandy (yawl) rig after this. The fleet continued until 1914, and deep water oystering was revived in the English Channel in the interwar years, but by this time the Brightlingsea men had bought old wooden Lowestoft steam drifters for the work.

STOWBOATER
(Colne smack)

The stowboater was a smaller, yacht-like version of a 1st class smack with a powerful hand spike windlass and a strong fairlead on the bow for hauling in the stow net. After the disappearance of the big Colchester smacks these craft were designated as 1st class smacks.

Because the channels in the Thames Estuary are narrow the Essex smacks could not use drift nets like the Suffolk sprat boats; instead, they anchored in the channel and lowered a 'stow' or stall net down over the bow to catch the shoals of sprat. Having to work up the channels and swatchways the smacksmen liked to have a fast, handy smack of about 45ft long. The Essex stowboating smack had a low bow and long counter stern which gave more deck space and, when heeled, increased waterline length which made for greater speed. The main boom always extended just over the stern to allow a powerful mainsail to be set, and a topsail was set on a separate topmast. Their weather helm was to some extent counterbalanced by a long bowsprit and large jib. The smack's running bowsprit was 'bowsed down', often so that it bent down, in order to keep the leading edge of the jib straight and prevent the mast from bending back. This, in turn, curbed the gaff's tendency to fall off the wind and improved windward performance. The Essex smack was fast but had a reputation of being a wet boat at sea.

The yards along the Colne built both smacks and yachts so the two types were closely related. Sometimes a hull was started 'on spec', which could be finished either as a yacht or a smack. The 50ft *Sunbeam* was one of these; she was started as a yacht in 1881, but was eventually bought for winter fishing. Since few records were kept it is now difficult to tell who built many of the smacks. Most were built at the Aldous yard at Brightlingsea and their smacks had the reputation of being useful workboats which were also quick, but they built whatever the smacksmen ordered.

The Essex smacksmen had an enviable reputation for their racing skills and many of the skippers and crews spent the summer months racing the big yachts as professionals. Those who did not get taken on might employ the stowboaters for summer shrimping and trawling. Often a yacht skipper who had taken a lot of prize money racing wrote to a builder and ordered a new smack for the winter and each owner stated precisely what kind of smack he wanted. The 36ft *Phantom*, for instance, was built in 1897 for an owner who wanted to be able to wildfowl in shallow water and she is quite different from the deep and fast 45ft stowboater *ADC*. Other smacks built in yacht yards were much sleeker, such as the 44ft *Ellen* built at Rowhedge in 1900, and the 44ft *Charlotte Ellen*, one of a few elegant smacks built by Kidby at Brightlingsea, but not necessarily any faster than the Aldous smacks.

The Essex smacks are still sailed and raced very competitively each summer.

OYSTER SMACK

The Essex oyster smack was a smaller version of the stowboater and was used for oyster dredging in the estuaries and creeks. Around 34ft to 36ft long on deck, they were pole masted and had a long bowsprit and boom to help them pull their dredges over the ground, while their counters were particularly long and the freeboard low to assist in the retrieval of the fishing gear.

MALDON SMACK

The little Maldon smacks were transom sterned, cutter rigged, carvel smacks with flush decks and a small low cabin top just aft of the mast. The eighteenth-century Essex smack used for oyster dredging in the Blackwater was about 35ft long, 11ft beam and drew an incredible 7ft with a transom or lute stern. While the eighteenth-century smack had a curved bow, rather like the later Galway hookers, *(qv)* the straight Victorian stem became universal, but Maldon smacks continued with the transom. Before about 1830 the Maldon smack was clinker built and by luck the 28ft *Boadicea*, built at Maldon in 1808, has survived. The *Boadicea* has been rebuilt twice but none of the original timber remains and she now has a carvel hull. However, although not as fast as the later slightly larger Victorian

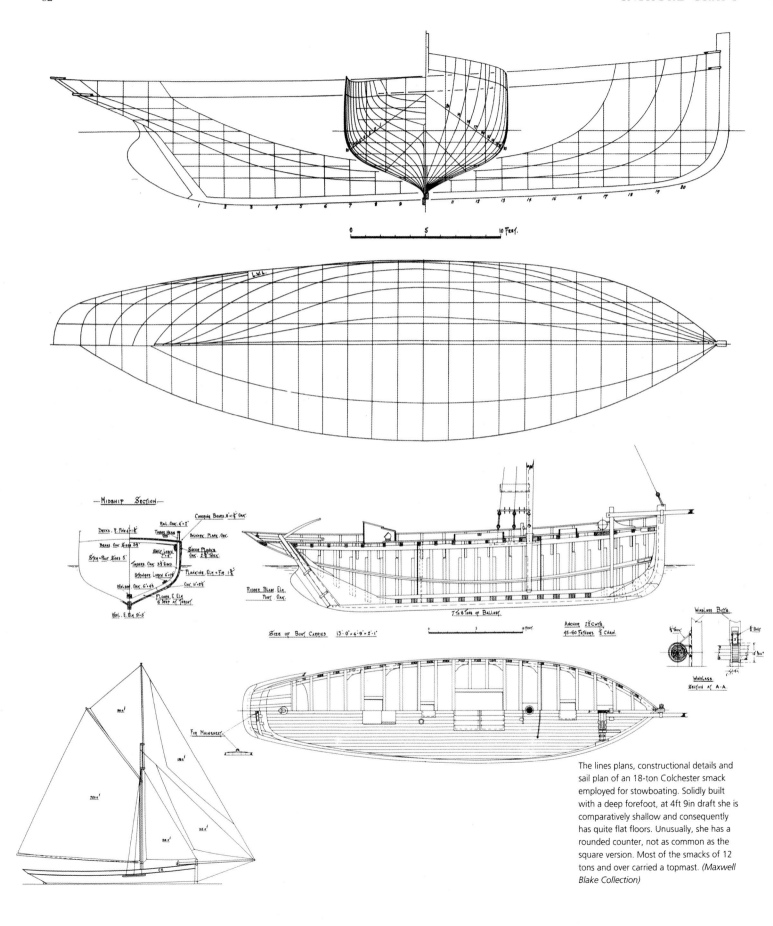

The lines plans, constructional details and sail plan of an 18-ton Colchester smack employed for stowboating. Solidly built with a deep forefoot, at 4ft 9in draft she is comparatively shallow and consequently has quite flat floors. Unusually, she has a rounded counter, not as common as the square version. Most of the smacks of 12 tons and over carried a topmast. (*Maxwell Blake Collection*)

The Essex smacks are one type amongst the few vernacular craft which have witnessed a revival in the last years of this century, even though they are used primarily as yachts. This photograph was taken in 1990. The oyster dredger *Mayflower* CK44, in the foreground, still fishes. This view shows well her low freeboard astern and the loose footed mainsail and long boom. In the middle distance is the *Sunbeam* CK328, a bigger stowboater with a tall topmast and well bowsed down bowsprit. *(Robert Simper Collection)*

The little 36ft oyster dredger *Harriet Blanche* is altogether more fine lined than her bigger sister, the stowboater, and the more rounded forefoot would help in going about smartly in narrow channels and creeks. The low freeboard and long counter, so typical of these vessels, can be clearly seen in these lines plans. *Harriet Blanche* was restored in 2006 by the Testers of Faversham. *(NMM, Coastal Craft Collection)*

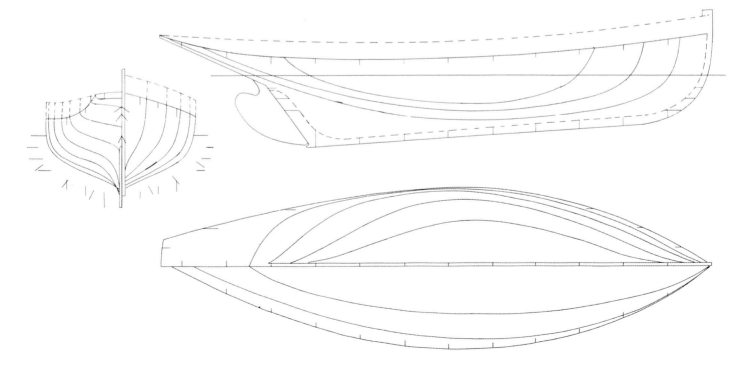

The Maldon smack *Joseph T* MN 9, photographed in 1960, sitting comfortably on her bilge on the shore just down river of the Hythe, her boom swung out to ensure that she lists into the hard. She has all the typical clutter of a working vessel: the oyster dredges on deck, peter nets hung up to dry on the mast, and sacks over the starboard pin rail, which might serve as aprons for the crew or for carrying the oysters. *(NMM, Oliver Hill Collection, neg no P75429)*

smack, she is a handy vessel. The lute sterned *Mary* of around 1860 still survives. After World War I the Maldon *Polly* and one or two others had counter sterns added. The Maldon smack of the Victorian period seems to have had a topmast and topsail, but by the 1920s a pole mast with larger mainsail and high cut peak was adopted as more convenient.

After World War II there were still fourteen smacks kept on the Mill Beach at Maldon and although most used sails while they dredged they also

had old car engines. Ernie Pitt's *Polly* was working under sail until 1956 and Alfa Pitt's *Skylark* and the Claydon brothers' *Joseph T* were still working until 1964. After this Alf Claydon bought the 27ft smack *Happy Days* to use in his retirement. In 1968 he sold her to sixteen-year-old Michael Emmett who fished with her and he eventually had the transom sterned Maldon smack *Ostrea Rose* built in 1980.

PAGLESHAM SMACK

The Paglesham smacks were smaller than the Colne smacks in order to work in the narrow River Roach and the adjoining network of creeks. They had a high bow and more hollow entry and a very long counter stern. Paglesham-built smacks still sailing include the 36ft *Mary* built before 1862 with a 10.5ft beam, a 5.3ft draft and a tiny V transom with a lute stern above it which seems to have been called a 'tucked' stern. The lute stern was replaced by the elegant counter stern by

the time the 32ft *Quiz*, built 1872, and the Hall-built 36ft *Kate*, built in 1883, joined the oyster fleet.

The smaller Essex smacks were among few of the working boat types – along with the Itchen ferry (*qv*) and the Bristol Channel pilot cutter (*qv*) – which were happily adapted to yachting, as witnessed by the two pretty little smack yachts, the 28ft *Secret* and the 30ft *Bird of Dawning*, built at the Paglesham yard of Frank Shuttlewood in 1932 and 1937 respectively.

WINKLE BRIG

Open, clinker boat with a centreboard, 15ft to 18ft long, rigged as a gaff sloop and used as a general runabout. These boats, which were originally old ships' boats with a gaff rig added by the Essex fisherman, were called winkle brigs at West Mersea and bumkins on the Colne. In about 1912 Charles Kidby built a new type of boat to work in the creeks and on the flats to replace the 20ft 'haul and towing' boat at West

Mersea. The new winkle brig was clinker built, but sometimes had grown frames so that they could carry the weight of oysters and winkles in bags. The last one working under sail seems to have been the *Boy George* from which 'Snowball' Hughes used to work oyster layings at Mersea until about 1964. By then the winkle brig had been replaced by the oyster skiff, a low sided motor boat built with grown frames. In 1996 up to seventeen brigs were racing, divided into high performance and the others who wanted to keep as near as possible to the traditional rig used by fishermen.

Sources
Hervey Benham, *Last Stronghold of Sail* (London 1948) and *Stowboaters* (London 1947), and John Leather, *Gaff Rig* (London 1970) are the best sources of information on the Colchester smacks. Arthur and Michael Emmett, *Blackwater Men* (Maldon 1992) covers Maldon smacks. John Leather, *The Salty Shore* (Lavenham 1975) and Robert Simper, *Essex Rivers and Creeks* (Ramsholt 1995) touch on winkle brigs.

Clinker built Gravesend Bawleys ashore at Bawley Bay in 1890 with their fine meshed shrimping nets hung up to dry. The stowed mainsail was hauled up by the throat to allow water to run off. The photograph shows clearly how the lines sweep round from the broad shoulders to the fine entry, a distinct characteristic of the bawleys. *(NMM. neg no G3605)*

Bawleys

The bawley was a very beamy, transom sterned, straight stemmed, decked smack with a cutter rig which incorporated a boomless mainsail with a long gaff. This mainsail, which was the bawley's most distinctive feature, was stowed with brails; a large topsail was set above. Technically, the bawley – as a decked, gaff rigged fishing boat – was a 'smack', but it always retained a separate identity. Their main employment was shrimping in the Thames estuary in summer while in the winter they went stowboating. A copper, in which to cook the shrimps before landing, was a noteworthy feature.

GRAVESEND BAWLEY

The late eighteenth-century fishermen of the lower Thames employed a 30ft peter boat (*qv*) for fishing and made voyages in the summer from Barking Creek and Gravesend as far afield as West Mersea; indeed, the increasing pollution of the Thames drove the fishermen ever further out into the estuary. As these craft grew in size and became too large to be rowed there was little requirement for the pointed stern, and in the 1820s to '30s there developed a type which was simply a peter boat with a transom stern. The main difference between the two types was that the clinker peter boat had a wet well for storing fish while the bawley had a shrimp boiler. This 'boilie boat' appeared in the 1850s when a copper was fitted so that the shrimps could be boiled on the way home. By the 1860s the Gravesend builders were producing a clinker bawley around 28ft long which did not work much below the Lower Hope and had a relatively shallow draft for trawling in the shoal waters, and a beamy, stable hull so that the hot water was not spilt from the copper.

The bawley's main work was to make daily trips out into the Thames Estuary and to do this they carried a very lofty sail plan; the loose footed mainsail, quickly and easily reduced by brailing, controlled their speed when trawling with the delicate shrimp nets. Unlike the spritsail barges (*qv*) the bawleys did not have wangs, and to prevent the head of the sail from sagging to leeward the peak of the mainsail was cut quite square.

A little fleet of bawleys was shrimping from Gravesend until the 1950s. The 28ft clinker Gravesend bawley *Ellen* was reputed to have been built in 1760 as a custom cutter and was still worked with a 15hp engine and hand operated capstan. She was sold to Medway owners in 1961. The boats at Gravesend were kept in an inlet known as Bawley Bay; the last here

was the *Thistle*, in fact a carvel built Medway bawley, which was sold when her owner, Bill Sunderland, died in 1970. The Gravesend bawley *Vivid*, built in 1882, is still sailing as a yacht while another one, *Lilian*, built by Waters at Gravesend in 1869, was taken to Maldon where a replica of her, the 29ft *Marigold*, was built at Cook's yard in 1981.

LEIGH BAWLEY

At Leigh and Southend a bigger carvel built bawley evolved which could venture further out in the estuary. One of these, the *Bona*, built by Aldous at

Above: The Medway bawley *Ethel* trawling off the Sheppey coast. The main brail around the leech of the mainsail can be seen and amidships is the chimney for the boiler. Even though she has a reef in, the photograph gives a good impression of the lofty and powerful rig of these craft. *(NMM, neg no P27471)*

Left and opposite page: The lines plans, constructional details and sail plan of the Harwich bawley HH65. This shows a typical Cann built bawley at 38ft overall, a beam of 13ft, and a draft of 5ft; they carried 6 tons of ballast. The planks were pulled down edge to edge with a mixture between them of tar, varnish and goat's hair and so required no caulking. The trawl was hoisted onto the wide side decks and so these bawleys were relatively squat and low amidships. *(Maxwell Blake Collection)*

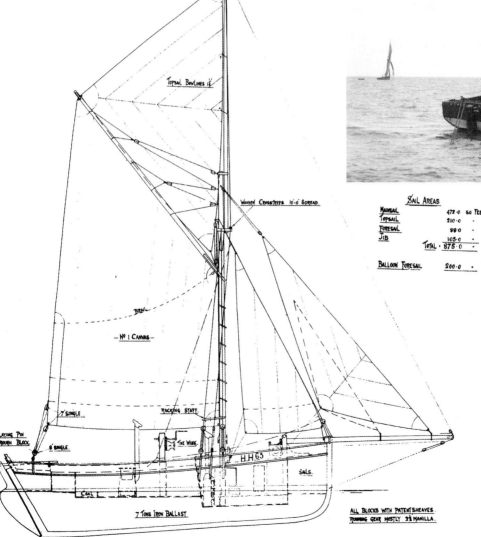

Brightlingsea in 1903 and still sailing, is 36ft overall, 13ft beam, and has a draft of 4.3ft The Leigh bawleys carried a very lofty sail plan, and even a small one, of around 37ft overall, might have a mast and topmast extending 50ft from the deck to the masthead truck. The hull had a very hollow entrance which quickly broadened out to the wide beam in way of the mast and, with the powerful hull sections, the bawley could carry its big sail plan in quite a stiff breeze. The 36ft *Helen & Violet*, built at Harwich for use at Leigh, used to race with a huge topsail, obtained second hand from a big racing yacht, and a large jib was set on a 17ft bowsprit. Ballast amounting to 6 to 7 tons was carried inboard.

Many of the Leigh bawleys were built by Aldous of Brightlingsea and J & H Cann of Harwich though Hayward at Southend and some of the Medway builders also supplied them. In 1890 there were eighty-six bawleys sailing from Leigh and another twenty at Southend although the two fleets were deadly rivals.

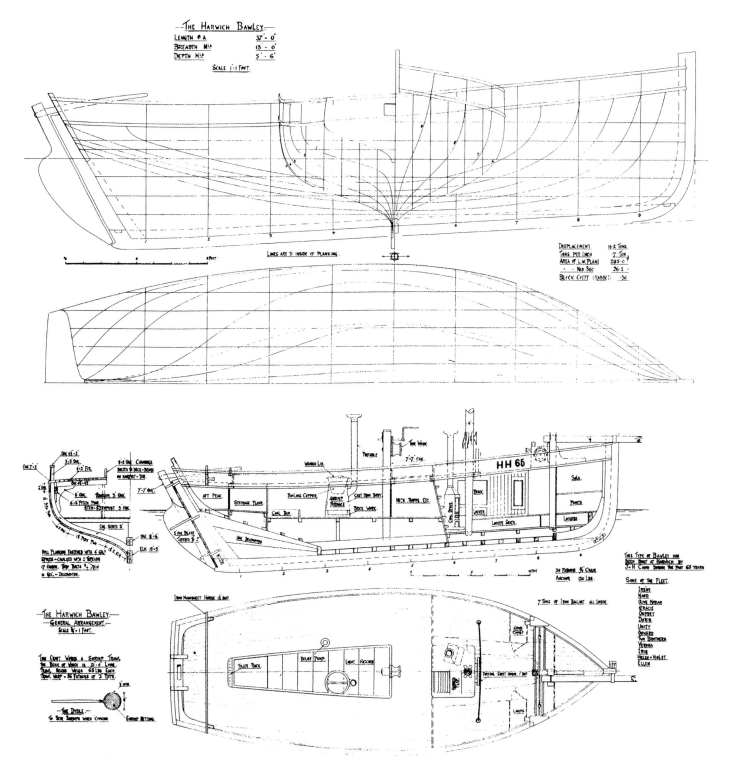

MEDWAY BAWLEY

There was a fleet of bawleys kept at Strood and Chatham on the River Medway and by the end of the nineteenth century the Medway bawleys were almost identical to the Harwich and Leigh vessels though they had rather less draft and, with their upright transom stern, were perhaps not quite so attractive to look at. The Medway bawley had a mast in a tabernacle so that it could be lowered to go under Rochester Bridge when they went

The shallow drafted Leigh cockler had a distinctly more rounded stem and forefoot than the larger bawleys. With no topmast the standing rigging was reduced to a minimum but these cocklers were fast and handy little vessels. This photograph was taken at Leigh on Sea in 1935. *(NMM, Oliver Hill Collection, neg no P74964)*

fishing for smelt upstream; their other important work was dredging Medway oysters. The main builders were Gill of Rochester and E Lemon of Strood. Some small clinker bawleys sailed from Faversham on the Swale and these had a loose footed mainsail and a tiny lug mizzen with an outrigger stepped right on the stern. This rig had been popular on the Thames during the early nineteenth century.

HARWICH BAWLEY

The Harwich bawleys were identical to the Leigh vessels and built at the same yards. Before World War I there were around sixty bawleys sailing from Harwich which had all been built in the town. Herbert and John Cann, at the Gas House Creek yard, built some of the best bawleys. Like the Leigh bawleys, they sailed every morning to

sea and returned in time to put their catch on the afternoon train. They carried heavy ground tackle and a powerful hand spike windlass so that they could 'fetch up' anywhere in the harbour to put the catch ashore by boat. In 1919 the first motor fishing boat built at Harwich was the *Lilian*, basically an open, transom sterned launch.

A few bawleys were sold for conversion to yachts and were given a boom. The loose footed mainsail was considered slow and clumsy and for over forty years there were no correctly rigged bawleys sailing. Attitudes towards the bawley rig changed when the *Helen & Voilet*, which appeared in 1982 with her original rig, beat all the fast smacks in the East Coast Old Gaffers Race. She went on to be unbeatable in the smack races showing that the bawley, correctly handled, was a fast boat. When sailing downwind

under a press of sail, the lofty rig sways gently like a pendulum as the loose footed mainsail alternately spills the wind and then fills again.

LEIGH COCKLE BOAT
(Cockle galley)

The Leigh cockle boat, or galley, was a smaller version of the bawley which was developed around 1900. The rig was identical, but the cockle boat was a shoal draft vessel and very strongly built to allow for the frequent groundings on the sands. The fishermen used to sail them down to the sands on the Essex and Kent coasts where they ran them ashore. When the tide went down four men filled them by hand raking into baskets.

When cockling started the Leigh men use to go across to the naval dockyard at Sheerness and buy old open

pulling galleys from the warships. At first the Leigh cocklers did not have to go far down the Maplin sands to be filled, but by 1900 they were sometimes travelling as far as the mouth of the Blackwater or to the Columbine near Whitstable. This required a larger, faster craft which could get out and home on one tide. Some of faster cocklers had centreboards, but although they were decked they were built with thwarts like the old pulling galleys, which gave them the extra strength needed to load about 4 tons of cockles. The first of these cocklers were about 27ft long, but the cockle men wanted even larger craft which resulted in Hayward building two 34 footers in about 1912. Then in 1914 Hayward built the 33ft *Reindeer*, now called *Viking*, and the *Mary Amelia*. These were built at his yard in Southend and then taken by traction engine out on to the sands where they floated when the tide came up. Two cocklers still sailing as yachts are *Mary Amelia*, rebuilt by Colin Fox, and the 30ft *Alice & Florrie* built by Peters at Leigh in 1905.

The largest cockler built before 1939 was the 40ft *Reliance*, with a beam of 12ft and a draft of 2ft, built at Leigh by Cole & Wiggins, and she would have had up to six men as crew. She had a 30hp Kelvin petrol-paraffin engine installed but still had a centreboard and pole mast for auxiliary sail. The shoal draft Leigh cocklers proved particularly useful in 1940 evacuating soldiers off the beach at Dunkirk and the *Endeavour*, *Reliance*, *Letita* and *Renown* were amongst the many east coast fishing boats that went to assist.

Sources
Derek Coombe, *Bawleymen, Fishermen and Dredgers of the River Medway* (Rainham 1979) tells the Kentish side of the story. W Edward Wigfull, 'Going A'Cockling', *Yachting Monthly*, Vol 14 (March 1913) gives a very good account of a trip in a working cockle boat. John Leather, *Smacks and Bawleys* (Lavenham 1991), describes the Leigh and Harwich bawleys.

PETER BOAT
(doble)

The peter boat was a double ended, clinker vessel, sometimes fitted with a wet well and a windlass for hauling nets. The sailing versions were rigged as spritsail sloops and sometimes set a topsail. They were employed for stop netting in the narrow creeks off the Thames and for trawling in the estuary. There were two types used: the 'above the bridges' rowing boats,

Lines and sail plan of a transom sterned peter boat built at Strood on the Medway. She was 27ft 6in overall, 9ft 6in on the beam and 4ft 2in draft aft, and had a wet well. She has the something of the look of a transitional craft with her distinctly eighteenth-century stem combined with the boomless cutter rig of the later bawleys. *(NMM, Coastal Craft Collection)*

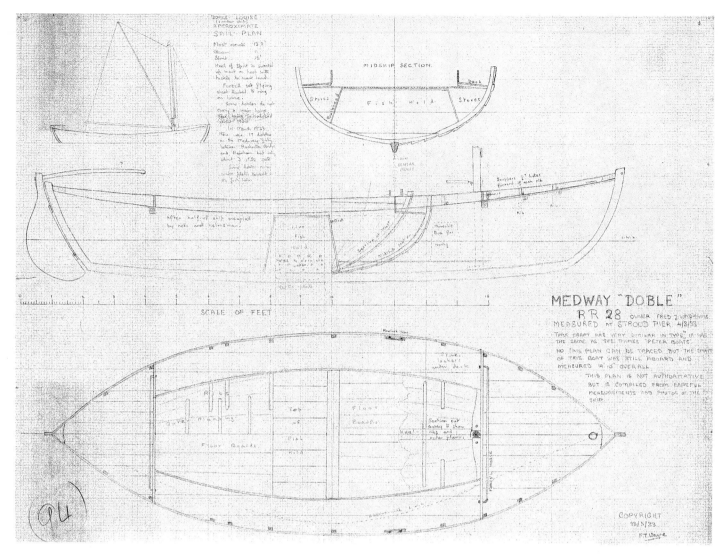

Above: The rough profile and plan of the Medway doble RR28, measured at Strood pier in 1933 by F T Wayne. They were half decked just below the level of the sheer. A note on the drawing states that in March 1933 there were seventeen dobles fishing in the Medway between Rochester Bridge and Rainham. *(NMM, Coastal Craft Collection)*

Right: A Medway doble, with its simple sprit mainsail and small foresail, underway below Rochester Bridge. The foresail sheet was often made up on a horse making the handling of the rig simplicity itself. *(NMM, Oliver Hill Collection, neg no P74970)*

which were about 12ft long, and were used up as far as Windsor; and those used below the Pool of London, which had sails and were from 18ft overall up to about 28ft long. The sailing peter boat, though it had a keel aft to grip the water, performed poorly to windward, but this mattered little as they were unable anyway to sail against the powerful Thames tide. The up river boats were rowed and sometimes had a canvas shelter on hoops so that the fishermen could live aboard. There was still an upper river peter boat kept at Putney in 1927.

The double ended peter boat probably has its origins in the Anglo-Saxon boat, and the name peter boat for the fishing boats of the Thames appeared in the fourteenth century; it is thought to have derived from St Peter, patron saint of fishermen, and there was a legend that he had been seen crossing the Pool of London in one of these boats.

The fishermen of Woolwich and Greenwich developed a peter boat with a spritsail and jib, while lower down, at Gravesend and Barking, an estuary version evolved which had a bowsprit and tiny cabin forward. These mid-Victorian peter boats made summer voyages to the Essex and Suffolk coast bringing their catch back alive in the wells.

One 18ft peter boat, built in 1835, was converted to the yawl *Dauntless* and owned by the artist and yacht designer Albert Strange. Although she had 6ft beam this yacht with her small sprit fastened to the mast several feet above the deck made a lasting impression on Strange and seems to have influenced his later passion for designing yawl yachts.

DOBLE

The doble was a version of the peter boat (*qv*) used on the Medway by the

An up-river stumpie barge off Butler's Wharf in the Pool of London. These narrow little barges, tiller steered with no mizzen and with their boats carried amidships, only navigated the Thames up-river from the Pool. *(NMM, neg no 3052)*

fishermen of Strood, Rochester and Chatham, and a typical example might have been 18.6ft overall, with a 6.6ft beam, and a 2.3ft draft. When they first started using them the Medway fishermen called them 'double boats' because the fish well divided the working space in the hull into two. Fishermen are good at corrupting words, and the double boat became known as a doble.

The doble was not a seagoing boat and had either a sprit or lug sail although much of the time they operated under oar. Often the fishermen who owned bawleys also had a doble for working above Rochester bridge or in the creeks. The last bawleys and dobles were still being used in the 1970s.

Long after the Thames peter boat had gone a type of peter boat was used at Mistley and Manningtree for mullet fishing with a fine net in the summer. When looking for mullet these boats were rowed along the tide line just as the old peter boats had been in the Thames.

Sources
White's *British Fishing-Boats and Coastal Craft* deals with the peter boat, as does John Leather 'Quest of the Peter Boat', *The Boatman*, No 6 (1993).

Thames Barges

LONDON RIVER BARGE

Flat bottomed barge with flat sides and a slopping bow and stern. They had a single hold, open or with hatches, and were rowed on the tide or towed by tugs. Because lightermen operated these craft people called them lighters, but on the London River they were always called barges. The very early barge had a rounded bow, rather like the Humber keel (*qv*) and this barge was used for ballast dredging until the end of the nineteenth century. The flat 'swimhead' bow seems to have developed because it was cheaper to build and did not require increasingly scarce large timbers. The secret of the swimhead barge's success was the 'budget' under the stern. This was, in fact, a fixed rudder and the lightermen could control the barge on the tideway by pulling the head round so that the budget acted as a rudder.

A smaller barge, carrying under 50 tons, was known as a punt, was usually wooden and could be 'driven' (rowed) by one man.

After steel hulls were introduced

barge sizes increased to around 180 tons capacity. Three watermen were required to drive them, although increasingly they were towed by tugs and just rowed into the wharves.

SWIMMIE

An early nineteenth-century, flat bottomed Thames sailing barge with sloping bow and stern, spritsail rigged and tiller steered. The early sailing barges on the London River were simply swimhead lighterage barges fitted with sprit, gaff or lug sails. Gradually the spritsail rig dominated because it was easier to control and stow. Leeboards were introduced to enable the barge to sail against the wind. The Thames barge was a purely local development but there was often confusion with the Dutch barge, which was a totally different craft. On the London River sailing barges were referred to as being 'sailormen' to distinguish them from all the other types of barges, but bargemen had terms for every type of sailing barge. In open waters the bow of the swimhead banged into the seas

Above: This well known photograph shows an old swimmie off Cubitt Town. She has a hand spike windlass, a very long sprit, and a flat cut topsail with no headstick, all typical features of the earlier generation of barges. *(NMM, neg no 3308)*

Below: These two stumpies, one at anchor and the other carrying a little tide and a dying breeze, are typical of their type. No topmast is carried nor a bowsprit, and their flat sheer has none of the elegance of the spritties and the bigger coastal barges. *(NMM, Oliver Hill Collection, neg no P38836)*

which made it unsuitable for a coastal passage. The last swimmies were used in the London River for the ballast trade until the 1930s.

STUMPIE

A flat bottomed, spritsail barge with a round bow and transom stern, leeboards but, significantly, no topmast. They were tiller steered before about 1885 after which a wheel was introduced. The most noticeable feature of the spritsail rig was a large spar, the sprit, or 'spreet' as it was called, running from the foot of the mast to the head of the sail. When sailing close to the wind 'wangs' were used to haul the head of the spreet in tight and this greatly improved windward performance, an important factor considering the high proportion of time spent negotiating the narrow channels of the estuaries. The barge's large mainsail could be quickly stowed by 'brails' which gathered the sail up to the mast. Although it was hard work a barge

could be sailed by just two people because there were winches to handle the sails and leeboards.

The stumpie had a very high peaked mainsail to compensate for the lack of topsail and to catch what wind there might be coming over the tops of waterside buildings. Stumpies worked mainly between the Medway and Thames carrying bricks and cement. If they were going 'up through the bridges' the mast was lowered to the deck and they were rowed on the tide. Some of the narrow stumpies just fitted through the locks into the canals around London and took cargoes far inland. The last stumpies traded until the outbreak of World War II after which lorries took over their work.

SPRITTIE
(Spreety)

A spritsail barge with a flat bottom, flat sides, leeboards, a topmast and topsail, a round bow and transom stern, employed for carrying all manner of car-

goes in and out of the London River. In the 1880s the spritsail barge, called a 'sprittie' by bargemen, had evolved away from the London River barge into a fine seagoing vessel though still able to be sailed up a narrow, shallow creek or into a dock. All the Thames barges were constructed so that the hull could take the strain of sitting in a berth at low water. An average spritty barge loaded 120-150tons, was 82ft long, 19ft on the beam, about 6ft 6in draft when laden and 2ft 6ft light. The keel was of elm, 14in wide by 4½in deep, but the strength of the hull was the 18in square Oregon pine keelson which was bolted on top of the keel inside the hold. The bottom of a barge, which was never painted, was made of 3in Oregon pine planks which were rabbetted together and made watertight with tar and cow hair, often called 'tar and set work'. Most of the wood in the rest of the hull was English oak. An average spritty had a 40ft pitch-pine mainmast, a 58ft Oregon pine spreet, a 39ft larch topmast, and a 22ft yellow

pine bowsprit. All wood is subject to rot and spars often deteriorated where they had iron fittings; in the 1930s the Ipswich and Mistley barges were given steel spars.

The Kent barges, because they were only making short passages from the London docks down to the Medway or Swale, had the inboard 'stemhead' staysail rig with just five sails. As the Essex and Suffolk spritties made longer passages down the Swin and through the Spitway channel they needed extra sail and had a bowsprit on which was set a jib and above this, in fine weather, a jib topsail. The bowsprit was called a 'borsprit', a corruption of boltsprit, because this was

The beautiful sight of the two spritties *James Piper* and *Clara*, beating to windward in the Medway. Well crewed for racing, they carry racing pennants on their topmast stays, then the usual practice. The *Clara* went on to win the 1896 Medway race. (NMM, neg no G415)

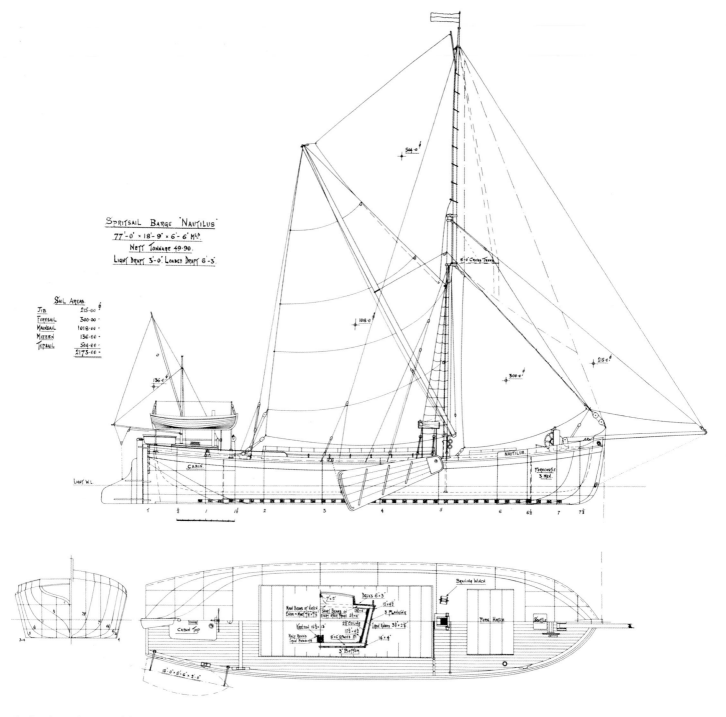

SPRITSAIL BARGE 'NAUTILUS'
77'-0" × 18'-9" × 6'-6" MLD.
NETT TONNAGE 49·90.
LIGHT DRAFT 3'-0". LOADED DRAFT 6'-3".

SAIL AREAS.

JIB	215·00
FORESAIL	300·00
MAINSAIL	1018·00
MIZZEN	136·00
TOPSAIL	564·00
	2173·00

The line plans and sail plan of the sprittie *Nautilus* – the classic profile of a bowsprit barge. She has a well cut away transom and a good sheer forward, and the barge boat in the traditional position, in davits, on the starboard side. *(Maxwell Blake Collection)*

lifted up when they came into a river. The little mizzen on the stern was sheeted to the rudder so that when the barge 'winded' it was pulled up to windward and helped to push the stern around. Even then the foresail on a barge had to be abacked with a 'bowline' to drag the head around.

The combination of the handy spritsail rig with winches enabled the large sail area to be handled by two men and

these craft were particularly handy in docks. A barge could sail with just the topsail set catching the wind coming over the tops of warehouses and they could be sailed through locks with the wind astern by sheeting in the main so that the whole rig was inboard; once in the confines of the docks they could stow their sails with the wind dead astern.

The barge matches, still run today,

were established in 1863 and these races also encouraged the development of the sailing barge. By 1900 there were about 2000 barges owned on the east coast of England and there was tremendous competition to obtain freights. Most barges were owned by 'seeking' owners and the bargemen literally raced to the next port to be first to get their 'turn' for the next freight. This competition produced a consummate barge which could carry 150 tons on a sea passage and which could still be managed by a very small crew of two plus the skipper. They carried mainly grain, timber, ballast, flour and cattle food. Although still called a Thames barge the sprittie was in fact built and owned all over southeastern England and travelled as far afield as even Liverpool, though their hull configuration and their rig were not suited to the open sea; the spreet with its wangs, in particular, could be a liability in a big sea, and if the spreet broke free it could spell disaster for the barge and its crew.

Some wooden barges, such as the Cann built *Beric*, *Edith May*, *Edme*, and *Gladys* and the Howard built *Mirosa*, are still extant today and are extremely handsome, but in practical terms the steel barge did not leak or wet the cargo and required less maintenance. Some of the most commercially successful steel barges were a series of seven built at Fred Horlock's Mistley yard. This series ended with the *Blue Mermaid* in 1930, which was the last full size sailing barge built. Of these Mistley 'iron pots' the *Xylonite*, *Repertor* and *Reminder* were still sailing in 1996 while *Adieu* was waiting to be rigged and the *Resourceful* was a houseboat at Chiswick.

Even after they had finished carrying cargoes the remaining barges continued to evolve. Everard's, the barge owners, developed the champion racing barges just for the Thames and Medway races. These carried massive gear and even a bermudian mizzen was tried. The champion barges *Sara*, *Veronica*, *Sirdar* and *Dreadnought* were abandoned after 1963, but one of their improvements, leeboard winches on blocks to save the crew bending down, has remained. Now, the remaining barges do charter and promotional work though they tend to carry a far larger sail area than would have been practical for two men to manage all the year round; and most have been fitted with auxiliary engines. When they are raced many barges have their props taken off, but in 1997 two fine wooden barges, *Mirosa* and *Edme*, were still being sailed without engines.

BOOMIE

A large, gaff ketch rigged, flat bottomed barge with leeboards. Some of the early examples had the curved cutwater more commonly associated with the coastal schooner, but those built from the 1890s often had a straight stem and bowsprit. The boomie barge was developed because the swimmies and spritties were not suited for the open sea. One of the larger wooden boomies, the *Lothair*, was 101.8ft overall, with a beam of 23ft and a depth in hold of 7.5ft. Very few boomies were built on

The boomies with their ketch rig came to dominate the coastal trade in the second half of the nineteenth century as, when reefed down, they were so much more able to stand up to a blow than a sprittie. *Cock o' the Walk*, photographed here, was a proud example of the type with the words 'While I Live I Crow' engraved on her stern. *(NMM, neg no P72109)*

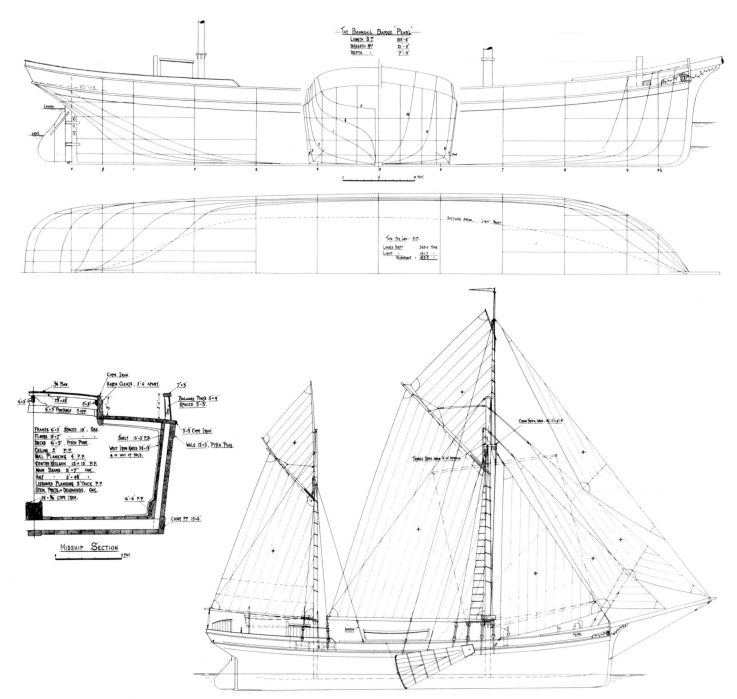

THE BOOMSAIL BARGE 'PEARL'
Length B.P.   85'-6"
Breadth M?   21'-0"
Depth   7'-9"

MIDSHIP SECTION

The lines plans and sail plan of the boomie barge *Pearl*. The well steaved bowsprit, carrying a good set of foresails to balance the comparatively large mizzen, is typical; not so usual, however, is the mizzen topsail. The combination of the hard chine with the profile of the coasting ketch encapsulates the the very nature of the boomie barge. *(Maxwell Blake Collection)*

the London River, and between 1879-1919 most were built at yards between Great Yarmouth and Littlehampton. They were always wooden hulled, and being built in yards used to building coasting schooners they were sometimes given elegant curved cutwaters and counter sterns. The schooner rig was even tried, but the shallow hull could not carry the canvas aft.

The chief trade of the boomies was coal from the northeast ports of England down to the east and south

coasts, but they went anywhere to find an economic freight. Some boomies traded to German and Dutch ports, while occasional freights were taken to the west coast of Ireland, and to Norway and Spain. Some boomies were sold to South America and sailed out there.

The disadvantage of the gaff mainsail was that they could not sail as close to wind as a sprittie and so were less suited to river work. Some boomies, such as the *Harold* when she was

owned at Mistley, had wangs fitted to stop the gaff falling off to leeward. The gaff mainsail was very heavy to hoist and the boomie carried a crew of four or five men. When the World War I shipping boom finished in 1920 the boomies were suddenly uneconomic and some were converted to a mulie (*qv*) rig. The last boomie trading was the Rye built *Martinet* which was 95.2ft long, 22.8 on the beam and 8ft depth of hold, but she sank in Hollesley Bay in 1941.

MULIE

Spritsail barge with a bowsprit and gaff mizzen, leeboards and sometimes a wheel shelter. The mulie, as its name suggests, was a cross between two established barge rigs, the sprittie (*qv*) and the boomie (*qv*), and grew from a demand for a vessel with the handling characteristics of the sprittie but the carrying capacity of a boomie. The result was the adoption of the gaff mizzen of the boomie, along with a sprit mainsail. The idea was to combine the advantages of the two rigs but in practice the gaff mizzen was too large and without the balancing effect of the boomies' headsails tended to push the bow up into the wind. But while the coasting boomies and schooners always had to hire a tug to get them in and out of ports the mulie could, like the sprittie, sail right up to the quay, although in some ports with difficult entrances, such as Great Yarmouth and the River Trent, even the mulie had to take a tug.

The mulies were originally sailed by two men and a boy – who also did the cooking and cleaning – but often, especially after the interwar Depression, it was just two men. In 1950 Everard's steel mulie *Greenhithe* was trading with coal from the Humber down to the Thames Estuary gas works with only a skipper and fifteen-year-old.

The introduction of steel for the hulls, mainmast and spreet pushed the coasting mulie barge to its limit in the 1920s. At Brightlingsea the Aldous yard built *Aidie* and *Barbara Jean* in 1924 which each loaded 260 tons. Pauls had these two in the London-Ipswich grain trade and although their crews found them a bit of a handful they were no doubt an economic form of transport in their day. Everards had four big steel mulies built at Great Yarmouth in the mid 1920s with wide sterns so that they could be converted to motor coasters when the capital was available. These were the 97ft long barges *Alf Everard*, *Ethel Everard*, *Fred Everard* and *Will Everard* which could load nearly 300 tons of cargo, and they earnt their owners and crews a good living trading around the ports of southeastern

England. The wooden Ipswich-based mulie, *Ena*, was bought new by Pauls and she is the only barge to remain in the same ownership until 1996. The *Ena* was built by McLearon at Harwich with the *Thalatta* in 1906 and both loaded about 160 tons though less when engines were fitted. Today, the *Thalatta* is a sail training barge based at Maldon.

BARGE BOAT

A clinker, 12ft to 14ft, shallow, beamy, open boat with a heart shaped transom stern, three thwarts, 'headsheets' – decking in the bow – and oak tholes. The barge's boat was elm planked with oak frames and had a full bow. This was because it was normally towed from high up on the barge's stern; while the slightly smaller smack's boat had a finer bow because it was towed from a low stern. The barge's boat was light enough for two men to hoist aboard, but had to be strong enough to withstand the knocks in the docks. There were 'headsheets' – a low deck in the bow – so that the

bargemen could step down onto it from the deck of the barge. In crowded docks the boat was usually sculled over the stern with a single oar. In fact, the barge's boat was seldom rowed and when anchored out in an estuary the bargemen set a lug sail and used an oar over the stern as a rudder to sail ashore.

Sources
There are over thirty books covering sailing barges. The standard work on details of hull and rigging is F S Cooper, *Handbook of Sailing Barges* (London 1955). Frank Carr, *Sailing Barges*, new edition edited by Robert Malster (Lavenham 1989) deals with the early history very well. Edgar J March, *Spritsail Barges of Thames and Medway* (Newton Abbot 1970) has a mass of detail, specifically on the Rochester barge *Kathleen*. The Kent coast is covered in Bob Childs, *Rochester Sailing Barges of the Victorian Era* (Rochester 1993), and Richard Hugh-Perks, *Sprits'l* (London 1975), while Essex and Suffolk barges are covered by Hervey Benham, *Down Tops'l* (London 1951). The Thames is recalled by Gordon Brown, *Mate of the Caprice* (London 1995). Robert Simper, *Thames Tideway* (Ramsholt 1997) covers sailing and lighterage barges.

Thames Open Boats

THAMES WHERRY

A clinker, open boat, usually double ended, though transom sterned in the late nineteenth century, used for ferrying passengers. The Thames wherry was the fast passenger boat which developed in the seventeenth century and remained in everyday use into the nineteenth century. It was a light, clinker pulling boat, a typical one measuring 26ft overall with a 5ft 8in beam, and had a long pointed stern. The wherry's bow was designed to lift the boat so that it glided over the water while its ample beam aft gave room for seats for passengers.

For river work the watermen had skiffs, 16ft rowing boats, which were much more heavily built and had small transom sterns. The skiff had a ring in the stern so that the apprentices could use them to tow lighterage barges away from wharves and out to the barge roads.

Built by Fellows of Great Yarmouth were four fine, steel mulies, *Fred*, *Ethel*, *Alf* and *Will Everard*. Here, on the *Alf Everard*, the gaff and boom mizzen combined with the slightly cut down spritsail, the defining features of these vessels, are shown to good effect. (*NMM, Oliver Hill Collection, neg no P72091*)

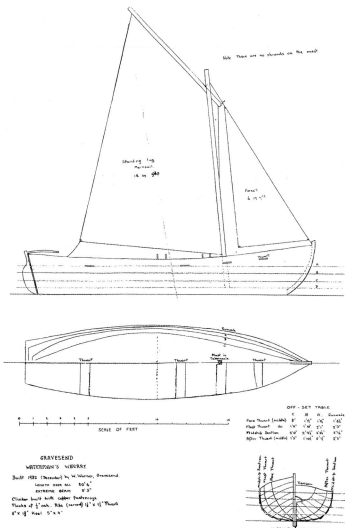

Rough lines and profile of a Gravesend wherry, drawn by F T Wayne in 1933. She is 20ft 6in long and the beam only 5ft 3in. She carried a standing lug sail and small foresail. *(NMM, Coastal Craft Collection)*

GRAVESEND WHERRY

Down near the mouth of the Thames, Gravesend watermen used a much heavier built version of the Thames skiff. Although still a clinker pulling boat, it was 21ft to 26ft long and narrower to make it row and tow more easily. The Gravesend men used to 'hook on' to a ship and be towed down to the Royal Sovereign lightvessel to meet an incoming ship and get the berthing work. The ships did not stop or slow down and the wherrymen simply hooked into the rigging in order to secure the job. William Warner of Gravesend built the last wherry in 1932.

Sources
Peter H Chaplin, *The Thames* (London 1982) describes the wherries.

WHITSTABLE YAWL
(Whitstable smack)

The Whitstable yawl was a cutter rigged, oyster dredging smack, heavily built with a square counter stern and recognisable by the square ports cut in the rail. They were very strongly built – with an elm keel, a hull constructed mostly of oak, and a yellow pine deck – because they were kept at anchor off Whitstable and had to withstand taking the ground and landing on the beach at low tide in every type of weather. They had a very full bow to give them enough buoyancy to lift the heavy anchor chains in a big sea, and each had a powerful windlass. The small har-bour at Whitstable was mainly used by commercial craft and it is said that if there was an onshore gale, which caused a heavy swell in the harbour, the smacks were taken out into the Thames estuary and left at anchor. The smacks had wide ports cut in the rails, mostly used for shovelling old oyster shells overboard, and it is claimed that in a really hard blow the smacks would lay at anchor and roll water in one port and out the other side. The Norse term 'yawl' or 'yoll' was widely used along the east coast of England and Scotland to denote an open boat and it appears that at Whitstable the term carried on when they started using decked smacks. The fishermen, or 'flatsmen', dredged for oysters off the Kent coast in the winter and in the summer a few went trawling or shrimping, while many were laid up and the men either ran trips for sum-

The Whitstable yawl *Seasalter* F322, built in 1875. She measured 51ft 8in overall, on a beam of 14ft 2in and a depth of 7ft 8in. Owned by the Seasalter and Ham Oyster Fishery she is photographed here with white sails which suggests that she was used mainly for carrying oysters and was thus set apart from her ochre-sailed sisters. She also has a load line which would have made her eligible for carrying her cargoes to overseas ports. White quarter boards gave some protection to the helmsman and made the vessel a little more conspicuous at night. *(Richard Hugh-Perks Collection)*

mer visitors or worked on the farms.

In 1910 there were around seventy smacks and a few bawleys with lug mizzens from the Swale working off Whitstable earning the flatsmen a 'comfortable living'. Some of the yawls

Lines and sail plan of the Whitstable oyster smack *Stormy Petrel*, F71, drawn by Ted Penny. She was built in 1890 by Richard and Charles Perkins of Whitstable and for a while was owned by Bob Roberts of the Harwich fishery. She has the typical buoyant forward sections and the distinguishing wide ports. She still sails without an engine and is one of the Core Collection of the National Register of Historic Vessels. At the time of her launch around 100 of these vessels were engaged in the oyster trade. *NMM, (Coastal Craft Collection)*

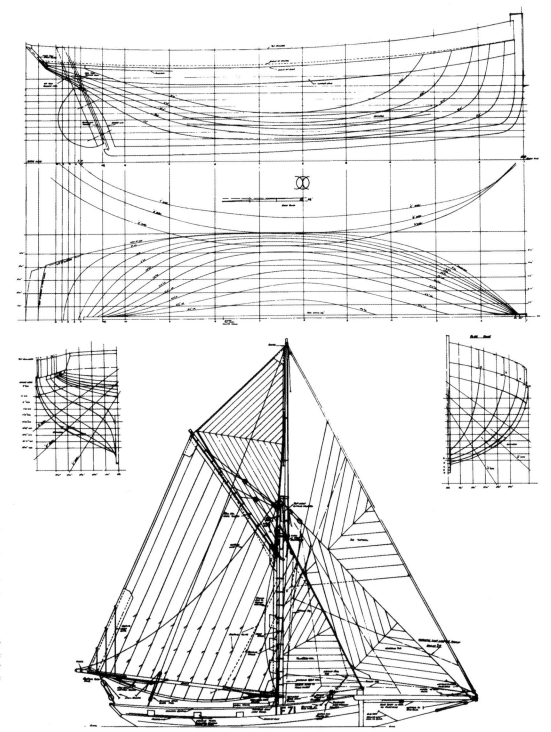

used to take freights of oysters across to Calais while *Thistle*, 44ft overall, with a beam of 12ft 10in and a 5ft draft, had an engine put in two years after she was built in 1908 so that she could carry bags of oysters from the Seasalter and Ham Oyster Fishery Co's smacks, back to the harbour. The clipper bowed ketch *Speedwell*, built as a motor dredger, also went dredging, but just for a couple of hours, and then went round and collected the oysters.

The oyster fishery started to dwindle in the 1930s and the smacks were sold. The 40ft *Stormy Petrel* became the watch vessel moored out on the oyster flats with a watchman aboard to stop poaching. She was bought and restored by Dick Norris in the early 1960s and has continued to sail without an engine. The 46ft *Rosa & Ada*, built by Collar in 1908, was restored in the early 1970s, while the 44ft *Emeline*, also built by Collar four years earlier, has recently been restored.

The 41ft Whitstable yawl *Gamecock*, built by Collar in 1906, with pitch pine planks on oak frames, was a motor vessel at Strood when, in 1963, Ronald 'Bill' Coleman bought her for oyster dredging at Whitstable again. Until about 1987 he worked her under motor in the winter and under sail in the summer, all with hand hauled dredges.

Sources
Derek Coombe, *Fishermen of The Kentish Shore* (Rainham 1989) covers the Whitstable yawls. Geoffrey Pike, John Cann and Roger Lambert, *Oysters & Dredgermen* (Whitstable 1993) has some descriptions of the boats.

THANET WHERRY

A narrow, open, clinker pulling boat with a single lug sail, and the blocks to hold the rowlocks fitted on the outside of the hull, employed for drift net fishing for herring. In origin the Thanet wherry appears to have been a cross between the Thames wherry and the Deal boat. It had a varnished hull and was lightly built and did not carry ballast. At Broadstairs the 18ft wherry was used for pilot work, but these had problems coming ashore in Viking Harbour where they were often holed by the flints on the beach. The Margate wherry was used in the summer for hiring out to holiday makers and when the Dunkirk Evacuation was taking place the Royal Navy sent a minesweeper to collect all the wherries on the beach.

Some of these were smashed when being lifting on to the minesweeper and few of them were seen again. In 1981 there were still several wherries at Broadstairs, but all in bad order.

Margate men also used 20ft to 22ft two masted luggers in the herring season which were launched into the sea from 'pole trucks'. There were also large open cutters of up to 50ft long used for carrying trippers in the summer.

Sources
Beach Boats of Britan deals with the craft along this shore.

Above: The deck views of two Whitstable oyster yawls laid up in the harbour in 1945 clearly showing the wide decks and broad shoulders so characteristic of these vessels. Laying outside are two double ended Whitstable boats which had interesting origins. In about 1907 several Sheringham crab boats *(qv)*, owing to poor local fishing, went to try their luck elsewhere – first to Harwich and then Whitstable – whelk fishing. They found favour with the local fishermen and by 1952 there were about a dozen small double ended motor boats at Whitstable, locally built but very much on the lines of the Sheringham boats. *(NMM, Oliver Hill Collection, neg no P74973)*

Below: Rough drawings by J W Holness of a Thanet wherry, or East Kent longshoreman's boat, using measurements taken at Herne Bay in 1968. Notes on the drawing state that the boat was thought to have been built at the beginning of the century at Margate for use as a hire boat. Similar boats were used for inshore fishing. A lug and foresail could be set. *(NMM, Coastal Craft Collection)*

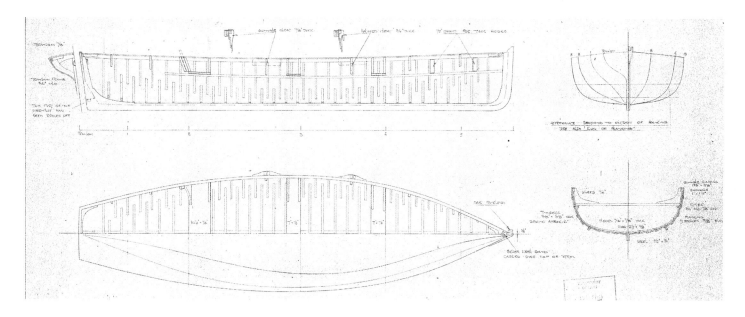

The South Coast

MUCH OF the southeast coast of England from the North Foreland to around the Isle of Wight is typified by steep shingle beaches, open to the prevailing southwesterly winds. These, along with the tidal steam coming in from the Atlantic, have torn away at the coast moving the silt eastwards, closing harbour mouths such as Shoreham and Newhaven and building up great headlands. The greatest of all, Dungeness, barely existed in Roman times. Each of these headlands – Portland, Selsey, Beachy Head and Dungeness – were important places of shelter for sailing ships making a passage in the English Channel, while the main place of shelter for ships leaving or entering the North Sea was the Downs off Deal. Here there was good holding ground for anchoring and it was sheltered from the easterlies by the Goodwin Sands. The Isle of Wight afforded the best protection from the southwesterlies, making the Solent a sheltered anchorage, but ships bound for London or the European ports did not come in here much as it was out of the way and prolonged their passages. The Solent was used mainly by the Royal Navy as a anchorage. The sailing ships that anchored off Portsmouth and Selsey, and particularly the Downs, gave employment to boatmen taking out passengers and supplies; in really bad weather they salvaged ships in trouble and as a last resort rescued the crews when they sank.

The whole southeast coast lacked good natural harbours, and in the early nineteenth century Brighton, and other south coast towns which were the major fish landing centres for London, worked their boats off open beaches; but once the North Sea fishing grounds were developed at the end of the nineteenth century they lost their importance.

Erosion closed Sandwich on the Kent coast as a major port, though a last attempt to open it was made in 1727; Ramsgate, where the harbour was begun in 1755, replaced it. The sea washed away the old town of Winchelsea on the Sussex coast and dumped the silt in front of Rye so that it became an inland port. Hastings lost its harbour and the haven leading up to Crowhurst, where William the Conqueror probably landed his ships, silted up altogether. From the eighteenth century onwards attempts were made to stabilise coastal erosion and piers were built at harbour mouths and dredging was carried out. Shoreham had its present entrance dug in 1760 and the mouth at Newhaven was finally stabilised in 1791. Like Dover and Folkestone, Newhaven's real importance grew as a cross-Channel ferry port, while Shoreham and Littlehampton had fleets of merchant sailing ships. However, the lack of good ports prevented any large-scale industries from becoming established along this coast, apart from the Royal Navy dockyard at Portsmouth. At the very end of the nineteenth century Southampton became an important passenger port, while Cowes in the sheltered Solent became the centre of yachting in the halcyon summers before World War I.

Before Southampton was developed as a transatlantic passenger port, Folkestone and Shoreham were the major shipping ports on this coast. In 1874 there were 161 sailing ships, mostly barques and brigs, owned in Shoreham. This was largely a result of the canal being built from Southwick to Aldrington Basin. Ships built and owned at Shoreham sailed all over the world. R H Penny & Sons progressed on to buying small steel barques built in the north of England which they ran in the New Zealand immigration trade. In 1865 there were thirty-five sailing ships registered at Arundel and Littlehampton; Harvey's yard at Littlehampton was building wooden deepwater merchant ships in the second half of the nineteenth century and continued with some very good boomie barges until the *Moultonian* in 1919. These were often called 'schooners with bottoms cut off' because of their similarity to deepwater ships.

The nineteenth century saw steady improvements to the har-

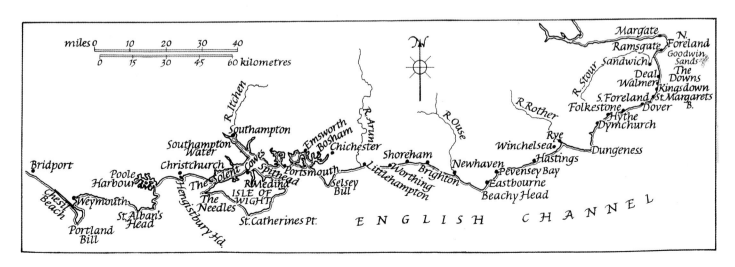

The Sussex beaches were home to the most significant fishing stations on the south coast in the middle and latter years of the ninetheenth century. Peaceful though this scene is – with nets and sails hung out to dry – the conditions were often considerably more ferocious, and the heavily built, bluff bowed Hastings luggers, like the *Primrose RX146* photographed here, were designed to withstand the great stresses and strains of beaching through breaking seas while carrying their catches. *(NMM, neg no 7043)*

bours. Ramsgate, Dover and Portland had massive stone break-waters built to create shelter, mainly as a response to a national out-cry about the number of ships and lives lost around the coasts. The merchant and fishing fleets were largely responsible for carrying much of the wealth of the nation, so that the building of 'harbours of refuge' was a major priority. Also the Royal Navy, protector of the seas, needed safe anchorages. While Dover seems to have been developed as a harbour of refugee, Portland Harbour was built as a safe place for naval ships.

The major beach landing on the south coast was Hastings, and during its heyday, from the 1850s to '80s, the fishermen went after herring in the southern North Sea in the autumn, trawling locally for flat fish in the summer, and long lining in the winter; in recent times they have worked gill and trammel nets, anchored to the seabed, and take every fish swimming past. While Hastings has survived as a fishing station, Brighton declined after the Diamond Grounds were worked out by over-fishing. Until around 1850, 300 English and French sailing trawlers would have been seen working these grounds and the English boats landed their catch for the Brighton fish market. Brighton beach boats were trawling until 1939 but since then the few remaining boats have been used for inshore potting.

To the east of Hastings, Rye had a small fleet of trawling smacks, while at Newhaven and Folkestone drift net fishing was the main occupation. The beach landings nearby had boats which worked pots for prawns and trammels for flat fish; in the late summer they went after herring. The waters off Selsey Bill were good breeding grounds for crab and lobster, while oysters were cultivated in the creeks around the Solent, and Emsworth became the centre of a considerable oyster industry.

Deal and Dover Boats

Open, clinker beach boats with high sterns and sides and, usually, small heart shaped transoms, employed mainly for servicing ships in the Downs, hovelling and some fishing. Open boats worked from the beaches at Deal, Walmer, Kingsdown and another group from the beach in Dover Harbour. They were lightly built of English elm, copper fastened and apart from the top strake being painted black, the hull was varnished and oiled with linseed oil.

In the nineteenth century the men of Deal and Walmer clubbed together and operated a 'set' of boats and the headquarters of each group was usual-

ly one of the many public houses. Their practice of sailing around looking for pilot jobs or salvage work, earnt the Deal men the name 'hovellers'. The boats, particularly the galleys, were fast but wet at sea and the men put on many layers of clothing in an attempt to keep warm.

In the age of sail all the Downs, a stretch of sheltered water between the Kent coast and the Goodwin Sands, was a safe anchorage in bad weather. Sailing ships from British and European ports, lay at anchor there waiting for a fair wind into the North Sea or down Channel. Up until the 1890s a hard blow could cause as many as a

hundred vessels a week to shelter there and this provided plenty of work for the luggers and the galleys. Royal Navy men-of-war also lay here and many navy captains ordered Deal boats because of their good sea keeping qualities. By 1900 the increasing number of steamers meant there was less work for the hovellers and so men switched to fishing.

Once motors were introduced the Deal galley's narrow hull proved quite unsuitable. A few galleys remained on the beach and were used for racing, but in 1952 only four remained. Around 1955 the eight-oared *Seaman's Hope* built of elm in 1907 was badly

smashed coming ashore and racing stopped. In 1996 only the galley *Undaunted*, which was owned by Dover Museum, and the *Saxon King* in Deal Museum, remained. The Deal men continued to fish and had motor boats which, like old sailing and pulling boats, were not painted and had a deep hull. The last wooden boat built at Deal was the *Golden Vanity* built by Bob Abel in about 1974.

FOREPEAKER
(Lugger)

This was the largest of the nineteenth-century Deal boats and the largest of

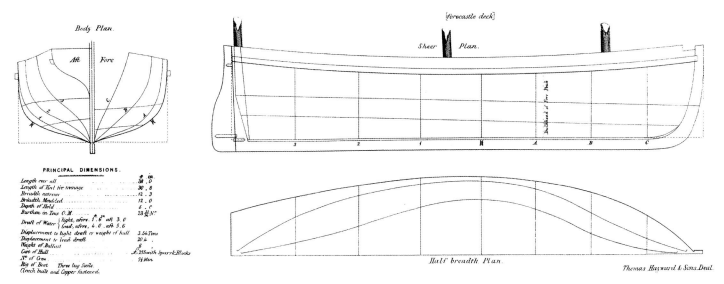

Body Plan.

Aft *Fore*

[forecastle deck]

Sheer Plan.

Bulkhead at Fore Peak

3 2 1 H A B C

Half breadth Plan.

Thomas Hayward & Sons, Deal.

PRINCIPAL DIMENSIONS.

	ft. in.
Length over all	38 . 0
Length of Keel for tonnage	30 . 8
Breadth extreme	12 . 3
Breadth Moulded	12 . 0
Depth of Hold	5 . 0
Burthen in Tons O.M.	23 ⁴⁵⁄₉₄ N°
Draft of Water { light, afore, 1'.6" aft 3. 0 { load, afore, 4. 0 . aft 5. 6	
Displacement to light draft or weight of hull	3.54 Tons
Displacement to load draft	20.4 .
Weight of Ballast	6
Cost of Hull	£ 275 with Spars & Blocks
N° of Crew	34 Men
Rig of Boat Three lug Sails	
Clinch built and Copper fastened.	

these were around 46ft long, though most were about 40ft long, with a 12ft beam. They had a small cabin forward in which was a stove and bunks. The lines fore and aft were as fine as the broad beam permitted. The rig comprised a jib, run out on a bowsprit, a large balanced lug sail and a smaller standing lug mizzen. These big boats were used mainly for salvage and servicing sailing ships anchored in the Downs and were large enough to carry out a spare ship's anchor. As work for them diminished they were sometimes seen hovelling far down Channel, and by the end of the nineteenth century, with the disappearance of sail from the Downs, they were

sold off for fishing around the coast. Like all the Deal boats, these big, heavy luggers were kept on the beach and had to be hauled up using hand capstans.

CAT BOAT

The cat boat was a slightly smaller version of the forepeaker, but had a 'caboose', a portable cabin, which was fitted between the fore and main thwarts. This type of boat did much the same work as the forepeaker but cost less to build and maintain and some evidence suggests that the small number built appeared after the last of the bigger forepeakers were built.

GALLEY PUNT *(Great galley)*

An open boat 22ft to 30ft long with a beam of only 6ft to 7ft, and also in other ways very different from the luggers described above. There were three classes of galley punt: the 1st class galley punt at 29ft to 30ft overall and a beam of 6ft 6in to 6ft 9in; the 2nd class version at 22ft 6in to 26ft overall and a beam of 6ft 6in to 6ft 8in; and the 3rd class galley punt at 22ft 6in overall and a beam of 6ft to 6ft 5in. The rig comprised a single, large, very square dipping lug sail on a mast stepped only just forward of amidships which could be removed if the boat was to be rowed, the men standing to their oars.

Lines and body plan of a 38ft forepeaker from the 1849 Washington Report. She is described as being rigged with three lug sails and is depicted with three masts. She has a fine, hollow entry but well rounded sections amidships. *(NMM, Coastal Craft Collection)*

These were heavy vessels to row and the crew usually depended on the sail. The galley punt was used mainly for hovelling, which could be anything from carrying messages and passengers to lending assistance to vessels in trouble on the Goodwin Sands. They would also go round the North Foreland or down the English Channel in search of a ship to put a pilot aboard.

GALLEY

Narrower version of the great galley usually about 29ft long, only 5ft 6in on the beam and with a draft of 2ft. They were very fine lined and could be easily rowed – pulled, not pushed like the great galley – by a crew of four. They also set a square, dipping lug sail on a mast just forward of amidships and sometimes raced in the summer regattas with two lug sails set. In the nine-

Deal luggers at South End station. In the foreground is the 33ft *British Pride*; behind her the 38ft forepeaker *Albion*, and next to her the 34ft *England's Glory*. Greased boards are ready, and in front of *Albion* can be seen a cable to an anchor for hauling out. In the distance any number of vessels ride at anchor awaiting the attentions of the Deal boatmen. The last registered lugger was *Tiger* of 17 tons. *(NMM, neg no 4610)*

104

INSHORE CRAFT

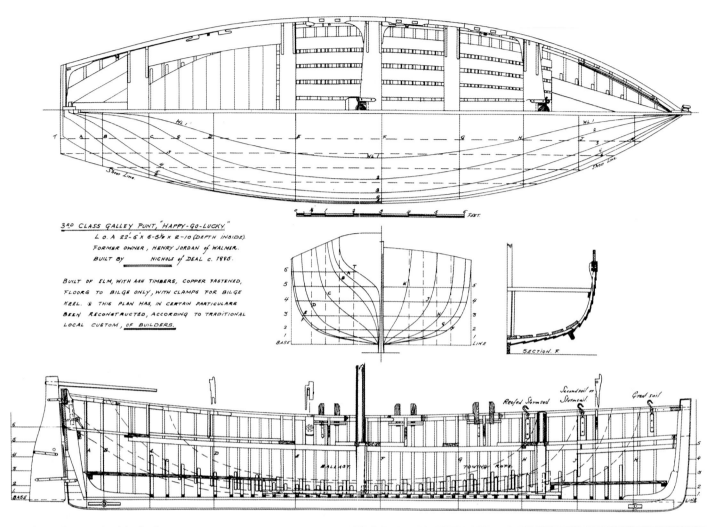

3ʳᴰ CLASS GALLEY PUNT, "HAPPY-GO-LUCKY."
L.O.A 22'-6" x 6-5½ x 2-10 (DEPTH INSIDE).
FORMER OWNER, HENRY JORDAN of WALMER.
BUILT BY NICHOLS of DEAL c. 1895.

BUILT OF ELM, WITH ASH TIMBERS, COPPER FASTENED,
FLOORS TO BILGE ONLY, WITH CLAMPS FOR BILGE
KEEL. & THIS PLAN HAS, IN CERTAIN PARTICULARS
BEEN RECONSTRUCTED, ACCORDING TO TRADITIONAL
LOCAL CUSTOM OF BUILDERS.

SECTION. F.

Lines plans and constructional details of the 3rd class Deal galley punt *Happy-go-Lucky*. Three hooks for the tacks of the lug sails can be seen as can the position for a second mast. (*NMM, Oke, Coastal Craft Collection*)

Two Deal galleys, amongst the last few to survive, photographed in 1952. Like the Cornish pilot gigs (*qv*) they had small, high transoms but were deep and fine lined aft to help give them directional stability. A lug sail lies across the thwarts but by this date their are no sailing ships on the horizon. (*NMM, Oliver Hill Collection, neg no P74977*)

The Deal galley punt *Happy-go-Lucky* photographed in 1937. These vessels, with their quite flat floors, sat easily on the beach. Galley punts usually carried two to three hands and relied more on their sail than on oar power and could stand up to pretty severe conditions. (*NMM, Oliver Hill Collection, neg no P74994*)

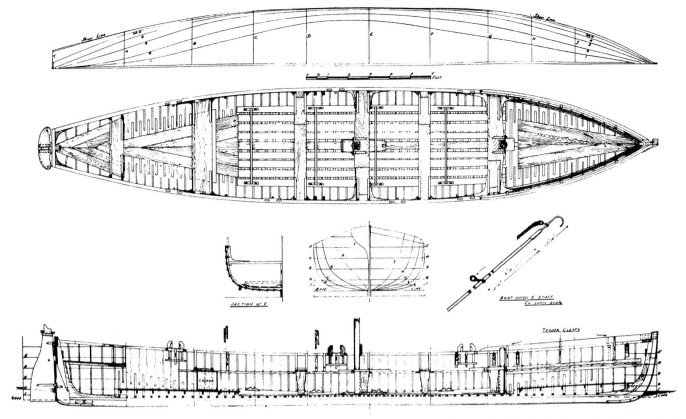

Above: The lines plans and constructional details of the Dover galley *Princess*, a typical galley of 29ft 1in overall, with a beam of 5ft 4in and a depth of 2ft. These long, fine craft tended to be used in more tranquil conditions than the sturdier galley punts and were easily rowed by four men; a fifth crew member steered with a rudder controlled by a yoke. *(NMM, Oke, Coastal Craft Collection)*

Left: A Deal galley punt runs along the Kentish coast under reefed lugsail. The position of the mast amidships and the very square cut lug sail were the most conspicuous features of the rig. The sail was quickly lowered when the vessel came alongside a ship. *(NMM, neg no N19094)*

teenth century this was the most common type of boat on the Deal beach and they were used mainly to take passengers out to ships anchored in the Downs.

FORE-MIZZEN PUNT

A small open boat 14ft to 18ft long with two masted, dipping lug rig used for fishing. These were the same type of punts which were used from Suffolk to Cornwall, and were really smaller versions of the luggers. In the 1920s most were given engines and the hulls painted.

DOVER SPRAT BOAT

Similar to the Deal fore-mizzen punt, but with lower sides. In the early nineteenth century there had been three masted luggers working from the beach at Dover in front of Harbour House. After Dover outer harbour was built, only small boats continued to be worked from the beach. In 1955 a few boats remained, and the last sprat punt was sailed from here until about 1976.

Sources
Inshore Craft of Britain, Vol 2, covers these vessels in good detail. G Appleton, 'Deal Luggers', *The Mariner's Mirror*, 45 (1959) describes all the types in some detail.

FOLKESTONE LUGGER

The Folkestone fishermen used two distinct types of two masted luggers for both trawling and herring drifting: the beamy, clinker hoggie, similar to the Hastings boat and, by the 1890s, carvel, decked luggers which were ordered from builders in east Cornwall. In the early nineteenth century the Folkestone boats were hauled up on the beach. These conditions favoured the bluff bowed, beamy hulls which were used to the west along the Sussex beach landings. Even after the harbour was built for cross-Channel ferries the inshore fishermen continued to use this type of boat. Probably the last of these was *The Sarahs* FE71 built by Tom Saunders on the Stade in 1920. The fishermen using the Cornish built luggers called her the 'Ugly Ducking'

By the end of the century, most of the Folkstone fishermen preferred to have carvel luggers, about 35ft overall, with sloping transom sterns, and these were imported from Cornwall. There were about twenty of these operating out of the port at the turn of the century. They set a standing mizzen, dipping fore lug sail and had a jib on a bowsprit. Because Folkstone Harbour dries out, all the luggers carried legs to hold them up at low tide.

After drifting died out in the 1920s some of the Cornish built luggers were converted to power craft. One of these Folkestone luggers, the *Three Brothers* FE93, built in Cornwall in 1901, was sold in 1994 and has been converted back to a sailing lugger for pleasure sailing.

Sources
John Leather, *Spritsails and Lugsails* (London 1978) covers them briefly.

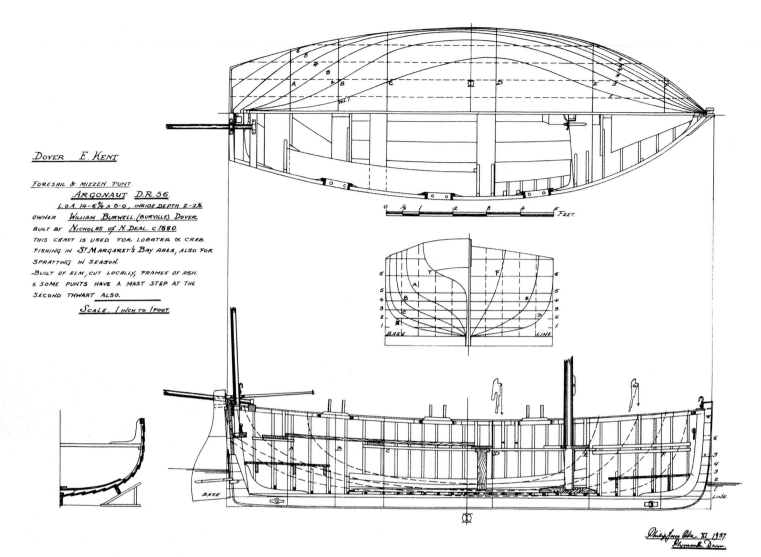

DOVER E. KENT

FORESAIL & MIZZEN PUNT.
ARGONAUT D.R. 56.
L.O.A. 14-6¾ x 5-0, INSIDE DEPTH 2-2½
OWNER WILLIAM BURWELL (BURVILLE). DOVER.
BUILT BY NICHOLAS OF N. DEAL. c 1880.
THIS CRAFT IS USED FOR LOBSTER & CRAB
FISHING IN ST.MARGARET'S BAY AREA, ALSO FOR
SPRATTING IN SEASON.
BUILT OF ELM, CUT LOCALLY, FRAMES OF ASH.
X SOME PUNTS HAVE A MAST STEP AT THE
SECOND THWART ALSO.

Scale. 1 inch to 1 foot.

Above: The Dover sprat boat *Argonaut* DR
56, built by Nicholas of Deal c1880 and
used for lobster and crab fishing in St
Margaret's Bay, just east of Dover, and for
spratting in season. The lines were taken
off in 1937. (*NMM, Oke, Coastal Craft
Collection*)

Right: A fore-mizzen punt photographed
at Deal in 1952. The Deal punts were used
only for inshore fishing and had
proportionately wider transoms than the
galleys, and like the bigger galleys and
luggers were built of English elm. (*NMM,
Oliver Hill Collection, neg no P74987*)

This Folkestone lugger, *Happy Return* FE5, with her wide transom stern, was of Cornish build and generally typical of boats from east of the Lizard. The forward raking mizzen and the long outrigger, typical of these craft, are clearly seen. Folkestone Harbour dries out at low tide and, in common with many of the luggers in the Westcountry, vessels were kept upright on legs bolted to the sides. Folkestone was unusual on the south coast for having a harbour - at nearly all the other fishing stations boats were hauled up on the beaches. This photograph was taken in 1937. *(NMM, Oliver Hill Collection, neg no P75000)*

A double ended Folkestone lugger, typical of the more traditional Cornish vessels which were imported, she is immediately identifiable as having originated in the Westcountry. The transom stern was a later development. The Folkestone luggers were seldom out for more than two tides and fished mainly on the Varne and Ridge Banks. *(NMM, neg no P32706)*

Sussex Barges

RYE BARGE
(Rother lighter, marsh barge)

A carvel, double ended barge, with a very shallow draft and a single, open hold. It set a single lug sail or was punted with a pole. Seagoing ships brought cargoes, mainly coal, into Rye Harbour which was off-loaded into the Rye barges before being carried into the network of waterways which reached the surrounding villages. In order to take the ground twice a day when loaded, the Rye barge was very heavily built with elm planks on oak frames, flat sided and flat bottomed. They were open with a small flush cabin for the crew of two, about 45ft long, had a beam of 12ft and carried around 20 to 30 tons. There was regular trade above Brede Bridge Wharf, about eight miles above Rye, which dated back to at least the eighteenth century when barges brought iron ore from Rye and returned with guns. There was also trade up to Newenden Bridge and Bodiam and, until 1909, through Iden Lock into the Royal Military Canal.

In 1993 the British Nautical Archaeology Society saved the 50ft Rye barge *Primrose* which had been built by W E Clarke in about 1875. She was worked until 1935 and finally abandoned on the mud in 1947. It was known that the Rye barges carried brick, wool, furniture, glass and livestock along the Rother and Brede. However, rescue leader Valerie Fenwick was told by a 91-year-old man that he could remember the barges taking hops across to France in the summer.

OUSE BARGE

A carvel, double ended barge which carried cargoes from Newhaven up the River Ouse to Lewes. These had a mast and set a single square sail or spritsail. The 20-ton barges, around 47ft overall, were poled or hauled manually with the tide, while bigger barges of up to 100 tons were either sailed or towed up to Lewis by a tug. In the summer some of the 50-ton barges carried cement on short coastal voyages. Others worked to the Phoenix Iron Works and were used for general farm work. Some of these barges were still at work in 1930.

ARUN BARGE

Carvel, transom sterned barges with an open hold. Several types were used on the River Arun and through the Wey and Arun Navigation to Guildford. Some of the smaller 20-ton barges were just pulled by horses while the larger 40- to 100-ton barges had a spritsail, stepped amidships, and often a very small cabin for the crew of two. Most of these barges were built at Pallington and their design had clearly been influenced by the Thames barges.

The Arun Navigation was closed in 1896 but the lower Arun barges were still active on the tidal waters until about 1935. Seagoing ships were still going up the River Arun to the Sussex port of Arundel until about 1914. Even after World War II the River Authority still used a barge, which was just poled on the tide, for moving chalk from Black Rabbit pit for making up the banks. When a man was lost overboard

they had a new 40-ton, 58ft long, 10ft beam, transom motor barge built by David Hillyard at Littlehampton. It was operated until about 1965 when it became a pontoon for yachts; a local society then set about its restoration, and in 1986 this was transported to Ellesmere Canal Boat Museum.

Page opposite
Upper: Rother barges reflect on a life of toil in the narrow gutway of the Rother at Rye. Two have their sails bent onto the yards. *(NMM, Oliver Hill Collection, neg no P73905)*

Lower: Two River Ouse barges photographed alongside a Thames spritty. A large rudder is visible on the well raked stern and a heavy sheerstrake gives protection when alongside. *(NMM, Oliver Hill Collection, neg no P73902)*

Below: Constructional details of the Rother lighter *Water Lily.* These strongly built, double ended vessels were well suited to hard work in the narrow confines of the River Rother. *(NMM, Coastal Craft Collection)*

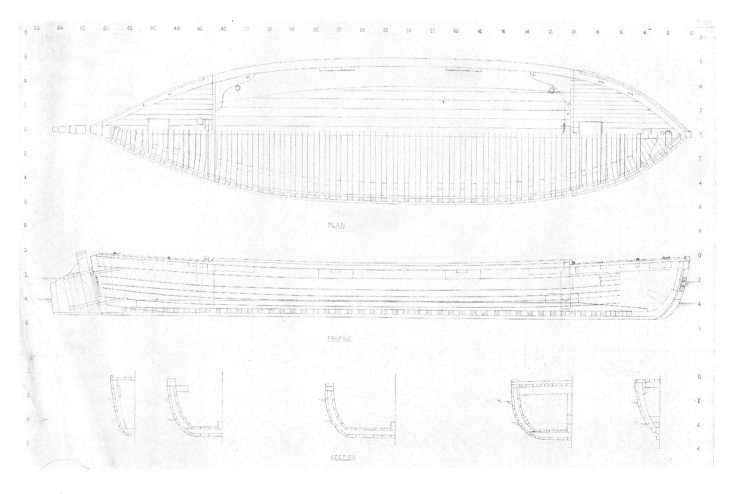

PLAN.

PROFILE.

SECTION.

Left: This photograph, taken by Oliver Hill in 1936, is captioned 'Rye boulder boat at Rye Harbour'. As fishing declined a number of Rye men took their boats round to Newhaven, the centre of the boulder trade, where between 4000 to 5000 tons of boulders would be built up awaiting a coaster. *(NMM, Oliver Hill Collection, neg no P75371)*

Page opposite
Upper: This photograph of *Industry* was taken in 1937 and shows her with an auxiliary engine installed, though she still has her sweeps, lashed alongside. The rig consisted of fore and mizzen lug, jib, mizzen staysail and topsail. The keel and the bilge keels were shod with iron, the end of which can be seen protruding at the aft end of the keel. She has an old fashioned lute stern. *(NMM, Oliver Hill Collection, neg no P75379)*

Lower: The lines plan and constructional details of *Industry* RX 94. The layout consisted of the fore room, used as the crew's cabin; the hold for fish and nets; and the aft cabin for stores and sails, with the capstan amidships, and this was pretty well universal for the trawl boats, or luggers as they became known, both at Hastings and Deal. The wide beam and flat floors of *Industry* are typical of boats regularly landing on exposed beaches. The smaller luggers at Hastings – less than around 27ft on the keel – were often referred to as 'bogs'. *(NMM, Oke, Coastal Craft Collection)*

Below: The lines plans of a three masted Hastings lugger from the Washington Report. Her overall length is given as 48ft with a beam of 14ft 11in and a draft of 7ft 3in. The three masts each carried a lug sail. These vessels were quite narrow compared with what was to follow, but they were not intended for local fishing and regular beaching but for more distant water work. *(NMM, Coastal Craft Collection)*

BOULDER BOAT

A gaff yawl with a counter stern, straight stem and open between the masts, used for collecting flints, or 'boulders' as they were known locally, from the Sussex beaches for use in the potteries. Often they were old boats bought in and some clinker boulder boats had laths nailed under the lands to prevent chaffing when they went on the beaches. The flint was taken back to Newhaven, stored until there was a cargo for brigantines, such as the *Sussex Maid*, built at Lewes in 1856, and then taken to Runcorn and down to Stoke-on-Trent where it was burnt in kilns to make it easier to crush before being used by potters to improve whiteness.

Sources
The Mariner's Mirror 21 (1935) contains an article by L Vidler about Rye Barges. Michael Bouquet, *South Eastern Sail* (Newton Abbot 1974), describes the Sussex barges.

Hastings, Eastbourne and Brighton Luggers

Bluff bowed, clinker built boats with elliptical or lute sterns. The larger ones were decked. In the mid-nineteenth century all the main Sussex beach landing at Hastings, Eastbourne, Brighton and Worthing had their own boat builders. Originally, the hulls were all Sussex oak, but as this became more difficult to obtain they used oak frames and elm planking. The decks were pine and the Brighton hoggies had ash transoms. Each landing had its own version of the lugger, but most were decked with very short beamy hulls which were almost flat bottomed. They had to be very strongly built to withstand landing on the beaches when heavily loaded with fish.

The early nineteenth-century boats appeared to have been transom sterned. By the 1870s the big boats had a lute, or 'beaching counter', stern which lessened the likelihood of the vessel being swamped as it rode onto the beach. By 1900 a short round or 'elliptical' stern was in use because the lute stern configuration was susceptible to water being pushed up through the rudder hole. Both Hastings and Brighton boats tried 4ft centreboards, but stones easily jammed in the casing and they were not a success.

HASTINGS LUGGER

Three masted, clinker lugger about 55ft overall, 15ft on the beam, and 7ft draft which carried a crew of eight men and a boy and had a small cuddy forward. These vessels were mainly employed in the North Sea autumn herring fishery when they would be based at Great Yarmouth, and, indeed, the Hastings luggers were not dissimilar to the Yarmouth ones. The Hastings lug-

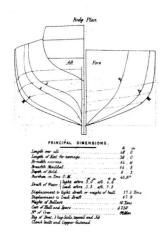

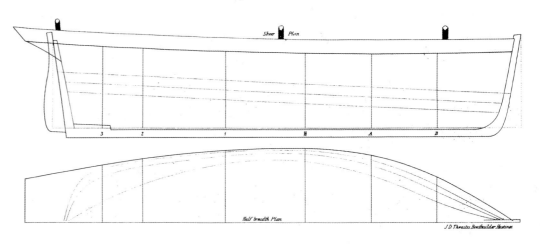

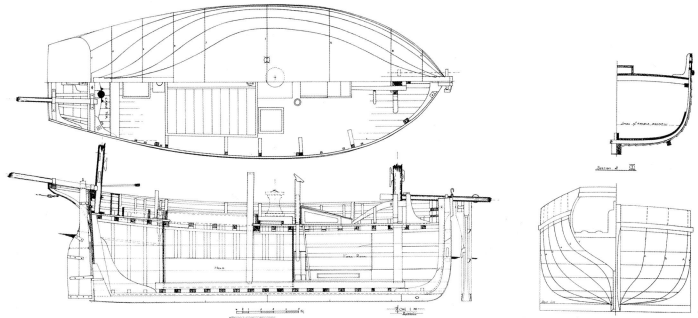

The Eastbourne lugger *Our Lassie* NN120, a smaller version of the bourne lugger. She has a very high cut sail and her mizzen mast is tall, two features which would have made for good performance. She carries the Newhaven registration as did all Eastbourne fishing craft. *(NMM, Oliver Hill Collection, neg no P75398)*

gers only returned to the beach between each fishing season and then they were hauled up between the tall 'net shops', and because of the relatively infrequent beachings they had quite fine lines. The big Hastings lugger was at its height between 1840 and 1865 when the town had about twenty-eight of them. With the development of harbours at Yarmouth and Lowestoft the Hastings fishermen either moved to the east coast or gave up the North Sea fishery. The last lugger built was the *Jane* in 1860.

TRAWL BOAT

A smaller, beamier version of the big lugger which was developed after the demise of the North Sea fishery. The trawl boat was a two masted lugger used for daily trips to the trawling grounds in Rye Bay and off Hastings. A typical vessel was 28ft long, 12.7ft on the beam and 5ft draft. Speed was not important, but they had to have a

beamy hull to ride through the breaking water. The first Hastings trawl boat with an elliptical stern was the 28ft *Clupidae* RX126, built in 1892. Once the three masters were forgotten the trawl boat was referred to as a lugger or 'big boat'. The last sailing big boat built was the *Mayflower* in 1913, but the class is represented today by the *Enterprise* RX278 which is on display at the Fisherman's Museum in Hastings. She is 27ft long on the keel and is 11.44 tons and was built at Hastings in 1912.

When boat building resumed in 1919, after World War I, the 28ft, decked *Edward & Mary* was built with sails and a 13hp petrol/paraffin Kelvin engine. Few more big boats were built at Hastings though the *Swan* was completed in 1923. In 1943 the *Beardmore* was built with an engine and sails in a barn at Pevensey for a Hastings fisherman. After this Alfred Philcox built the 30ft *Wendy Mary* at Hastings in 1948

This rough lines plan and constructional drawing gives a clear view of the extraordinary beam of the hoggie. However, they were well suited to landing on the very exposed beach at Brighton. Instead of a bowsprit they carried a small bumpkin. Often, they carried only one leeboard which was changed from side to side when beating to windward. *(NMM, Coastal Craft Collection)*

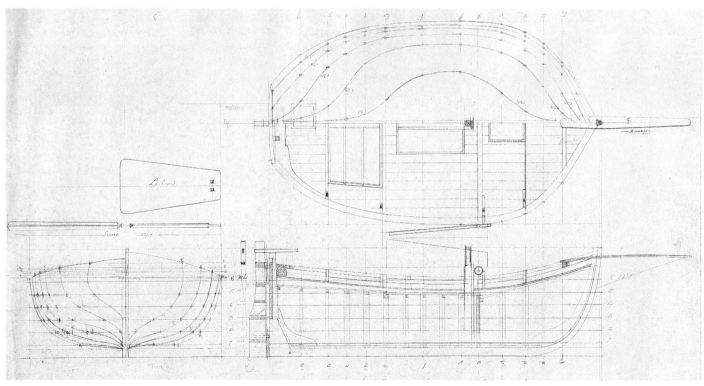

Two Brighton luggers on the shore and a beach capstan, photographed in 1910. The hoggie was superseded by a two masted lugger whose beam was altogether less and which had a bowsprit traditionally reeved past the stemhead. *Elizabeth II*, 29ft on the keel, was built at Hastings while *Belinda* was built at Aldrington, near Shoreham. *(NMM, Oliver Hill Collection, neg no P72830)*

The Brighton lugger *Victory* at the end of her life. Though the lute stern is in bad condition, the arrangement of the rudder can be seen, and the photograph shows clearly the flat floors and the well rounded midship sections of this typical Brighton beach boat. *(NMM, Oliver Hill Collection, neg no P72847)*

and then the *Gertrude*, which proved too large for beach work.

Most of the sailing boats were motorised and worked until the 1950s when another series of boats, called trawlers, big boats and sometimes even luggers, were built. By 1964 all the former sailing big boats were replaced by new Rye-built, decked craft with wheelhouses. In 1980 a further wooden decked boat was built for Hastings. This was the 31ft *Our Pam & Peter* which was built for Denis Barton by H L Phillips at Rye.

BOURNE LUGGER

A 35ft to 40ft lugger used from the beach at Eastbourne and rather similar to the Hastings lugger. These vessels made voyages to southern Ireland and Yorkshire drift net fishing and they only returned to Eastbourne between voyages when they were hauled up on the beach by steam capstans. A smaller, two masted, half decked lugger, the 'shinaman', was used to fish daily off the beach.

In the 1880s a certain F W Leybourne Popham, a rich individual, decided to develop fishing at Eastbourne and several luggers, auxiliary steam drifters and yachts were built here for him. Popham was very keen to promote luggers and had George Gausden at Eastbourne build luggers for fishing, and others as racing yachts. The first of this series was the 50ft *Queen of Sussex* which had a centreboard, later removed. The hotel operators at East-

bourne drove the fishing fleet off the best landing beach in front of town, but they continued until 1914 and in 1984 a group of Sussex beach boats were fishing off the east beach.

HOGGIE
(Brighton hog boat)

The Brighton hog boat or 'hoggie' was about 28ft long with an extreme 16ft beam, tiny transom and very bluff bow which enabled it to drive through the breaking water and float on to the beach like a duck. The hull was decked and had leeboards to counteract the excessive leeway made by these beamy vessels, and carried a two masted, spritsail rig. The true hoggie was out of fashion by about 1880, although Brighton boats, which were usually luggers built at Hastings or Rye, continued to be known as hoggies. In 1886 there were only three hoggies left on Brighton beach: *Cambria*, *William and Mary* and *Who'd Have Thought It*; a fourth, *Nil Desperandum*, was burnt on the beach on a 5th November celebration. The last Brighton lugger working under sail was Alfred Cobbett's *Victoria* SM25 which was still long lining for flat fish in Rye Bay at the beginning of World War II.

Sources
The main sources are James Hornell, *The Fishing Luggers of Hastings* (London 1974, reprinted from *The Mariner's Mirror*) and Steve Peak, *Fishermen of Hastings: 200 years of the Hastings Fishing Community* (Hastings 1985).

A typical example of an east Sussex beach boat. This photograph of *Gratitude*, taken at Hythe in 1930, shows off the elegant elliptical stern and the flat floors. The iron rudder lifts up and though she has been fitted with an auxiliary engine she still retains her sailing gear. *Gratitude*, rather than being an open punt, was, in fact, decked. (*NMM, Oliver Hill Collection, neg no P75367*)

Sussex Beach Boats

EAST SUSSEX BEACH PUNT

Open, clinker built boat with a bluff bow and a short counter or elliptical stern, usually varnished, and employed for inshore fishing along the coast from Hythe in Kent and under the lee of Dungeness, and as far west as Brighton. The nineteenth-century, clinker sailing punt was 14ft long with a transom stern and a dipping lug. In the 1930s open motor punts developed which had the same hull shape as the old sailing boats but were lengthened to around 20ft long. They were beamy amidships and full bellied to make them buoyant, and were rounded off with a narrow elliptical stern similar to the bigger Hastings trawl boats (*qv*). The bluff bows allowed the boat to ride up on the beach rather than plough into it, and, to avoid damage, the rudder could be lifted up into the stern on landing. The punt had two short masts and usually a small mizzen set as a steadying sail.

After World War II this type of open boat became very popular for working from beaches and harbours, and although built up to 26ft overall the fishermen still called them punts. They were used for trammel net fishing, whereby nets are anchored to the sea bed, and did not need to be as powerful as the trawlers.

There were two main builders of these punts: H L Phillips & Son at Rye, and R Lower & Son at Newhaven. These punts had fifteen planks aside, but the two firms used different methods of building. Phillips preferred lute sterns with grown and laminated floors and did not start to use steam timbers until about one third of the way up the side making a one seam tuck on the 3rd/4th

A Hastings punt hauled up alongside the net houses. Her fishing number has been removed and she has a roller fitted in the stern. The last feature is quite unusual and might have been associated with laying moorings. (*NMM, Oliver Hill Collection, neg no P75376*)

The Eastbourne sprat punt *William and Dorothy* NN45, photographed in 1937. Compared with the Hastings punt she is altogether more finely lined. She has a fine entry and quite a fine run aft where she is surprisingly deep. She has a very small rig which quite possibly is her winter rig, and only a single line as a sheet for the fore lug sail. Eastbourne was well sheltered by Beachy Head and the vessels from there seem to have been lighter and more finely lined than those found at Brighton and Hastings. *(NMM, Oliver Hill Collection, neg no P75399)*

lap. Lower favoured the elliptical stern with simpler framing, longer timbers and an early tuck. Phillips built with wych-elm because it was only about 75 per cent dry, so that when the boats were hauled up on the beach they did not dry out and leak. They were soaked in linseed oil and lasted well.

Lower's last boat was the *Nguyen Van Troi* of Eastbourne, built in 1977 and named after the Vietnamese revolutionary. Derek Phillips, whose great-grandfather started the firm in a shed beside the Rock Channel at Rye in 1904, built all the new boats for fishermen between Hythe and Dungeness but stopped building wooden punts in about 1985 because of the scarcity of decent timber. He then developed a class of 26ft GRP boats with elliptical sterns.

WEST SUSSEX BEACH BOAT

Open, lute sterned boat, under 20ft overall, employed for fishing off the beaches of West Sussex. These were, in effect, just rowing boats with a 'lute' built out over the stern. Early nineteenth-century drawings of boats on Bognor beach show just transom sterned vessels so the lute seems to have been a mid-Victorian development. Most of the wooden boats used in West Sussex were built at Littlehampton. Horses were used to drag the craft over the flat foreshore.

SELSEY GALLEY

In the nineteenth century a large galley was used for salvage work and to attend ships anchored for shelter about a mile from the landing on East Beach in an area known as the Park. The galley was up to 40ft long and was pulled by eleven pairs of oars; it also carried two lug sails. It was similarly proportioned to the Deal galley *(qv)* and Cornish gig *(qv)* but considerably larger.

SELSEY CUTTER

Clinker or carvel, decked, gaff cutter, which was kept on a mooring off East Beach, and employed in the good crab and lobster grounds near the Owers Lightvessel. These boats, built at Littlehampton, were about 24ft to 26ft long, with a good beam, a deep draft and a wide transom stern. They were cutter rigged but could be rowed in calms with 12ft oars. They carried a tall 37ft pole mast, a 16ft boom and a 22ft bowsprit and in fine weather they set a large jackyard topsail. A smaller Sussex beach boat was used to get off to them.

In the 1870s a race was started for

Page opposite
Upper: A Selsey galley photographed on the beach in 1927. These were big and powerful vessels, powered by twenty-two oarsmen. In the background are three of the Selsey cutters, two clinker built and one of carvel construction. *(NMM, Oliver Hill Collection, neg no P75413)*

Lower: A carvel built Selsey cutter, or Selsey lobster boat as they were sometimes called, with the bow of a clinker version in the foreground. They were distinguished by their sharp bows and low, wide transom sterns. Two lobster pots lie under the bilge. Though shown ashore here, they spent most of the year riding at moorings just off the beach. In 1903 there were seventeen 2nd class (26ft on the keel) fishing boats recorded at Selsey. *(NMM, Oliver Hill Collection, neg no P75409)*

This page
Upper: A small Selsey seine net boat photographed in 1961. Though being used at that date for seine netting, similar, small rowing punts were used by the Selsey fishermen to reach their bigger, cutter rigged lobster boats moored offshore. *(NMM, Oliver Hill Collection, neg no P75412)*

Lower right: A small open crabber at Selsey in 1934. These beach punts were also used for prawning. All the vessels at Selsey carried the Littlehampton registration. *(NMM, Oliver Hill Collection, neg no P75410)*

these sailing crabbers and this was held, apart from during World War I, until 1939. It was revived in 1979 for the motor crabbers, over a 4½-mile course. Two men in a sailing crabber could haul fifty pots a day, but the motor crabber, with powerful capstans, hauled two to three hundred pots a day.

Sources
Mike Smylie, 'The Fishing Boats of East and South Coasts' *Boatman* (May 1996) covers some of these craft. Robert Simper, *Beach Boats of Britain* is a further source. The Selsey boats are described in Thurston Hopkins, *Small Sailing Craft.*

EMSWORTH LUGGER

An open, clinker boat with a transom stern and a high bow and short fore-deck, which was rowed, or sailed with a single tall lug sail, and employed for dredging oysters and beam trawling in Chichester and Langstone Harbours. A typical lugger was 15ft long overall with a 5ft 6in beam. They carried a very square, dipping lug sail, tanned black, though it was often found to be easier to row them to windward over short distances. The Emsworth lugger did not have a centreboard but instead had a false keel of about 18in. Their V-formed hull made them rather cranky

to sail. The last lugger built appears to have been the *Matilda*, built by Felsham at Portsmouth in 1945 for Emsworth owners. As well as working in the sheltered harbours these luggers were sometimes taken off the coast in summer where they drifted for mackerel.

BOSHAM BOAT

The luggers used at Bosham sometimes had centreboards which greatly improved their performance to windward and they also had the lug tack rope through a hole on the weather bow, otherwise they were very similar to the Emsworth boats (*qv*). Like them, they mainly dredged for oysters and trawled in Chichester Harbour. Overall length was around 16ft, and

they were given a small foredeck and a fish tray aft just below the rail.

Sources
David J Rudkin, *The Emsworth Oyster Fleet* (Emswoth 1975), is a good source for these boats.

EMSWORTH OYSTER SMACK

Although John Kennet operated four ketch rigged oyster smacks, the description here is confined to those built and owned by James Duncan Foster, because they are well-documented and many of the hulks survived into the 1950s when they could be measured and studied. Foster built four ketches in 1888-1890, ranging in size from 55 to 35 tons, the smaller ones having register dimensions of 60.2ft x 15.3ft x 9.2ft. Then came three cutters

Upper left: The Emsworth lugger *Matilda*, built in 1945 and photographed in 1952. These shallow boats were ideally suited to working the shoals of Chichester and Langstone Harbours. The tack of the lug sail is made fast on the weather side as is the halyard. *(NMM, Oliver Hill Collection, neg no P75430)*

Lower left: Rough drawing of an Emsworth lugger which gives a clear indication of the shallow draft of these craft. *(NMM, Coastal Craft Collection)*

Below: A Bosham boat with its very tall, narrow cut lug sail. These broad little craft had a very tight turn to the bilge to accommodate the shallow draft. They employed drift and seine nets and also trawled. *(NMM, Oliver Hill Collection, neg no P72683)*

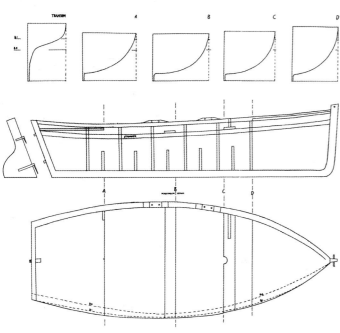

of 22 tons each, which were 8ft shorter. These were followed in 1894 by the large ketch *Nonpareil* of 69 tons with dimensions of 86.7ft x 19.3ft x 10.0ft. Two more ketches were built prior to the large non-typical auxiliary ketch *Echo* of 1901.

The ketch rigged Emsworth oyster dredger *Nonpareil* photographed in October 1931. She is laid up in this photograph with her sails removed and her hull painted white in order to prevent the seams from opening up. The bowsprit, which in 1898 was 31ft, has been unshipped. *(NMM, Oliver Hill Collection, neg no P71987)*

Foster wanted fast vessels and used half-models for the design. The result was a hull with rounded bilges, a fine entrance and run, a square counter stern, a cut-away forefoot, low bulwarks and tiller steering. They were constructed with oak frames and were planked with larch and oak. All had wet wells connected to the deck by one or two trunks and these wells required massive timber beams. The cutters and smaller ketches hauled in the dredge warps by hand winches, but the larger smacks were each fitted with three vertical steam capstans, steam being raised by a boiler below deck.

All the smacks had lofty sail plans, and when *Nonpareil* was given new masts in 1921, the overall length of the mainmast from heel to head was 64ft, being of recently cut English larch. In addition, she carried a tall topmast. The mizzen had an overall length of 55ft and was of spruce or Douglas fir which had been seasoning in the sea for four years. The rigging was of 2½in galvanised steel wire.

The warps for the oyster dredges were of hemp with wire core and averaged 350ft-600ft long. When dredging, sails were sheeted right in and the vessel kept broadside on to wind and, if possible, to tide. *Nonpareil* might have five dredges out simultaneously, the smaller vessels perhaps three. In 1935, a warp and dredge cost £10; they were frequently lost. The oysters were stored in the wells but the scallops were placed in small nets.

The season operated when there was an 'R' in the month; so in the summer the smacks were laid up and the external planks white-washed to protect them from the sun. The cutters were crewed by four strong men, the smaller ketches by six. Each steam capstan needed two men to work it and there was also an engineer; so *Nonpareil* had a crew of seven. An average wage was £5 per week. The cutters usually worked close inshore, and so were usually away less than a week. Up until the First World War, the ketches dredged anywhere between the Dogger Bank and Cornwall but after 1920 the favoured area was about 20 miles south of Newhaven and off the Chesil Bank. Sometimes they were away for several weeks. The last year in which the smacks put to sea was probably 1935.

Sources
Peter Norton, *The end of the Voyager* (London 1959) and David J Rudkin, *The Emsworth Oyster Fleet* (Emsworth 1975) are the best sources. Surviving hulks were measured by David R MacGregor between 1951 and 1965.

Spithead Wherries

1ST CLASS WHERRY

Double ended, two masted, spritsail rigged, clinker built, copper fastened, open boats employed as general runabouts, operating from the hards at Portsmouth and Southampton. They took passengers out to ships anchored in the Solent and across to the Isle of Wight. They also took merchandise from shops out to ships and even carried cattle. They were about 27ft to 30ft long. One of the larger ones, *Turkish Knight*, was 34.6ft long, 9ft on the beam and 3.11ft draft aft. They were decked forward under which was a cuddy with a stove. They carried up to 4 tons of ballast and some of this was portable so that when sailing in a stiff breeze it could be moved to the weather side. Built of oak and copper fastened they lasted for many decades, being worked by the same families of boatman.

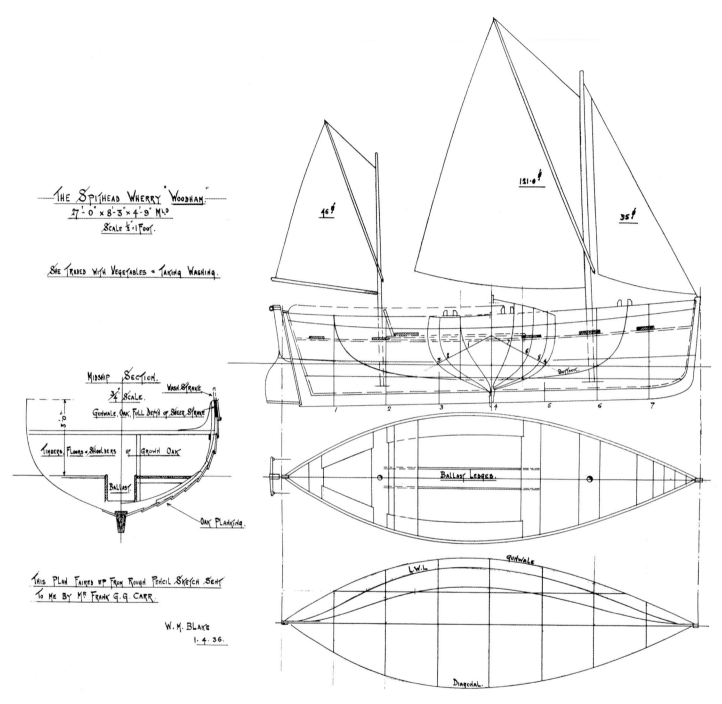

THE SPITHEAD WHERRY "WOODHAM"
27'-0" x 8'-3" x 4'-9" M'L'D
Scale ½:1 FOOT.

SHE TRADED WITH VEGETABLES & TAKING WASHING.

MIDSHIP SECTION.
¾" SCALE.
WASH STRAKE
GUNWALE, OAK, FULL DEPTH OF SHEER STRAKE
TIMBERS, FLOORS & SHOULDERS OF GROWN OAK
BALLAST
OAK PLANKING.

THIS PLAN FAIRED UP FROM ROUGH PENCIL SKETCH SENT
TO ME BY MR FRANK G. G. CARR.

W. M. BLAKE
1. 4. 36.

16⁵   121·0⁵   35⁵
BUTTOCK.
BALLAST LEDGES.
L.W.L.   GUNWALE
DIAGONAL.

The lines and sail plan of the 1st class Spithead wherry *Woodham*. She was 27ft overall, with a beam of 8ft 3in and a depth of 4ft 9in. The drawings show the side benches and thwarts for the passengers and the yoke and lines for steering. With the gently rising floors and the rounded bilges, her section was almost semi-circular. A washstrake was fitted in rough weather which offered a little more protection to the passengers. (*Maxwell Blake Collection*)

They appear to have used the sprit rig because they could brail up the sails up above their passengers' heads. Carrying their beam quite a long way aft, they were very weatherly little craft and were often working in the Solent when short, steep seas kept other vessels ashore; often the anchored warships could not get crews ashore in their own boats and had to hire the wherries. The wherries also made smuggling trips to the Channel Islands.

2ND CLASS WHERRY

The 2nd class wherries were mostly found at Portsmouth and were smaller pulling and sailing boats, used mostly in the harbour. Clinker built and double ended, they were considerably lighter and had less freeboard than the 1st class wherry. When there was no wind the mast was taken down and they were easily rowed. The wherries were very busy in the days of the sailing Royal Navy while in the final

decades of the nineteenth century they were used to run passengers on trips around the warships laying at anchor off Portsmouth. The last wherries were laid up at Portsmouth in the 1920s.

Sources
Inshore Craft of Britain, Vol II, describes the 1st class wherry in some detail.

SOLENT BARGE (*Cowes ketch*)

A carvel barge with round bottom, single hatch, a transom stern, tiller steer-

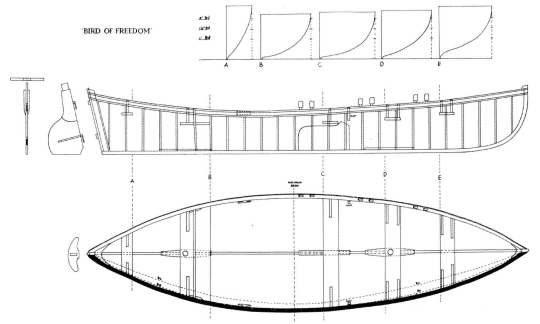

'BIRD OF FREEDOM'

Above: The 2nd class Portsmouth wherry *Bird of Freedom* at the hard at Portsmouth in 1952. The keel is quite deep aft which would have given her good directional stability. *(NMM, Oliver Hill Collection, neg no P75415)*

Left: Rough drawing of *Bird of Freedom*, a 2nd class wherry. Though chiefly a rowing boat, it could be sailed with a small lug sail. As with the 1st class wherry, steering was done using yoke and lines. *(NMM, Coastal Craft Collection)*

ed, and ketch rigged. There was a small fleet of these shallow draft barges which carried cargoes between the ports and creeks of the Solent and Spithead, east to Chichester Harbour and west to Poole. Most of their trade was grain and coal, but they carried any freight. The early barges like the *Bee* had a pointed stern, but by the 1870s they were transom sterned. The *Arrow*, built by Shephard Bros at Cowes in 1875, was 50ft long, with a 14ft beam, and an average depth in hold of 4ft 2ins. The 34-ton *Emerald*, built at Landport in 1877, had leeboards and so did *Fortis*, built at Emsworth in 1904, but most managed to sail on their shallow draft.

These barges had very long main and mizzen gaffs which were almost as long as the booms and allowed them to carry plenty of sail in the sheltered Solent waters. They also had long bowsprits which could be run in and they had thin, tall topmasts. Most of these ketches were built by Hansen at East Cowes or White at West Cowes. There were also spritsail and boomie barges built in the Solent area, but they were in the general coastal trade. The 27-net ton barge *Bee*, built at Cowes in 1801, was 51ft long overall, 10ft beam and 6ft deep in the hold, and she was believed to have served as a victualling vessel serving the fleet before the Battle of Trafalgar. She was also known to have carried oak to Beaulieu for the building of Royal Navy ships. The *Bee* was last

owned by Shepherd Bros, Newport merchants, and they also operated the last of these barges, the 50ft, 20-ton *Arrow*, built in 1877 by Hansen, which was still sailing until 1938.

Sources
John Leather, *Barges* (London 1984) has coverage of the Solent barges.

BACK OF THE WIGHT BOAT

An open, clinker built, two masted lugger with a sloping, heart shaped transom. The maritime artist E W Cooke used to visit this coast in the mid-nineteenth century and his paintings show tarred luggers with slopping transoms

and a red top strake, hauled out on a sort of jetty under the cliff at Bonchurch; there are no harbours on the south side of the Isle of Wight, only small beach landings at the foot of the cliffs facing the English Channel. By the 1880s landings to the east of St Catherine's Point were mainly involved with running trips for visitors. The Wheeler family at Blackgang Chine kept a 20ft back of the Wight boat until 1914 for mackerel fishing in Chale Bay. The last back of the Wight pot boat was the 14ft *David*, built in about 1930, which Jim Richard worked from Atherfield. This was a difficult place to work from because after use the boats had to be hauled some 50ft up the cliff; and in 1983 the *David* was abandoned.

ITCHEN FERRY
(Solent punt, Solent smack)

The Itchen ferry was a carvel, straight stemmed, transom sterned, half decked, pole masted, tiller steered cutter used for inshore fishing and oyster cultivation. The Victorian yachtsmen who came down to the south coast used to see the little fleet of fishing

The Solent barge *Attempt*.
The earlier, pointed stern
has been replaced by a
counter stern which was
the more common sort by
the latter part of the
nineteenth century. The
big sail area drove these
vessels well in the
sheltered waters of the
Solent. *(NMM, neg no
P39523)*

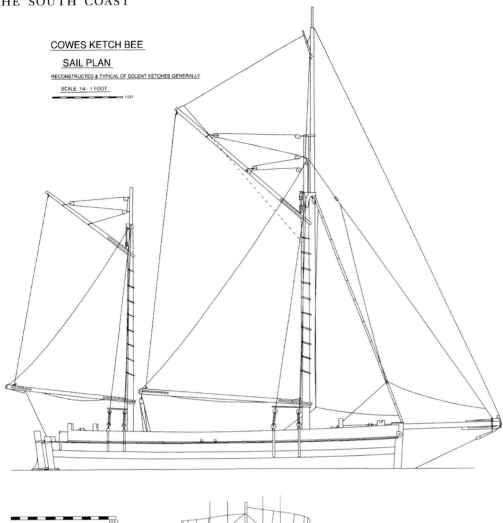

COWES KETCH BEE

SAIL PLAN

RECONSTRUCTED & TYPICAL OF SOLENT KETCHES GENERALLY

SCALE 1/4 - 1 FOOT

FEET

DIMENSIONS

LENGTH O.A	50' - 0"
LENGTH W.L	49' - 0"
BREATH	14' - 6"
DRAFT FORWARD	3' - 6"
DRAFT AFT	4' - 3"

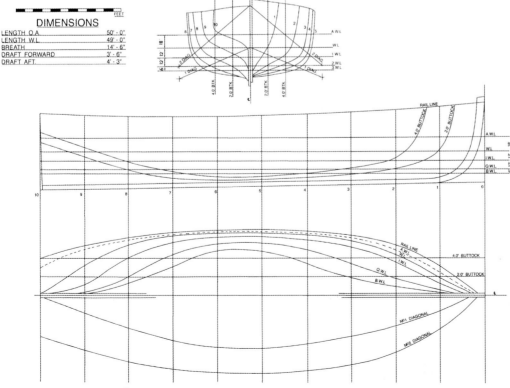

Sail plan of the Solent barge *Bee*. The rig was characterised by a short bowsprit, a large mainsail with a topsail set above and a large mizzen, with no topmast. *(NMM, Coastal Craft Collection)*

boats in the River Itchen near the ferry to Southampton. Itchen, then a pretty fishing village, was certainly a centre for this type of cutter but they were used all around the Solent. The true Itchen ferry was about 19ft long, 8ft beam and 3.6ft draft but boats of up to about 30ft long were built to trawl further out, and these were sometimes referred to as Solent smacks although there was no clear definition between the two types. Some of the smacks were completely decked or had side decks and topmasts.

The original Solent fishing boat was the punt. This was a 13ft to 14ft open, carvel rowing boat with a wide stern for working nets from. By the mid-nineteenth century the punt was a spritsail rigged boat and the next development was a deep keeled hull with a gaff cutter rig. Those used for shrimping had a loose footed gaff mainsail, foresail set, unusually, on a bumkin, and a jib on a long bowsprit. The 21ft 9in *Nellie*, built by Dan Hatcher in about 1862, carried a loose footed mainsail until the 1920s. The fishermen, like the Essex smacksmen, used to ship as yacht hands during the summer so they became very keen on racing and developed a fast sailing half decker of about 20ft long. The beamy hull became increasingly deep and powerful and fast. In an 1875 race between two fishing boats, from Northam Bridge to Millstone Point, spinnakers were set on the downwind leg, an unusual occurrence for a work boat at this date. The *Foam II* built by Arthur Payne was 20ft long, 7ft 10in beam and drew 3ft 6ins and once averaged an extraordinary 7 knots on a reach for the 35 miles from Southampton to Portsmouth.

Most of the Itchen Ferries were built to work, but intended to race as well. An early successful racer was the 21ft *Star*, built in about 1845 of red pine on oak frames for Mr Paskin, the oyster merchant, and she was a constant winner at regattas.

Sources

J Holness, 'Itchen Ferry Boats' in *Yachting World Annual* (1972).

The lines and body plan of the transom sterned Solent barge *Arrow* showing the flat rise of floor and the shallow draft. *(NMM, Coastal Craft Collection)*

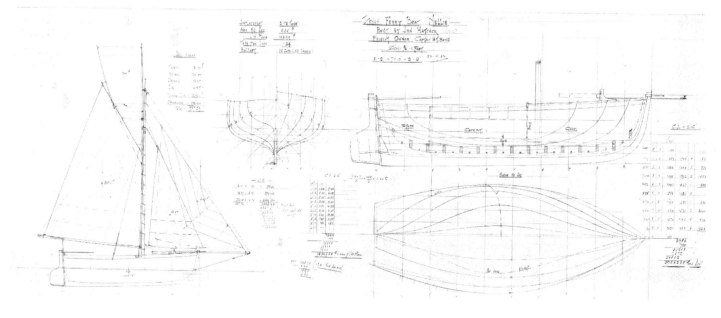

Above: Lines and sail plans of the Itchen ferry *Nellie*, built in 1862. These lines were taken off in 1932. These were pole masted vessels and the topsail was hoisted on the head of the lower mast. The wine glass midships section and the hollow entry made them fast and weatherly craft. *(Maxwell Blake Collection)*

Left: This Itchen ferry boat is typical of the later versions. She is very deep, has sharp floors and a well rounded forefoot. She would have been fast and good to windward. This photograph was taken in 1937 at Southampton. *(NMM, Oliver Hill Collection, neg no P75416)*

POOLE BOAT

In the last decade of the nineteenth century about forty boats were fishing under sail out of Poole Harbour. These were a larger version of the boats used in the Solent.

In the 1870s the Poole boats were spritsail rigged and about 18ft long and worked from the quay at Poole and out in Poole Bay where they met the yawl rigged boats which worked from Swanage. By 1890 Barfoot was the leading builder and his boats were half deckers 20ft to 25ft long. There was a constant need to go trawling further out in the English Channel so that by 1900 they had 30ft half deckers which had a broad head to meet the higher seas, but still retained the hollow underwater lines of the fast punt. They had a high freeboard and wide transom, but retained the pole masted cutter rig of the small inshore boats.

In 1906, Barfoot launched the 35ft

This photograph shows Solent smacks – larger versions of the Itchen ferry. They were photographed in Portsmouth in 1928. (NMM, Oliver Hill Collection, neg no P75414)

sail on a bumkin. The boats used for crabbing originally had two spritsails until a gaff mainsail was adopted. The same type of boat worked from the beach in Portland Harbour and along the coast at Worbarrow Bay, before that bay became a firing range. Most of these had been replaced by motor launches by the late 1940s.

Sources
McKee's *Working Boats of Britain* contains a brief description.

PORTLAND LERRETT
(Chesil Beach lerrett)

The lerret was a varnished, open, double ended, clinker boat rowed with oars fixed by a 'copse' to the oar loom that fitted over a single throle, used mainly for seine netting off Chesil Beach. The flat floored, level keeled, lerret was the traditional boat working off the 18-mile-long Chesil Beach in Dorset. In the early nineteenth century 20ft, eight-oared lerrets with fore lug and spritsail mizzen were used for smuggling trips to the Channel Islands. There was also a six-oared lerret with two spritsails. The eight-oared version had gone by about the 1870s and the last six-oared lerrets were fishing in the 1920s. In recent decades the 17ft, four-oared boat became the most practical for fishing off the beach. The four-oared lerret *Ena*, built around 1905, had a pitch pine keel and twelve planks a side of wych elm. The steamed timber appeared to be Canadian rock elm. By having the oars fastened on a single throle they could be left safely while the fishermen handled their pots and nets.

The main work of the lerret was to take the mackerel shoals which went past Chesil Bank in the autumn. Each village had its own 'seine company' which had a section of the beach. In the last decades of the nineteenth century there were nearly one hundred lerrets kept along Chesil Beach. The six-oared lerret needed a team of fourteen men; only seven men went out in the boat for the rest were needed to haul the boat up the beach and sort out the catch. Once off the beach the man in the wide stern paid out the seine net. The net was hauled ashore and the boat hauled in stern first with the

Boy Bruce with a centreboard which was about the largest sailing boat two men could handle at sea. After this most boats had centreboards although some later had them removed after engines were fitted around the time of World War I, and sails were only set with a fair wind. One of the these, the 28ft *Margaret Catchpole*, built by Adams in 1928, drew 4ft and an extra 2ft with centreboard down. Motor sailing fishing boats continued to be built. One designed by Eric H French in 1939 was 27ft long, transom sterned, and drew 3ft but 6ft with steel centreboard down. The 24hp Ailsa Craig engine was in the forward cuddy which meant a long prop shaft. Some of French's fishing boats had a bermudian rig with a hollow spruce mast and a jib on a

bowsprit. After World War II French designed more motor sail boats, usually with raised foredeck to give a large cuddy. The draught was increased to about 4ft but no centreboard was included. By the 1950s some were wheel steered and by then the engine was installed further aft.

POOLE PUNT

Used for mullet fishing on the mud flats of Poole Harbour, the Poole punt was a flat bottomed boat about 17ft long with a transom stern, sloping stem and drew only a few inches in order to work in shallow water. The sides were clinker and made up of four planks. They were rowed with oars on single tholes; and the net was worked over

the stern. A similar carvel built boat was used for mullet fishing in Portsmouth Harbour.

Sources
John Leather, 'Fishing Boats of Poole', *Boatman*, No 7 (1993).

WEYMOUTH BOAT
(Stuffy boat)

Open, clinker boat with high sides and transom stern employed for lobster and crab fishing. At the end of the nineteenth century the watermen at Weymouth Harbour used an open boat, locally called a 'stuffy boat', which was about 20ft long and rigged with a triangle mizzen on an outrigger, a loose footed gaff mainsail and a fore-

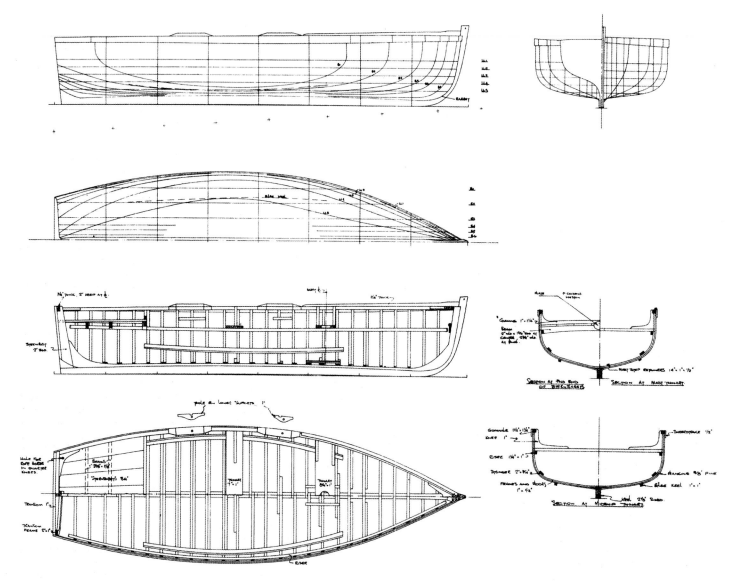

Above: The 14ft punt *Mullett* SU88 drawn by J W Holness. This boat was 14ft 2in overall with a beam of 4ft 7in and drew only inches in order to float in the shallowest waters. *(NMM, Coastal Craft Collection)*

Left: This small Weymouth lobster boat, or stuffy boat, is rigged with a spritsail mizzen, a gaff mainsail and a jib. *(NMM, neg no C4562A)*

'start rope'. As it approached the beach the men leapt out and hauled the boat up the beach. In early times the boat was always carried up the beach and there is no record of any turning over in the surf. Even after tractors and winches were introduced in the 1950s it still required about eight men to operate a four-oared lerret.

Local folklore has it that the first lerret was built in 1682 and was modelled on a boat called *Lady of Loretto* which was brought back from the Mediterranean. There is a local superstition that for good luck a boat should have a stone with a hole in it in the bow. In 1983 the square ended *Sea Rover* at East Beckington and the *Liza* at Burton Bradstock still had their lucky stones. In 1996, although there were plenty of mackerel only Richard Andrews used his lerret *Vera* to shoot a seine. The only other lerret on the beach was *Silver Star*, while *Blessing Two* and *Maroga* were used until 1993.

SQUARE STERN CHESIL BOAT

The pointed stern of the lerret is very difficult to fix an outboard to so the fishermen had boats built with the same lines but with a transom stern. These square stern boats were mainly

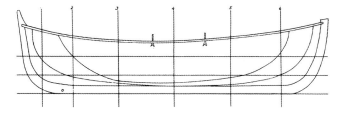

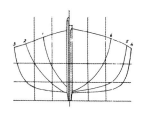

Lines plan of the Portland lerrett *Pussyfoot*. She was 17ft 2in overall with a beam of 7ft, and was built at Weymouth. She is considerably fuller in the stern than the bow and has very flat floors. These, with the wide beam, made the boats very seaworthy and well suited to landing on the very steep Chesil Beach. *(NMM, Coastal Craft Collection)*

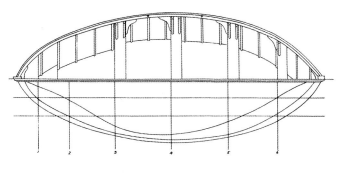

built by Nobby Clark on Portland and became popular for lining and crabbing. On the Isle of Portland there was a beach landing at Church Ope until 1914 by which time waste from the stone quarries closed the landing . The fishermen got old cranes or 'whims' from the quarries and began lowering their boats about 40ft over the cliff from points just east of Portland Bill. Because of the tidal race off Portland this is a very dangerous place to work a boat, but fishermen go potting for crab and lobster and lining for bass from March until November. Originally, the fishermen used double ended lerrets and the fishery almost died out by 1970, but with new faster boats it revived and there were sixteen boats in 1981.

Sources
The booklet *Lure of the Lerret*, produced by the Leisure and Tourism Department of the Weymouth & Portland Borough Council, is the most comprehensive source of information on these boats. Details of their construction are given by Percy Roberts who started working on these boats in 1894.

FLEET TROW
(Backwater boat)

A flat bottomed boat used mainly on the Fleet, a 7½-mile lagoon running behind Chesil Beach. Though flat bottomed boats occur widely in Europe, and even more widely in North America, they occur rarely on the British coasts. The classic exceptions are, of course, the boats of the levels

(qv); the Orkney flattie, still in use on some lochs in the archipelago in the 1990s, and apparently introduced in a deliberate immitation of the Canadian Banks dory in the early years of this century; and the Fleet trow.

The Fleet trow is a handsome version of the type, 14ft to 18ft overall and some 4½ft on the beam. Very similar in construction to some Swedish and Danish boats used in shallow waters, she provides transport for fishermen across the Fleet to Chesil Beach. Fitted with raised seat in the stern for a marksman, she is also used for wildfowling and as a fishing boat. Trows are either double ended or have a small transom. They are not dished nor have fore-and-aft rocker. They are rowed with balanced oars with a single

metal thole pin. They are still being built in the 1990s, both in wood and GRP, and one, complete with wildfowler seat, is displayed at the Abbotsbury Swannery.

Fleet trows have been seen in use in Poole Harbour, as well as transom sterned derivants. There is also a version at Wareham for reed cutting and another used used at Christchurch for commercial salmon fishing. (Photo page 10).

Sources
Eric McKee, *Working Boats of Britain* contains descriptions and lines plans.

LYME BAY BOAT

A fishing and 'freight' (tripper) boat, almost identical to the Beer lugger *(qv)*, which operated from the drying harbour loosely called the Cobh at Lyme Regis. Frequently built by the same builders as the Beer boats they were also employed in a similar fishery but, because they could dry out on the ebb on the sheltered sand of the harbour floor and did not have to be beached, they were developed into slightly larger forms. However, they had to be equally strongly constructed because when a ground swell is running in West Bay, despite the protection of the Cobh, on the last of the ebb and the first of the flood, boats are liable to pounding on the hard sand. Rigged like the Beer boats as luggers the Lyme boats, like them, were motorised at an early date but retained their masts and sailing gear up to as late as World War II.

Sources
J C Wilcocks, *The Sea-Fisherman* (London 1884) describes these craft. McKee, *Working Boats of Britain* also has coverage.

The Portland lerrett *Comrades*, photographed at Portland in 1938. Note the hole in the keel, just forward of the sternpost, through which the 'start rope' was led. This was used for hauling the boat up the beach. When not in use it was coiled, as shown in the photograph, over the protruding sternpost. *(NMM, Oliver Hill Collection, neg no P75417)*

The Coasts of Devon and Cornwall

THE COASTS of the southwestern peninsula of Britain are characterised by tidal estuaries which stretch relatively far inland. Those on the south coasts of Devon and Cornwall – the Exe, the Teign, the Dart, the Kingsbridge River, the Kingston River, the Yealm, the Tamar, the Looe River, the Fowey, the Fal and the Helford River – are in varying degrees deep on the tidal flood, with soft mud banks and each has several tidal creeks which provide waterways to inland villages. In contrast, the relatively few estuaries of the north coast – the Gannel, the Camel, the Torridge and the Taw and the Parrett – although each provided with their tidal creeks, are, on the whole, shallower than those of the south with sandy or mud beds and shores.

This is a coast exposed to the North Atlantic, to the southwest gales of autumn and winter, which can be savage, and to the Atlantic swell, the 'ground sea', as it was known to local seamen. Boats and

vessels using Boscastle, for example, had frequently to withstand very bad pounding when the ground sea rolled in. By contrast, nearby Porth Gaverne did not have the same problem. The boats and vessels of this coast had to be heavily built to withstand launching from the beaches and lying in exposed drying harbours, especially on the northwest coast where the absence of harbours meant a much smaller fishing industry, north of Padstow, than in the south. The main fisheries varied over the years with herring, mackerel and at some periods pilchard, being taken in great quantities. There was the 'cracks in the rocks' fishery for crab, lobster and shrimp, while the Fal and the Helford River had the specialist oyster fishery. The beds of the latter had their own carrier boat to take the crop to Plymouth, the fast sailing *Rob Roy*, built on the lines of a Bristol Channel pilot cutter but ketch rigged.

Pilot cutters were built at Porthleven in Cornwall as well as in

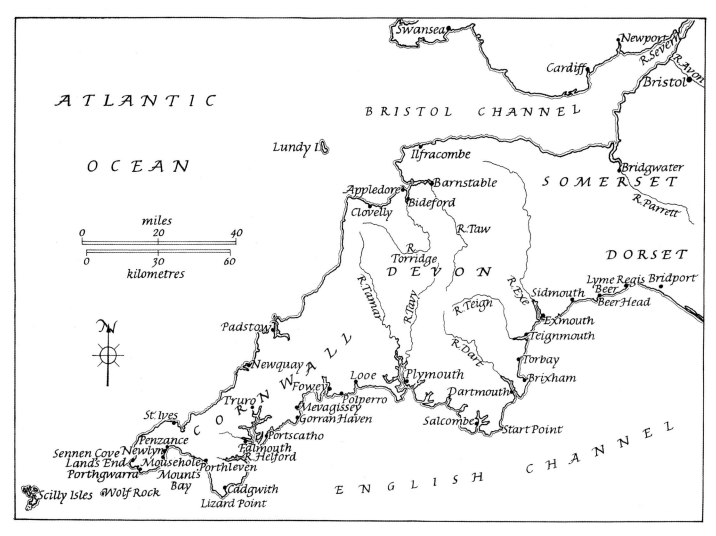

THE COASTS OF DEVON AND CORNWALL

Cadgwith Cove, a typical Cornish cove, photographed around 1899. The boats hauled up above the tide line are mostly crabbers. Chocks and skegs lying on the beach indicate that a number of boats are still at sea, while at the head of the rough paved slip a big seine boat is poised for launching. *(NMM, neg no G2958)*

greater numbers at Crockerne, Pill, Cardiff, Barry and Swansea, while the pilot gig is especially associated with Cornwall. The gigs serviced the local harbours of both the north and south coasts and of the Scillies while the cutters and schooners from the Bristol Channel ports serviced the deep sea vessels making their landfall on the southwestern peninsula and bound for the big ports – Swansea, Cardiff, Barry, Bristol, Sharpness and Gloucester.

The Fal estuary, Carrick Roads, is one of the world's great natural harbours where for many years before radio, vessels from all over the world called to await orders as to where in Britain or Europe to discharge their cargoes, which may have changed hands several times on the commodity markets during passage. To service them the quay punts and many other boats provided a living for local watermen.

The largest fishing vessels of southwest Britain in the nineteenth and early twentieth centuries were the smack and ketch rigged beam trawlers of Brixham and Plymouth. These vessels sailed far up the North Sea and around the land to the Welsh fishing grounds. Based in relatively sheltered harbours with plenty of water on the flood, though drying on the ebb, they could be of substantial size

and powerful enough to drag the beam trawls over the banks. Particularly after the development of the railways in the nineteenth century, which opened up wide markets, the local industries became prosperous enough to finance larger and larger vessels. These were among the most spectacular and finest of British sailing fishing vessels.

The inshore grounds of southwest Britain were rich with many varieties of fish and for a thousand years or more such local communities as there were utilised them as a source of food. It is to be remembered that until well into the twentieth century each of these small places was largely self-dependent, with its own fish dealers, boat builders, net and sailmakers, blacksmiths, and indeed, shoemakers, butchers, tailors, carpenters, carriers, and so forth. Socially also the communities tended to be self perpetuating, suspicious even of relatively near neighbours. In these circumstances, given that coastal conditions varied greatly and that many of the boat launching and landing places were little more than cracks in the rock with their own patterns in the very local behaviour of the sea in different conditions, it is not surprising that a multiplicity of boat types grew up all around the coast as different from one another as the deep keeled boats built for oyster dredging in the waters of Carrick Roads and the clinker built, round bottomed luggers which were beached on the shingle at Beer and Sidmouth in south Devon. Nor is it surprising that these types continued to differ from one another until the introduction of marine motors, shortly before World War I, began the long, slow process of the development of a degree of uniformity which even at the end of the twentieth century has only been partly achieved despite the very widespread introduction of plastics into the building of even the smallest and simplest fishing boats. There appears to have been little influence from the standardised small craft built for the navy and most boats were built of locally available timber in which the region was rich.

The great tidal range of the inner Bristol Channel and the soft mud of its rivers produced the specialised flatners while the wild weather and the very limited coastal shelter produced the small but strong and seaworthy Sennen Cove boats, types utterly remote from one another. There was really no predominant type widespread, like the cobles of the northeast coast, which were the result of fairly uniform geographical and weather conditions over a long stretch of coastline. A fair measure of uniformity could be achieved in the boats of one fishing place – such as the Mounts Bay or St Ives luggers but even these, the products of different conditions of sea and land, differed from one another as the drawings of the *Lizzie*, and the *Ebenezer* in this section of this book clearly show.

Before the development of motor transport, which was a phenomenon the beginning of which followed immediately on World War I with the massive disposal of surplus army transport at low prices, goods could be carried far inland on the waterways, and the products of the river valleys carried to the ports on the coasts far more quickly and economically by sailing barge than by any other means. One or two men could move a dozen wagon loads or more on one tide which would have taken many days to move by land. I have used the term 'sailing barge', but in fact, of course, the prime mover

in these barge trades was the tide; sailing, like poling, kedging, rowing with sweeps and towing from the boat, was essentially auxiliary propulsion. This barge work was a highly skilled branch of the craft of the watermen, no less skilled in its way than the skill of the men who manned the smacks and ketches which traded on the local coasts. The work which often involved loading and discharging the barges was extremely arduous. Unlike the men of the smacks and ketches, however, the bargemen were often able to sleep at home, especially after the pedal cycle became available.

The exception to these sailing limitations was provided by the 'outside' barges of the Tamar and Fal which worked between those ports and the shipping places in between them and to the beaches on the east side of the Lizard. Their men lived in both worlds. They had the skills and hazards of the men of the trading smacks and at the same time the very special skills of the bargemen in working tidal waters.

Exceptional in this section of this book are the Bideford polacca brigantines. These vessels operated essentially local trades, like the Tamar barges, feeding the lime kilns of the Taw and Torridge with limestone and small coal, but some sailed more widely in the home trade, in foreign trade, and even across the north Atlantic. They are included because they were local craft with a rig unique to one small area of the southwest, essentially the river Torridge, where almost all were built.

Beer luggers pulled up on the beach under the lee of Beer Head with nets hung out to dry. The lugger on the extreme left of the group is double ended but most of the others have the more usual transom stern. Most of the craft here have had motors installed. *(NMM, neg no G3313)*

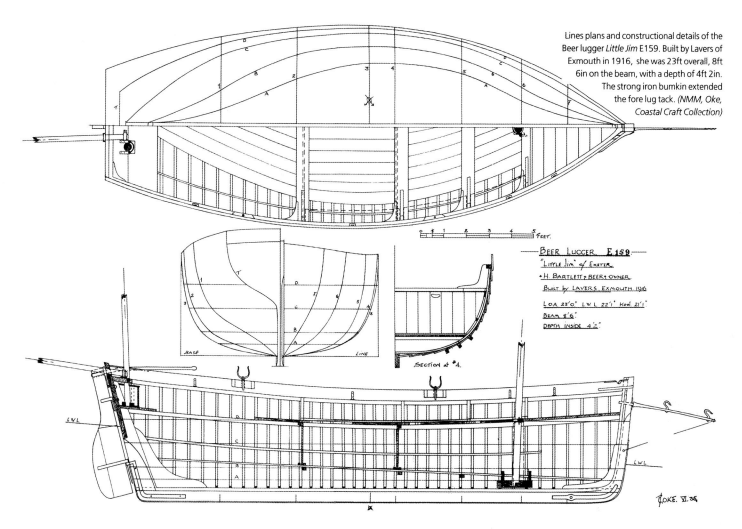

Lines plans and constructional details of the Beer lugger *Little Jim* E159. Built by Lavers of Exmouth in 1916, she was 23ft overall, 8ft 6in on the beam, with a depth of 4ft 2in. The strong iron bumkin extended the fore lug tack. *(NMM, Oke, Coastal Craft Collection)*

Devon and Dorset Beach Boats

BEER LUGGER

Strong, clinker built, lug rigged, open sailing boat, with good carrying capacity, full lines and stout bilges for beaching on the shingle ridges, which was used for general fishing all year round, and pleasure sailing and mackerel whiffing in the summer. These boats were very similar to those found at

The sail plan of *Little Jim*. The late abandonment of the three masted lug rig, occurring at about the time that engines were adopted, resulted in a marked gap in the sail plan and the corresponding hull space was taken up by engines. The foremast continued to be stepped well forward in the bows while the reduced mizzen mast was shifted aft against the transom. *(NMM, Oke, Coastal Craft Collection)*

Hastings and Eastbourne, and at Polperro up to the 1870s. As well as fishing some were also used as market boats and local general carriers. All the boats on this stretch of coast were essentially similar, and came under the Port of Exeter. Between 1869 and 1884, though some seventy-nine boats were registered at Exeter as working from Beer, there were probably less than thirty boats in use at any one time. Although one of the smaller fishing stations within the port, the Beer luggers and their crews enjoyed an enduring reputation for sea keeping and seamanship.

The earlier three masted luggers carried dipping fore and main lug sails, with a standing lug mizzen. Worked out of this relatively isolated cove, the three masted lug rig seems to have held on longer at Beer than at any other coastal station. The last of these, the *Beatrice Annie* E80 was one of the

bigger luggers at 28ft overall, 11ft 6in on the beam, with a depth of 5ft and she worked up until 1917. Their beamy, buoyant hulls required a lot of stone ballast to be shipped for sailing. The third mast or the mainmast, generally fell out of use towards the end of the nineteenth century, leaving a dipping fore lug and standing lug mizzen, usually of slightly larger sizes than previously, but with a notable break in the sail plan. During the first decade of the twentieth century, with the adoption of marine motors the boats were reduced in size to keep their overall weight down to one which could be hauled up the beach with the same number of men and existing capstans. Later the foremast was generally discarded, with only the lug mizzen retained as a steadying sail.

Like most Westcountry clinker built craft, the majority of these were constructed of oak and elm – elm keel and

oak stem, sternpost and transom, with elm planking on oak frames – and were built all along the coast. While some must have been turned out by Charles Chapple, and Thomas Restorick, both working at Beer around the turn of the century, others were built by Lavers [Lavis], and Dixon Bros, at Exmouth. By the twentieth century, if not earlier, a distinctive feature of these boats was their bright varnished hulls above the waterline.

Today, a couple of traditionally built descendants of these craft are still working off the beach at Beer.

SIDMOUTH LUGGER

These craft were essentially the same as the Beer luggers. Although not so well known as a fishing station, after Exmouth and the Exe Estuary, Sidmouth was the next largest within the limits of the Port of Exeter. Some 180

fishing boats were registered as working from Sidmouth during the closing years of the nineteenth century. Builders included W H Hart, at Sidmouth, and William Clarke, of Seaton.

EXMOUTH LUGGER

Exmouth and the Exe Estuary accounted for about half of the fishing boats registered on this coast. These too were essentially of the same build and appearance as the Beer luggers. However, the sheltered berths in the river estuary enabled slightly larger boats with deeper draft to be employed here.

The adminstration of this coast came under the Custom House Port of Exeter, which included Lyme Regis from 1880. Here, some 786 fishing boat registrations were recorded between 1869 and 1884. However, these figures include two block re-registrations of previously registered boats, and the maximum number of boats registered at any one time was 323 in 1871. Fully two-thirds of these were small open rowing boats, 3rd class fishing boats, and mostly under 3 tons. The remainder were 2nd class boats, open sailing craft of about 5 tons, with only three or four 1st class boats registered here between 1869 and 1913.

Sources
There is a useful study on the Beer luggers by H Oliver Hill in *The Mariner's Mirror*, 38 (1952). An account of their build and usage appears in Edgar March, *Inshore Craft of Britain*, while M G Dickenson covers some different aspects of these craft in his *A Living from the Sea* (Newton Abbot 1987).

Upper left: The Lympstone fishing boat E214, photographed in May 1939. She has quite steep dead rise and sits up with legs. At this date she is motor driven with a propshaft through the sternpost and a small petrol tank on the port side. She was most likely used for hand lining and general fishing within the Exe estuary. *(NMM, Oliver Hill Collection, neg no P74139)*

Left: This clinker built Lympstone fishing boat, E79, was photographed in May 1939. She is quite similar to the Beer boats but is heavier and deeper with more dead rise. She is clearly a sailing vessel, having an iron horse on the transom. She was probably used in the herring fishery but by the date of this photograph, at the outset of World War II, has probably been laid up for the last time. *(NMM, Oliver Hill Collection, neg no P74134)*

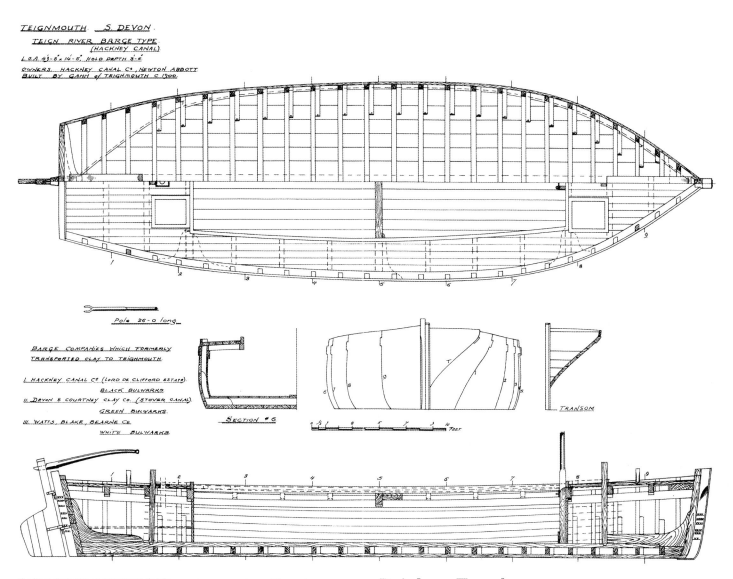

TEIGNMOUTH. S. DEVON.
TEIGN RIVER BARGE TYPE.
(HACKNEY CANAL).
L.O.A. 49'-5" x 14'-5", HOLD DEPTH 3'-5".
OWNERS. HACKNEY CANAL Cº., NEWTON ABBOTT.
BUILT BY GANN of TEIGNMOUTH c 1900.

Pole 26'-0 long.

BARGE COMPANIES WHICH FORMERLY
TRANSPORTED CLAY TO TEIGNMOUTH.

I. HACKNEY CANAL Cº. (LORD DE CLIFFORD ESTATE).
BLACK BULWARKS.
II. DEVON & COURTNEY CLAY CO. (STOVER CANAL).
GREEN BULWARKS.
III. WATTS, BLAKE, BEARNE Cº.
WHITE BULWARKS.

SECTION # 6.

TRANSOM.

The lines plans and constructional details of a Teign river barge, owned by the Hackney Canal Co. She measured 49ft 5in overall, with a beam of 14ft 5in and a depth in hold of 3ft 5in. She was built by Gann of Teignmouth around 1900. *(NMM, Oke, Coastal Craft Collection)*

TEIGN BARGE

Flat-bottomed, hard bilged, smooth planked, non-edge joined, barges about 50ft long used to transport china clay from workings along company canals and into the estuary to Teignmouth for transhipment into seagoing vessels. They mostly worked the tides, though many had a small single square sail set from a mast right forward and used only with the wind more or less dead aft. Latterly they were towed in trains by steam tugs, and in the 1930s

by motor tugs. These barges were built of local timbers, notably, latterly by Messrs Gann and Palmer, boat builders, at Teignmouth.

There were in the early twentieth century at least three fleets of barges, each owned by a clay company. The barges prospered into the 1930s but passed out of use with developing road transport.

Besides these vessels there were smaller barges of 40ft or so overall in the aggregate business. A drawing of one of these, a motor barge built by Upham at Brixham in 1924 is reproduced in McKee's *Working Boats of Britain*. She is of slightly more sophisticated shape than the clay barges as represented in Oke's drawing.

Sources
H J Trump, *Westcountry Harbour* (Teignmouth 1976).

Brixham Trawlers

MUMBLE-BEE

Cutter rigged, full bowed and broad beamed, fully decked vessel, with a fine run aft to a flared transom. Up to about 40ft long, 14ft to 15ft beam, and 6ft to 8ft deep, they registered between 30 and 40 tons. All had a long straight keel, with a deep drag aft taking a firm grip on the water. Though heavily used they were strongly built, and many attained a good old age. The *Dart*, built at Topsham in 1760, was staunch enough to be re-registered for a further term of service in 1828.

Sloop rigged at first, these were the fishing vessels that established Brixham and Torbay's reputation for trawling during the eighteenth century. From the end of the French Wars this

fleet expanded rapidly and began exploiting new fishing grounds off South Wales and up the southeast and English Channel coast. With some relaxation in the anti-smuggling laws, they adopted the 'cutter' rig, but were always known as sloops.

Those fishing off the Welsh coast out of Tenby, working the grounds in Mumbles Bay, acquired the collective term 'Mumble-Bees'. This was in part coined because of the numbers of them 'buzzing' around the Mumbles like bees round a hive, and also arose by their adopting some of the features of the established Mumbles boats encountered.

On the south coast they worked out of Dover, where three older sloops were transferred between 1826-28;

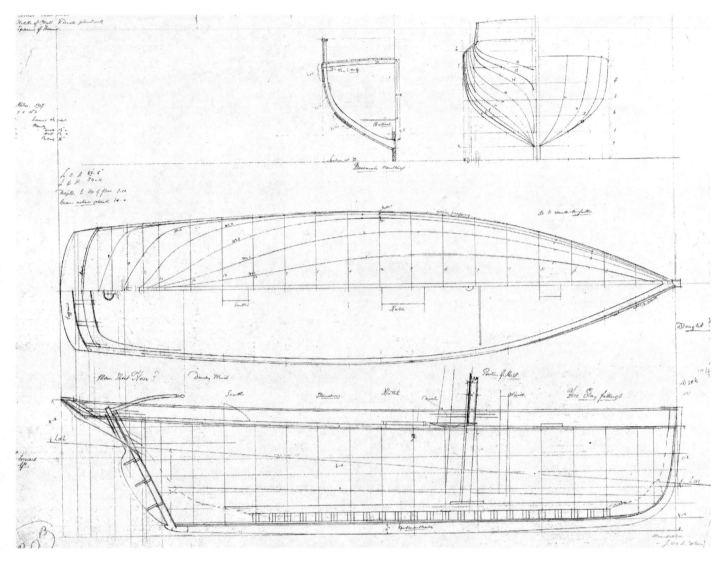

Rough lines drawings and sail plan of the
Mumble-bee *Nisha*, built in 1907. She was
55ft between perpendiculars and 14ft on
the beam. She had a deep drag aft with a
draft of 7ft 10in aft but only 4ft forward.
The sail plan shows a snug cutter rig with a
comparatively short luff to the mainsail.
(NMM, Coastal Craft Collection)

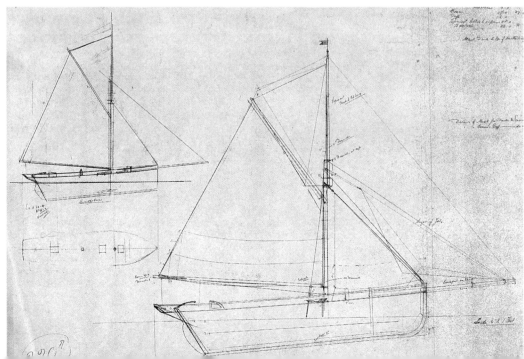

This Mumble-bee was photographed at Brixham in 1937. She has no fishing number and has acquired some davits on the starboard side which suggests that she has, by this date, been converted to a yacht. A wonderful impression is given of their deep, sharp hulls, while the ladder in the background clearly indicates the size of these big vessels. (NMM, Oliver Hill Collection, neg no P72866)

Ramsgate, where another three newer ones were transferred between 1833-36; and Rye. Within a decade the Brixham men had moved up into the North Sea.

Crewed by three men and a boy (parish apprentices), or four men in later years, these sloops worked heavy beam trawls. The massive towing hawser, the 'warp', was heaved in by the crew tramping round a small con-ventional capstan on deck amidships, or by hauling on a hand-spike windlass – a laborious task that took up to two hours. Agreement with France limited the length of the trawl beam, and thus the width of the mouth of the trawl, to 38ft. This helped determine the maximum size of the early trawlers, as the trawl beam (when fished alongside) extended from the aft side of the main rigging to port, to just overhang the stern. The beam was about the same length as the keel of the vessel. The key requirement of these craft was the ability to carry sail and to stand up to their work in heavy weather. A towing speed of about four knots over the ground was required, and this usually meant a wind of Force 4 or above.

By the 1890s they had been pretty well eclipsed by the mules (qv) and by sloops (qv) though the rig continued in use until the end of sail.

MULE

With the coming of the railways (Brixham Road in 1861), faster vessels were required to catch the fish trains to the more distant markets. Bigger sail plans were tried on the sloops, but proved beyond the abilities of the small crews. The massive booms, over-hanging the sterns, became too big to handle, even killers, and so the ketch rig then came into vogue, keeping sail handling within manning limits. These ketches were increasingly bigger than their predecessors, though the tonnage rule changes of 1854 meant that they still registered about 30 tons. These small ketches acquired the name 'mules', a term alleged to allude to their hybrid rig derivation. As a class they were under 40 tons register, and were generally under 60ft overall length. Using beam trawls they fished their home waters and the nearby English Channel.

BIG SLOOP
(Smack)

Towards the end of the nineteenth century relaxation in the legislation permitted longer trawl beams; in turn, bigger and more powerful craft were required to work the heavier gear. And, as the home grounds became worked out, bigger craft were also required to work fishing grounds ever more distant from Brixham. These big sloops searched as far afield as south-west Ireland, the Irish and North Seas.

This increase in size was facilitated by the introduction of steam capstans in the 1880s. As well as hauling bigger and heavier trawling gear, hauling time was now reduced to 15 minutes. At the same time, steam capstans were used

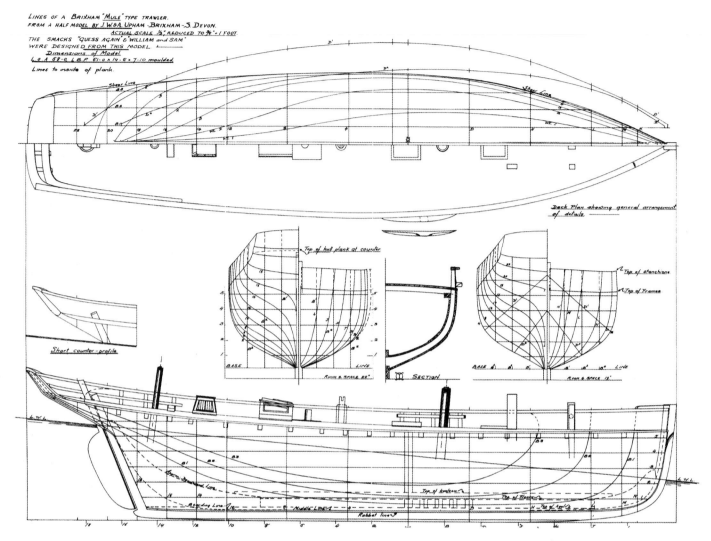

LINES OF A BRIXHAM "MULE" TYPE TRAWLER.
FROM A HALF MODEL BY J.W. & A. UPHAM. BRIXHAM - S. DEVON.
            ACTUAL SCALE ½" REDUCED TO ¾" = 1 FOOT.
THE SMACKS "GUESS AGAIN" & "WILLIAM and SAM"
WERE DESIGNED FROM THIS MODEL.
        Dimensions of Model.
L.O.A. 68·0. L.B.P. 61·0 × 14·6 × 7·10 moulded.
Lines to inside of plank.

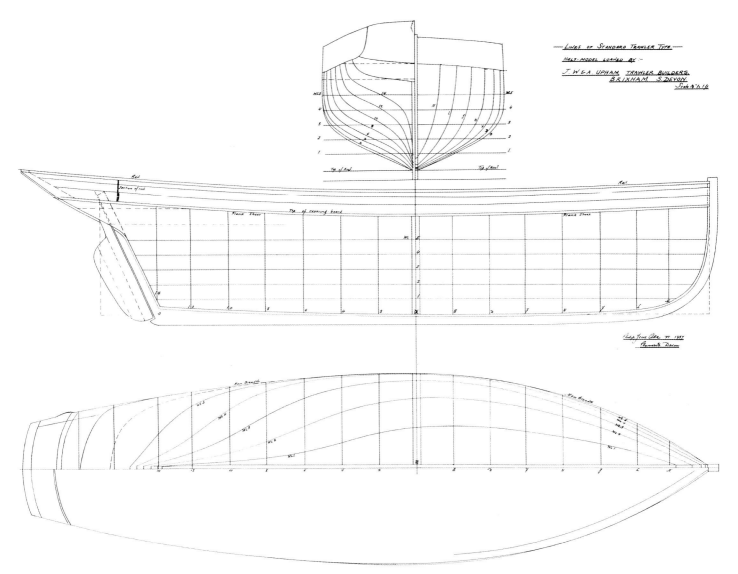

Page opposite

Top: The lines plans of a mule taken from a half model by J W & A Upham of Brixham. The mules *Guess Again* and *William and Sam* were built from this model. These mules were smaller and narrower than the big sloops but were proportionally deeper, exploiting to the full the depth of the harbour. *(NMM, Oke, Coastal Craft Collection)*

Bottom: Smacks drying their sails inside the breakwater. The photograph predates 1902 as all the boats are registered under Dartmouth – DH. These big cutters, with their massive booms, were to convert to ketch rig. *(NMM, neg no G2472)*

Above: Lines plans of a standard Brixham trawler, or big sloop, taken from a half model by J W & A Upham. She has a beautiful clean sheer, so typical of these craft, and a long, straight keel. *(NMM, Oke, Coastal Craft Collection)*

for sail handling, and working the boats generally. This allowed the crew size to remain as before – four hands – though by the early years of the twentieth century apprentice boys were becoming harder to find.

Although ketch rigged, these vessels were known locally as the 'big sloops'. This class embraced all those ketches of over 40 tons register and the biggest registered 70 tons, or more. A typical vessel was 78ft length overall, 69ft between perpendiculars, 60ft on the keel, 18.25ft beam, 9ft internal depth and 11ft draft. These were the ultimate development of the Brixham trawlers and, with local variations, their hull form and rig was emulated all round the coast of the British Isles. Other ports referred to them as 'dandies', though they never carried a lug mizzen, and their build and form also found favour in France and Belgium, where they

were known as 'dundees'. Most were built within the port limits of Dartmouth, to the demanding requirements of their owner skippers, and the principal builders were Sidney Dewdney, William Allen Gibbs, Robert Jackman, and John William & Andrew Upham.

The dogged adherence to sail after World War I was due on the one hand to the lack of capital to build steam trawlers, and on the other to the lack of suitable, reliable, compact, marine internal combustion engines. Some of the smaller mules were able to fit motors with some success, but such were not available for the big sloops, and their hull size and shape were unsuitable for installing steam engines. The factors combining to keep the Brixham fleet sailing had the historical spin-off of making them one of the best, photographically, documented class of sailing vessels.

In 1913 there were 'upwards of two hundred dandies of 50 tons, costing about £1200; twenty to twenty-five mules of 33 to 37 tons, costing about £500; and seventy to eighty mumble-bees of 20 to 25 tons, costing £400-£500.' By 1935 only twenty-five remained, and by 1939 only a handful.

In their final form, the 'big sloops' of Brixham were among the largest British sailing fishing boats, fully equal to the best in the British Isles. A vision of these craft in their prime can be drawn from the words of a Mousehole fisherman, the late Leslie Hicks. Recalling an occasion when working long lines in the motor lugger *Emblem*, PZ26 during the 1920s:

'We was N.W. of the Scillies, getting gear in and ditching everything below decks. It was blowing a hurricane, and the Yorkies near alongside had a reef in their mizzens, and their 'fiddlers'

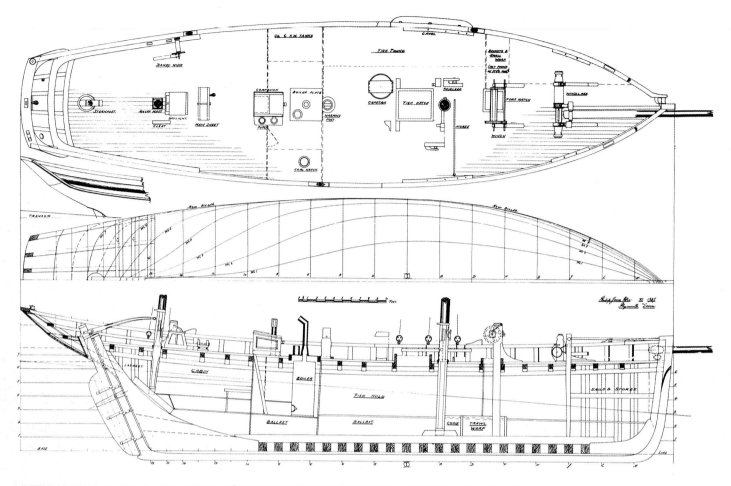

Above: The lines, layout and constructional details of the big sloop, *Competitor* BM241. She was 74ft 2in overall and 18ft 7in on the beam, and was built in 1904. *(NMM, Oke, Coastal Craft Collection)*

Left: Four- and five-thwart Brixham trawler punts. These were heavy but very buoyant work boats which were carried on transverse deck blocks on the trawlers. Most of them in this photograph have central sculling notches in their sterns. *(NMM, Oliver Hill Collection, neg no P73255)*

[their big funnels], battened down. An hour or two after dark the heavy cracking sea was full of phosphorescence. We were clearing lines when the old man called, "Look! What's coming here lads!" Away to starboard we could see a ball of fire coming up – and you could hear it roaring. Within moments, with a heavy slatting of sails a 'brickie man,' *Abide With Me*, hauled her wind close aboard to windward. Her skipper hailed, "You all right men!" "Aye!," yelled father. After a brief exchange, and remarking that, "If this weather

holds we shall make Berry by dawn," he filled on her . . .

I shall always remember that. The sea came in up to his hatches. You never seen his lee rail, and she was nothing but one mass of fire, the phosphorescence. My father yelled out, "Have a look at that, Boy! Thats a man's Toy. You wain't see many sights like that in a lifetime!"'

The Brixham smacks remained one of the last strongholds of British working sail, carrying on well into the interwar years. Sturdy, powerful, seaworthy, ketch rigged vessels, with clean lines; capable of keeping the seas in all but the most extreme weather, and of making fast passages.

Sources
In addition to numerous 'Notes and Queries', two good accounts of aspects of these fine craft have appeared in *The Mariner's Mirror*, one by H Oliver Hill, 16 (1930) and the other by A E Dingle, 19 (1933). They are given full coverage in Edgar March's *Sailing Trawlers*, while Rob Robinson covers the movement of the Brixham fishermen into the North Sea and the establishment of the trawl fishery at Hull in *Trawling – the Rise and Fall of the British Trawl Fishery* (Exeter 1996). Devon's fisheries in general are well summarised by Anthony Northway and Mark Porter, *The New Maritime History of Devon*, Vol 2 (London 1992).

The deck of the Brixham trawler *Compeer* BM21, photographed in 1929 alongside at Newlyn, a port to which they often resorted for shelter during the interwar years, all too frequently with broken trawl beams from working the rough 'western' grounds. This shot gives a clear idea of the massive spars, heavy rigging and deck gear carried by these relatively small vessels. Note the longitudinal chocks on the grating, added to give the helmsman some grip. *(NMM, Oliver Hill Collection, neg no P72910)*

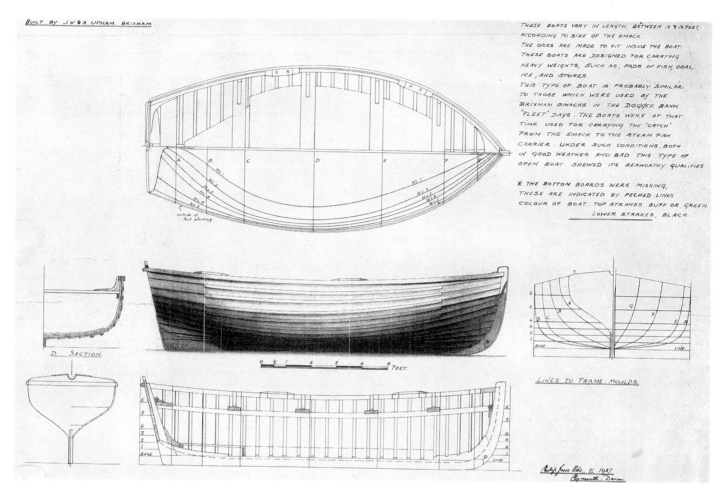

Above: Lines plans and profile of the Brixham trawler's boat from the trawler *Forseti*. These craft, with their very flat floors and wide beam, needed to be extremely seaworthy and able to carry heavy loads. The arrangement here is for four rowers pulling single oars. *(NMM, Oke, Coastal Craft Collection)*

Right: The Hallsands crabber *Sylvia*, photographed in 1935. The sprit rig, common to these craft and also used in the Orkney Isles, was not usual on small fishing vessels but it lingered in the southwest up until the end of sail. The chocks used to keep the boat upright are clearly visible. *(NMM, Oliver Hill Collection, neg no P74174)*

The stern view of a Hallsands seine boat. She has a very full hull for carrying the bulky seine net, and the thole pins are all forward of amidships, leaving the stern sheets free for working the net. This photograph shows clearly the cut away heel at the stern which suited working off the shingle bank. *(NMM, Oliver Hill Collection, neg no P74181)*

Hallsands Beach Boats

HALLSANDS AND LANNACOMBE CRABBERS

The Hallsands Crabbers were beamy, clinker built, open beach boats, similar in build to the Beer luggers, but smaller. Though quite full in the bilges, chocks were used to keep them upright onshore. These were essentially two man craft and as there were few beach capstans used here, the boats had to be light enough to be manhandled on the beach for launching and recovery. In this several crews worked together in mutual co-operation. From 12ft to 15ft in length, with about 5ft beam, and 2ft to 3ft depth, these crabbers set a main spritsail laced to a stumpy mast, with a foresail setting from a short spar bumkin.

Those of Lannacombe were very similar, but of heavier construction on account of the rockier shore west of the Start. The Lannacombe men worked alongside their Hallsands neighbours in manning and maintaining the seine boats and gear, essential for catching bait for their crab pots.

Crabbing, or 'potting', was the mainstay fishery at Hallsands, Beesands, and Lannacombe. Grouped under 'Torcross', in the decade prior to World War I, annual shell fish landings here ran at about £1,500. These accounted for nearly two-thirds of the total value of fish landed here. Between the Wars the Southampton 'well ketches', *Ceres, Gem, Macfisher,* and *Mary Leek* – successors to the earlier 'well smacks' – were still collecting fortnightly consignments.

In addition to crabbing the bigger boats worked long lines, or 'bultows'. On these occasions two crabber crews worked together, four hands being required. These boats also worked hand lines, and occasionally drift nets for herring.

HALLSANDS SEINE BOAT
(Hauling boat)

Beamy, clinker built, open beach boats, perhaps 20ft to 25ft long, and similar in shape to the smaller seine boats at other fishing stations. Rowing boats, with a fine entry and great carrying capacity aft, they were pulled by four oarsmen. When shooting, two hands shot the seine net over the quarter. The boats were known locally as 'hauling boats'. Their 'tuck nets', or 'tuck seines', were elsewhere known as 'ground seines', or 'drag nets'. The peculiarity in seining here lay in the method of working the gear, not in the design of the boats. These were beach seines, which after the boat's crew had shot the net some 600 fathoms offshore, was drawn in onto the beach by two shore parties of six men each. Working the 'tuck net' was a communal project in which the men of Lannacombe co-operated. Most of their catch was used to bait the crab pots, though some was sold, or eaten fresh.

Sources
There are few published accounts of these small craft, but M G Dickenson, *A Living from the Sea* (Newton Abbot 1987) devotes a chapter to the fishing communities of Start Bay, and the way they worked their craft. Some further references to the crabbing trade appear in Edgar March's *Inshore Craft of Britain.*

Plymouth Fishing Craft

PLYMOUTH TRAWLER

Heavy, staunch, weatherly, decked vessels, with a reputation for speed, and massively built to withstand the rigours of the trade. The Plymouth trawlers were in most respects very similar to those at Brixham (*qv*), and although only about one-third of their numbers, they had followed a similar line of evolution. The earlier craft were heavy cutter/sloop rigged boats, averaging about 30 tons register. Over time these gradually became finer and faster, while retaining their power. In the later nineteenth century, ketch rig came into vogue for the larger boats. The smaller boats retained the cutter/sloop rig, and there was considerable overlap with the 'hookers', many of which also went inshore trawling.

Plymouth trawlers, sketched by Philip Oke in 1932. They were very similar to their Brixham cousins but one notable difference was the parallel set of the masts which the artist has clearly shown in this sketch. *(NMM, Oke, neg no PAI7368)*

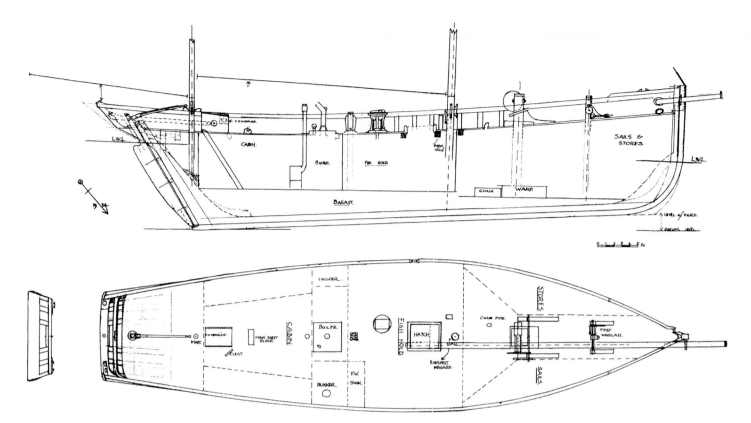

At Plymouth the trawlers fell into two classes, those over 33 tons, and those between 10 and 33 tons. The bigger boats increased in numbers, to peak around 1889, at 100 1st class boats, while their mean tonnage continued to increase until 1900, when it peaked at just under 44 tons.

In 1913, for insurance purposes, the 'Port of Plymouth Fishermen's Insurance Society' limited total loss on the largest class to £300, decreasing after thirteen years, which must have been considerably less than true cost. The limit on the smaller craft of £130, decreasing after five years, would have been much closer to a realistic valuation.

The greater concentration of capital at Plymouth enabled the port to aquire a number of steam trawlers. By 1913 there were six of these, but only thirty 1st class trawlers still working under sail.

In many eyes the Plymouth boats were not as good-looking craft as their Brixham cousins. The cutters were fine craft, but some of the later ketches looked positively ungainly and even crank. W H Shilston had a reputation for turning out fine cutters, but the *Erycina* PH63, and the *Vanadura* PH 119, both built as 46-ton cutters in 1882 and 1880, lost their looks when converted into ketches about 1894.

Despite her hollow floors, fine entry, and slight beam, *Erycina* had a very heavy appearance when dried out.

A ready home market meant that quite indifferent catches could attract fair prices. So, the Plymouth boats were less inclined to fish far away from home, though many worked the grounds of Mount's Bay, much to the annoyance of the local drift fishermen. They never gained the exposure, nor the reputation, of the Brixham smacks.

PLYMOUTH HOOKER

Modest, sturdy and seaworthy, sloop/cutters, and crewed by two or three men, these boats supplied much of the daily fresh fish demand of Plymouth. Fishing up to 50 miles off Plymouth, the hookers rarely remained at sea for more than 24 hours, and invariably worked out of their home port. Originally working several thousand hooks (hence their name), from long lines, by the twentieth century many also worked light trawl gear in the inshore fisheries.

In appearance they were smaller versions of the trawlers (*qv*), with straight stems, steep floors with rounded bilges, long keels with a drag aft, and raking transom sterns. Rudders were hung 'out of doors', with the tiller working through a port in the transom at deck level. In size they ranged from 25ft to 40ft overall, 9ft to 14ft in the beam, and 5ft to 7ft depth of hold. Drawing from 4ft to 8ft of water, they registered between 5 and 14 tons. As such they were nearly all registered as 2nd Class fishing vessels. In the main they were sloop rigged in winter and cutter rigged in summer. They set a loose footed gaff mainsail, bald headed in winter, but with a lofty jack yard, gaff topsail in summer. They also set a flying jib from the long running bowsprit. A few of the larger boats were dandy rigged, and there were one or two yawls.

The bigger boats were fully decked with a small hatch to the space for gear under the foredeck, larger hatches to the fishroom amidships, and a companion to the cabin aft. Prior to the introduction of steam capstans, the gear was hauled by double handed, flywheel, capstans – 'Iron Men'. From the turn of the century a number of these carried the smaller size Elliott and Garrood steam capstans. Boilers for these were usually in the cabin aft, as in the western mackerel drivers. Patent line haulers, mounted on the rail, were also introduced after World War I.

The smaller hookers were half-decked, with a cuddy under and hauled their gear with a 'dandy wink'.

Above: Rough drawings of the layout and profile of a Plymouth trawler. The layout is very similar to the Brixham trawler but the counter is distinctly shorter and squarer and there is, as a result, very little deck aft of the rudder head. *(NMM, Coastal Craft Collection)*

Page opposite
Top: Lines, layout and constructional details of a Plymouth hooker. They show very clearly the deep sailing hull and the steep rising floors. There is a 10ft cuddy with a stove which would have offered reasonable shelter for the three crew. Note the handspike 'wink' across the boat amidships with its 'clicker' or ratchet to prevent the loss of line under tension. Later boats had steam capstans. *(NMM, Oke, Coastal Craft Collection)*

Bottom: The Plymouth hooker *Dayspring* PH339, photographed in Plymouth in 1935. Though she still has her sails, this vessel has embraced the age of the motor. Tyres have been adopted for fenders and much of the well is taken up by an engine and its cowling. Note the heavy chock inside the waterway to starboard which would have carried one end of the handspike 'wink' for hauling the long lines. *(NMM, Oliver Hill Collection, neg no P74280)*

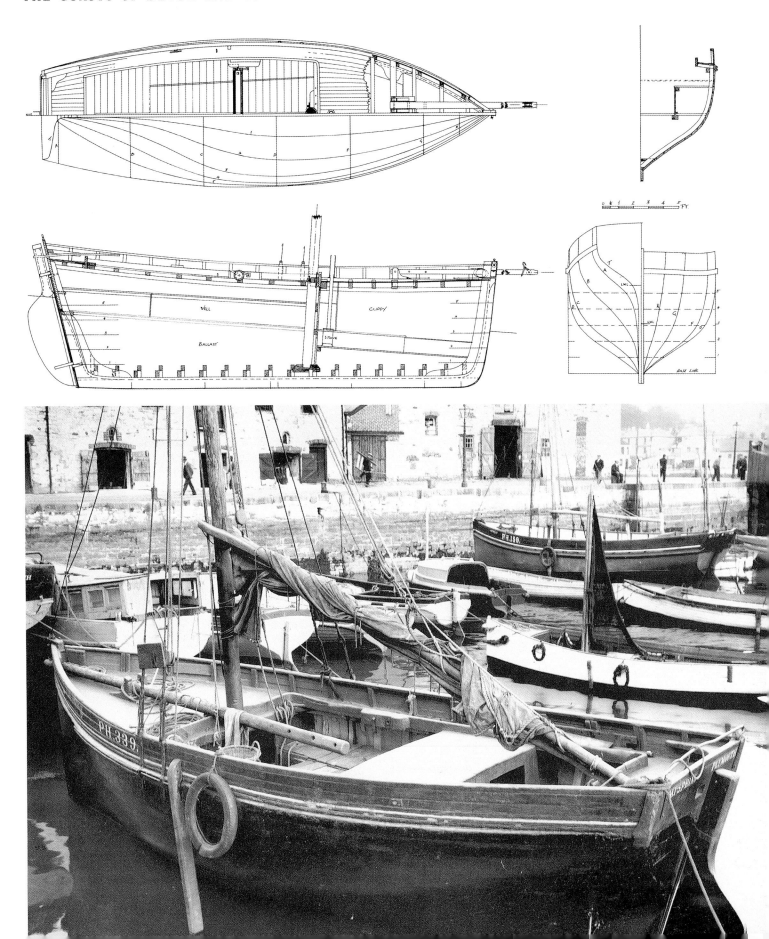

In many respects these were quite similar to the Polperro gaffers (*qv*), and the Mevagissey toshers (*qv*). As a very general class of boats they were built by builders all round the southwest.

Class numbers peaked in the 1880s and 90s, with 190 hookers and drivers registered at Plymouth. By 1913 numbers were down to under 100, at which time the 'Port of Plymouth Hookers' Insurance Society allowed £150 as maximum cover for total loss on these vessels.

PLYMOUTH DRIFTER

These do not fit easily into any classification. Many different types of drift net fishing boats worked out of Plymouth, having migrated from other ports. One Plymouth drifter 50 PH pictured aground at Newlyn in the early 1870s, was a big clinker built lugger, after the style of a Deal forepeaker (*qv*). Straight stemmed, with what appears to be a lute stern, her painted waterline is about 7ft 6in deep forward (fifteen strakes), and 8ft aft, and she is about 40ft overall. Fore and mizzen lug rigged, she carries a 20ft running bowsprit, Mevagissey fashion. She appears fully decked, certainly there is chimney smoke from accommodation under the foredeck, and what appears to be a companion aft, fore side of the mizzen.

Within a few years of this photograph most Plymouth drifters were of the East Cornwall, or Mount's Bay, types.

Sources
As with the Brixham trawlers, the fullest account of the Plymouth version appears in Edgar March's *Sailing Trawlers*. Plymouth hookers and drifters have had little written on them though Edgar March devotes a couple of pages to the hookers in his *Inshore Craft of Britain*.

TAMAR BARGES

Sailing barges of distinctive hull form working within the port limits of Plymouth and to Falmouth in the west and occasionally to the Channel Islands. The most developed of them overlapped in occupation with the local trading smacks and small ketches. These were the 'outside barges', statutorily registered vessels, subject to survey and with load lines. There was also a large group of 'inside barges', smaller vessels, similar in hull form but usually unregistered, whose activities were normally confined to the tidewater north of Plymouth breakwater.

The Tamar 'inside' barge *Macadam* photographed in 1934. She was built by F Hawke at Stonehouse in 1894 and lasted until at least 1940. She was used mainly for carrying stone. The horse at the stern, the 'Plymouth gallows', is very clear. *(NMM, Oliver Hill Collection, neg no A1065)*

Tamar barges were beamy and of shallow draft with a shallow external keel, flat floors and a hard turn of bilge. There was little or no drag. The sternpost ended in a broad flat transom with the bulwarks pieced for the tiller and a massive timber sheet horse, locally known as the 'Plymouth gallows'. Both outside and inside barges were of this general shape immediately recognisable as of the Plymouth area. The big outside barges had low bulwarks and usually a fidded topmast from which a jackyard, later jib headed, topsail was set. Points reefing was always used. Bowsprits were running and a staysail and a jib were normal. The inside barges, or Tamar sloops as they were sometimes called, had a high peaked mainsail, a staysail and some had a bowsprit and jib. The gaffs and booms of inside barges tended to be long, but the mast, stepped often in a tabernacle on deck, was short, as were the luffs of the sails. Inside barges, depending on size and work, frequently had very low bulwarks, or even none at all. The Tamar barges in the twentieth century worked a multiplicity of cargoes: timber transhipped at Plymouth for the riverside quays, limestone for the numerous kilns on the tidewater, hard coal from Plymouth for the same kilns, grain for the mills on the Cleave at Cotehele, stone for building and for the roads from the great quarries at Treluggan and the Lynher, groceries for the shops of Callington, bricks from Gunnislake, 'dock dung', the sweepings of the droppings of the hundreds of horses employed in Devonport naval yard, for use as fertiliser on market gardens, and general work in connection with the dockyard. All these cargoes meant tide work, poling, towing, kedging, as well as sailing, and the bargemen had very highly developed specialist skills. Two men normally comprised the crew.

Barges were built at a number of yards in Plymouth, notably that of F Hawke at Stonehouse, and David Banks at Queen Anne's Battery. They were built at Saltash, and by Edward Brooming and later James Goss at a yard in Devon opposite Calstock. Most of them were built of readily available

local timber, oak, elm, and larch and imported softwoods for the planking.

The considerable scale of the barge trade is shown by the numbers of vessels employed. Ian Merry identified over 130 vessels in use on the river in the nineteenth century. Bearing in mind that very few of the inside barges were registered or recorded in any other way, the total is likely to have been at least twice that number. They were mostly of 20-30 tons and 30ft to 60ft in length. Tamar Barges continued in trade in some numbers until World War II, by which time many had been fitted with auxiliary motors. After the War the improvement of roads and the further development of road transport rapidly eliminated their trades. The last to work were the *Mayblossom*, built by Banks in 1889, and the *Shamrock*, a shallow draft ketch barge, built by Hawke in 1899. These two were still in the stone trade in the early 1950s. *Shamrock* has been splendidly restored by the National Trust and now lies at Cothele Quay. The very pretty inside barge *Lynher*, built by

Goss in 1896, has also been beautifully restored by private enterprise and lies at Morwellham.

Sources
Ian Merry, *Shipping and Trade of the River Tamar* (London 1980, reprinted 1984). A full and comprehensive history of the barges and a master work of local maritime history.

East Cornish Luggers

LOOE AND MEVAGISSEY DRIFTERS

Fine lined, yachty little luggers, with a rather delicate appearance, seemingly unsuited to the rigours of fishing. They were carvel built, with steep floors, and raking transom sterns. Running to about 40ft overall, 33ft on the keel, 12ft beam, and 6ft internal depth, they were relatively lightly framed. In a

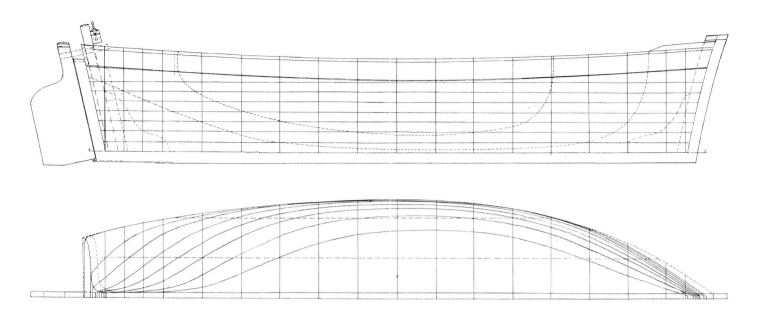

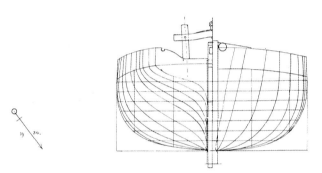

Lines of Tamar barge "Flora May". 22 tons register.
Builder F Hawke Stonehouse, Devon 1897.
Designed by Capt C A Daymond, Plymouth.

The lines plans of the Tamar barge *Flora May*, built by F Hawke at Stonehouse in 1897, drawn from a builder's half model. The straight keel and the flat floors are clearly seen as is the high, broad, flat transom. *(NMM, Oke, Coastal Craft Collection)*

class of their own, the east Cornish drifters were generally smaller than their west Cornish contemporaries. In the main the best boats here were close to the 15 tons borderline.

Decked fore and aft, full width hatchways occupied the middle of the boats. What accommodation there was lay under the foredeck, with access via the fish room hatchway and a small doorway in the bulkhead. Their evolution from open boats was marked by calling the underdeck beams 'thwarts'. Lug rigged, they rarely set topsails, but when passage making set a jib from a running bowsprit, and occassionally a mizzen staysail. They were essentially pilchard drivers that doubled as long liners. In the 1860s, a few larger,

decked, counter sterned, luggers were built purely for mackerel driving. These were not a success, and were sold away within a decade or so.

Against the local, lightly built and finely finished boats, those from Porthleven, in Mount's Bay, were considered 'rough as rats, but strong and sturdy'. Whatever local opinion as to their build and finish, in the early twentieth century, most of the large boats at Mevagissey had been bought second hand from West Cornwall. Boats from Looe and Mevagissey came under the Port of Fowey, and there was very little difference in their appearance and build. If anything the sterns of the Looe boats were more upright.

During the first decade of the twentieth century there were on average 90 1st class luggers registered at Fowey, against 85 at St Ives, and 135 at Penzance. However, the tonnage of those at Fowey averaged only 16½ tons, against 22 to 23 tons, at St Ives and Mount's Bay.

About that period the principal boat builders at East Looe were Jas Angear,

and R H Shapcott; at West Looe, Peter Ferris and Hugh Stephens and Sons; and at Mevagissey, Frazier Bros, William D Lelean, Henry Roberts & Co, and a little later Percy Mitchell, round the corner at Portmellon.

Sources
H Oliver Hill's study of these craft was published in *The Mariner's Mirror*, 21 (1935), and they are well covered in Edgar March's *Sailing Drifters*. More background and related information can be found in H A Behenna, *A Cornish Harbour* (Privately published 1995).

MEVAGISSEY TOSHER

A local class, the toshers were carvel built, open sailing boats. Good sea boats with clean lines, they were mainly employed hand lining for mackerel and hake in their respective seasons, along with other inshore fishing.

They were very similar in size, rig and build to the Polperro gaffers (*qv*), though generally smaller, registering at about 5 tons. It has been suggested that toshers were kept under 20ft over-

all in order to avoid increased harbour dues, and although vaguely worded, the 1886 schedule of dues supports this view. Some of the larger toshers had a short cuddy deck forward. The hull was divided into compartments by bulkheads under the thwarts. In earlier times they set a single dipping lug, but adopted a cutter rig in the last quarter of the nineteenth century. Worked by one- and two-man crews, the toshers were economical and popular. Many were successfully converted to motor propulsion. During the interwar years motor toshers were built in good numbers by Percy Mitchell at Portmellon.

In recent years the toshers have seen a revival as a class of traditional sailing boats, both for pleasure and racing, though most of these are GRP.

Sources
Mevagissey toshers are covered briefly in Edgar March's *Sailing Drifters*, while further information on them appears in H A Behenna, *A Cornish Harbour*, and a general account of their construction was published in Percy Mitchell, *A Boatbuilder's Story* (Mevagissey 1968).

Left: The Mevagissey lugger *Jane* FY42, dried out at the back of the old harbour in 1936. With her hull cleaned and tarred she will soon lift to a rising tide. The sheen of the fresh tar gives a good impression of her underwater shape and shows the run of the thick bilge strake. By this date she probably had an engine with the prop on the port quarter, well clear of the nets which were worked to starboard. *(NMM, Oliver Hill Collection, neg no P74354)*

Below: The old harbour at Mevagissey, photographed in 1904. The many craft here follow the natural ranking imposed by the shoaling water. Small toshers and crabbers are nearest the camera; bigger pilchard drivers are in the middle ground; the biggest, the mackerel drivers, occupy the deeper water in the centre of the harbour. *(NMM, neg no G3080)*

Page opposite
The Mevagissey tosher *Charm* FY260, photographed in 1936. The short foredeck and cuddy stop well forward of the mast and would not have afforded any shelter. Their lines were very similar to those of the bigger lugger. *(NMM, Oliver Hill Collection, neg no P74375)*

The Polperro Fishing Craft

POLPERRO LUGGER

A short lived class of inshore herring and mackerel drivers, little is known about them. Four are mentioned by T Q Couch as having been built in 1858, when they were described as being about 35ft in length, and 10ft beam, and costing about £100 each. They were possibly clinker built with transom sterns. They proved too expensive for the little port in terms of both men and resources, requiring four or five hands to work them, and being too large for other out of season work; they consistently failed to earn an economic return. When badly damaged in gales that swept into the harbour in the 1870s, they do not seem to have been repaired. The class fell out of favour and the boats were abandoned or sold away.

POLPERRO GAFFER

Fine lined, lightly built, half decked fishing boats, carvel built and gaff rigged, employed in the hook and line fishery out of Polperro. Much the same size as the Mevagissey toshers (*qv*), these renowned little craft replaced undecked, sprit rigged boats of about the same size between 1860 and 1880.

Up until the 1860s these were mostly clinker built boats, running up to 30ft overall, 27ft on the keel, by 9ft to 10ft beam, 6ft deep in the waist, and 7ft to 8ft at the ends. They registered under 10 tons. A little smaller than the luggers of the same period, they were in many respects similar to the luggers at Beer (*qv*). But with less full bilges and a greater rise of floor amidships, they required legs to keep them upright when aground. Their transom

sterns were more upright. Reputed to cost about £250, with their gear and nets, this seems high. Even allowing for gear costing as much again as the price of the boat, this was as much as the 40ft Mount's Bay luggers.

In about 1856 seventeen of these boats worked out of Polperro. Single masted, they set a loose footed, sprit mainsail, and a foresail set on the forestay, carried to an iron beak on the stemhead. In fine weather they set some sort of topsail, while a few occasionally rigged a small mizzen, and/or a jib from a running bowsprit. Essentially open boats, they adopted a short foredeck between the stem and the first beam, with a cuddy under, in about 1850. When hooking they were crewed by two men, but when driving a crew of three or four were carried. By 1870 there were only ten of these boats costing about £85 (a much more acceptable figure), and fifteen smaller boats of 22ft to 24ft by 8ft beam, cost-

ing about £65. Apart from two gaff rigged boats, the smaller boats were then still all spritties, or 'spreeters'.

Due to wholesale destruction in storms, by the 1880s most of these had been replaced by gaff rigged, carvel built boats, of similar dimensions. The reason for the change of rig has not been noted, but by this time they were as much pilchard drivers as hookers, and the sprit mainsail when brailed up, still held a lot of wind, presenting a problem when driving. The contemporaneous change in construction appears to have occurred because of the way in which the light, clinker built boats were so badly smashed up in the gales of the 1870s. In addition, much of their boat building was now handled at Mevagissey, Looe and Fowey, where shipwrights were more accustomed to building carvel craft – shipwrights such as Lelean, Roberts, Shapcott, and Hugh Stephens, and later on, Oliver, and Angear. The 27ft

Two Sisters FY 253 built by Angear, cost £42, hull and spars.

A few Polperro craft adopted motors, and on their introduction the foredeck was extended back to the mast, to protect the engine, not the crew. Prior to this the boats had to be worked out from the confined cove by sweeps which was once a regular sight. One distinctive trait at Polperro, was the way in which they stowed their gaffs, head down in the boat and throat up the mast.

Sources
While these craft are only mentioned in passing in T Q and J Couch, *History of Polperro* (manuscript), and are merely touched on in Andrew Lanyon, *Rooks of Trelawne* (London 1976), Edgar March gives Polperro and the gaffers good coverage in *Inshore Craft of Britain*.

CORNISH COVE CRABBERS

Small, but strongly built, staunch, open boats, with good carrying and sea keeping abilities. The conflicting requirements of sailing and carrying led to a compromised hull shape of fine ends and full bodies which resulted in some very hollow waterlines. Even so, many crabbers were swift sailers enjoying considerable local repute. The

Two early Polperro lugger hulls, one badly damaged after one of the many disastrous storms that drove into the harbour, even after the completion of the Duke of Cornwall Pier in 1861. *(Royal Institution of Cornwall)*

An undecked Polperro spritty, the precurser of the gaffer, being worked out of the little harbour around 1884, prior to the construction of the short counter pier off the eastern side which created a narrow gap, small enough to be closed by baulks in bad weather. *(NMM, neg no G2442)*

term 'crabber' covered all boats employed in fishing for crustaceans – crabs, lobsters or crayfish – with pots.

Crabbers worked out of most of the Cornish coves from Seaton (near Looe) and Gorran Haven in the southeast, round to Port Isaac and Boscastle in the northeast. They generally worked in larger numbers out of the rocky coves of south and west Cornwall, and in smaller numbers on the more hostile northern coast. Most of the western

coves had a large communal capstan for hauling up the boats. Usually the property of the landlord, they were manned and maintained by the community. These coves were of necessity close to the fishing grounds as the strings of pots had to be lifted at least once a day. Both carvel and clinker craft were built for crabbing, and though quite similar in general form and arrangement, most crabbers adopted specific features peculiar to their coast and locality.

At Penberth, a hard, rock bound cove, with a boulder slip and a small head of population, the craft were of rarely more than 20ft in length. The big exception here was the 48½ft, 21-ton mackerel driver *White Star*, worked by the Jackson brothers between 1861 and 1873. The Porthgwarra crabbers were relatively fine lined with fair carrying capacity, but rarely of more than 18ft. Usually lug rigged, these boats were as often rowed as sailed by their

Lines plans and constructional details of *Cuckoo*, a Gorran Haven crabber, built in 1881. She is quite shallow with a well rounded midships section and good carrying capacity. The position of the mizzen may be 'as built' but suggests a compromise upon the introduction of a motor. There is a hole in the forefoot for the hauling up strop. *(NMM, Oke, Coastal Craft Collection)*

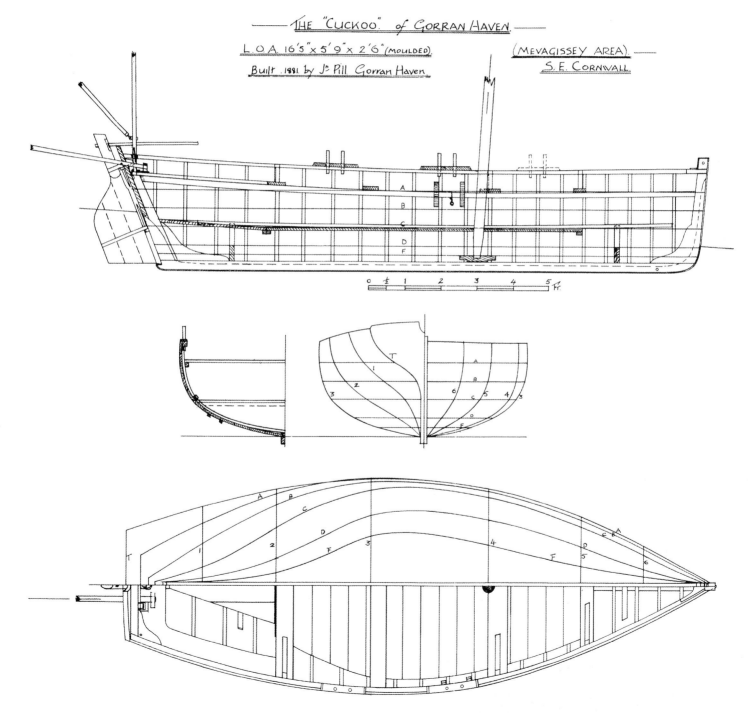

THE "CUCKOO" of GORRAN HAVEN.

L.O.A. 16'5" x 5'9" x 2'6" (MOULDED).

Built 1881 by Jⁿ Pill, Gorran Haven.

(MEVAGISSEY AREA).
S.E. CORNWALL.

Right: These Gorran Haven crabbers are Fowey registered boats and were photographed in 1933. Their small mizzens evolved after the introduction of engines. *(NMM, Oliver Hill Collection, neg no P74424)*

Below: Lines plans and constructional details of *Waterfall* FH26, a crabber from Cadgwith Cove. At first glance she is quite similar to *Cuckoo (qv)* but closer inspection shows her to have flatter floors and a sharper turn to the bilge. This gave her a greater carrying capacity which in turn required the addition of a centreplate to enable her to sail reasonably. Note the large midships well either side of the centreplate casing. *(NMM, Oke, Coastal Craft Collection)*

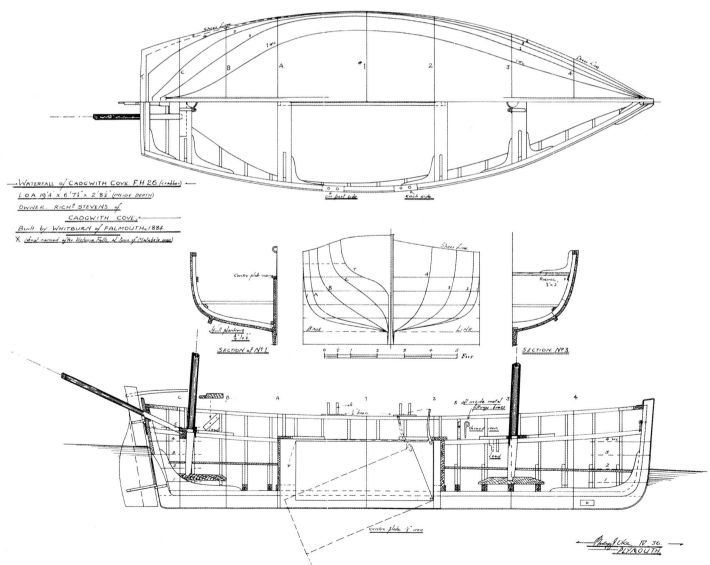

Left: A Portloe crabber, photographed in 1952. This little crabber has been converted to motor power and has no spars rigged. Behind her is visible the sheer of a bigger crabber, still sporting a steadying mizzen. There is a wire strop lashed to the bow for hauling up the steep beach. *(NMM, Oliver Hill Collection, neg no P74428)*

Below: Lines plans and constructional details of the Sennen Cove Crabber *Nile* PZ439. She is much the same length as *Waterfall* of Cadgwith (*qv*) but beamier and nearly a foot deeper. There are some exaggerated tucks in the stern to fair up the lines. She has a demountable fairlead for hauling pot lines, shown in the inset detail. *(NMM, Oke, Coastal Craft Collection)*

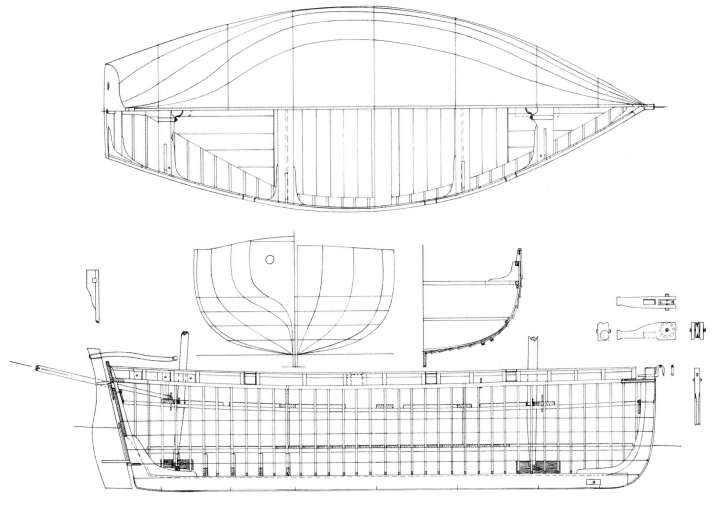

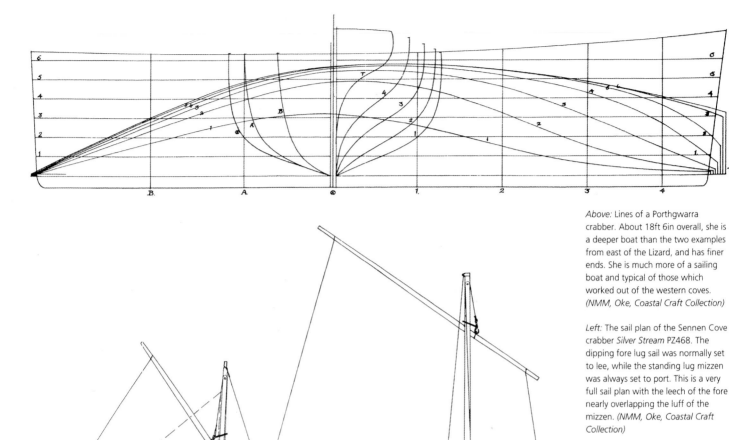

Above: Lines of a Porthgwarra crabber. About 18ft 6in overall, she is a deeper boat than the two examples from east of the Lizard, and has finer ends. She is much more of a sailing boat and typical of those which worked out of the western coves. *(NMM, Oke, Coastal Craft Collection)*

Left: The sail plan of the Sennen Cove crabber *Silver Stream* PZ468. The dipping fore lug sail was normally set to lee, while the standing lug mizzen was always set to port. This is a very full sail plan with the leech of the fore nearly overlapping the luff of the mizzen. *(NMM, Oke, Coastal Craft Collection)*

Page opposite
Top: Sennen Cove crabbers photographed in 1937. The cutouts on the washstrake for rowing are clearly visible. A crab pot lies on the ground. *(NMM, Oliver Hill Collection, neg no P74942)*

Bottom: Alaska, a small pilchard driver cum crabber. There is a cuddy stove pipe forward and the spikes of the 'forkel' or lantern spear show between the luff of the mizzen and the head of the helmsman. She is setting a big fore lug sail and a heavy second mizzen. *(NMM, Oliver Hill Collection, neg no P74740)*

two- or three-man/boy crews. As at Sennen, the older clinker built boats carried washstrakes, with shuttered cutaways for rowing. On some boats a midships section of the starboard washstrake could be removed for working the gear. The later, carvel built boats rigged pairs of thole pins for rowing. Most carried a steadying mizzen when working under oars.

Round Land's End the Sennen Cove crabbers were marginally bigger, partly on account of the larger slipways here, but also the larger population. Again crewed by two or three men,

some ventured as far as the Scillies. Though mostly carvel built, the *Nile* PZ439 was a clinker built, lug rigged crabber, with a full washstrake, in which were shuttered cutaways for rowing. *Nile* appears to have a slight tumblehome to the wings off her transom, perhaps the last trace of past connections with Irish and north Devon boats. Built in 1889 for Mathew George, and drawn by Oke in 1935, she was full bodied with quite flat floors, but with a fine entry and hollow run. A Paynter's draft exists of a Sennen Cove crabber for a 'Mr.

George, about 1886'. With dimensions of 22ft 1½in overall, by 7ft 4in beam, and 4ft moulded depth amidships, this shows a longer, deeper boat with greater rise of floors, closer to a pilchard driver. This was possibly the *Ark* 311PZ, built for George George in 1884. However, the fore and aft sections are over sketched with a shallower hull with flatter floors, as in Oke's plans of the *Nile*. Many a boat's form and build was derived from modifications to an earlier craft, and it seems likely that *Nile* evolved from the *Ark*. Both drafts indicate a shifting thwart

amidships, a common practice to create working space for handling gear, also found in the seine boats.

Sources
A brief note on the Sennen Cove crabbers, by H Oliver Hill, with a delightful sketch, appears in *The Mariner's Mirror*, 41 (1955). The construction of crabbers and other local fishing boats is covered well in A S Oliver, *Boats and Boatbuilding in West Cornwall* (Truro 1971), while supplementary information can be found in Keith Harris, *Hevva: Cornish Fishing in the Days of Sail* (Redruth 1983).

The Falmouth oyster dredger *Mayflower*, photographed sometime in the 1950s, being worked single-handed. She is setting all her working sail and is not dredging, but she makes a fine sight as she works along the land. She was built as a Porthleven lugger and acquired this rig when bought for the oyster fishery. *(NMM, Oliver Hill Collection, neg no P74524)*

Falmouth Working Boats

FALMOUTH OYSTER DREDGER

Powerful little gaff cutters, with fair lines and deep hulls. Carvel built in the main, they set a lofty sail plan for their length, and were employed between October and March dredging for oysters within the Fal and Helford estuaries. They still work today under sail, motor fishing for oysters being prohibited by by-laws. They are similar in size and form to the quay punts (*qv*), but generally finer and not quite so deep, from 22ft to over 30ft in length. Some of the smaller ones were open boats, but most had a short forecastle deck and waterways, with 22in side decks with 'tables' for working the dredges. Steep floored and long keeled, with heavy keel irons as well as internal ballast, they are crewed by two or three hands when working, depending on the size, but more when racing.

When dredging, by skilful backing and scandalising of the sails, these boats are worked across the wind. Deliberately making excessive leeway, the bigger boats can then stream three oyster dredges: one off the beam, one off the quarter, and one off the stern, each dragging over its own line of sea bed. Smaller boats, working single-handed, stream two dredges in the same manner.

Many local boatbuilders, with long standing family names of repute, turned out working boats over the years; builders such as Ferris, Hitchens, Burt, Jacket, Green and Rutson. In addition to those still employed as working boats, many others are sailed for pleasure, including a number of modern GRP boats. These now carry increasingly bigger sail plans, with tall jackyard topsails, and ever more ballast to keep them up to their work. Representative amongst the traditionally built survivors are *Victory* (ex-*Royal Oak*) (27ft 1in x 8ft 8in x 5ft) built by T Hitchens at Yard, Devoran, in 1884; *Florence* (28ft 5½in x 8ft 11in x 5ft 4in)

built in Pill Creek, Feock, by William Ferris in 1895; and *Winnie* (28ft 4in x 9ft 4½in x 5ft 4½in), built by William Brabyn at Calenick, Truro, in 1897. Paul Williams' *Serica*, was built at West Looe in 1912, by Peter Ferris, as the *E.R.C.*, while *Softwing* is maintained in working condition by the Cornwall Maritime Trust.

FALMOUTH QUAY PUNT

Seaworthy, carvel built, yawls, with fuller lines and deeper hulls than the fishing boats, and employed servicing the needs of vessels calling at 'Falmouth for Orders'. They were smaller than, and not to be confused

with, the Falmouth pilot cutters. Quay punts normally worked within the port limits, but occasionally went seeking off the Lizard. As with pilotage, the first punt to make contact with an incoming vessel had their business for the duration of their stay – ferrying, fetching and carrying of all kinds.

The quay punts varied in length from 20ft to 30ft, 7ft to 10ft in beam, 5ft to 8ft deep internally, and drawing from 3ft to 6ft of water. Half decked forward, with a cuddy under, they had a large open cockpit aft, with waterways and combings on either side, terminating with a fairly upright transom. A vertical stem turned through a more or less rounded forefoot to a long, deep

keel with a external keel iron of about a ton. Another ton of scrap iron, or stone, was carried as internal ballast, stowed amidships, away from the ends. Some had a pronounced rocker in their keel to improve manoeuvrability. They all had an exaggerated rise of floors with deep 'V' underwater sections.

Easily handled by one man, or even a boy, to work alongside square riggers they carried a low ratio, stumpy yawl rig, consisting of a fore staysail, set up from a short iron bumpkin; a bald headed gaff mainsail, loose footed to a boom; and a 'leg-o-mutton' mizzen, also loose footed to a boom and sheeted to a short outrigger.

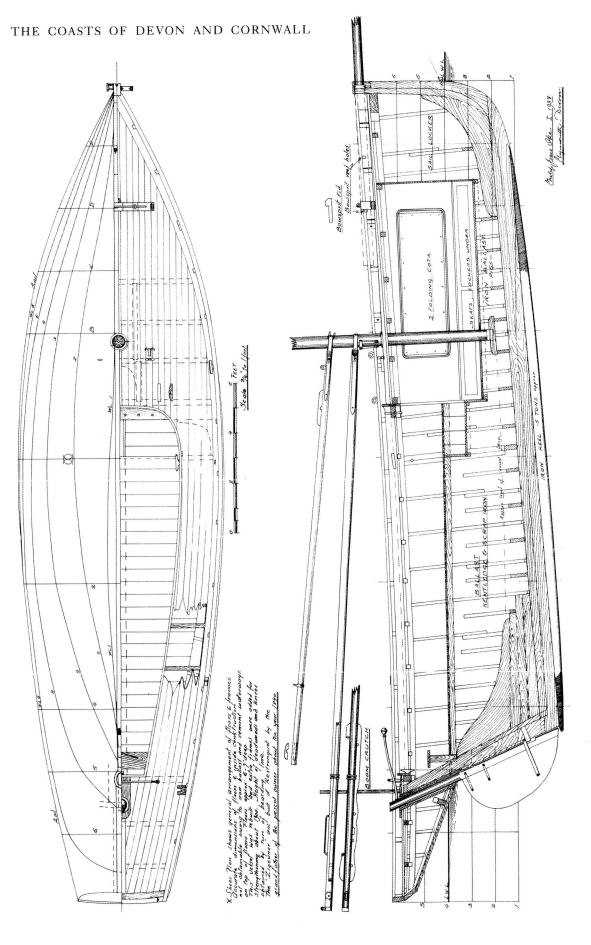

Philip Oke drew the lines of this Falmouth oyster dredger in 1938, but she is as atypical of the class as you could get, a class composed of a greater variety of converted vessels than purpose built ones. Oke's note that she was built at Restronguet around 1840 should be treated with caution. Current research suggests that she was originally a deep, clinker built German yacht. She was too deep for oyster dredging, which takes place over shallow estuary banks, and when she was acquired the lower part of her clinker hull was cut away and replaced with a shallower one of carvel construction. Laid up in Restonguet Pond in 1951, she eventually fell to pieces. (NMM, Oke, Coastal Craft Collection)

Costing from £30 to £45 (up to World War I), these boats were built by most of the boatbuilders on the Fal, though William Edward Thomas enjoyed a high reputation at Bar Yard. There are several fine half models of quay punts in the Cornwall Maritime Museum, Falmouth. One presented by Captain Dowman, of the *Cutty Sark*, is endorsed on the back – '24ft x 8ft x 5ft., Not built from ye ordinary Quay Punt'. It carries a sketch of a dandy rigged yawl, with a flying jib set from a long running bowsprit, working boat fashion. She was probably built for him as a pleasure boat.

Sources
A joint note on the Falmouth oyster dredgers, by Oliver Hill and Basil Greenhill, appeared in *The Mariner's Mirror*, 41 (1955). Since then Alun Davies has published his full and lively account of these craft, *The History of the Falmouth Working Boats*, (Falmouth 1989, reprinted 1995). Quay punts have generally been ignored, though Dixon Kemp, in the seventh edition of his standard work *A Manual of Yacht and Boat Sailing*, gives these craft a short chapter, and Edgar March covers them in *Inshore Craft of Britain*.

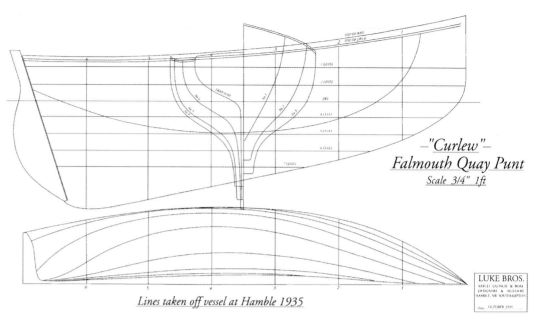

—"Curlew"—
Falmouth Quay Punt
Scale 3/4" 1ft

LUKE BROS.
YACHT LAUNCH & BOAT
DESIGNERS & BUILDERS
HAMBLE, NR SOUTHAMPTON
Date OCTOBER 1935

Lines taken off vessel at Hamble 1935

The lines of the Falmouth Quay punt *Curlew*. Note the contemporary yacht-style keel and the much deeper draft than found on the fishing boats, the cutaway forefoot and the very deep heel. *(NMM, Coastal Craft Collection)*

A Falmouth Quay punt, photographed in 1923. Despite the deeper draft and their greater ballast carrying capacity, they set a less lofty sail plan than the fishing boats. This enabled them to work alongside the square riggers without becoming entangled in their sheets and braces. *(NMM, Oliver Hill Collection, neg no P74633)*

A small, unidentified Fal 'inside barge' aground at Malpas, on the confluence of the rivers Tresillian and Truro. With her shallow draft and flat floors, her lack of bulwarks and pole mast, she is a good representation of the smallest type of barge working between the riverside quays. Similar, very small barges worked on the Tamar. (Basil Greenhill Collection)

THE SAILING BARGES OF THE FAL ESTUARY

Sailing barges working within the port limits of Falmouth. There would appear to have been fewer sailing barges on Fal tidewater than on that of the Tamar and this is perhaps not surprising as there was no equivalent enterprise to the Devonport Dockyard or the great quarries of the Lynher. Moreover, the barge trade appears to have been principally inside the great harbour and its tidal tributaries and to the Helford River and adjacent beaches with relatively few locally owned 'outside barges' sailing up-channel.

Nevertheless, the barge trades appear to have been extensive. Almost every local industrial plant seems to have had its own barges, if not a group of them. They were gaff rigged, often pole masted, vessels with no bowsprit or, on the bigger ones a running bowsprit. All had been built by the shores of the creeks, usually of local timber. Often, like the Cornish merchant schooners, they were of good hull form and they were probably better sailing vessels than their Tamar equivalents. The Truro River-built *Mystery*, whose lines are reproduced here, is very similar in dimensions and sections to some Tamar 'outside barges', but as perhaps might be expected of a Cornish shipbuilder, she was a little narrower, rather finer both in the bow and in the run, the sternpost sloping much more steeply and the stem gracefully rounded. The *Mary*, whose lines are also reproduced, was known among bargemen as the 'little big barge' because, although she was a seagoing vessel, she was small and had some of the characteristics of the inside barges.

The sail plan of the Falmouth barge *Mystery*. She was built in 1885 by Charles Dyer and remained afloat until World War II. On the luff of her mainsail she has lacing as far up as the second reef and mast hoops thereafter. (NMM, Oke, Coastal Craft Collection)

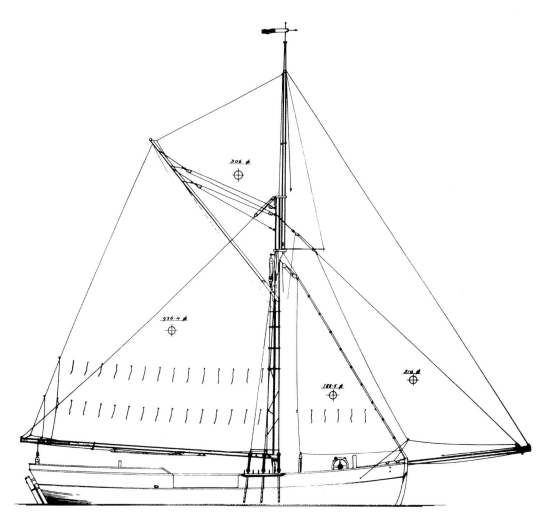

The lines plans, and layout of the Falmouth barge *Mystery*. She has well rounded midships sections but really quite fine ends. (NMM, Oke, Coastal Craft Collection)

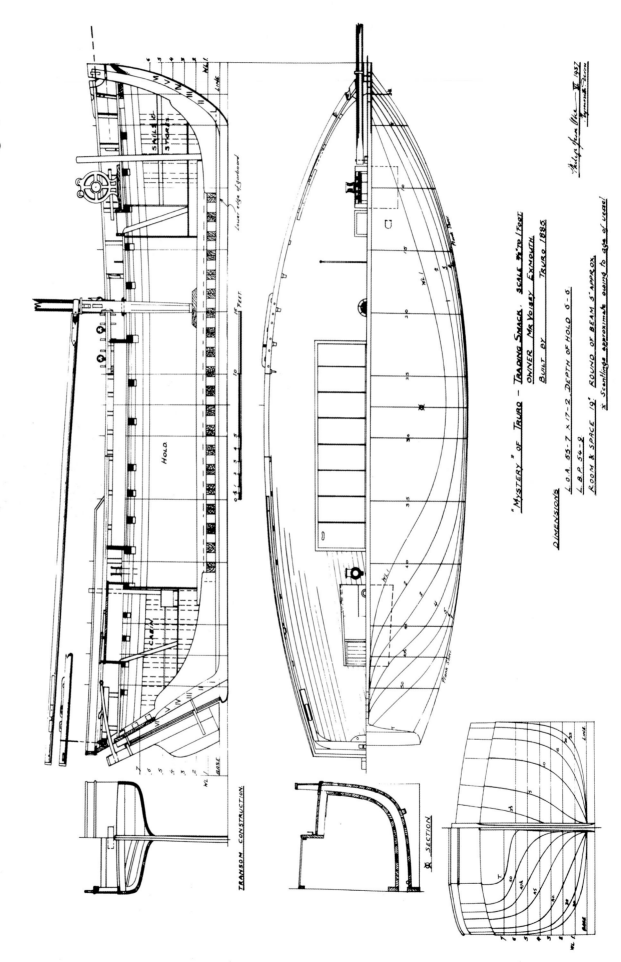

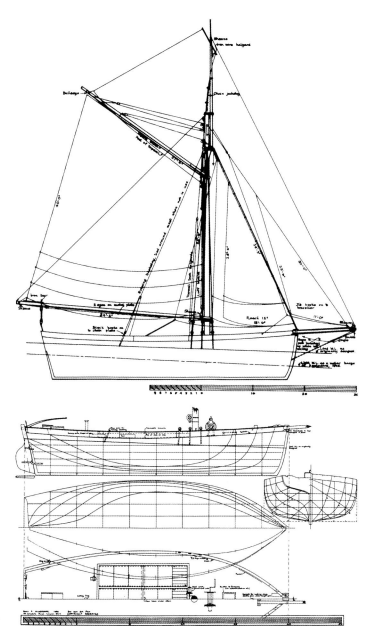

Above: The Falmouth 'inside' barge *Industry*, often referred to as *Little Industry* to avoid confusion with an 'outside' barge of the same name. She is pole masted and has no bowsprit. She is photographed here bound for the head of Gillan Creek on the evening tide with her well known skipper, Harry Ditch, at the tiller. She was owned by Collins who were coal merchants and millers, with a mill at Gillan Creek. *(NMM, Oliver Hill Collection neg no P72213)*

Left: The lines plans and deck and sail plans of the Falmouth barge *Mary*. This small seagoing barge traded between the Fal and the Tamar. She is beamy and has quite flat floors and these characteristics would have made her stiff in a blow. *(David R MacGregor)*

In the 1920s at least thirty specialised inside barges worked around the Fal, each serving a particular local trade. The *Industry*, owned by local coal merchants and millers, traded to Porthallow where she discharged on the beach. Her owners had a mill in the village and another at the head of the Gillan Creek at the entrance to the Helford River. The *Industry* carried about 25 tons of cargo and had very low bulwarks. The *Maggie* and the *Marion* had tabernacles and used to trade to a factory above the bridge at Devoran. The *Betsy*, the *Spritely* and the *Tregothnan* had little fiddleheads and fixed bowsprits. They were rigged with a gaff mainsail and a staysail and worked from Roundwood Quay. The *Graham* regularly carried beer from Falmouth to Truro. The *Trelonke* was unique among barges in that she had a dipping lug sail. The *Sunbeam* and the *Swift* were pretty little barges without bulwarks, decked only at bow and stern which carried cargoes of grain and timber transhipped from the ships in Carrick Roads up to Truro. None of these vessels has been preserved.

Sources

Little has been published on the sailing barges of the River Fal except in Basil Greenhill, *Sailing For a Living* (London, 1962). There is also the article 'The Mary of Truro' by Greenhill and MacGregor which gives a detailed account of the history of this vessel, published in *The Mariner's Mirror*, 46 (1960).

Cornish Seine Boats

Cornish seine boats were heavily constructed, open rowing boats which fell loosely within three groups: those fishing for pilchards, mackerel, or mullet.

PILCHARD SEINE BOATS

Depending on the fishing station, each 'company' worked a two- or three-boat operation. Confusingly, the names applied to different craft varied between stations, and too often the same name had different meanings at different places. Basically, the operation consisted of the main seine boat, a 'follower', and sometimes a 'lurker'. Where 'huers' directed operations from the shore there was no lurker. Pilchard seine boats worked all round the Cornish coast, wherever there were sandy bottoms.

The seine boats were heavily constructed, beamy, open rowing boats. Their form was another compromise between carrying ability, and speed. Usually carvel built, they ran to between 36ft to 40ft in length, 11ft to 12ft beam and 3ft to 4ft moulded depth. Most were double ended, and had their maximum beam in the 'net space' abaft, which was contained by under-thwart bulkheads. Here they

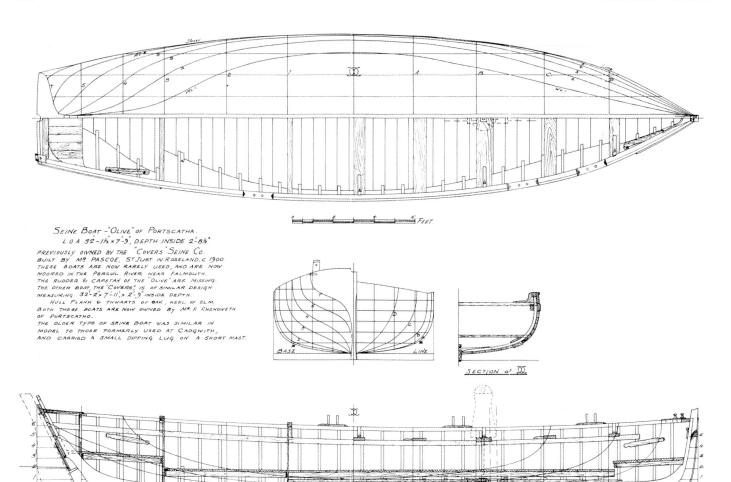

SEINE BOAT - "OLIVE" OF PORTSCATHA.
L.O.A 32'-1½" x 7'-9", DEPTH INSIDE 2'-8½"
PREVIOUSLY OWNED BY THE "COVERS" SEINE CO.
BUILT BY MR PASCOE, ST JUST IN ROSELAND.C 1900
THESE BOATS ARE NOW RARELY USED, AND ARE NOW
MOORED IN THE PERCUIL RIVER NEAR FALMOUTH.
THE RUDDER & CAPSTAN OF THE "OLIVE" ARE MISSING.
THE OTHER BOAT, THE "COVERS", IS OF SIMILAR DESIGN
MEASURING 32'-2" x 7'-11", x 2'-9" INSIDE DEPTH.
    HULL PLANK & THWARTS OF OAK, KEEL OF ELM.
BOTH THESE BOATS ARE NOW OWNED BY MR F. CHENOWETH
OF PORTSCATHO.
THE OLDER TYPE OF SEINE BOAT WAS SIMILAR IN
MODEL TO THOSE FORMERLY USED AT CADGWITH,
AND CARRIED A SMALL DIPPING LUG ON A SHORT MAST.

Above: Lines plans and constructional details of the Portscatho pilchard seine boat *Olive.* Her sheer reflects that of the local pilot gigs and gives her the characteristics of a shallow skimmer. Compare her lines with the one photographed at Cadgwith (page 129). *(NMM, Oke, Coastal Craft Collection)*

Below: This photograph of a Portscatho seine boat demonstrates most of the features of the big pilchard seine boats. She is shallow draft with a full beam, and yet has fair lines for rowing. The thole pins are forward, along with the capstan for drawing the ends of the seine net together after it was shot. Aft are the transverse beams and bulkheads enclosing the net room and a broad flare to the transom with quarter timberheads to act as fairleads for the net lines. The sharply raking transom was a feature of this part of the coast. *(NMM, Oliver Hill Collection, neg no P75431)*

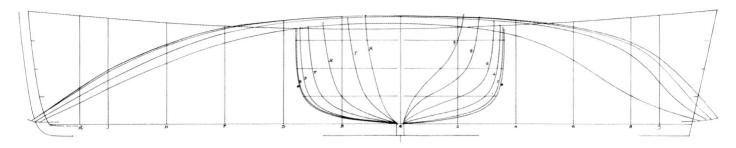

Lines of a mackerel seine boat from Sennen Cove. At around 25ft overall she is about 5ft to 7ft shorter than the pilchard boats, but otherwise is much the same shape and style – a beamy, flat, carrying boat. (NMM, Oke, Coastal Craft Collection)

The lines and constructional details of a Penberth tuck or seine boat. At 25ft 11in she is about the same length as the mackerel seine boat but she is double ended and has finer ends. She was employed in 'tucking' (removing) pilchards from the seine. (NMM, Oke, Coastal Craft Collection)

carried the seine net, or 'great seine', an immense, dense, close meshed net, from 320yds to 440yds long, and weighing some 3 or 4 tons in all. In action, five or six men pulled the boat while two or three shot the net, and one steered.

The 'followers' were also heavily constructed, carvel built, open rowing boats, similar to but smaller than the seine boats. From 20ft to 30ft long, 6ft to 7ft beam, and 3ft deep, they were usually double ended. These boats carried a stop seine, or tuck net, as required. In the early 1860s, a 28½ft fol-

lower, built at St Ives by William Paynter, cost £33.

'Lurkers', where used, were sleek, clinker built, rowing boats, 16ft to 18ft long and manned by three or four men. They carried the master seiner, when directing operations afloat. These cost from £11 to £13 in the 1860s, less than 15s per foot.

Once the pilchards were enclosed, any number of boats, barges and luggers were employed to ferry the catch ashore. At St Ives there were some purpose built 'loaders' which were heavy, beamy craft with no pretensions of

speed. A new loader built for the Gurnards Head Fishing Co, by John T Short of St Ives in 1874, cost £26.

It may be surprising to learn that all these purpose-designed craft were only employed for six to eight weeks each summer, so an immense amount of capital was tied up in this speculative business.

St Ives was by far and away the largest pilchard seining station, and the fishery was heavily regulated. Here, seine ownership peaked about 1870 when there were 286 seines, loosely organised into five general

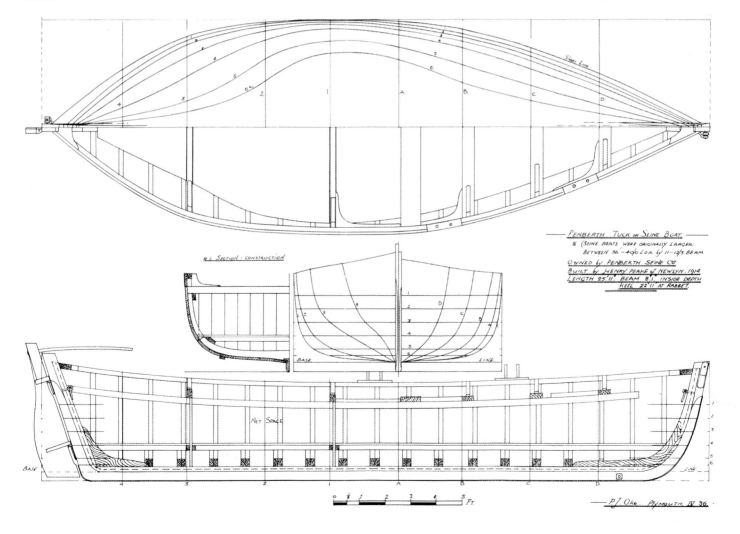

A Sennen Cove mullet seine boat, photographed in 1935. She is quite similar to the crabbers in form and size, though rather fuller aft in order to carry the seine net. To the right of the boat is the round house which housed the communal capstan, while on the wall behind is an old ship's winch for hauling up the smaller boats. *(NMM, Oliver Hill Collection, neg no P74934)*

companies. But, of the 286, only 71 registered for fishing in that year. A distinctive bow marking system evolved here to identify the boats of the different concerns. All the registered seines worked the six fishing 'stems' (designated locations) in a strict rota, decided by a seine boat race at the commencement of each season. Once the rota was established, it was then pot luck who held stem when any fish came in. This fishery declined around the turn of the century, reducing the numbers of seine boats manned up until 1922, but the last enclosure recorded at St Ives was made in August 1908. Despite the great capital investment in these craft, there was little sentiment amongst their owners. Commercial logic determined that most of the old boats were broken up for scrap value. The few that were not were too far gone for conservation. Not one of the hundreds of St Ives seine boats was preserved for future generations, the last being reportedly broken up in 1928.

At each of the other fishing stations there were rarely more than a dozen vessels or concerns operating at any one time. Steam seine boats were tried at Sennen (1870-95), Porthgwarra (1893), and Cadgwith/Falmouth (1881-84), but were not successful as propeller noise agitated the fish. For the same reason motors were never adopted.

Even before World War I the coves had become so severely depopulated that only smaller boats could be manned. Probably the last of these was built for Penberth, at Newlyn, by Henry Peake in 1914. Her cost may have been recovered, as the last enclosure of pichards in Mount's Bay was a large one, made off Porthcurno in 1916. Tucking, and landing by motor luggers, took all week, and on the Friday the 'dead tuck' was released. These were the last known seine pilchards taken off Cornwall. The industry had failed after hundreds of years. Pilchards continued to be caught by the driving boats, but have rarely been seen since in the old seining grounds.

MACKEREL SEINE BOATS

Mackerel shoaled in smaller schools, so the boats and seines employed were smaller, usually under 30ft in length, and often only 20ft or so. Otherwise they were much the same shape and build. They tended to work alone, with an occasional attendant 'cock boat'. Mackerel seining was mainly a Mount's Bay fishery, the boats being manned by four or more men, with a master seiner at the helm.

MULLET SEINE BOATS

Mullet schooled in tight shoals, and were usually caught close in shore by drag seines, or ground seines, and principally in the crabbing coves of west Cornwall. Though the schools appeared off Sennen most frequently, if somewhat irregularly, they were occasionally taken as far up channel as Par. These boats, working off a beach, were about 20ft long, relatively light, and manned by three or four men. In later years a number of gigs were used for this fishery. One built by William Paynter, for Sennen, in the early 1860s, cost £22.

Sources
The standard work on this fishery is Cyril Noall, *Cornish Seines and Seiners* (Truro 1972), while supplementary information on the seine boats can be found in both A S Oliver, *Boats and Boatbuilding in West Cornwall* (Truro 1971), and Keith Harris, *Hevva, Cornish Fishing in the Days of Sail* (Redruth 1983). John Bartlett, in his recent classic *Ships of North Cornwall* (Padstow 1996), devotes a chapter to seine companies and fishing vessels.

Mount's Bay Luggers

MACKEREL DRIVER

Fully decked, carvel built, lug rigged, fishing boats, employed in the Cornish and Irish mackerel fisheries, and in the Irish, Manx, Scots, North Sea, and Plymouth herring fisheries. In these fisheries they worked fleets of drift nets of up to 1½ miles in length. Fine, weatherly sea boats, they ultimately sacrificed a little of their sea keeping abilities for speed. In the latter part of the nineteenth century they developed finer lines with a wedge shaped bow, vertical stem, sharp forefoot, with a long straight keel. Their underwater body was fuller forward, drawing into a long hollow run with a deep heel. The pronounced rake of their sternposts being accentuated when afloat.

The relationship between the early fishing boats and the three masted smuggling luggers of the late eighteenth century is clearly seen in contemporary portraits. Indeed, many of the smaller of these were ostensibly fishing boats, the fishermen being active smugglers prior to 1815. The hull form of the 'Penzance Fishing Boat', in the Washington Report is little changed from these with their shallow hulls, full lines and rounded bilges. Open boats prior to the 1830s, the crew slept wherever they could in heavy oilskin capes. Foredecks appeared, offering better shelter, soon after entering the Irish fisheries in the late 1820s. Half decks followed in 1832, and it was a plan of this type of boat that was sub-

mitted to the Washington inquiry. These had a deck from the bows to the fore side of the fish room, wide hatchways over the fish and net rooms, with narrow waterways on either side, and open stern sheets.

Though the Mount's Bay luggers had effectively stopped using their mainmasts by then, the Custom House

Page opposite
Top: Lines plan of the double ended Mount's Bay mackerel driver *Lizzie* PZ596, from a builder's model by Harold Legg of Penzance. She is 50ft 9in overall. She was actually built 10 years earlier than noted by Oke, in 1896. This vessel represents a typical 1st class Mount's Bay lugger at their peak. Note the inset sketch with the foremast nearly vertical, and the mizzen mast now with a distinct forward rake. *(NMM, Oke, Coastal Craft Collection)*

Bottom: Typical Mount's Bay mackerel drivers working out from Penzance in the 1880s, probably after a gale. Prior to the building of Newlyn Harbour in 1885-94, the only shelter was Penzance – at all other times the boats avoided the place like the plague. All the vessels have their big fore lug sails set and their mizzens, while a few in the distance have their mizzen topsails set. Note the 'jenny' booms extending the foot of the big mizzens without the need for even longer outriggers. There are no punts on deck so this is the home mackerel season, between March and June. *(NMM, neg no B5783)*

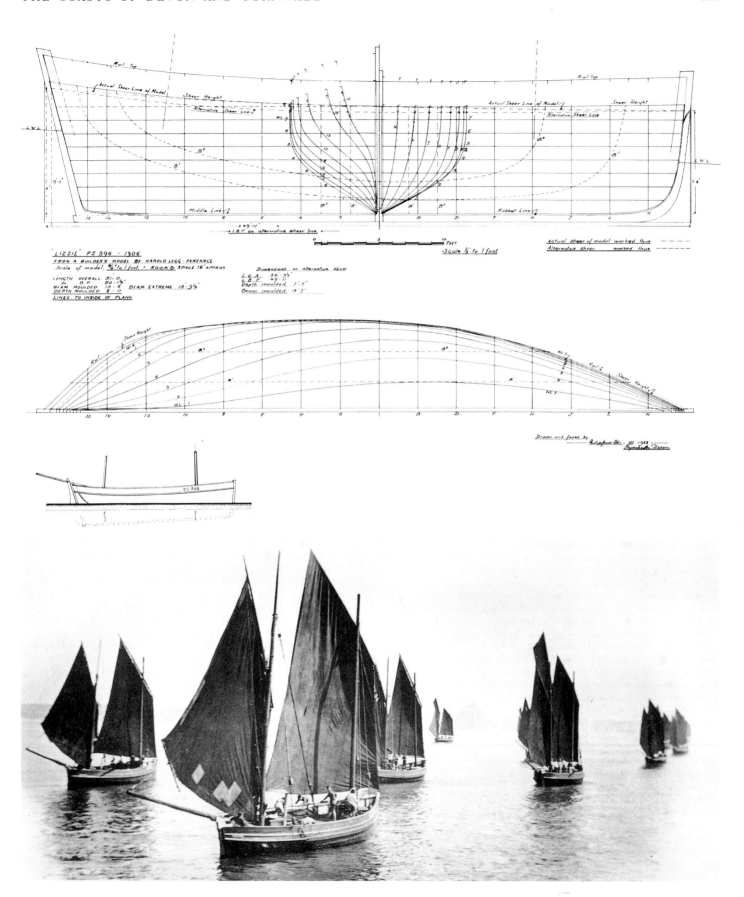

"LIZZIE" PZ 596 — 1906
FROM A BUILDER'S MODEL BY HAROLD LEGG-PENZANCE
Scale of model, ¾" to 1 foot. ~ ROOM & SPACE 18" APPROX

LENGTH OVERALL 51-0
    do   B P   50-1½
BEAM MOULDED 13-6   BEAM EXTREME 13-9½
DEPTH MOULDED 8-0
LINES TO INSIDE OF PLANK

Dimensions in alternative sheer
L O A   50-9½
L B P   49-11
Depth moulded 7-7
Beam moulded 13-7

Actual sheer of model marked thus
Alternative sheer   marked thus

Scale ½ to 1 foot

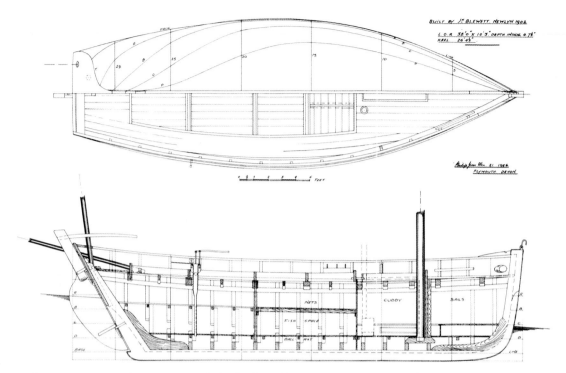

BUILT BY J.^S BLEWETT, NEWLYN 1902
L.O.R 52'0" X 10'3" DEPTH INSIDE 4 7/8"
KEEL 26'05"

officers continued to register them as such for some time. The last new three masted Mount's Bay lugger to be registered being the *Charles Pearce*, on 1 July 1848.

Fully decked boats appeared from 1848, but large numbers of half decked boats remained in use well into the 1870s. The *Gleaner* PE187/163PZ, a model of which exists in Penlee House Museum, was such a boat. Built before 1851 she was broken up in 1871.

From the 1860s the Mount's Bay boats featured increasingly deeper 'V' shaped hulls than their St Ives counterparts, with considerably less bilge, requiring legs to keep them upright when taking the ground. Mostly double ended boats, or 'double-bowed' as they were known locally, they were described as 'round-sterned' in the Custom House registers. Claims that the west Cornwall boats were double-ended to fit more effectively in the small harbours is untrue. The traditional shape of their hulls was set while they were still beach boats. They were not exclusively double ended however. Following construction of Jas Wills' renowned *Colleen Bawn* PE104/PZ12 in 1867, a number of elliptical and counter sterned boats were built in Mount's Bay and at St Ives. All very fine underwater aft, skillful 'tucks' in the planking flared the hull above the waterline, thus increasing the deck space and giving additional buoyancy for the hull to lift to a following sea.

Ranging from 40ft to 50ft long on the keel, 45ft to 55ft overall, between 12ft and 15ft in the beam, and 6ft to 7ft deep under the deck aft, they registered from 14 to 25 tons. In sailing trim these boats drew about 4ft to 5ft forward, and from 7ft to 8ft aft. Permanent ballast, iron and cement, was stowed under the warp and fish room, near the centre of the boat; shifting ballast, half-hundred weights, was stowed in the wings on either side of the warp.

Their stout fore and mizzen masts were stepped about 10ft or 11ft in from the ends. The foremast measured about 40ft from deck to truck, reducing from 11in to 6in diameter. This mast was part lowered when fishing, considerably easing their motion when riding to the nets. The taller, permanently stepped mizzen mast, rose about 38ft from deck to hounds, 48ft to 50ft to the tip of the 'mizzen-pole'. The mizzen boom, or outrigger, ran out through a raised chock on the port quarter, where it was clamped. About 30ft long, two-thirds of its length was rigged outboard. Its inboard heel was squared, and secured to the deck. It was sometimes rigged parallel to the centreline, but was more often set at an angle so that the outboard end canted inwards, to pick up the centreline of the boat.

All plain sail consisted of a large dipping lug foresail, a smaller standing lug mizzen, and a mizzen topsail. These boats usually reduced their sail area by changing down to smaller sails as re-

quired. Each boat carried several different size lug sails, permanently bent to yards for this purpose: the foresail; big mizzen; second mizzen; small mizzen, jigger or a triangular storm sail.

The foresail was set to leeward of the mast, with both the fore burdon (burton) and the fore halyard rigged to windward to support the mast. The tack was taken to the 'scud hook', usually set in the stem head, but occasionally in the form of a short bumpkin carried out beyond the stem head. For passage making, when long boards (tacks) were expected, two additional sails might be set. A fore-reaching foresail was set flying to a lash-up bowsprit, and a staysail to the mizzen jump stay.

The mizzen topsails, originally continuing the line of the luff and leech of the mizzen, were elongated to set even higher when the Mount's Bay boats adopted higher peaked sails in the late 1870s. This extended their clews well beyond the peak of the mizzen, and the foot near the clew had to be stiffened by a 'jinny-boom'.

Working away from home the boats carried a punt on deck, on the starboard side during the passage.

Transom sterns, which were the norm in the east Cornish ports, were also common at Porthleven, west of the Lizard. These spread with the introduction of motors, giving more working room on deck and, in the cabin below, a triple berth against the transom.

Above: Lines plans and constructional details of the Mount's Bay pilchard driver *Veracity* PZ111, built in 1902. Note the broad waterways, hatches and well. Although a sailing boat the mizzen has been stepped right aft to make way for an engine, and this became a feature after the turn of the century. In earlier times the mizzen mast would have been stepped forward of the tiller. The raking transom appeared on Porthleven-built boats from around 1900 and quickly found favour, offering more deck space and stowage under. *(NMM, Oke, Coastal Craft Collection)*

The cost of a Mount's Bay mackerel driver was usually quoted as between £240 and £300, fully equipped for sea with nets and gear. Harvey & Co, of Hayle, built a number of luggers in the 1860s. Amongst them was the *Excelsior* 67PZ for John Humphrys of Mousehole. The contract, agreed on the 4 January 1861, specified – '40 feet Keel; 12 feet 6 inches Beam; 6 feet 8 inches Deep: Outside planking and frames all English Oak – finished inside in usual manner – 1 fore mast – 1 mizen mast – 1 outrigger. Together with all fixed bolts – 1 wood pump and shaft – Keel-iron fore and aft – Handed over in May for £125.' She was delivered on 28 May 1861, when there was an additional £2 charged for '. . . sundry alterations and copper fastenings'. Nets and sails would have cost about as much again as the boat.

Transom sterned pilchard drivers putting out from Porthleven for the fishing grounds; *Advance* PZ60, *Grace Darling* PZ345 and *Boy Warry* PZ363. *(Tony Pawlyn Collection)*

A boat load of pilchards on a 'half-'n-halfer' at Pothleven. Note the cabin companion aft and the double flywheel hand capstan mounted on the main beam for working mackerel nets. Amongst the 'jaffle' of gear strewn around the decks are a water anker, leather thigh boots permanently set at the knees, a coil of hawser laid rope, a raft of sails, spars in irons, and numerous half-hundreds on the port side aft – ballast brought up from the wings to trim the full load of fish. *(Tony Pawlyn Collection)*

Two of the last big luggers built at Newlyn by H N Peake were *Breadwinner* PZ238 (56.1ft x 15.6ft x 7ft – 39 tons) in 1903 at a cost of £272, and *Our Lizzie* PZ109 (54.2ft x 15ft x 7ft – 37.47 tons) in 1905, costing £235.12.6., after allowing for old materials which were worked up. *Breadwinner* was sold to Arklow in 1914, and the *Our Lizzie* was broken up in 1930 after having been badly damaged in a collision.

PILCHARD DRIVER

Fine, little seaworthy craft, employed in the drift pilchard fishery in Mount's Bay from July to December, they were rarely at sea for more than ten or twelve hours at a time. A little bigger, and finer lined, than the crabbers, they ranged from 20ft open boats to 30ft half decked boats. These latter were fore decked with a cuddy under, and hatched aft with waterways and a short stern deck. In many respects smaller versions of the 1860s mackerel drivers, they measured from 3 to 5 tons and from 1900 they were increasingly transom sterned. Setting a fore and mizzen lug sail plan, they were crewed by two or three men, and/or a boy. The practice of stepping the mizzen mast right aft, as in a yawl, did not occur until after the introduction of engines, the first being installed in the *Aliza Craig* PZ157 in 1910. This opened the sail plan, leaving a 6ft gap between the leech of the fore lug and the luff of the mizzen. To balance the rig the new mizzens were made much smaller than previously.

In the days of sail, an intermediate class of luggers spanned the gap between the mackerel and pilchard drivers – 'half-'n-halfers'. Of between 30ft and 40ft long, and measuring 10 or 12 tons, they were half decked boats capable of working fleets of pilchard, herring, or mackerel drift nets. These worked the local fishing grounds, lacking the accommodation for fishing away from home. With the introduction of marine engines, these intermediate hulls were decked over, to become the motor pilchard drivers and long liners of the interwar years.

Penzance fishing boats fell within the main groups of Mount's Bay luggers – they were not a class in their own right. This widespread misconception arose from Penzance being the Custom House Port for Mount's Bay – the Port of Registry. Thus all fishing vessels working from the harbours, porths and coves, within the Port limits of the Lizard to Cape Cornwall, were required to register at Penzance. Hence the distinctive fishing marks *PE* from about 1843 to 1869, and *PZ* ever since.

This fiction was aggravated by the fact that the Mount's Bay types noted in the Washington Report were recorded under 'Penzance or Mount's Bay'; and compounded by Dixon Kemp, in immortalising the Newlyn lugger *Colleen Bawn* as a Penzance lugger.

Over the years there were many different builders of Mount's Bay luggers, associated with each of the harbours, including at:

Newlyn: James R Wills (1867-71)*; Richard Warren (1871-77); William

Warren (1877-85); J & T Blewett (1877-1902); Joe Peake (1897-1930s); Henry Peake (1897-1903), (Tolcarne) Triggs Bros (c1915).

Mousehole: J Warren, (1871); William Williams (1871-1902).

Porthleven: Richard Kitto/Kitto & Sons (1864-1904+); John Bowden/ Bowden Bros (1877-1905); Pascoes, (1905); Symons (1930s), and the Gilberts and Olivers in later years.

Hayle: Harvey & Co (1860-1870).

Penzance: Martin Mathews, Penzance Dry Dock (1836-77); Robert Corker Symons, (1836-52); Joseph Watty, and Harold Legg (1878-1910); Edwin Semmens (1878-85); Samuel Richards (1877).

Samuel Richards, after building three boats at Penzance for Lowestoft owners in 1877, moved to Kirkley Hill, Lowestoft, where he built the first of a long line, the *Nil Desperandum*, in 1879. He soon moved on to build some of the earliest steam drifters, and many others followed.

Mathews, and Symons, were modest ship builders and ship repairers rather than boatbuilders, but Richard Kitto of Porthleven, destined to become one of

the finest and most productive of the Mount's Bay boatbuilders, was apprenticed to Symons, just prior to 1850.

The dates refer to the first and last recorded boat built by the particular firm.

Sources
Many notes and queries on these craft have appeared in *The Mariner's Mirror*, over the years, and the early history of the west Cornwall luggers was covered by R Morton Nance in Vol 30 (1944). They are covered extensively in Edgar March's *Sailing Drifters*, with further detail in A S Oliver's *Boats and Boatbuilding in West Cornwall* (Truro 1971), and Keith Harris's *Hevva*.

___

PENZANCE PLEASURE BOAT

Light, clinker built, open sailing boats, with lute sterns, used in carrying summer visitors on pleasure trips in Mount's Bay, they are recorded in photographs taken between 1870 and World War I. These boats not previously having been noted, there are no accounts of their construction. They were sharp hulled and straight keeled, with an angular forefoot and a modest

drag aft, a fair entry and fine run, and their rise of floor was sufficient to necessitate legs to keep them upright when aground. They measured from 15ft to 20ft long, perhaps 6ft to 7ft in the beam, and 3ft to 4ft deep in the hull. In the photographs, the smaller ones were rigged as cutter or sloops, and the larger as yawls, or even ketches. At least two of the ketches have a pronounced sheer, with slightly flared bows.

A singular feature of these boats is a form of roller reefing on the fore staysail (attached to stemhead stay). The earliest known account of any such mechanism was described by Dixon Kemp, under *The Bembridge Rig* in 1891, as having been devised by Captain Ernest Du Boulay. However, photographs of them at Penzance having been dated at 1880, at the latest, these clearly predates this. This is not to claim the first usage of such a device, only to illustrate an early adaption.

These boats were probably built by Joseph Watty Legg, whose boatbuilding loft – demolished in the 1920s – was behind the Penzance Dry Dock

Several Penzance pleasure boats taking the ground on a falling tide sometime in the 1870s. The time exposure has washed out the ripples on the water. These craft have furling headsails which was most unusual for that date. In the background are the local mineral schooners, lying alongside the Albert Pier. *(Tony Pawlyn Collection)*

which appears in one of the photographs. He and his son Harold operated similar pleasure boats up to World War I, for the visitors to enjoy a 'penn'orth of sea'.

CORNISH PILOT GIGS

The Cornish six-oared gig in its working days was a fast, narrow, lightly built, rowing boat used for general services, pilotage, hovelling, for salvage work and life saving, as an inter-island work boat, and, in some areas, as a fishing boat, on the coasts of Cornwall and the Scillies. A length/beam ratio of 6.5:1 was not uncommon and a typical gig was 30ft long and about 5ft in the beam. Recently built gigs, many based on the crack gig *Treffry* built in 1838 and still raced at Newquay in the

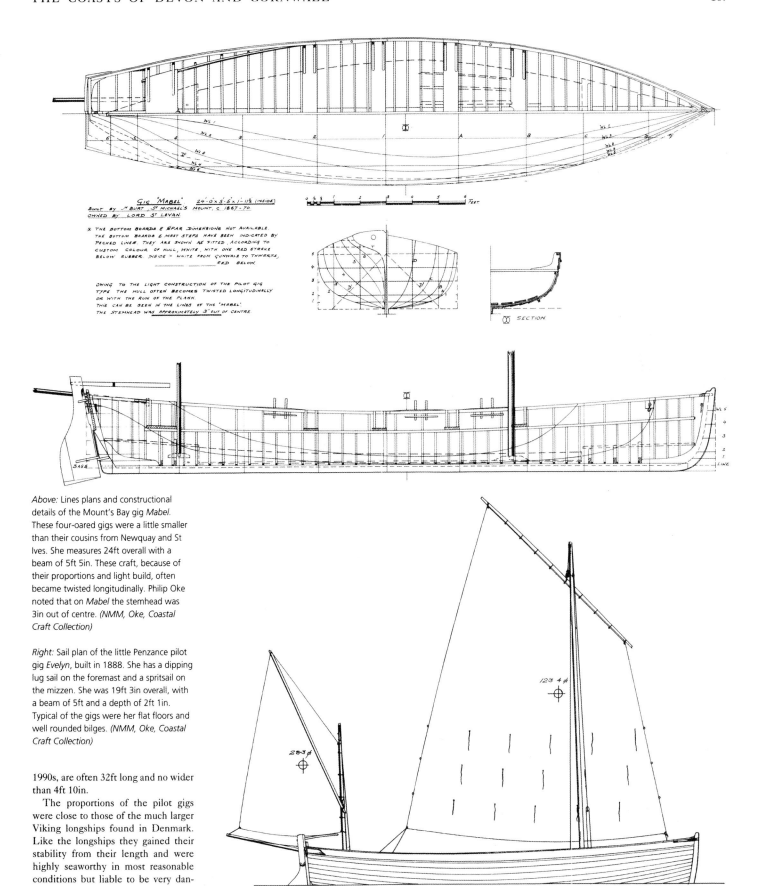

Above: Lines plans and constructional
details of the Mount's Bay gig *Mabel*.
These four-oared gigs were a little smaller
than their cousins from Newquay and St
Ives. She measures 24ft overall with a
beam of 5ft 5in. These craft, because of
their proportions and light build, often
became twisted longitudinally. Philip Oke
noted that on *Mabel* the stemhead was
3in out of centre. *(NMM, Oke, Coastal
Craft Collection)*

Right: Sail plan of the little Penzance pilot
gig *Evelyn*, built in 1888. She has a dipping
lug sail on the foremast and a spritsail on
the mizzen. She was 19ft 3in overall, with
a beam of 5ft and a depth of 2ft 1in.
Typical of the gigs were her flat floors and
well rounded bilges. *(NMM, Oke, Coastal
Craft Collection)*

1990s, are often 32ft long and no wider
than 4ft 10in.
  The proportions of the pilot gigs
were close to those of the much larger
Viking longships found in Denmark.
Like the longships they gained their
stability from their length and were
highly seaworthy in most reasonable
conditions but liable to be very dan-

A Mount's Bay pilot gig leaving Newlyn in about 1923. Each mast is rigged with a standing lug sail; a boy pulls with an oar to help them clear the harbour. *(NMM, Oliver Hill Collection, neg no P74889)*

gerous in water rough enough to bring their rudders out of the water. Working gigs, when on passage in favourable conditions, carried a small dipping lug mainsail with a jib headed mizzen. There were variations on this sail plan. Gigs were limited to three pairs of oars by government decree, against smuggling. The customs cutters could not catch eight-oared gigs upwind.

The gigs were clinker built with American elm or oak keels, planking ideally was of Cornish elm. I have a 14in piece of a strake removed from the *Newquay* (built in 1812 and the oldest gig still in commission in 1996) when she was repaired in 1955 and the pit sawn elm is an even and pretty exact ¼in thick, demonstrating great skill with the big pit saw. The fastenings are 3in apart, copper nails clenched over square roves roughly ⅜in sided. Scientific tests have shown the copper to be of Cornish origin. Frames were steamed and joggled. They were very lightly built, a finished gig weighing about 7cwt. Tholes were always used. These details varied with the place of build and the intended use of the gig.

Principal builders were Peters of St Mawes, Tiddy & Julyas in the Scillies, Tredwen of Padstow and Burt of St Michael's Mount. In the revival of gig building since 1970 the name of Ralph Bird of Devoran has been the most prominent.

Very little is known of the origins and ancestry of the Cornish six-oared gig. Richard Gillis tended to date them from the building of the first gig by the Peters family of St Mawes in 1790. This family became the most prominent gig builders for the next century. But the type of long, narrow, light, shallow, fast rowing boat for rough water occurs to this day in arctic Finland and Norway and historically with other north European types and is part of the broad boat culture of Europe. The Cornish gig probably goes back in history for many years, perhaps centuries.

The crews were men who lived on islands and the exposed western coast and were accustomed to hardship and exposure to the weather and to a very low standard of living. They not only spent many hours at the oars in any reasonable weather but sometimes beached their boats overnight and slept underneath them.

Gigs operated from Fowey, Polruan, Falmouth, Truro, St Mawes, Porthallow, Coverack, Penzance, St Ives, Newquay, Padstow, Porthquinn, Port

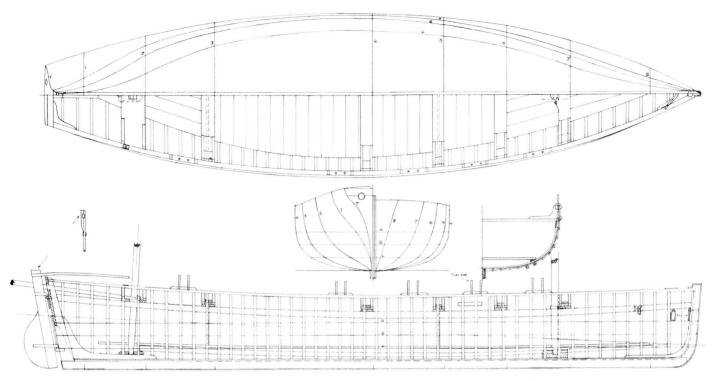

Isaac and Boscastle. Some were used for fishing. There was a Cornish-style gig used by the pilots at Appledore in north Devon. Generally similar in proportions, the gigs varied a great deal from place to place and builder to builder in size and in details of construction. Harris lists nearly 150 known gigs of the nineteenth and early twentieth centuries and there were certainly many more.

With the development of powered boats, the introduction of radio-communication into the pilot service, the rising standards of living and of expectations in the first half of the twentieth century the gigs virtually dropped out of use. By 1945 there were only half a dozen or so still working and an unknown number stowed away in various places ashore. Only at Newquay and in the Scilly Isles were gigs used. At the Newquay Rowing Club, under the vigorous leadership of the late Richard Gillis, there was a re-birth of the gig. The club purchased derelict gigs and repaired them, racing regularly and stirring such interest that the gigs have now acquired something of a cult status in western Cornwall. Many new ones have been built and Harris lists by name 130 built in the last thirty years, half of them in the 1990s. Around fifty now race each summer. This is a British working boat type now fully assimilated into leisure use.

Above: Lines plans and constructional details of a St Ives gig. The North Cornish gigs were generally larger than those on the south coast. This craft was 26ft 6 ½in overall, with a beam of 6ft 4in and a depth of 2ft 6in. *(NMM, Oke, Coastal Craft Collection)*

Right: These Newquay pilot gigs were photographed at Padstow in 1957. Stretchers for the rowers' feet are angled to give maximum leverage. These vessels are relatively deep below the small, high transoms and this gives them directional stability. *(NMM, Oliver Hill Collection, neg no P75433)*

Sources

The Cornish gigs are amongst the best documented British working boats. The research of Richard Gillis is conveniently summarised in his lecture to the Society for Nautical Research in 1969, published in *The Mariner's Mirror*, 55 (1969). March, in *Inshore Craft of Britain*, gives an account of the gigs which, though heavily dependent on Gillis, has some additional material. Keith Harris, *Azook!* (Redruth 1994) gives valuable construction detail and an A-Z list of the gigs past and present. A S Oliver, *Boats and Boatbuilding in West Cornwall* (Truro 1971) has useful information on the St Michael's Mount gigs.

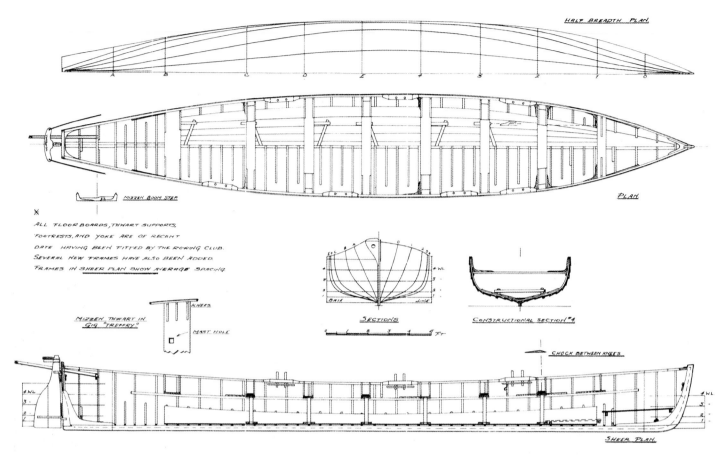

HALF BREADTH PLAN

MIZZEN BOOM STEP

PLAN

X

ALL FLOOR BOARDS, THWART SUPPORTS,
FOOTRESTS, AND YOKE ARE OF RECENT
DATE HAVING BEEN FITTED BY THE ROWING CLUB.
SEVERAL NEW FRAMES HAVE ALSO BEEN ADDED.
FRAMES IN SHEER PLAN SHOW AVERAGE SPACING.

KNEES

MIZZEN THWART IN
GIG "TREFFRY"

MAST HOLE

SECTIONS

CONSTRUCTIONAL SECTION #1

CHOCK BETWEEN KNEES

SHEER PLAN

Above: Lines plans and constructional details of the Newquay pilot gig *Newquay.* Built for pilotage work in 1812 at St Mawes, when George III was on the throne, and still used today for leisure rowing by the Newquay Rowing Club, she is probably the oldest wooden boat in regular use in the western world. She has never been refastened. She is 29ft 11in overall, with a beam of only 4ft 9in and a depth inside of 2ft. *(NMM, Oke, Coastal Craft Collection)*

Below: Newlyn bummers' gigs working off the beach in the harbour having landed the mackerel catch. The catch and stores were landed and loaded using one-horse dead-carts. The gigs are loading bags of ice, empty pads (fish baskets) and trunks and other stores for the waiting craft. (See page 172 for text.) *(Royal Institution of Cornwall)*

Above: These stout punts were photographed around 1885. The rough ground and the frayed rope ends mark their hard usage with little time for niceties. (See over for text.) *(Tony Pawlyn Collection)*

Below: Lines plans of a St Ives Punt, built by William Bryant for the *Jonadab* in 1910. Dicon Nance's drawing shows a lighter-built boat than that at Brixham (*qv*). The scantlings are lighter all round and the boat measures 13ft against 14ft 6in. The transom is narrower with a greater tuck underneath. (See over for text.) *(NMM, Coastal Craft Collection)*

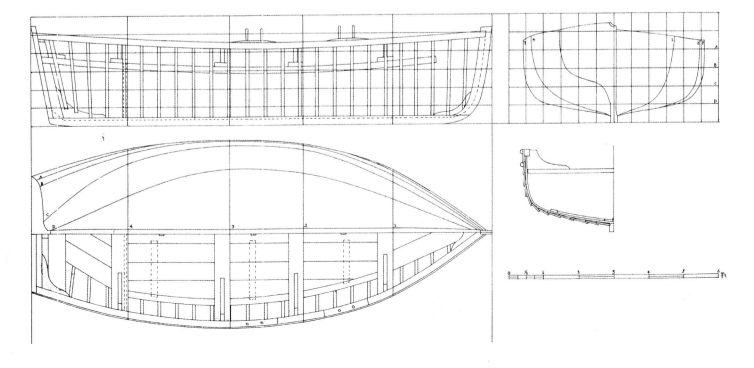

Out of season, coal barges are laid up at Newlyn, within the old quay. The enlarged portion gives a better view of them. Beamy, with little sheer, they were good coal carriers. *(Tony Pawlyn Collection)*

NEWLYN BUMMERS' GIG

Strong but light, clinker built rowing boats, of good carrying capacity. Employed in ferrying catches of mackerel from fishing boats at anchor off Newlyn, to the salesmen onshore. Very similar to the herring gigs of St Ives Bay (*qv*), and occasionally shipped there in that season, they were not normally used in fishing in Mount's Bay. From 20ft 25ft in length, they cost about 15s per foot to build.

These gigs serviced the needs of the visiting east coast drifters, and were at first operated by freelance crews, 'bummarees' after the Billingsgate middlemen – hence their name. After the completion of Newlyn Harbour in 1894 many were owned and operated by companies of salesmen. Fishermen were often contracted to salesmen whose gigs carried distinctive markings.

Their use gradually declined from 1905, the first year that the east coast steam drifters carried 'swing gaffs', landing derricks, on their foremasts, to swing their catches ashore directly onto the piers. Even so some continued in use up until World War I.

Sources
There has been no material published on these craft.

NEWLYN AND ST IVES PUNTS AND MOUSEHOLE JOLLY BOATS

The standard work boat – strong, but relatively light and clinker built – with full lines and good carrying capacity, was common all round the coast in one form or another. Here employed serving the fishing luggers, their size varied from 12ft to 16ft. The Mousehole jolly boats, descendants of the eighteenth-century 'yoles', being between a punt and a gig, were by the latter part of the nineteenth century about 18ft long. When the mackerel drivers fished away from home they were carried on deck. But in the home season they were left in the care of a lad or older fishermen who was paid a few shillings a week to tend her, and watch out for the lugger. Usually sculled over

the stern by a single oar, they could be pulled by up to four oars if required.

A number built by William Paynter at St Ives, about 1864-65, cost from £6 10s to £12. Over sixty years later H N Peake built one at Newlyn for £13 6s 3d, together with a pair of ash oars for 14s, and a pair of brass rowlocks for 3s 6d.

Sources
The ubiquitous small ships' boat, these are frequently mentioned in passing, but are rarely given space of their own. However, March quotes a good account of the Mousehole 'yawlers' and their jolly boats in *Sailing Drifters*.

NEWLYN COAL BARGE

Burdensome, heavy, carvel built, open boats, propelled by oars, used for carrying coal from the hulks to the visiting Lowestoft and Great Yarmouth steam drifters based at Newlyn during the mackerel season, from about 1905 to the early 1950s.

There are no known drawings or specifications for these boats, and the only surviving visual evidence of them lies in occasional glimpses of them in photographs of Newlyn Harbour. Size is difficult to estimate, as they were rarely the subject of the photographs.

However, from recent talks with Raymond Peake (ex-shipwright and boatbuilder at Newlyn), it can be estimated that they were about 30ft long, 10ft to 12ft in the beam, and 5ft 6ins to 6ft deep, keel to gunwale. As a boy he recalls falling into an empty one and having great difficulty climbing out again. When loaded they could carry up to 10 tons of bagged steam coal, and drew perhaps 3ft to 4ft of water: when light they drew about 1ft or so.

Carvel built, and heavily constructed, they had full lines with a large flat bottom and hard chines with a broad transom stern. A heavy, iron capped rubbing strake, was set high on the hull, almost flush with the gunwale. Inside there were one or two transverse beams, heavily braced and, again, nearly level with the gunwale. A feature peculiar to these boats were the multiple sculling notches in their broad transoms, two or three depending on size. With no free space inboard when loaded, they were propelled by two or three men, standing on one of the transverse beams, or on the coal, and sculling over the stern. The oars were substantial ash spars, 20ft long, costing about 12s each in 1929.

It is thought these barges were peculiar to Newlyn, the home ports of Lowestoft and Great Yarmouth having more sophisticated coaling facilities. They were certainly not of a local form, and were the property of the coaling companies, such as Craske & Co, Bessey & Palmer, R R Bath, and the North Sea Coaling Co (Sherwood Hunter). Between the various companies there were probably twenty or so of these coal barges just after World War I. These were left at Newlyn out of season, when they were hauled up as near the high water mark as possible, only floating on a few tides each month. This kept them reasonably staunch, with a minimum of wear and tear.

Possibly the last of these was built at Newlyn by Theodore Peake, in about 1934. At that time there was also a smaller double ender, with a motor installed, possibly a double diagonal ex-ship's lifeboat, employed as a tow boat for these heavy barges.

Sources
Discussions with Raymond Peake of Newlyn in 1997. No material has been published on these craft.

St Ives Bay Luggers

MACKEREL DRIVER

Full bodied, carvel built, seaworthy fishing luggers, that evolved in the waters of the Western Approaches. Although close neighbours to Mount's Bay, and working in the same fisheries, these boats possessed different characteristics. The lines of William Paynter's St Ives Fishing Boat, submitted to the Washington inquiry, show that by the 1840s, they had a more advanced hull shape than those of Mount's Bay, with a sharper entry, finer run, and more upright stern. Further major improvement in hull form at St Ives was prevented by the harbour conditions: the very hard, shoaling, sandy bottom, and the all too frequent severe run of heavy ground seas. Because of this a full body with heavy bilge pieces prevailed here throughout the sailing era which allowed them to take the bottom safely, without falling over. Though many rigged legs, for taking the ground, these were liable to be ripped off in a ground sea. This fullness amidships lead to very hollow lines in the run, yet the St Ives boats sailed well. It also gave them greater burthen, so that size for size the St Ives boats registered a higher tonnage than those of Mount's Bay. The liability of bumping and boring was also reflected in the heavy, solid timber rubbing strakes built into them, as opposed to the fine, iron-capped bends usually found in Mount's Bay.

Although adopting a better hull form, the St Ives luggers did not progress to hatches and waterways at this time, continuing as open boats with a short forecastle deck. By this they retained their ability to set a three masted sail plan well into the 1860s. The last three masted mackerel driver registered at St Ives was the *James*, on 7 March 1866, with the first two masted one being the *Star of the West*, registered on 1 April 1867. This late rig development tended to keep their fore and mizzen masts nearer the ends of the boats, with a taller, short footed sail shape. On the adoption of two masted, fully decked boats, the mizzen mast was moved forward a little to balance the sail plan, but the mainmast remained proportionally closer to the bows. In later years, to sustain power as the luggers approached 50ft in length, they rigged even taller masts, retaining the tall, short footed, sail shape. St Ives boats were regarded as faster in light airs, but Mount's Bay boats could hold their sails in a stiffer wind.

As in Mount's Bay the double ended hull prevailed, but boats with counters and transoms were also built.

Harvey & Co built a number of mackerel drivers for St Ives owners, including four, 19.56-ton, iron boats in 1864. These cost £150 each, and lasted about 30 years. Paynter's draft of the *Boomerang*, 40ft on the keel, indicates that she sold for £140 complete on 11 December 1862.

PILCHARD DRIVER

Carvel built, as in Mount's Bay, the pilchard drivers were again smaller versions of the mackerel drivers. But,

at St Ives, their lines had an even closer similarity, because of the need for the full midships body form. Here, the pilchard drivers did not adopt the transom stern, with double ended pilchard drivers working well into the 1930s, being successfully converted to auxiliaries from about 1910 onwards.

At St Ives the pilchard drivers also doubled as herring boats, as both fish appeared in the late autumn and early winter. Takes of either were often made unexpectedly when fishing for the other kind. Open boats at first, they adopted full decks with large hatches in the 1890s. At times the boundaries between the mackerel drivers and the pilchard drivers were less clearly defined here than in the Mount's Bay, though the term 'half-n'-halfer' was not much used at St Ives. Boats of 30ft to 40ft, carrying small flywheel capstans for working mackerel nets with foot lines, were built in good numbers. Such a boat was the 36ft, 8-ton, *Barnabas* 634SS built in 1881 by

Lines plans of a St Ives mackerel driver, built by William Paynter, and drawn for the Washington Report, 1849. Double ended, at this time the St Ives mackerel drivers were less full bodied and deeper heeled than their Mount's Bay contemporaries, and had a finer run aft. However, with only a short forecastle deck, they were virtually open boats. The masts are relatively further in from the ends of the boats, but with much the same rake as the Mount's Bay vessels. As there, the pilchard drivers were smaller versions of the same. *(NMM, Coastal Craft Collection)*

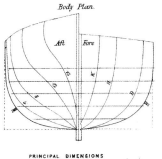

Body Plan.

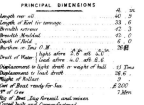

PRINCIPAL DIMENSIONS		ft	in
Length over all		40	9
Length of Keel for tonnage		33	6
Breadth extreme		12	3
Breadth Moulded		12	0
Depth of Hold		6	0
Burthen in Tons O.M.		26 44	
Draft of Water { light afore 2.6 aft 4.0 in			
{ load afore 4.0 aft 6.6			
Displacement to light draft or weight of hull		11 Tons	
Displacement to load draft		26.6	
Weight of Ballast		9	
Cost of Boat ready for Sea		£200	
N° of Crew		7 Men	
Rig of Boat. Lug foresail and mizen			
Carvel built and Copper-fastened			

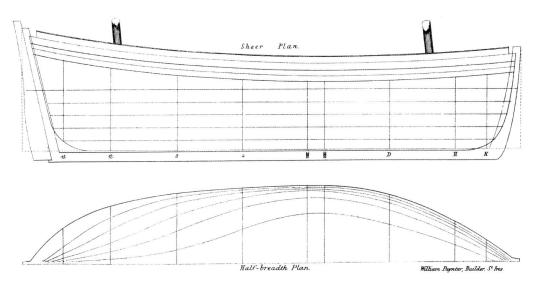

Sheer Plan.

Half-breadth Plan.   William Paynter, Builder, St Ives.

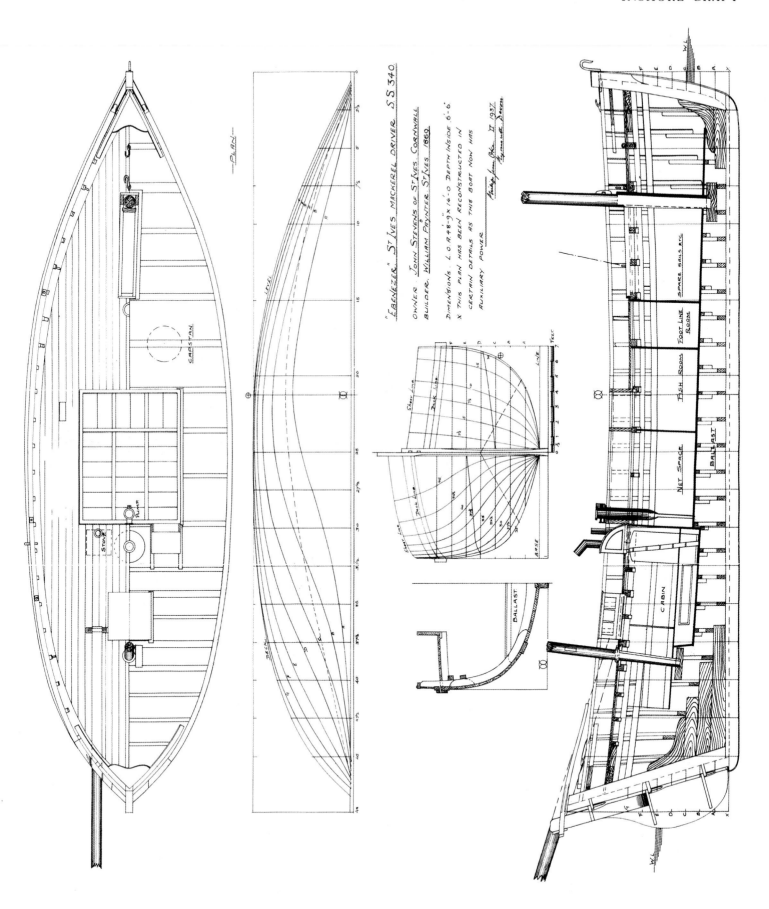

—PLAN—

CAPSTAN

PUMP

STOVE

"EBENEZER" ST IVES MACKEREL DRIVER SS 340
OWNER JOHN STEVENS OF ST IVES, CORNWALL
BUILDER. WILLIAM PAYNTER ST IVES 1869
DIMENSIONS. L.O.R 48-9 × 14-0 DEPTH INSIDE 6'-6
× THIS PLAN HAS BEEN RECONSTRUCTED IN
CERTAIN DETAILS AS THIS BOAT NOW HAS
AUXILIARY POWER

Philip Jones Oke. II 1937
Plymouth Devon

FEET

BALLAST

SPARE SAILS ETC
FOOT LINE ROOM
FISH ROOM
NET SPACE
BALLAST
CABIN

Page opposite and right: Lines plans, constructional details and sail plan of the fine mackerel driver *Ebenezer* SS340, built in 1869. She shows a modest rise of floors while retaining full round bilges. When she was drawn by Oke in 1937 her rudder had been modified for use with motors – the original would have been taller. The sail plan shows her rig at about the 1890s. The original foremast would have been stepped a couple of feet further aft and she would have set a squarer headed dipping lug. Note the heavy, timber rubbing strake with four scuppers cut through which were a constant source of rot. *(NMM, Oke, Coastal Craft Collection)*

Below: The lines plans of the St Ives pilchard driver *Godrevy* SS92. Although she was built at Porthleven the hull form is strictly St Ives; the rubbing strakes with twin, half round capping irons reflect Mount's Bay practice. These irons were usually omitted at St Ives where they ripped off so easily. The preferred solution was wood on wood. *(NMM, Oke, Coastal Craft Collection)*

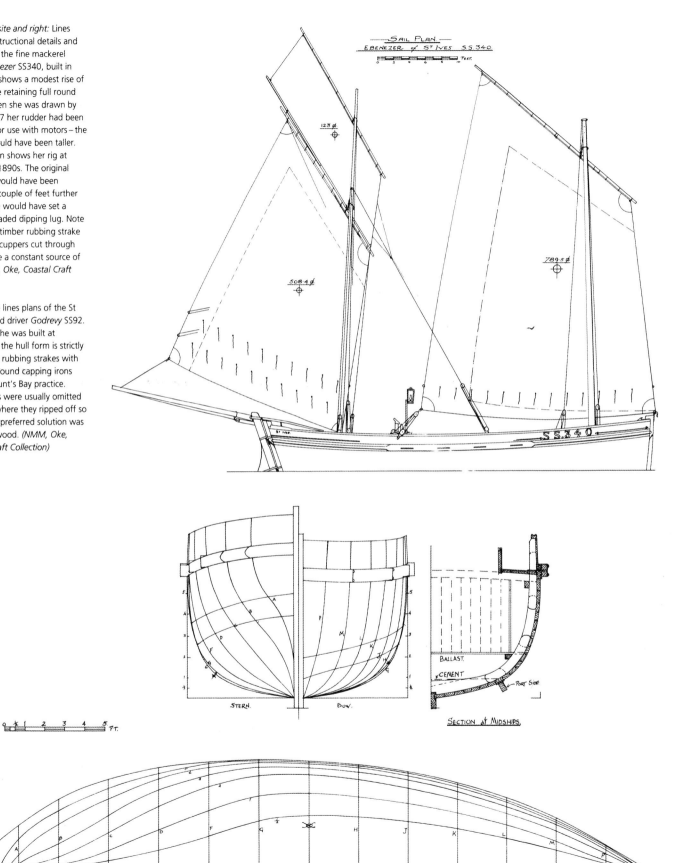

Henry Trevorrow, and still afloat and cared for by the Cornish Maritime Trust. These boats sometimes went to Ireland, but rarely to the Isle of Man or beyond. Many of these intermediate luggers did not set mizzen topsails, and neither did the pilchard drivers.

A Paynter's draft for a pilchard driver gives, 'Length of Keel 30ft. Breadth Mould 10ft. Depth Amid 6ft. do. Fore 6ft. 6ins. do. Aft 7ft. 7ins. Room & Space 16ins. . . .' Price £50, or £1 16s 8d per foot.

Amongst the many boat builders at St Ives were: Francis Adams (1812); William Paynter (1840); Robert Bryant (1862-82); Tonkin (1862); Thomas Hambly (1862-82); William R Williams (1862-1902); Arthur Rosewall (1878); William Bryant (1879-85); Henry

Right: The St Ives pilchard driver SS62 (not traced) working out of Newlyn under sail in 1920. Having had an engine installed she is rigged with a cut down mizzen and outrigger, and the mizzen mast has been stepped fore side of the engine. In the light wind the fore lug sail has been allowed to draw against the unstayed mast, but she will soon go about on the other tack once she has cleared the pier head. She is decked as far aft as the engine and there is a small hatch into the fish room. She has relatively high bulwarks. *(NMM, Oliver Hill Collection, neg no P75432)*

Below: A copy of William Paynter's draft, not re-drawn, showing the St Ives jumbo, built for 'John Uren & others'. *(NMM, Oke, Coastal Craft Collection)*

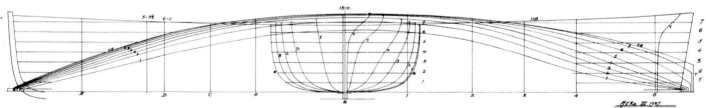

26 FOOT GIG BY WM PAYNTER ST IVES.
SCALE 1 INCH TO 1 FOOT

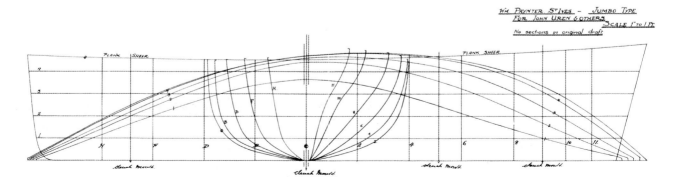

WM PAYNTER ST IVES – JUMBO TYPE
FOR JOHN UREN & OTHERS
SCALE 1" TO 1 FT
No sections in original draft

Trevorrow (1882-1902); William Paynter (1860-76 & 1883-1902); N Congdon: John Tregarthen Short (1878); J R Cothey; and Thomas Thomas.

Sources
See 'Sources' for Mount's Bay luggers.

The dates refer to the first and last recorded boat built by the particular boatbuilder or firm.

ST IVES JUMBO

The jumbo was a light, one-man, sailing and pulling fishing boat, exclusive to St Ives. A draught of those built by William Paynter, for 'John Uren & others', depicts a double ended, clinker built boat. The boat shown is similar to the local herring gigs but deeper and fuller. In typical Westcountry fashion, they had a straight stem, distinct drag aft to grip the water, and a raking sternpost. The lines show a clean

Herring gigs, schooners and pilchard drivers in St Ives Harbour, where the white hulls of the gigs stand out in strong contrast to the other vessels. *(Tony Pawlyn Collection)*

wedge entry, full midships body, with a hollow run aft. About 22ft on the keel (6in by 3in timber), 25ft overall, 7ft 9in beam amidships (maximum beam 8ft just 1ft abaft the midships station), depth forward 4ft 2in, amidships 3ft 9in, and aft 4ft 7in. Afloat they drew about 18in of water forward and 27in aft, when ready for sea; with a catch of fish on board, this could perhaps be 30in aft. Paynter's draught also indicates the positions of the four 'clench moulds' used in construction.

A painting of one sailing shows a single mast, rigged with a standing lug main, and fore staysail. Essentially 'old men's' boats, and fair weather craft, they probably worked a few pieces of herring or pilchard drift nets or hand lines.

Sources
Briefly mentioned in A S Oliver's *Boats and Boatbuilding in West Cornwall*, these craft have not otherwise been previously noted.

ST IVES HERRING GIG

Herring gigs were most common at St Ives, but were also worked out of Newquay in the late summer season.

Very similar to the bummers' gigs (*qv*) at Newlyn, they could set sails – a dipping lug foresail and gaff mizzen – but were usually worked under oars. Typically about 26ft long, 6ft 3in beam, and 2ft 6in deep inside. Clinker built, and fairly fine lined, they had more body than pilot gigs of the same length. One or two strakes deeper in build, they carried more drag aft for sailing, drawing about 1ft of water forward, and 2ft aft.

With a crew of four, in working to and from the grounds three pulled conventionally, while the man at the tiller pushed on a fourth oar. A 6ft space, abaft the beam, was left clear for the nets, with a 3ft space forward of this for the fish. These spaces were partitioned by light bulkheads up to thwart level.

Working the inshore grounds in the late summer and autumn herring fishery, they carried ten or so pieces of herring drift nets. Each piece 60yds long, as made, drawn in 40yds when secured to their light head lines and corks; of 29 to 32 meshes per yard, and 18 score meshes deep they extended for about 400yds when fishing.

Sources
Briefly mentioned in A S Oliver's, *Boats and Boatbuilding in West Cornwall*, these craft are usually ignored because of the higher profile of the six-oared pilot gigs.

CLOVELLY LONG BOOMER

Heavy, carvel built, decked, smacks, which worked the strong tidal waters of the upper Bristol Channel. Features of the earlier sloops were a curving stem with a broad cutaway forefoot, and a tapering narrow gutted stern, with a pronounced tumblehome aft, producing a heart shaped transom, as in the *Teazer* 218 BD. Similar features were to be found in the Galway hookers, evidence of the strong maritime links between north Devon and Ireland. Later cutters adopted a straight stem and square forefoot, with a fuller deck line aft, and broader transom. Edgar Marsh mistakenly placed the chronological change in hull styles the other way round.

Called 'long boomers' because of the length by which their booms overhung their sterns, they ran up to about 30ft in length. They were mostly 2nd

Clovelly in the 1890s. This wonderfully
atmospheric photograph features a
number of pleasure craft in the
foreground, but to the left of the central
tier lie three Clovelly long boomers. The
long booms are not that evident from this
angle, but the heads of the trawl beams
can be seen and the two outer boats have
their trawls hauled to the masthead to dry.
Pulled up on the beach behind are a
number of picarooners, distinguished by
their heart-shaped transoms and the
distinct tumblehome of the top strake.
(NMM, neg no G2519)

class fishing boats of less than 15 tons,
registered at the Port of Bideford.

An unusual feature for British trawlers was their habit of working their
beam trawls over the starboard side,
the drift fishermen's practice.

Sources
Just mentioned in Marsh's *Inshore Craft of
Britain*, little has been written about these
craft.

THE CLOVELLY
PICAROONER

A small, smooth planked boat rigged
with two lugs used in some numbers in
the herring fishery from Clovelly in
north Devon.

Holdsworth, writing in the early
1870s, records that 'Drift fishing is carried on by the inhabitants of the romantic little village of Clovelly but the
herring fishery has for many years
been subject to great fluctuation. Long
lines or spillers are in general use along
this part of the coast'. He shows
Bideford (including Clovelly) as having more boats than anywhere east of
St Ives on the south coast of the Bristol
Channel and, after the 1880s, a substantial number of these must have
been picarooners.

The picarooner was usually about
13ft in length with a deep heel and
wide waterways surrounding a small
well for fisherman. A model in the
Science Museum of the *Rattling Jack*,
built in 1886 at Clovelly of local oak,
shows a bigger boat measuring 19.2ft x
7ft x 5.4ft. She was rigged with a dipping lug forward and a standing lug on
the small mizzen. As with the Beer luggers (*qv*) the tack of the main was
secured to a hook at the end of a small
iron bumpkin projecting from the stem.

Clovelly herrings were a staple food
for the poorer people of Appledore and
the adjacent coasts in the nineteenth
and early twentieth centuries. These
high protein fish could be purchased
for one penny each.

A Clovelly picarooner photographed in 1934. She has the standard two masted lugger rig with bumkin and outrigger. Shallower than the older local boats, and able to enter the harbour earlier on the tide to dispose of their catch, they were dubbed picarooners, derived from a Spanish word meaning 'searobber'. *(NMM, Oliver Hill Collection, neg no P74110)*

Sources
Holdsworth, *Deep-Sea Fishing and Fishing Boats* (London 1874) and White's *British Fishing-Boats and Coastal Craft.* Vernon Boyle, *Devon Harbours* (London 1952) mentions the derivation of the name.

THE BARGES OF THE TAW AND THE TORRIDGE

Small smack rigged sailing barges used in lightering cargoes, mainly timber, from deep-sea vessels anchored in Appledore Pool to Bideford and Barnstaple. They also carried clay from Fremington Pill to the then thriving potteries of Bideford and Barnstaple, and general cargoes on the two rivers. In the twentieth century barges fitted with hot bulb semi-diesel engines continued to be employed until as late as the 1960s in the business of extracting gravel from the river beds for transhipment into ketches which carried it to south Wales and Bristol for use in dock and other construction work.

These barges were broad-beamed with a hard turn of bilge and flat bottomed. Because of local conditions they depended on sail more than did some of their contemporaries on the south coast. They had a good run aft and less full waterlines forward. Latterly, as the gravel trade became their principal employment they were increasingly massively built. This trade required them to take the ground on the gravel ridges during the ebb. They were then filled, with perhaps as much as 30 tons of gravel, shovelled up from the ridges by the crew of two and thrown up and into the barge. This was killing work for the men and the subsequent banging on the ridges and floating off of the fully-laden barge imposed great stresses on her fabric.

This photograph of Appledore sand barges gives a good impression of their shape. The flat bottom and the hard turn to the bilge are quite clear. Having loaded with gravel, these three barges are waiting for the returning tide to float them off. Note that the gravel is piled high on the decks. The peaks of the mainsails have been lowered while loading but will easily be hoisted with the billy tackle, clearly visible on the vessel in the foreground. *(NMM, neg no P38252)*

This photograph of a north Devon salmon boat gives a good impression of the layout and shows the space in the stern for the seine net. Note the salmon lying on the bottom boards. Similar boats are still in use on the Tamar and Teign. *(North Devon Maritime Museum)*

decade and the Appledore shipyards were developed into some of the most modern and efficient in Europe.

Sources
There is a very good account of the north Devon barges in Grant and Hughes, *North Devon Barges* (Appledore 1975).

NORTH DEVON SALMON BOAT

These were sturdy, clinker built rowing boats used for salmon netting.

Barnstaple and Braunton boats fished the lower Taw, and Bideford boats the lower Torridge. These river boats were up to 22ft long, some having rockered keels to help them slew in restricted waters. Some Barnstaple boats had a mast with a lug sail to help them reach the fishing grounds, but from the 1950s Seagull outboard engines were increasingly used by all boats for this purpose. Appledore boats, used in the estuary of the two rivers, were around 18ft by 5ft by 2ft deep, with four thwarts.

The boatbuilder first set up the backbone (oak or elm keel, oak stem and sternpost etc), fitted the oak or elm transom, then planked the boat with ½in larch, at least eleven strakes a side. The lowest three were steamed, as were the oak or larch timbers, fitted at 6in centres. The boat was riveted out, then tied with gunwales, risings, bends, thwarts and knees, all of oak. From the 1880s until 1970 these boats were built by P B Waters & Sons and J Hinks & Sons, both of Appledore, and M W Blackmore of Bideford.

Seine nets, up to 200 yards long and 8 yards deep, of hemp, or manilla and cotton, had lead weighted footropes, and were very heavy when wet. A crew shot their net five or six times in the two-hour low-water period, two rowing out in a semi-circle, leaving a shoreman holding one end, while the fourth man paid the net out, jumping out with the 'boat end' as the boat grounded. The 'shore end' was brought up, and all pulled in the net, a 15 minute job, with or without a catch.

Nets of synthetic fibre, needing fewer men to work them, changed boat design after 1970. Several 14ft wooden boats were built, then 12ft and 14ft GRP boats, made by H Ford & Sons of Appledore. Today, with fine nylon nets, there is no need for specially designed salmon boats.

Sources
Alison Grant and P B Waters (eds), *Salmon-Netting in North Devon* (Appledore 1997) is based on information from boatbuilders and fishermen, notes and sketches from the V C Boyle Collection held in the North Devon Maritime Museum, and local newspapers and other archival material held in North Devon Record Office.

Henry Williamson, *Salar the Salmon* (London 1935) is set in north Devon and the author, who knew local fishermen well, describes salmon netting in evocative detail.

Locally built barges lasted for many years in this business, but a few Tamar barges, such as the *Secret*, the *Princess May* and the *Mary* from the Fal, brought round when the gravel trade was booming, were soon sold again.

Taw and Torridge barges were otherwise all locally built of local timbers in half a dozen yards at Appledore itself, at Bideford East-the-Water, and at Cleave Houses. As long as the yard at P K Harris & Sons survived at Appledore in its old form as the maintenance base of the local fleet of ketches and schooners the barges could be maintained there. In the 1950s there were still a dozen of them or so working but, like the local coasters, they melted away in the next

This remarkable photograph of the polacca brigantine *Peter and Sarah* was taken sometime in the 1850s. It gives a very good impression of the type's characteristic features. The pole mast forward set a course and a deep topsail, while a gaff mainsail and gaff topsail were set on the mainmast. With her flat floors she sits upright when aground and her very full sections are clearly seen. *(Basil Greenhill Collection)*

BIDEFORD POLACCA BRIGANTINE
(homophradite brig, Muffie, Polacca)

A small merchant sailing vessel rigged with a pole foremast carrying two yards and no gaff sail, a rig occurring in Britain almost solely in north Devon. Employed principally in the trades of the western part of the Bristol Channel, most often with limestone and coal from south Wales to the north Devon and north Cornish coasts, some polaccas were also employed in the general coasting trade and some sailed to the Iberian peninsula and the Mediterranean and to and from Prince Edward Island in eastern Canada, an area with which Bideford had close trading connections in the nineteenth century and where some of the polaccas were built.

Documentary and iconographic evidence both suggest that the polacca rig was already in use in north Devon in the late eighteenth century. The evolution of the hull form appears generally to have followed that of small merchant sailing vessels in the first three-quarters of the nineteenth century. Early vessels were of very full hull form, apple bowed with little rise of floor like the *Peter and Sarah*, built in 1809, illustrated here. The last polaccas of the 1860s like the *Two Sisters*, still afloat as a ketch in 1950, were much sharper.

The rig comprised a forecourse and a deep single topsail, staysails between the masts and an orthodox gaff mainsail and gaff topsail. This was a handy and economical rig for a small full-hulled vessel with few pretensions to windward ability. Oral traditions still extant in the 1930s indicated also that this simple square rig was particularly suited to conditions met when entering and leaving the difficult Bideford river. When they mis-stayed in going in or out of this dangerous channel (and the old full-hulled vessels often did mis-stay), they could in a few minutes be made to go astern and thus the crew regained control of the vessel which did not go aground. As long as the tide was carrying her out or in she did lose much ground while making the stern board.

Bideford polaccas were the smallest of British square-rigged merchant sailing vessels. The *Sarah* built at Bideford in 1831 measured 61.4ft x 19.1ft x 11ft; the *Nugget*, launched in Prince Edward Island in 1852, was just 68ft long; the *Newton*, built in 1788 on the Torridge and broken up at Appledore a century later, measured 53.4ft x

15.6ft x 8.8ft; while the *Joe Abraham* built in Prince Edward Island in 1850 was only 46ft long. Crews normally comprised three or four men.

Polaccas were conventionally constructed, fully skeleton built vessels usually of very heavy scantlings since many of their trades involved discharging coal or limestone on exposed beaches. Among their builders were Thomas Geen, Thomas Evans, William Clibbett, Richard Chapman and Thomas Waters on the Torridge, and James Yeo in Prince Edward Island. A few polaccas were built in Wales and one or two in Ilfracombe. Graham Farr identified thirty-three statutorily registered polaccas but there were probably a hundred or more in trade in the mid-nineteenth century, the balance registered as brigs, brigantines or schooners without specific use of the adjective 'pol' in the registers.

At least three early surviving contemporary paintings, of the *Sarah* referred to above, the *Henry*, built at Bideford in 1833, and the *Newton* show pole masted brigs. It is probable therefore that the polacca brigantine was, in fact, a normal economic development from the pole masted brig in the second half of the nineteenth century, some vessels, like the *Newton* herself, being converted from brig to brigantine rig to save a man, perhaps two, in the crew, and also to reduce maintenance costs. Pole masted vessels were common in the Baltic and Mediterranean in the early nineteenth century – polacca brigantines persisted, as Sir Alan Moore shows in *The Last Days of Mast and Sail*, in some numbers in the Levant until World War I. Bideford had trading connections with both the Baltic and the Mediterranean and influence could have come from either or both seas, or the rig could simply have developed locally independently.

It would be nice to think that, in these days of reconstructions and replicas, a polacca brigantine, say 45ft long, might be built to grace once more the small harbours of the southwest and perhaps even to sail to Prince Edward Island.

Sources
Numerous notes and articles on polaccas of all kinds have appeared in *The Mariner's Mirror*. The most important are Vernon Boyle, 18 (1932), Michael Bouquet, 49 (1963), Grahame Farr and Basil Greenhill, 47 (1961) and 51 (1965). See also Slade and Greenhill, *Westcountry Coasting Ketches* (London 1974) and Sir Alan Moore, *The Last Days of Mast and Sail* (Oxford 1925) for the Levantine polacca brigantines of the early twentieth century.

The boats of the Levels

A group of flat bottomed boats with no keels which between them present what Eric McKee described as 'an almost Darwinian progression of forms', used on the rivers and inundation areas of the Somerset levels, which lie immediately inland of the coast between Watchet and Clevedon. They were, in ascending order of sophistication of shape and construction, the turf boat, the withy boat, the parrett flatner and the watchet flattie and the Bridgwater barge. There were two other related types, the Weston-super-Mare flatner, and the Clevedon boat.

These boats, entirely products of their environment, were for local service in the shallows off the coast, on the heavily tidal rivers of this part of Somerset with their soft mud banks and on the man-made 'drains' and canals. The first three were simple to build and could be, and were, put together by any skilled carpenter. They might be thought of as a group of manifestations of the great European flat bottomed building tradition of boats for the shallows which was demonstrated in such widely diverse boat types as the Fleet trow (*qv*), the Gotland Flätaska, the Danish and German Kåg and Praam types, and, in the south of Europe, the boats of the shallow shore of the Gulf of Lions around Sète and, later, developed for

The photograph of this turf boat under construction was taken at Westhay, near Glastonbury, in 1970. The main features of their simple build – the bottom made of a single piece and the two plank clinker sides – are well demonstrated here. *(NMM, neg no B4454/23)*

A turf boat demonstrates her stability and her load bearing capacity. These simple craft were ideally suited for work when the levels flooded as they have here. *(Basil Greenhill Collection)*

other purposes, the Grand Banks dory. This tradition reached its high point perhaps in the Hanseatic cog. Graffiti clearly illustrating cogs large and small have been found in a medieval context at Crane Godrevy near Hayle on the north Cornish coast.

THE TURF BOAT

A double ended, flat bottomed boat with the bottom made from one piece of timber used for carrying cut turf, peat, from the peat beds of the levels down canals and streams to the points of sale. Poled or paddled they were also used as general farm transports especially in periods of inundation of the levels. 13ft or 17ft long and 2ft 4in to 4ft 8in in the beam, these boats had two strake clinker sides flared at 45 degrees and identical ends raked at the same angle. Widely used until the draining of the levels and the coming of motor transport, one or two examples are to be found in museums.

THE WITHY BOAT

Used, poled or paddled, in numbers on the rivers Tone and Parrett in connection with the farming of osiers for basket making. 18ft long and 5ft or 6ft in the beam, their bottoms were made up of several strakes, non-edge joined, with four strake clinker sides flared at 20 degrees. The stem raked at about 45 degrees. These boats were almost startlingly similar in form and construction to the flätaska of the shallows of the south Gotland coast. One or two may still be in use.

THE BRIDGWATER FLATNER AND THE WATCHET FLATTIE

Used on the Parrett and the adjoining coasts in numbers as farmers' fishing boats, rowed or sailed under spritsail and jib with a daggerboard. 17ft to 22ft long, the bottom of these boats was cambered fore and aft and athwartships, and made up of five strakes non-

This Bridgwater flatner was photographed in 1946 and is shown fitted out for scoop netting for shrimps. There is a mast step in the forward thwart. *(Basil Greenhill Collection)*

edge joined. They had a hard chine, and the 30 degree flared sides were made up each of two single pieces of timber, scarfed just aft of amidships. As with the bottom of the turf boat this form of construction assumed the existence of very large, readily available trees. The stem was slightly curved as well as raked. The stern was a raked tombstone, like that of a dory. The type lends itself to plywood construction and some flatners have been built of this material. The Watchet flattie was similar, but with reinforced floor for beaching. There may be one or two flatners still in use for their proper purpose and there is one of them in the possession of the Bristol City Museum. A replica of a Watchett flattie was built and sailed there in 1997.

THE BRIDGWATER BARGE

Used on Somerset waterways as a general cargo carrier, using tidal flow, tracking and tugs. Canal locks limited the length of these barges to 52ft and the beam to about 12ft. They were flat bottomed with non-edge joined multistrakes, hard chine and flared curved clinker multi-strake sides, raked stem and raked tombstone stern. These sophisticated boats may possibly share an ancestry with the up-river Severn trow (*qv*).

THE WESTERN-SUPER-MARE FLATNER AND CLEVEDON BOAT

The Western-super-Mare flatner and the Clevedon boat were sophisticated clinker built boats with dished flat bottoms, 10ft to 23ft long, rowed and sailed under spritsails. They were used for fishing and freighting trippers.

Sources
By far the best account of these boats is to be found in different chapters of *Working Boats of Britain*. Basil Greenhill, *The Archaeology of Boats and Ships* (London 1995) has an account of the building of a turf boat. There is a nice account of the contemporary use of the Parrett flatner together with an engraving showing two of these boats employed in the shrimp fishery in *Deep-Sea Fishing and Fishing Boats*. Holdsworth also reports the existence of sixty-nine 2nd class fishing boats, presumably mostly flatners, operating from the port of Bridgwater in 1872.

This drawing of a flat bottomed, or up-river, trow was made by Eric McKee from a drawing in the Tewkesbury Town Council Chamber. Her open hold, clinker sides and simple square sail are all depicted. (*Eric McKee Collection*)

The Severn trows

The term 'trow' was used locally rather indiscriminately for the wooden sailing vessels up the river Severn and its tributaries. The vessels were in fact of two main types, which were structurally and in ancestry quite different from one another.

THE FLAT BOTTOMED TROW

A flat bottomed, clinker sided, towing, sailing and poling vessel used on the upper Severn until the 1880s.

Knowledge of the up-river trow, which ceased to be used with the decay of the up-river trade in the nineteenth century, was confined to what could be deduced from drawings and old photographs until the summer of 1992 when the remains of what is believed to have been an up-river trow embedded in the river bank just north of the entrance to Lydney Dock in Gloucestershire were recognised and excavated by the Ironbridge Gorge Museum Archaeological Unit. The excavation revealed the remains of a much rebuilt hull, roughly 40ft in length, the basic structure of which appears to have resembled the vessel in the drawing in the Tewkesbury Town Council chamber reproduced here. As

originally built she had a non-edge joined, smooth planked flat bottom, without a keel, the strakes being fastened only to the massive floor timbers. There was a hard turn of bilge, a chine, above which the sides were of clinker construction. The stern of the vessel had been destroyed. The strakes at the bottom were of oak and Scots pine. Frames and the clinker laid strakes above the turn of the bilge were also of oak.

This shape and the form of construction is reminiscent of the early cogs of the eastern coast of the North Sea. Cogs, both seagoing and sheltered water types, are clearly depicted in graffiti found on the north Cornish coast. The construction generally appears to have been similar to that of the Bridgwater boats (*qv*). It is possible that the up-river trow was an example of the very strong north European flat-bottomed building tradition which developed in north Germany into the cog of the Hanse and became a very widespread building tradition. Farr, in his splendid paper listed below, tells much of the work of the up-river trows of the seventeenth and eighteenth centuries.

The up-river trow which also traded down into the estuary, and may, old

photographs suggest, have had variants and derivants operating on the Bristol Avon, the Wye and the Parrett, was usually rigged with a single square sail ideal for river use.

THE ROUND HULLED TROW

A round hulled, fully skeleton built sailing vessel of distinctive hull shape used in the tidewater trades of the Severn estuary in the later nineteenth and early twentieth centuries. These vessels were distinguished by the absence of continuous fore and aft decks and the use of sidecloths on metal stanchions, sometimes lined with boards, in place of bulwarks, by virtue of which they were called 'open moulded' trows. They were usually smack or ketch rigged.

With the building of the railways and the changing industrial scene the up-river trow dropped out of use. Some vessels, like the Lydney trow, were partly rebuilt to adapt them to estuary use. The development of the docks at Gloucester, Sharpness, Avonmouth, Barry, Cardiff and Swansea and the enormous expansion of the coal trade, especially for bunkering steamers, gave rise to the development of a

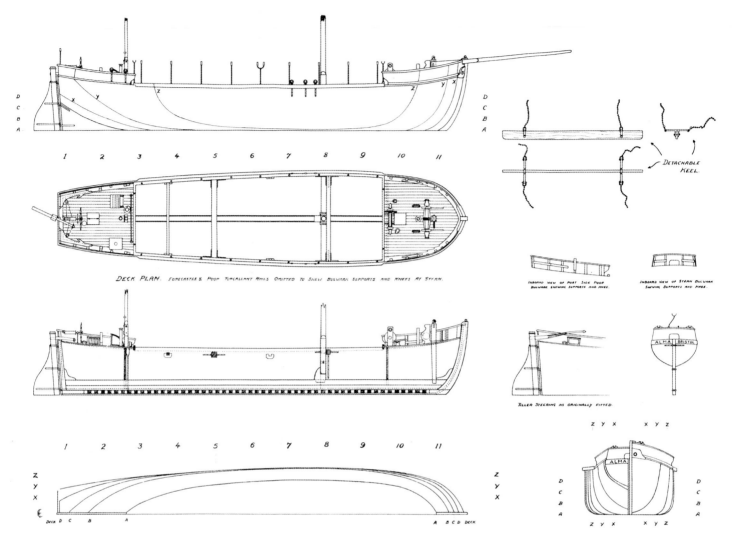

Lines plans, constructional details and layout of the round hulled trow *Alma*. The absence of side decks is clear, and the stanchions for the sidecloths are illustrated. Note also the details of the detachable keel. *Alma*'s registered dimensions were 77ft overall, with a beam of 17ft and a depth in hold of 6ft 3in. (NMM, Coastal Craft Collection)

smack, later ketch rigged, fully skeleton built vessel type, flat floored, with a hard turn of bilge, very full in the bows and with a massive transom stern shaped like a letter D on its back. They had no external keel.

This hull form was not suited to sailing. It was evolved to maximise cargo capacity in a given length, draught and beam. Such are the tides of the Severn estuary and the inner Bristol Channel that much of the work of these vessels comprised tidal drifting, the sails being used to give steerage way and control.

As the drawing of the *Alma* shows, these vessels, to enable them to make some showing to windward when light, carried removable keels. These were slung overside by supporting chains which were worked forward from the stern to avoid the bowsprit. To these vessels, completely different in construction from the old up-river trows, the name 'trow' was transferred.

Apart from their hull form, the distinctive characteristics of these vessels was the absence of a fixed deck, except for short lengths forward and aft which covered respectively the forecastle and gave space for windlass and winch and which protected the Master's accommodation and provided space for the helmsman at the tiller or, later, the wheel; the hull space was completely open. Though they carried many other cargoes these open moulded trows were specialist vessels for the coal trade. The coal was tipped into them straight from the railway trucks

and only the bare minimum of trimming was necessary. To discharge them, grabs could work unimpeded by hatches or even deckbeams. Their crosstrees were hinged so that they could be dropped to keep them clear of the grabs. Many of these vessels were statutorily registered with a loadline. They were, tradition has it, customarily limited to the Channel east of a line from Milford to Bude and during and after the 1890s to the east of a line from Watchet to Barry Island. There are, however, excellent photographs showing big open moulded trows in Ilfracombe.

These trows existed in scores and even in the 1920s could be seen on almost every tide working their way up the Bristol Avon from Cardiff, Barry or Newport with cargoes of bunker coal. They were generally of up to 70ft in length. Earlier trows had been built at Ironbridge, Bridgnorth, Shrewsbury, and Worcester, but after 1868 no trows

were built north of Gloucester. The later vessels were launched at Framilode, Gloucester, Bridgwater, Longney, Newnham, Bullow Pill, Lydney, Berkeley, Chepstow and Appledore.

THE BOX TROW

In a box trow, the sidecloths gave way to a boxed-in hold, still open, and usually the full width of the vessel. It was a vessel of similar construction and shape to the open moulded trow. She had her hatchcombings, however, built up all around her and sometimes waterways. She still had the enormous open hold. It is not certain that sailing trows were ever boxed. Boxing may have occurred after trows were reduced to towing barges.

THE FLUSH-DECKED TROW

The flush-decked trow was of the distinctive trow shape but was fully decked with small hatches and ordinary bulwarks and had the appearance of a very full hulled Westcountry trading ketch. Such vessels sailed in the general home trade and were really coasting ketches of locally distinct shape.

The last rigged trows, ketches, were the *Alma* and the *William*, and both operated in the bunkering business in the late 1930s. A smaller trow, the smack rigged *Spry*, built as a ketch at Chepstow in 1894, has been rebuilt at Ironbridge.

Sources
The paper on the trow by the late Grahame Farr, published in *The Mariner's Mirror*, 32 (1946), is a classic which remains the best account of these vessels. Farr, however, wrote before the development of archaeological studies into the construction of vessels and could not be aware of what appear to have been the characteristics of the upriver trow and the gulf between her and the later vessels. The report on the Lydney excavation of a probable up-river trow is in Williams, *A River Severn Trow*, Ironbridge Archaeological Series No 27 (1992).

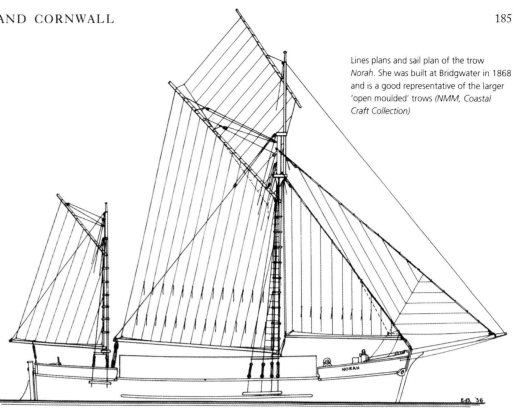

Lines plans and sail plan of the trow *Norah*. She was built at Bridgwater in 1868 and is a good representative of the larger 'open moulded' trows *(NMM, Coastal Craft Collection)*

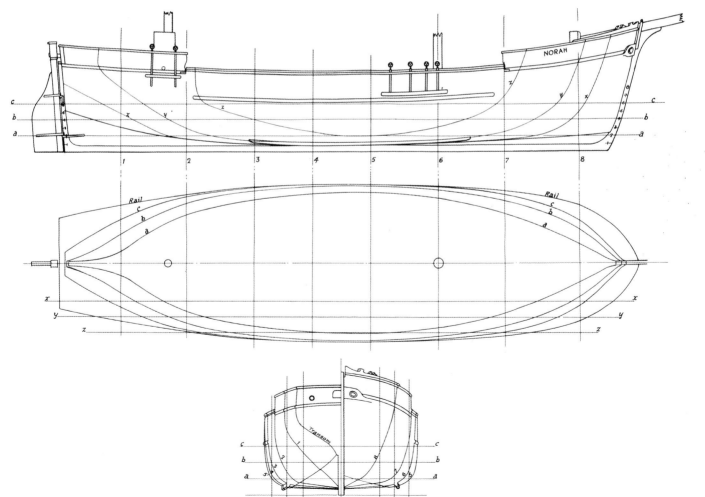

Bristol Channel Pilot craft

BRISTOL CHANNEL PILOT CUTTER

(Known as yawls in Wales and skiffs in England)

Deep draught cutter employed for pilotage in the Bristol Channel.

Pilotage in the Bristol Channel can be traced back to the fifteenth century and from these beginnings developed

'Making port in a storm'. The Newport registered *Spray* No 19 is shown running into Ilfracombe in December 1900. A big sea is running but she seems comfortable enough under a well reefed mainsail, staysail and spitfire jib set on her reeved bowsprit. *(NMM, neg no B2348(B))*

The lines plans of the Bristol pilot cutter *Herga*. She measured 41ft 10in overall, with a beam of 13ft 5in and a draft of 7ft 2in. She was built by John Cooper at Pill in 1902. Though she has a hollow entry below the waterline she is quite full in the head. Choice of underwater lines was a matter of individual taste and vessels varied considerably. *(NMM, Coastal Craft Collection)*

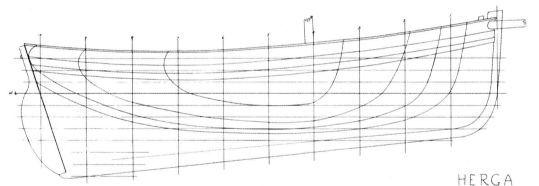

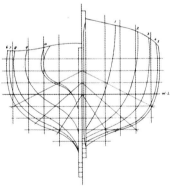

HERGA

BUILT COOPERS BRISTOL 1902

L O A   41' 10"
L W L   40' 0"
DRAUGHT   7' 2"
BEAM   13' 5"
26 TONS T M

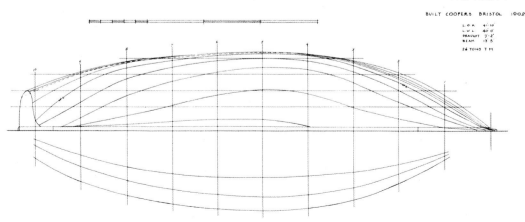

New Wave No 2, photographed in about 1896, was licenced for both Barry and Cardiff. The pilot ports and their relevant hull and sail markings were as follows: Glo'ster/Sharpness, number on hull and 'GS' on the mainsail; Bristol, number on the hull and same number on the main and foresails; Newport, number on the hull and 'N' on the mainsail; Cardiff, number on the hull and 'Cf on the main and foresails; Barry, number on the hull and 'By' on the main and foresails; Port Talbot, number on the hull and 'PT' on the mainsail; Neath, number on the hull and 'N' on the mainsail; Swansea, 'S' and number on the bow and 'S' over number on the mainsail and foresail. *(NMM, neg no A1999)*

the magnificent craft so admired today.

From the middle of the nineteenth century to their final demise as working craft early in the twentieth a typical Bristol Channel pilot cutter would have been between 40ft and 50ft in length, 13ft beam and drawing 8ft or 9ft aft, straight stemmed with a long straight keel. The materials used were, typically, keel of elm, stem- and sternposts of oak, keelson of pitch-pine; the top plank of oak, pitch-pine to bilge, bilge elm, and the remainder elm or pitch-pine. Decks were of yellow pine, fastenings of galvanised iron, concreted over.

The mast was stepped just short of amidships and usually had a short fidded topmast, although some of the latter-day boats had pole masts. Standing rigging was cut to a minimum but was enormously strong. Running backstays were seldom, if ever, used when working but sometimes used with a racing mainsail, especially bent on for regatta days.

The mainsail was usually of flax for winter and cotton for summer work. Older boats used point reefing on a loose footed mainsail but 'Appledore' roller reefing was introduced in the late 1800s and soon became universal and gratefully accepted by the small crews. Halyard falls were led back to the cockpit, as were the headsheets.

An essential part of the cutter's equipment was the 12ft 6in boarding punt, strongly built to withstand very rough handling, being the means by which the pilot boarded ships at sea. The punt was normally stowed on deck in chocks, to port and just forward of the cockpit. In the Welsh boats she was launched over the bulwark, which was low with the capping rail protected by two lengths of half-round iron strip, but the Bristol boats launched through an opening section in their higher bulwark. After putting the pilot on board a ship the punt, returning to the cutter, would be retrieved by means of a wire strop fastened between the stem- and sternposts and hooked on to a burton from the cutter's masthead and thus hoisted inboard. It was usually the apprentice who manned the punt—a daunting task for a youngster, especially in heavy weather. The crew of a pilot cutter usually consisted of the pilot himself, one or sometimes two men and an apprentice or a boy. In the Bristol boats the men were referred to as 'Westernmen' and in the Welsh boats as 'Men-in-the-Boat'.

Piloting in the Bristol Channel was a highly competitive business and it was the pilot who was prepared to keep to sea, often more than 100 miles to the westward, who made the best living. Hence the reputation enjoyed by both the boats and the men who sailed them. Lundy Island was the western limit of pilotage, so a Bristol pilot had to sail some 70 miles before he could claim 'Lundy Pilotage', provided that a rival had not beaten him to it.

The method of boarding a ship was to sail the cutter through her lee with the punt in tow, the pilot and boy on board. When abreast of the ship the punt was cast off and left to row or scull across to her, while the cutter sailed clear to eventually come about and pick up the punt again. It was never the regular practice to lay the cutter alongside a ship at sea, due to the possible damage to her top hamper.

The days of the sailing pilots came to an end just prior to World War I when the various ports introduced a system of amalgamation. The immediate effect was a reduction in the number of cutters required and a surplus of these wonderful boats resulted. Many were sold off as yachts or finished their days as small carriers, while others became stripped out 'gadgets' in the docks – merely platforms for steam winches to serve the cargo derricks of ships unloading – or simply laid up in the rivers or creeks to quietly rot away.

Bristol – or more accurately Pill, on the Avon, – was the last service to use a pure sailing cutter on regular station, in the form of the famous *Cariad*, whose pilot flag was lowered for the last time in December 1922. This event was witnessed by her well known builder Edwin 'Cracker' Rowles, who had built her in 1904 at his yard in Pill. He had the reputation for building very good looking boats which were notably fast, as in the case of his famous *Marguerite* of 1893. Like the *Cariad* she had the pretty elliptical counter characteristic of his building whereas the other Pill yard of John Cooper produced very fine pilot boats, but possibly less elegant, with a squared-off counter or transom stern though with the reputation of being the better seaboats. Rowles and Cooper were the last builders to survive into the twentieth century.

There were, of course, many other builders of high repute within the confines of the Bristol Channel and far beyond. There were yards at Gloucester, Saul, Chepstow, Newport, Penarth, Cardiff, Bridgwater, Bideford, Appledore, Porthleven, and even Fleetwood. Many of these are represented in boats surviving, and sailing, to this day, living testimony to the skill and craftsmanship of the shipwrights of a hundred years ago.

Sources
Peter J Stuckey, *The Sailing Pilots Of The Bristol Channel* (Newton Abbott 1977). Grahame Farr, 'Bristol Channel Pilotage' *The Mariners Mirror*, 39 (1953).

Sail plan, sheer draft and deck layout of the Swansea Bay pilot boat *Bensen* S4. This schooner rig was very unusual in British working boats and the origin of it on these vessels is obscure. *(NMM, Coastal Craft Collection)*

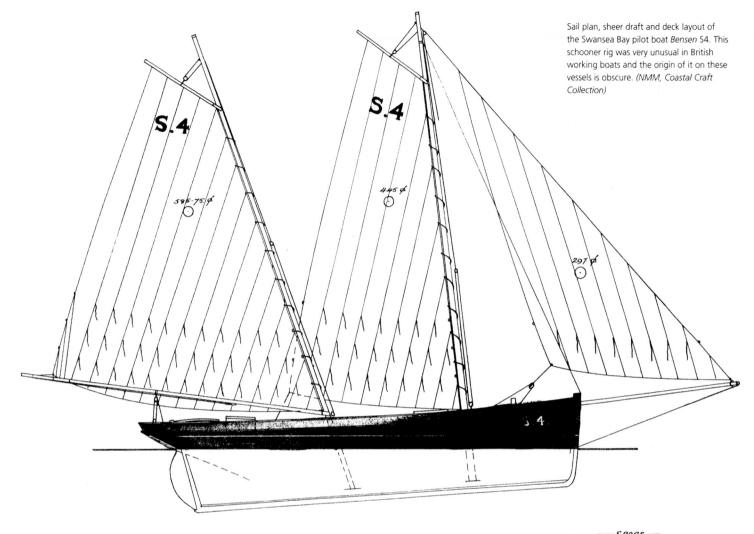

585·75 ◻

445 ◻

297 ◻

SAIL PLAN - SWANSEA BAY PILOT BOAT — C 1870.
FROM SAIL PLAN DRAWN BY A SAILMAKER.

---SPARS---
BOWSPRIT. LOA 25.0". OUTB'D 17.6".
FOREMAST — 51.9". GAFF 9'6".
MAINMAST — 52.10". GAFF 10'0".
MAINBOOM 34'5".
---SAIL AREA---
JIB   297 ◻.
FORESAIL. 445.0 ◻.
MAINSAIL 585.75 ◻.
TOTAL SAIL AREA. 1327.75 ◻.

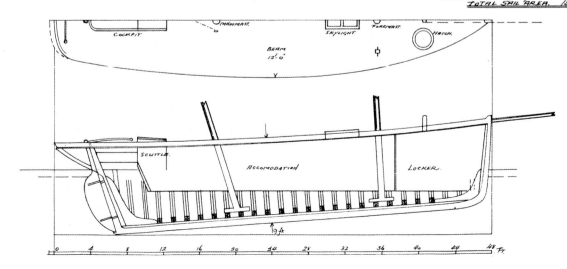

SWANSEA BAY SCHOONERS

It is a curious fact that, whilst every other pilot service in the Bristol Channel used gaff cutters, the pilot craft of Swansea employed a unique form of schooner rig, the origin of which is obscure. Described technically as two masted schooners, the mainmast was heavily raked and, like the foremast, unsupported by any standing rigging. The gaffs were short and the sails were laced to the mast instead of by the usual hoops. A boom was used on the loose footed mainsail. The sail plan was completed by a jib set on a bowsprit positioned to starboard of the stemhead. In their day they were often referred to as luggers and it is thought that the very early boats were, in fact, lug sail rigged; contemporary illustrations show them as being almost indistinguishable from the eighteenth-century shallop. They are sometimes shown at this time as being clinker built with no bowsprit and the foremast stepped right in the eyes of the boat.

Until about 1860 they were open boats, as they worked mostly within the Mumbles Roads though they had to be capable of putting out to into Swansea Bay to secure the pilotage of ships running for shelter in the port during the frequent southwest blows. However, the building of the South Dock in 1859 attracted larger ships and competition for the pilotage of these compelled the pilots to 'seek' far out to sea off Lundy Island and beyond, requiring much larger boats. This resulted in a decked hull identical in form and size to that of their gaff rigged cousins up Channel but retaining their traditional schooner rig, albeit increased in mast height. A deck plan by Mr J F Coates shows provision for stowing a dinghy but in practice the pilots almost always sailed right alongside of a ship as they had no standing rigging to worry about, thus obviating the need of a boarding punt at sea. However, by 1890 the copper ore trade had faded and the character of pilotage requirements had changed to working inshore again. Ships now required pilotage into the port at all times so it became usual for the pilot schooners to tow a 10ft punt for use in light airs. For use in calms the schooners also carried 20ft sweeps, worked from crutches between the masts.

The early open boats were quite small but the later decked vessels were between 42ft and 50ft in length with a mast length of 40ft and a draught from 6ft to 8ft. There were sometimes three pilots to a boat plus a master and two paid hands. Unlike on the cutters, there was no horse for the mainsheet. This was shackled to an eye-bolt abaft the rudder head and the foresail sheets led back to points on either side of the companion hatch where they were secured to cleats in the deck. The schooners were good sailers and could hold their own with the cutters when racing, except in light airs.

At its height the pilot schooner fleet numbered eleven boats, most built by Bevan or Bowen of Swansea but one, the *Charles Bath*, by Cock of Bideford. Some ten years before the introduction of a steam cutter, tradition was broken by the purchase of a Portsmouth gaff cutter, the *Mary*, to replace the schooner *T.W.T.* which had been cut down in the bay.

The Swansea pilots amalgamated as long ago as 1898 which created a surplus of boats and, as in later years with the other pilot services in the Bristol Channel, they were sold away as yachts. Only two of the biggest boats were retained, namely the *Grenfell* (S9) and the *Benson* (S4) until they, too, were disposed of, the *Grenfell* becoming a 'gadget' in Bristol, and the *Benson* a yacht.

Sources
J F Coates 'Swansea Bay Pilot Boats' *The Mariner's Mirror*, 29 (1943)

The two Swansea pilot boats S4 and S7. This photograph gives a good view of the remarkable rake of their mainmasts. There is no standing rigging and the bowsprits have been run in while the craft are in port. Their booms lie along the deck and the mainsails, attached to the short gaffs are under cover. *(NMM, neg no C3594)*

Wales

WALES IS better known for its hills and mountains rather than for a coastline which, with two navigable rivers flowing along the borders after rising within her, gave access by boat and ship to almost all inland activities at a time when overland routes were an excruciating brake on the movement of people and goods. In earlier centuries a number of lesser rivers made possible the growth of maritime activities based on produce gleaned from the sea and from the hinterland, most of which by now are subjects for historians and theme parks as new development covers past glories.

Prevailing winds are mainly westerly and southwesterly so that safe anchorages and harbours are judged with that in mind. Afon Menai (the Menai Straits) and the east and north coasts of Anglesey, St Tudwal's Roads, Porth Dinllaen, Fishguard Bay, parts of Carmarthen and Swansea Bay are still used in bad weather. Apart from a fetch across the Irish Sea, the Atlantic Ocean makes itself felt on occasions. Big tidal ranges are the bane of otherwise good harbours, since bars lie across their entrances so that they become inaccessible except towards half flood. The ports on Afon Dyfrdwy (the River Dee), Rhyl, Conwy, on the Afon Menai, Pwllheli, Porth Madoc, Abermaw (Barmouth), Aberystwyth, Aberteifi (Cardigan) and many more were not reliable places of refuge. This was the reason for building the large harbour of refuge in the 1850s at Caergybi (Holyhead). Placed strategically near a dangerous tide- and wind-swept series of headlands on the route from north to south in the Irish Sea, early photographs show how essential it became to ships of all sizes. The next safe port south was Abergwaun (Fishguard), eighty miles on, if the land to leeward could be weathered.

Two major estuaries mark the northern and southern limits of the Welsh coast arising from the River Dee and the River Severn, as one pours into Liverpool Bay and the other into the Bristol Channel. Whereas south Wales made coal and copper its economic base at Abertawe and Caerdydd (Swansea and Cardiff), creating complex dock systems and major shipping companies, north Wales left its mark in slate on the roofs of towns and cities from the Baltic to North America over a longer period with smaller vessels and simpler facilities, sailing out of the Menai Straits ports and Porth Madoc.

Wool, metals, grain and timber were amongst other products which depended on a vast coastal fleet sailing from any convenient creek, beach and haven to reach the markets of the increasingly industrialised areas of Britain. From those same creeks, beaches and havens also came a steady stream of new build wooden ships and fishing boats of all sizes, built in such unlikely places that it is hard to believe except for photographic proof and ship registers. Some places became pre-eminent for this such as Amlwch, Caernarfon and the other Menai Straits ports, Porth Madoc, Barmouth and Cardigan. Iron and later steel shipbuilding was typical of the south

Wales coal ports and also along the shores of the River Dee under the influence of the advances made in the shipyards of the River Mersey. Concentration of shipbuilding was nearly always linked to a specialised trade or product on which a place was dependent.

References to north and south Wales do no justice to a third area of coast, generally lying directly to leeward of a passage up the Irish Sea, that of Bae Ceredigion (Cardigan Bay), which is geographically separate because of the massive cliff coast of Pembroke to the south and the rocky Lleyn Peninsula and Anglesey to the north, both swept by a tremendous tidal flow. The ports of south Wales, facing across the Bristol Channel, had easy access to industrial England, while from the Lleyn eastwards Liverpool had a considerable influence on north Wales and, it must be said, north Wales on Liverpool. The steam packet service, begun early in the last century from Liverpool, linked all the coastal towns as far as Caernarfon until well into this, showing the importance of Liverpool Bay to all aspects of maritime endeavour in that part of the country. Apart from Porth Madoc, which grew on the export of slate from the southern aspects of Eryri (the Snowdon massif), the Cardigan Bay towns saw few industrial incursions of significance and stayed with the export of wool in part-worked form, timber, stone and agricultural produce. The bay is devoid of harbours accessible at all states of tide and weather except for Fishguard at its southern end. In its northern half a submerged causeway, Sarn Padrig, extends for 12 miles southwestwards, ready to wreck any ship uncertain of her position in that end of the bay. It is the kind of hazard which sends a frisson of fear through a coasting skipper as he contemplates the chart. The many small, restricted harbours and quays which dot the coast and were essential for trade, developed capable pulling and sailing beach boats that were necessary providers of muscle and expertise to assist cumbersome trading craft making harbour or attempting to depart from what was often a lee shore. These were the origins of the double enders of Aberystwyth and Pembroke and the basis of the local Cardigan Bay herring fleets which made Aberystwyth a very important landing port, though others along the whole bay shared in the bounty. More substantial fishing boats, nobbies, were built in the more northern end and were used for beam trawling. The Bay was a fisherman's cornucopia and attracted larger fishing craft from Devon and Cornwall as well as others from Fleetwood. The mixed mud, sand and shingle bottom, over half within the 10 fathom line and all within the 20 fathom line, was prime fishing ground. Under sail it was inexhaustable but the fleets of steam trawlers and drifters from Aberdaugleddau (Milford Haven), and further afield soon changed that.

The Welsh coast along the Bristol Channel is a series of bays capable of providing temporary anchorage from strong winds or foul tides, except for Milford Haven which is safe from all directions. The larger bays of Carmarthen and Swansea, supported fisheries based at Dinbych-y-pysgod (Tenby) and the Mumbles for many centuries. So attractive were these that local craft were almost always outnumbered by those from far afield. Fish caught here and, indeed, in Cardigan Bay, were needed to feed the fast-growing industrial conurbations of the Welsh coalfields and ports just along the coast.

From the Lleyn Peninsula to the River Dee working the strong tides was essential for those who fished off the Anglesey coasts and the Liverpool Bay along the sandy flats off Conwy, Rhyl and the West Hoyle Bank. Anglesey vessels were built to be pulled up stoney beaches due to a lack of small harbours except for those fishing out from both ends of the Menai Straits. A variety of nobby was built in the Lleyn, at Conwy and Rhyl for the rough conditions encountered over the flats. Many boats found work as hovellers in Porth Penrhyn and Amlwch at the height of the sailing coastal trade in slates and copper. The Llanddwyn pilot station was manned at the west end of the Menai Straits so that incoming vessels could be safely conned over the changing bar and up to Caernarfon or Porth Dinorwic. Similar work was found at all of the other ports. Old photographs of Rhyl show the harbour with three masted ships and barques discharging timber from North America and indicate the level of skilled ship-handling that was possible by working sail and oar.

GLAMORGANSHIRE CANAL BARGE

A double ended, heavily built barge for carrying coal from the valleys down to Cardiff.

Out of the Industrial Revolution the small town of Cardiff grew enormously important as an outlet for the anthracite mined from far up the valleys of the River Taf. In 1790 an Act of Parliament allowed the canalising of the Taf as necessary from Merthyr Tydfil, the major coal producing centre, to Cardiff. This was followed by constructing a canal from Aberdare in 1793 to link with the River Taf. A railway line joined the Taf below the confluence of the canals close to Porth.

The descent from the Brecon Beacons required many locks and No.6 below Merthyr Tydfil had the greatest fall in Britain of a single canal lock at 14ft 6in, second only to the Manchester Ship Canal.

The canal tolls were related to cargo. Since this was always coal a system of weighing a barge both empty and loaded was devised using a long scale-beam connected to the cradle on which the barge was dried out. This must have stopped disputes between the coal producer, the canal operator and the coal merchant in Cardiff over quantities being handled. Only on one other canal was this used and that also

A rough drawing of the Glamorganshire canal barge which measured 60ft overall, with a beam of 10ft. The drawing includes a section through the cabin. The stempost is measured as being 12in by 5in. (NMM, Oke, Coastal Craft Collection)

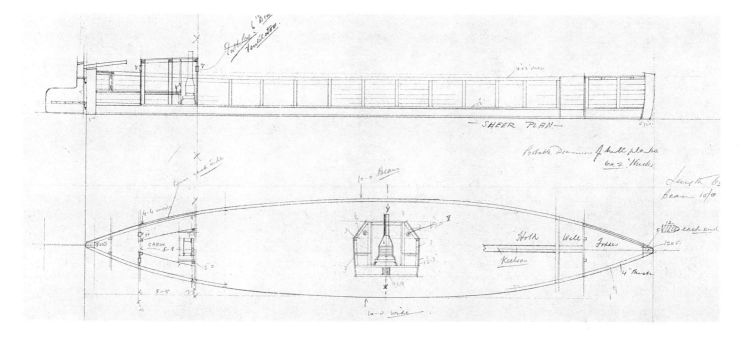

A Glamorganshire canal barge shows off her fine forward lines, a graceful sheer and her heavily built structure. There is no cabin. (NMM, Oliver Hill Collection, neg no P74089)

was dedicated to the movement of coal.

On canals a boat's length includes the rudder because of locking requirements. Boats used on the Glamorganshire Canal were, without the 5ft of rudder, about 60ft long and had a beam of about 8ft 6in. That measured by P J Oke in 1937 at Cardiff had a beam of 10ft. Their draft was about 13in when empty and they had a 'mass per unit immersion' of 1 ton for every 1in. The usual load was about 20 tons. Contrary to usual canal boats, which are parallel sided and have bluff ends, these vessels had no parallel mid-section and the ends were quite fine. The canal boat found at Tredunnoc and used on the Monmouthshire Canal, built in 1792, has remarkably similar form

and dimensions. This shape greatly eased propulsion. Construction of the Glamorganshire Canal boat was very basic. Materials used were mostly deal held with iron spikes and nails. The athwartship bottom planking 6in by 2in, is nailed to a massive kelson 9in by 9in. L-shaped frames were fastened to the bottom. Heavy stem and stern posts fitted the kelson ends. Side planking 2in thick ended at a heavy inwale sat on top of the frame ends. Apart from the hold there was a pump well, suggesting pump problems with coal dust, and a fodder store for the towing horse though no towing post is shown. Rudimentary accommodation for two, plus a large coal stove, was fitted ahead of the steering position. From Cardiff to Melin Griffith the boats were towed by steam tugs.

In 1830 the Bute Canal was built to link the Glamorganshire Canal to the new coaling docks opened for the increasing trade. Confidence in canals was unshakable as is shown by the *Illustrated London News* even in 1874

when it printed 'They are not likely to be superseded by railways, as they afford an economical means of carriage of heavy goods, at the uniform speed, continued day and night, of two miles and a half per hour.'

Sources
Peter Smith, *Waterways Heritage* (Luton 1971) contains details on these craft. See also S McGrail and S Parry, 'The Tredunnoc Boat', *International Journal of Nautical Archaeology*, 18, 1 (1989).

MUMBLES OYSTER SKIFF

The Mumbles, including the Parish of Oystermouth or Ystumllwynardd, is tucked in behind the most easterly of the headlands which fringe the Gower coast, facing across Swansea Bay and overlooking what at one time was an exceptionally rich ground for oyster dredging. In the eighteenth century the oyster beds were regarded as the best in Britain. During that time and until well into the next century oyster fishing was done from open boats

some of which developed a distinctive two masted rig supporting two gaff headed sails. This rig was to be seen also in Aberystwyth beach boats, in the Swansea pilot boats and in prints of maritime scenes of places further north in Wales. The need to exploit more distant grounds and an awareness of the oyster fishing vessels which came from other distant ports, including Colchester, prompted early orders for fishing smacks from yards along the coast of Devon and Cornwall, during the second half of the nineteenth century. Thereafter, most of these gaff cutters were built locally along the shores at Cardiff, Swansea and the Mumbles. Within the Mumbles oyster dredging community they were known as skiffs. When oysters were 'out of season' the skiffs would go trawling in Swansea Bay and Carmarthen Bay using a beam trawl. Dredging for oysters always began to windward of the patch to be worked so that power and control was easily maintained sailing downwind while towing the dredges.

At the end of a haul the skiff would lift her two dredges aboard then sail back up wind to sail down nearly the same track once again, as often as was necessary. The skiffs dredged with a three-man crew. If oysters were not sent to market at once then they were discharged into a type of holding tank, carved out of the beach between tide levels, one to each skiff.

Skiffs were mainly between 37ft and 40ft in length in order to be powerful enough to tow the dredge, but not too fast. The *Emmeline* was 40ft long with a beam of 10ft 7in. Her keel was 31ft long and depth in the hold was 5ft 3in. The graceful sheer ended in low freeboard aft to make hauling dredges easier. The vertical stem rounded quickly into the straight keel which was much deeper aft. The short counter was squared off. Low bulwarks secured the

deck and the dredging gear. The keel would be of elm, the framing of oak and the planking of larch, all iron fastened. Maximum beam was about the middle of the waterline which would make for an easily handled craft under sail. Plenty of space was allowed for the favoured ballast, which was dense copper dross from the smelters at Swansea.

The skiff *Emmeline*'s gaff cutter rig was absolutely typical of the arrangement given to cutters of this size whether work boat or yacht. The high peaked mainsail was set below a large topsail on a mast with a fidded topmast. The bowsprit was nearly 17ft ahead of the stem so plenty of sail area was available. Light weather performance was essential for work boats and sail could always be reduced.

Over-fishing and diseased oysters plus a loss of the safe traditional moorings area to railway development led to the demise of oyster dredging at the Mumbles. Many of the skiffs were sold off to fish as smacks in other parts of the country.

Sources

R J H Lloyd, 'The Mumbles Oyster Skiffs', *The Mariner's Mirror*, 40 (1954). C Matheson, *Wales and the Sea Fisheries* (Cardiff 1929). R Carl Smith, 'The Mumbles Oyster Fishery', *Cymru a'r Mor/Maritime Wales*, Vol 3 (1978).

PEMBREY GUN PUNT

Double ended gun punt used for wild-fowling on the marshes of Carmarthen Bay. The rivers Taf, Tywi, Gwendraeth and Bwri at low water have vast sand banks flanking their depleted channels and their estuaries are extended by a seemingly horizonless green sea marsh riddled with narrow tidal creeks. Such wet areas are a major attraction for large flocks of local and migratory wildfowl. In the nineteenth century Lord Ashburnham was the owner of a large estate near Pembrey which included the ten square miles of marsh to the west and north. A special kind of boat was needed which could negotiate the shallows, and it was from his estate that the Pembrey wild-fowler's gun punt was sold.

The Pembrey gun punt has very little in common with other wildfowling punts which carry very long, large-bore guns requiring the aiming of the boat as part of the hunt. Yet a boat like the Pembrey gun punt would not have been unusual since a young sportsman's book from 1833 gives instructions for building a similar craft, 'For shooting from the creeks with a large shoulder gun'. The Pembrey gun punt was built about 1850. She was a small, double ended boat having no keel

since her bottom was flat and made up from three 1in thick, knot-free, pine boards fitted edge to edge and caulked with oakum. The bottom is rockered which would have made her responsive to rowing and manoeuvering in shallows. The sides were fitted at nearly a right angle to the bottom and each comprised two yellow pine clinker strakes, less than ½in thick, which ran out to the raking stem- and sternposts. These were carefully rabetted to take the hood ends which were fastened with copper nails as were the garboard edges to the pine bottom and the sheer to the inwales. The laps of the clinker strakes are rivetted using copper nails and almost square roves less than ½in sided. The bottom planks were linked together by seven floors, 1in square in section, fastened with iron screws. The frames, which have been delicately shaped and finely finished, were fastened with copper nails and roves like the topsides. The stem and stern knees and the breast hooks were also fine examples of craftmanship and timber selection. Parts of this interior framing, all of which was of ash, had decorative moulding lines carved parallel to their edges.

The guns might have been stowed beneath the broad flaps of canvas fixed to the sides ahead of the thwart. The

The deck layout and constructional details of the Mumbles oyster skiff *Emmeline* 14SA. With her straight stem, low freeboard and counter stern she is immediately reminiscent of a Colchester stowboat (*qv*) on which she was based. She was built by William Paynter of St Ives around 1865 and survived until after World War I. *(NMM, Oke, Coastal Craft Collection)*

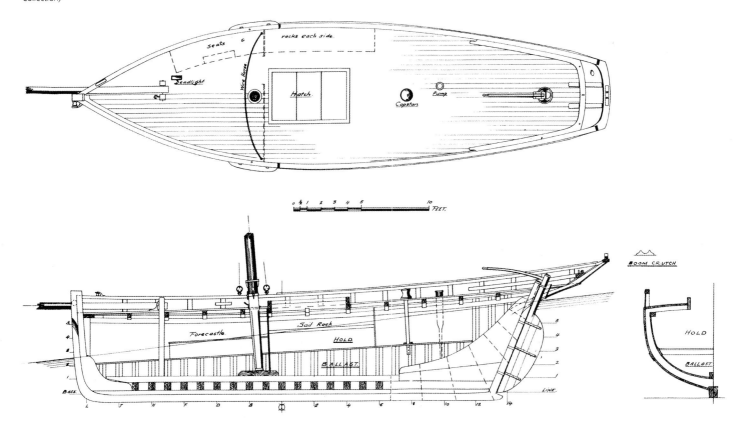

A Pembrey gun punt photographed looking aft, which shows the delicate nature of the framing. This craft still has the canvas flaps under which the guns were stored. *(Owain Roberts Collection)*

oars would have had cleats with holes which would fit over the single thole pins. Bottom boards were fitted over the frames and floors. An iron ring was stapled to each breasthook for mooring. Into the stem and stern knees was fixed a substantial ring for hoisting the punt to the roof of a boathouse

The Somerset turf boat (*qv*), used on the quiet waters of the Levels could be mistaken for a poor relation of the finely built but technically similar Pembrey gun punt. The Pembrey wildfowler's gun punt was recognised and rescued from a farm outbuilding in 1968 by Mr Fred Lyne of Burry Port and since then has been stored safely in a workshop at Cwm Bwri Honey Farm by Mr Brian Jones.

Sources
B Greenhill, *Archaeology of the Boat* (London 1976) describes the boats of the Somerset levels. See also Lt Col P Hawker, *Instructions to Young Sportsmen in Guns and Shooting* (Seventh edition, London 1833).

THE TENBY LUGGER

Two masted, carvel built lugger employed mainly for herring fishing in Carmarthen Bay. Tenby had been renowned for herring since the fourteenth century. In the early nineteenth century it was exploited by Brixham and Torbay trawlers but when the railway arrived the number of local boats increased dramatically since fish could be sent to the industrialised south Wales, especially Swansea. The Tenby fishing grounds trawled by bigger craft lay within Carmarthen Bay. Locally built luggers of various smaller sizes, though all similar, engaged in long lining, drift net fishing and oyster dredging. Their numbers grew from about twenty-five in 1864 to at least forty-nine by the end of the century, when sizes tended to increase so that the largest had a keel length of around 27ft.

Some Tenby luggers were built with carvel planking though most of the early ones had clinker strakes. They had vertical stems and slightly raked transoms. The keel was straight with noticeably extra depth, which made

Sheer plan and constructional details of the Pembrey gun punt which shows the thwarts in position. She is 12ft 7in overall. *(Owain Roberts Collection)*

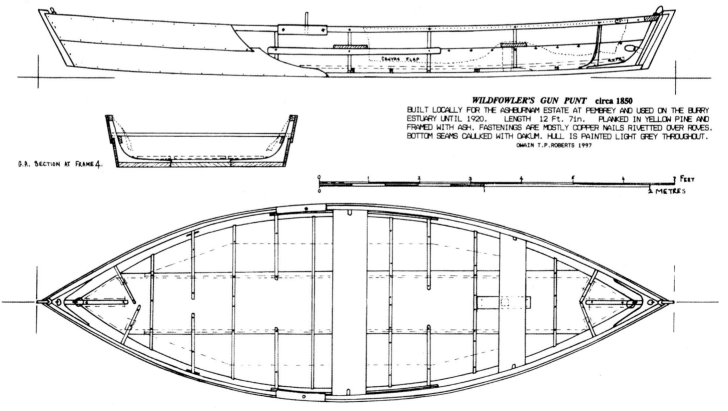

G.A. SECTION AT FRAME 4.

WILDFOWLER'S GUN PUNT circa 1850
BUILT LOCALLY FOR THE ASHBURNAM ESTATE AT PEMBREY AND USED ON THE BURRY ESTUARY UNTIL 1920.   LENGTH 12 Ft. 7in.   PLANKED IN YELLOW PINE AND FRAMED WITH ASH. FASTENINGS ARE MOSTLY COPPER NAILS RIVETTED OVER ROVES. BOTTOM SEAMS CAULKED WITH OAKUM. HULL IS PAINTED LIGHT GREY THROUGHOUT.
OWAIN T.P.ROBERTS 1997

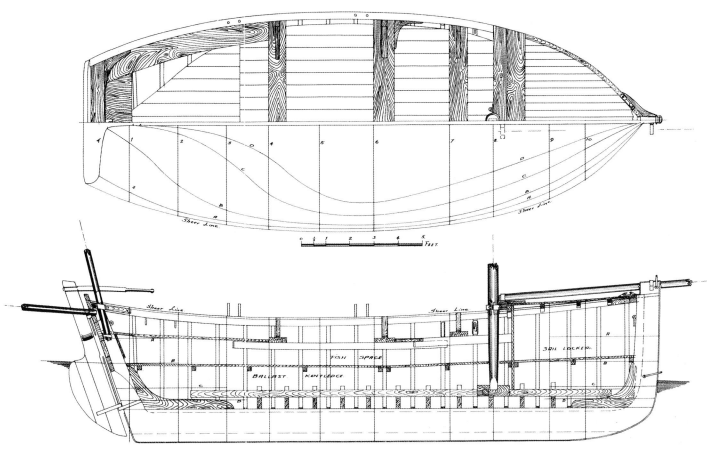

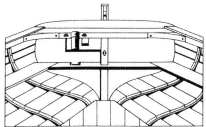

— PROJECTION of TRANSOM —
SHOWING
MIZZEN STEP & BOOM DETAILS.

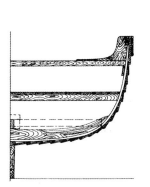

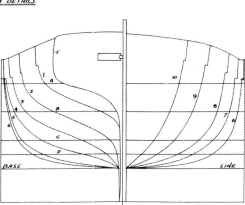

the luggers better sailers than would have been the case with their flat floors. There was a cuddy forward, decked over as far as the mainmast which was stepped about one-third of the hull length from the stem.

It was clamped against a mastbeam referred to as a crosspiece and stood in its maststep fastened to the kelson. This was bolted down over floors which alternated with sawn oak framing. Being a buoyant hull much ballast was needed to settle the lugger down to her waterline. Over this was a close-fitting deck upon which the catch was landed. One may imagine the distinctive stink that would be the inevitable result of such an arrangement, no matter how careful the fishermen were. No doubt this was addressed before giving 'trips round the bay' to holiday-makers as became the summer norm.

Normally, two men and a boy were sufficient, though for drifting an extra man and boy would be included in the crew. Oars were used when needed. The mizzen, about half the height of the mainmast, was raked in line with the transom and stepped over to starboard. It carried a spritsail sheeted to a mizzen or jigger boom. The mainsail was a dipping lug tacked to the stem.

Lines and constructional details of the Tenby lugger Seahorse M170. She has very flat floors amidships and is buoyant forward, but has a good, fine run aft. There is a small cuddy forward which was entered by a sliding door in the bulkhead. This cuddy was used as a sail locker but it would have given the crew a little shelter as well. (NMM, Oke, Coastal Craft Collection)

Its halyard was made fast to windward to support the unstayed mast. If a jib was set then a bowsprit was carried. This practice became common towards the end of the last century which suggests that setting a jib helped to reduce the weather helm which may be deduced from the lines of the *Seahorse*. The jib halyard was made fast on the opposite side to that of the main.

The decline of Tenby was due to the growth of Milford Haven as a major fishing station so that commercial fishing from that ancient harbour is now a very minor factor in its economy.

Sources
J Leather, *Spritsails and Lugsails* mentions the luggers. More detailed information can be found in R J H Lloyd, 'Tenby Fishing Boats'. *The Mariner's Mirror*, 44 (1958).

Left: The Tenby lugger *Florence* M81, photographed in 1936, probably with trippers aboard. She has the standard rig of sprit mizzen, dipping fore lug sail and a jib set flying on a long bowsprit. This had a bobstay but no shrouds. *(NMM, Oliver Hill Collection, neg no P75420)*

Below: Lines plans of a Pembroke longboat which were lifted in 1996 by Dai Williams. She measures 22ft 6in overall on a beam of 4ft 11½in. These craft have a long and distinguished past and are now built in GRP. *(Owain Roberts Collection)*

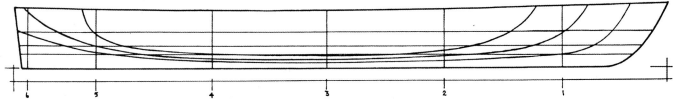

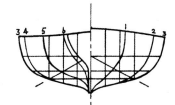

TONNAU GLÂS --- A PEMBROKE LONGBOAT

Length 22'-6"   Beam 4'-11.5"
Now built in g.r.p. since the late 1970's
Lines lifted 1996 by Dai Williams
of Ynys Marine, Aberteifi, (Cardigan)

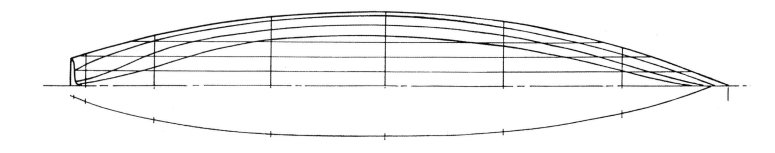

PEMBROKE LONGBOAT

Clinker built, four-oared gigs used for racing along the Pembroke coast.

The skills of boat handling for fishing and hovelling in Cardigan Bay were channelled into the pursuit of racing at regattas with the inducement of good cash prizes, and from out of this nineteenth-century phenomenon grew the continuing interest in longboat racing in Pembroke. The longboats were clinker built boats or gigs, about 23ft overall with transoms. The double ended development at Aberystwyth had spread south so that the wooden longboats racing up to the 1970s were all double ended, as indeed are some on the eastern Irish coast even now.

This long tradition of racing, centred on Cardigan, now supports longboats based in many of the towns and villages around the Pembroke coast. Competition is keen, encouraged by large sums of prize money and much betting on the side. Fleets of fifteen are not at all uncommon.

Desmond Harris of Aberporth intended to build a new fast boat in the 1970s as a multi-chine plywood hull but was persuaded to build the first in GRP based on the old form. She was an instant success on which all the others have since been modelled, leading to the complete demise of the wooden longboat in Pembroke. The boats are four-oared in the standard manner and carry a coxwain. Oars are crutched on outriggers and as the hulls are narrow the rowers sit in line. It is doubted if any of the GRP longboats are the same in section even though out of the same mould, since various ways of cutting, rebuilding and tweeking-in have been employed to try to gain that elusive competitive edge. All have small transoms which is a reversion to the form of their nineteenth-century origins. There is a Regatta circuit extending from Aberystwyth southwards round the Pembroke coast. Longboats are raced in three classes, Senior, Ladies and Junior. Some have raced in the Celtic Challenge from Arklow to Aberystwyth, and some have been raced on the Thames and against the Cornish gigs when they were found to be highly competitive. The Pembroke Longboat League as the organising body, has now changed to Welsh Longboat League Cymru.

Sources
R J H Lloyd, 'Aberystwyth Fishing Boats', *The Mariner's Mirror*, 41 (1995), and correspondence with Mr D Williams of Ynys Marine, Aberteifi.

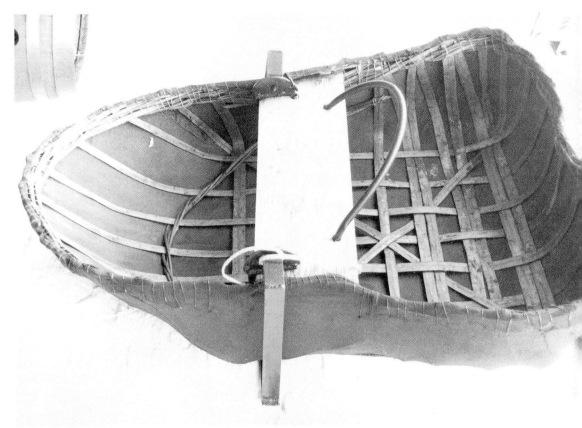

The most ancient of boats – a coracle from the River Teifi. The gunwale here is made of woven withies and the thwart rests on top, through which a strap is passed for carrying. *(Owain Roberts Collection)*

WELSH CORACLE

A boat built with a light, flexible framework with a membrane stretched over it, once employed throughout the Welsh river system, mainly for salmon fishing. These types of craft, dating at least from the Bronze Age, are still found on both maritime and inland waters on the western Celtic fringes and the very qualities which have enabled the Irish curragh (*qv*) to continue on the Atlantic coast are the same as are found in the Welsh coracle. Being extremely light, such craft are very buoyant so rise to any rough water that threatens. Skilfull handling ensures safety.

These Welsh rivers were fished for salmon and sewin, both in their tidal reaches as well as further upstream. Coracles worked in pairs to draw a net along a section of a river. Techniques varied from river to river as did the technology of net making and handling. A coracle was easily carried by one man, and most have a strap of leather or woven hazel, fixed each end of the thwart, which is slipped over the man's head and across his chest. To describe a coracle from one river does not do justice to all the others. All have a frame woven in different but similar ways

perhaps of split willow or sawn ash. The gunwale may be solid wood or, more likely, made of twisted or woven withies. In some the thwart is placed on this and on others a little below. Early last century flannel had superseded hide as the coracle's skin but this gave way to canvas or calico which is shaped then fitted by sewing it into the twisted-withy gunwale or clamping it within the gunwale's wooden structure. The 'skin' was tarred to render it waterproof. Size was related to the user's height in that it should clear his head when carried. Coracles from Cardigan and from the River Dee tended towards a slightly tapering oblong plan form with rounded corners. The end behind the paddler curved upwards quickly while the end towards which he faced was near vertical for maximum buoyancy when handling nets or fish. Those from the River Severn at Welshpool and Shrewsbury tended towards an oblate or even oval form which in some gave an almost saucer-like appearance. The single paddle showed as much variety as there are coracles though two basic types were used: one with a long loom and another shorter, with either a claw shaped end or finished as a crutch. Using one hand with the loom against the shoulder, or

tucked into an armpit, a combination of continuous sculling strokes allowed the coracle to manoeuvre with agility.

The demise of Welsh coracles started during the last century and continued into the 1930s after the banning of their use in non-tidal waters by riparian landlords in order to reserve salmon stocks for sport fishing. Coracles are now only semi-active on the tidal Teifi below the bridge at Llechryd, while a few have been built on the River Severn.

Sources
J Hornell, 'British Coracles', *The Mariner's Mirror*, 22 (1936). Reprinted as Monograph by Society for Nautical Research (Greenwich 1973). J Geraint Jenkins, *Nets and Coracles* (Newton Abbot 1974).

ABERYSTWYTH BEACH BOAT

Clinker built, transom sterned, three masted vessel employed in the herring fishery in Cardigan Bay.

Many larger fishing vessels visited the grounds to the southwest of

Aberystwyth from the English fishing ports of the northwest. However, over seventy fishing boats were registered locally, though only nine were 1st and 2nd class trawlers, the remainder being open or half decked small herring drifters and hand liners. In 1883 Aberystwyth was described as 'the most considerable fishing station in Cardigan Bay'. The lucrative herring fishing season in Cardigan Bay occurred in the last third of the year as the shoals moved up the coast. Most of the local boats were small. The small herring drifter had settled at a size and catching capacity which made it a viable economic unit within its locality. Larger boats shot between fifteen and twenty-five nets each on a continuous line. Smaller boats such as gigs and smaller beach boats would shoot between six and eight.

Aberystwyth had grown as a resort, helped by the railway, and in the summer many small drifters turned to carrying holiday makers on 'trips around the bay'. The boats were clinker built and had a transom. Those about 24ft long had a three masted unstayed rig. The combination of sail was not common though a variation on it was to be seen, just a hundred miles over the horizon, on the east Irish coast on the larger Wexford herring cots (qv). The three masted Aberystwyth beach boat's first two masts set loose footed gaff sails which were quite long in their luff, ahead of a spritsail mizzen. The rig is known to have been in use at least as early as 1844.

The practice of beaching bows first was not popular with the tourists as the waves tended to break against the transom, and as a result beach boats were gradually replaced by double enders in the late 1880s. A number of three masters with double ends were built. Their rigs changed to all gaff sails and these were given brails, making them much more handier when carrying passengers. These new boats were built by David Williams of Aberystwyth and at other yards. By 1890 the smaller gigs gave way to his new design of double ender, which was about the same size. These were 18ft long and 6ft beam with a well rounded stem and a raking sternpost. Though intended as rowing boats they would carry sail if the wind was free. In season they would be used as herring drifters. By the turn of the century there was a considerable number of them and the fishermen had a high regard for their seaworthiness. They were built quite lightly, which made them such good sea boats, of high volume but combined with fine waterlines forward and well flared topsides for nearly the first third of the hull. Rowing off a beach would be done quickly yet the flare would turn away the threatening wave crests. At sea, lying to five or six drift nets from the bows, the double ender would ride easily and rise to the waves without fuss, being more buoyant than the older craft. Returning to what was usu-

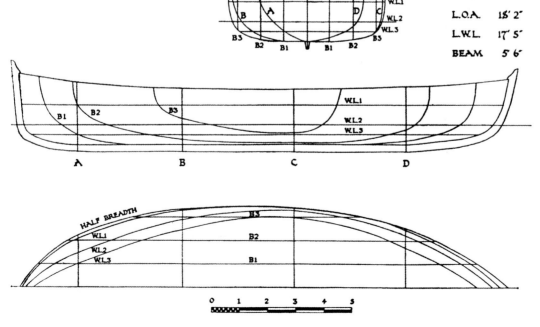

L.O.A. 18' 2"
L.W.L. 17' 5"
BEAM   5' 6"

HALF BREADTH

0   1   2   3   4   5

Top left: An Aberystwyth beach boat with its unusual three masted rig of two loose footed, boomless gaff sails and a sprit mizzen. No foresails, topsails or standing rigging were ever employed. The luffs of the gaff sails were surprisingly long and were seized to the masts. This craft sports the older transom stern. (*Society of Nautical Research*)

Left: Lines plans of a small, double ended Aberystwyth beach boat, a type which was introduced sometime in the 1880s. Unlike the larger three masted craft, these were primarily rowing craft and were used for carrying passengers. However, they did carry standing lug sail which was used off the wind when the boats were employed in herring and line fishing. (*Society of Nautical Research*)

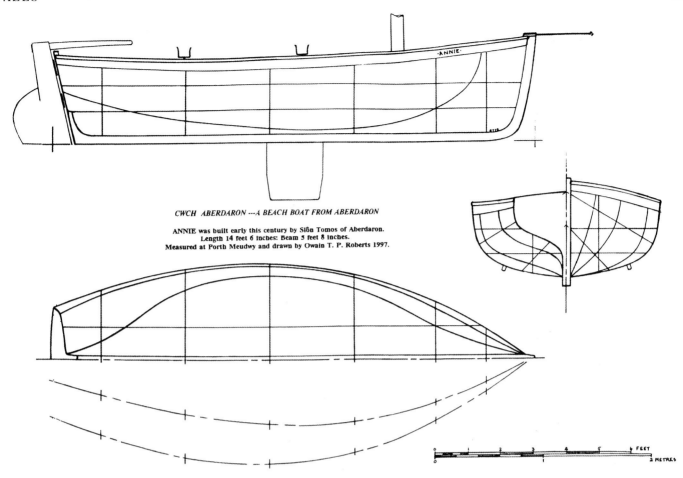

CWCH ABERDARON ---A BEACH BOAT FROM ABERDARON

ANNIE was built early this century by Siôn Tomos of Aberdaron.
Length 14 feet 6 inches: Beam 5 feet 8 inches.
Measured at Porth Meudwy and drawn by Owain T. P. Roberts 1997.

ally a lee shore, the single lug sail would have driven the drifter back to the beach or into the harbour with ease. Plying for passengers off the beach continued as a business until recent memory as did the various methods of fishing.

Sources
R J H Lloyd, 'Aberystwyth Fishing Boats', *The Mariner's Mirror*, 41 (1955). C Matheson, *Wales and the Sea Fisheries*, (Cardiff 1929).

BEACH BOATS OF ABERDARON

Clinker built, transom sterned, single masted vessels employed in fishing for lobsters and herring along the Llyn peninsula. Aberdaron has been the main departure place for tide-swept Ynys Enlli (Bardsey) since time immemorial. These clinker planked boats were all built under 15ft in length so that it was possible for two men to handle them on the beach. Those measured are all close to 14ft 8in overall, with a beam of 5ft 7in. This is not surprising since beach boat construction over the last hundred years at least was confined to two boatbuilders.

The lines plans and sail plan of the Aberdaron beach boat *Annie* built early this century by Siôn Tomos. A feature of his craft was the hollow entry at the waterline. She has quite a wide transom with a pretty tuck. The rig was reconstructed by Owain Roberts in 1997. *(Owain Roberts Collection)*

Siôn Tomos built his last Aberdaron beach boat when he was 83 in 1963 for the village postman. He employed three moulds plus the transom to establish the shape of his boats but would vary their positions slightly. This shows in those of his craft which are still afloat. However, he always produced a fine entry to the waterline and gave the transom a tight tuck like a wine glass so that it remained almost clear of the water. All the deadwood was planked over down to the keel. Some fishermen preferred this because it gave the ability to row in either direction easily, like a double ender. Because of deep water close in, lobster pots were set at the cliff edges and in the gulleys, so this manoeuverability was valued.

The other boatbuilder, Wil Jones of

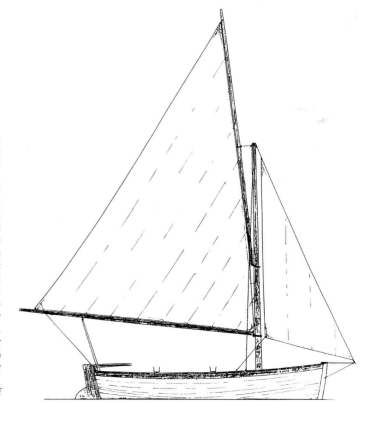

Ty Tanfron, who died before Siôn Tomos, built his beach boats with no tuck or reverse curve to the transom, which sat on the end of a long wedge of deadwood built over the keel, rather like later clinker racing classes. His waterlines tend to more fullness forward. Both builders favoured full rounded bilges and deep hulls which suggests a no-nonsense approach to bad weather.

Wil Jones fastened his steam-bent, oak frame-tops between an inwale and the sheer strake. He did not fit a capping which is convenient for cleaning. Siôn Tomos would fit a capping which might, in places, touch the frame tops. Another idiosyncracy was an over wide frame spacing of 9in and even more towards the fore end where frames tended not be fitted. If time is the test then the boats built early this century have all passed. Perhaps it was the quality of the larch planking and the oak centre-line which helped. Incidentally, no two stems were exactly alike due, no doubt, to the selection of crooks.

The Aberdaron lobster pot was spherical, made from green willow withies, with a neck-like entrance from where the weaving was begun. More lobsters were caught before the advent of mechanised fishing but plenty are still caught. Herrings were caught after October but only two drift nets were set because of the boat size and the rough tidal conditions. Mackerel still give excellent hand line fishing during the late summer.

In the last century daggerboards were introduced in the beach boats which until then used a single leeboard. Masts were stepped against the forward thwart and supported a high peaked, gaff mainsail balanced by a jib hooked onto the end of a modest iron bowsprit which clamped over the stem.

Many of the remaining Aberdaron beach boats, about thirty, race as a restricted class, length and construction being the only limits. Modern rigs make for excellent sailing during a summer race programme and the annual regatta which was established in the last century.

Sources
Interview with Mr Gruffyd Jones of Aberdaron. J Geraint Jenkins, *Crefftwyr Gwlad* (Llandysul 1971). J Geraint Jenkins, 'Herring fishing in Wales', in *Cymru a'r Môr/Maritime Wales*, 4 (1979). See also Eric McKee, *Working Boats of Britain*.

BEACH BOATS FROM YNYS ENLLI

Clinker built, double ended, two masted vessels, with noticeable drag aft.

The coastline of Bardsey (Ynys Enlli) is steep-to and ruggedly indented allowing very limited beach access. Having been inhabited since prehistoric times the entwining of farming and fishing seems always to have been a feature of the island, coupled with a long period of importance as a place of pilgrimage. Three pilgrimages to Enlli were equal to one to Rome.

Images of boats specific to Ynys Enlli are limited to a very few old photographs but it is clear that an identifiable type was in use. Interpretation of those from the nineteenth century give details of beach boats about 25ft overall. They were softwood, clinker planked on sawn oak frames, with oak keel and posts. The hulls were double ended, the stem curved but scarphed to the keel at a steep angle reminiscent of eighteenth-century practice, resulting in a sharper entry through the water for the bottom planking. The sternpost was moderately raked but its main feature is that it is clearly longer than the stem. When afloat this would give the keel drag, that is more draft aft, improving the sailing quality and making the hull more manoeuverable. Eric McKee, in defining groups of

A rare example of a posed photograph of fishermen and their boat. This wonderful image depicts an Enlli boat on the beach at Aberdaron in 1886. The distinct drag aft of these boats is well described in this view. Both masts are sprit rigged and a small jib extends on an iron bumkin. *(National Library of Wales Collection)*

working boats, identified what he called the 'western skiff' representing boats including Cornish drivers, nickies and nobbies from the Isle of Man, and the Lochfyne skiffs. All are double enders having firm bilges and keels drawing distinctly more at their after end. The Ynys Enlli boat should be considered in this grouping.

The Ynys Enlli boat had five oars whose looms were left square where they lay in their crutches. These were the product of a local blacksmith but must have suited the rough water practice of not feathering between strokes. The sprit rig was used on both masts with the jigger needing a long jigger

Northeast Anglesey beach boats racing at Moelfre in 1926. The boat in the foreground is from Amlwch. In the background is a vessel setting a small sprit mizzen. *(Owain Roberts Collection)*

Lines plans of a northeast Anglesey beach boat which demonstrate a distinct deadrise. These lines were taken off a model which was an accurate scale representation of a vessel 22ft long overall, with a beam of 6ft 3in. *(Owain Roberts Collection)*

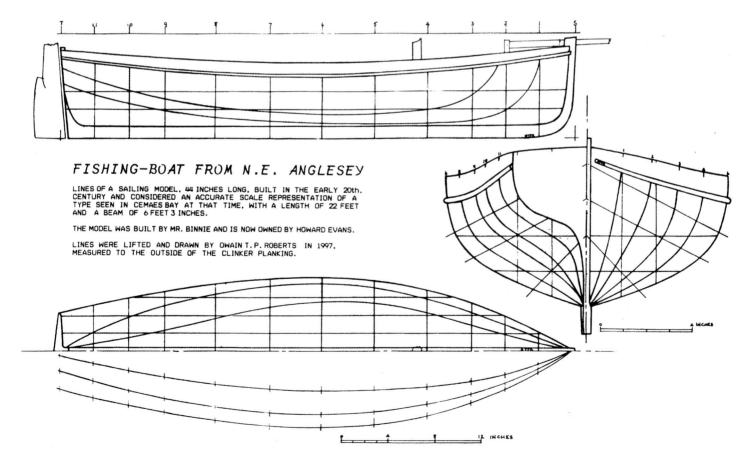

FISHING-BOAT FROM N.E. ANGLESEY

LINES OF A SAILING MODEL, 44 INCHES LONG, BUILT IN THE EARLY 20th. CENTURY AND CONSIDERED AN ACCURATE SCALE REPRESENTATION OF A TYPE SEEN IN CEMAES BAY AT THAT TIME, WITH A LENGTH OF 22 FEET AND A BEAM OF 6 FEET 3 INCHES.

THE MODEL WAS BUILT BY MR. BINNIE AND IS NOW OWNED BY HOWARD EVANS.

LINES WERE LIFTED AND DRAWN BY OWAIN T. P. ROBERTS IN 1997, MEASURED TO THE OUTSIDE OF THE CLINKER PLANKING.

boom for its sheet. The jib's tack was hooked to an iron bumpkin protruding from the stem. Both the mainsail and the jib had reef points.

Drifting for herring was seasonal towards the winter. Hand lining over the rocky bottom and laying pots for lobster and crab were the other methods of fishing. For Ynys Enlli the boats were also immensely important both for communication with the mainland and for moving stock, produce and supplies. Aberdaron was and still is the most convenient fishing village for this traffic.

Sources
Enlli Ddoe a Heddiw/Bardsey Past and Present (Gwynedd 1987). J Geraint Jenkins, 'Herring Fishing in Wales', *Cymru a'r Mor/Maritime Wales*, 4 (1979).

NORTHEAST ANGLESEY BEACH BOAT

Clinker built, transom sterned, gaff rigged cutters and yawls employed for

fishing in the inhospitable waters off the north Anglesey coast.

A few moorings are used in the various creeks along this coast but none are safe in all weathers, unless behind a harbour wall as at Cemaes and so the boats in use were all capable of being manhandled up a beach. This was such a necessity that special keel rollers were devised for the rather rough, stoney beaches to ease the task.

Photographs of nineteenth-century craft show gaff cutters and cutters with a small sprit mizzen. These were beach boats of between 18ft and 25ft which had to be able to sail well because of the strong tides in which they worked. First impressions are of fairly standard clinker planked boats having larch planking on oak framing, either steamed or sawn. However, the lines taken off an accurate turn-of-the-century sailing model show a hull having a distinctive high deadrise for the bottom planking. This improvement on the usual flat floored beach boat would have been welcome in such waters

where speed and weatherliness were required. Fishing here was dominated by the tides as well as weather and winds blowing across strong tidal streams often produce sea conditions out of all proportion to their strength.

Inshore, close to the cliffs, there would be lobster and crab pots to tend, while over the rocky patches offshore, and at the down-tide side of islets and headlands, hand and long lining were practiced. In a couple of the bays there are long patches of clear sand and gravel over which beam trawls could be drawn. Even now small otter trawls are used in these areas. These beach boats were manned by two or three. Off Amlwch there were always work for hovellers in the days of sailing coasters, and then as the villages along the coast attracted holidaymakers in the latter half of the nineteenth century some of the beach boats were used for 'trips around the bay'. Yachting, already part of the scene, grew in importance but in boats still indistinguishable from the beach boats whose per-

formance the amateur owners attempted to match in local regattas of the sort organised in Port Llechog (Bull Bay).

Sources
J Geraint Jenkins, 'Herring Fishing in Wales', in *Cymru a'r Mor/Maritime Wales* 4 (1979). Also recorded conversations with longshore fishermen.

CONWY NOBBY

Carvel built, high peaked, gaff cutters, with a broad beam and a rounded counter. The nobbies built at Conwy, Criccieth and elsewhere on the north Wales coast were variations of a distinctive type of inshore fishing boat which was developed to work the eastern margins of the Irish Sea from the Solway Firth to Tremadoc Bay, where extensive offshore shallows are linked with broad tidal estuaries. Prevailing lee shore conditions required fine sailing ability, stability in short, rough seas and moderate draft.

It is said that there is not a single

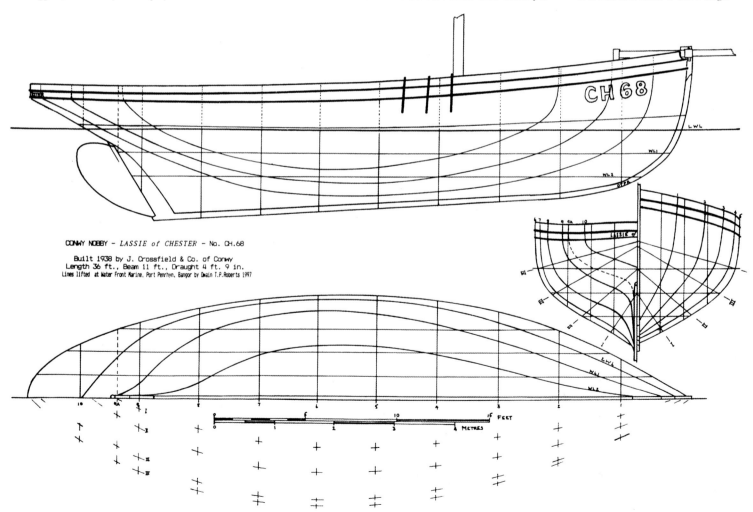

CONWY NOBBY – *LASSIE of CHESTER* – No. CH.68

Built 1938 by J. Crossfield & Co. of Conwy
Length 36 ft., Beam 11 ft., Draught 4 ft. 9 in.
Lines lifted at Water Front Marine, Port Penrhyn, Bangor by Owain T.P.Roberts 1997

straight line in a nobby, including the rockered keel, though seemingly not always in those of the Welsh variants. Photographic evidence from the last quarter of the nineteenth century shows the presence of the nobby type as far south as Aberaeron, and not all of them, by any means, would have been built in the northwest of England. Though yacht-like in their lines these are not yachts that are being considered but fishing boats in which the concepts of underwater form developed within the average nobby hull, whether Welsh or Lancastrian, were up to sixty years ahead of contemporary yacht practice prevailing at the turn of the nineteenth century.

The low headroom under the foredeck, barely adequate for overnight fishing, was a result of moderate draft and low freeboard aft. The cockpit was the safe working area. Its positition from just abaft the mast to the beam ahead of the rudder trunk gave access to almost all of a beam trawl, extending from the shrouds to the end of the counter. The wide side decks eased the sorting of the catch. Both ends of the cockpit are rounded to prevent snagging of net and lines.

The fitting of engines gave the nobbies the power to drag an otter trawl net far bigger than that allowed by the old beam trawl, whose main catch was the various flatfish feeding over the banks. As a result of engine power new nobby lines changed subtly in the run to increase the hull volume so that the large three-bladed propeller, usually fitted out of the starboard quarter, even from new, did not cause the hull to squat too much. Quarter installations kept the propeller on one side and the nets on the other. Inevitably the use of engines led to a gradual reduction in the sail area carried.

A resurgence of interest in the type has led to the restoration to original sailing condition of many old nobbies. The *Lassie* of Chester was returned to Wales for rerigging and her long cockpit and general deck arrangement are as they were for fishing.

Of the *Benita*, built at Criccieth, only Eric McKee's brief recording of her in 1973, and an early photograph in the Gwynedd Archives, remain. Being clinker planked she represented a nobby development from out of the many and varied clinker fishing boats which had been built in the Tremadog and Cardigan Bays, mainly for the vast shoals of herring.

Sources
L J Lloyd (ed), 'The Lancashire Nobby', *North West Model Shipwrights*, Extract No 15 (1994). E McKee, *Working Boats of Britain*.

Lines plans and sail plan of the Conwy nobby *Lassie* CH68, drawn by Owain Roberts 1997. *Lassie* has recently been restored and her general deck arrangements and rig are as they would have been for fishing. The Conwy nobby is of the same family as the Morcambe Bay prawner (*qv*) and they are of a type which fished on the inhospitable eastern margins of the Irish sea from Tremadoc Bay to the Solway Firth – a true measure of their adaptability and seaworthiness. Such a wide distribution is matched, perhaps, only by the coble (*qv*). *(Owain Roberts Collection)*

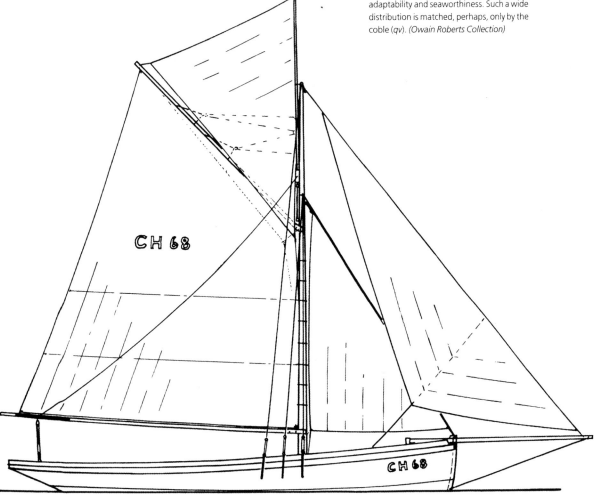

CH 68

CH 68

The Northwest Coast

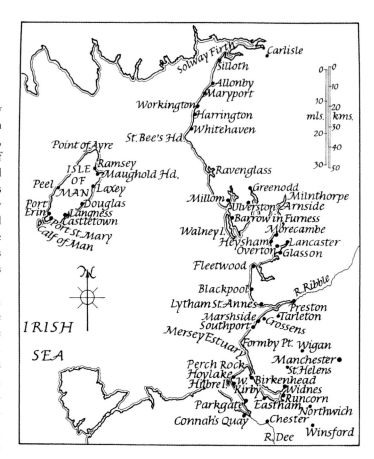

THE NORTHWEST coast stretches from the Dee estuary to the Solway Firth and includes the Isle of Man. The Irish Sea in this area is shallow, no more than 20 fathoms deep, with two large bays, Liverpool and Morecambe. The tidal range of the Isle of Man is 20ft and 27ft at Liverpool at spring tides. Tidal currents are strong and reach 5 or 6 knots in some places such as Langeness on the southern point of the Isle of Man and the Mersey estuary. The bottom is predominantly sandy with a mixture of mud and sand further out from the shore. On the whole, the coasts are low-lying sand hills except for the Cumbrian coast north of St Bees Head, which has some significant sea cliffs. The prevailing wind is from the west.

Maritime activity can be traced back as far as the Romans, with their legionary headquarters at Chester and the coastal forts on the Cumbrian flank of Hadrian's Wall. Viking settlers left their place names, and in the Isle of Man two ship burials have been uncovered. In the Middle Ages, English kings used Chester and Liverpool as maritime bases for campaigns in Wales and Ireland. Trade with Ireland and, to a lesser extent, with France and Spain, was well established by the sixteenth century. The major commercial expansion did not begin until the late seventeenth century. Liverpool, closely rivalled by Whitehaven until 1750, became one of the main ports for the developing of North American and West Indian colonial trades, especially the slave trade. Liverpool had inherent advantages such as a fine harbour and a densely populated hinterland with water links delivering textiles, salt, coal and other manufactures. It grew to become a port of international significance. Its dock system was one of the engineering wonders of the eighteenth century. The Industrial Revolution saw a major upsurge in maritime commerce throughout the northwest and, by 1851, Liverpool had grown to such a position that it exported more goods than London and overall was second port of the kingdom, dominating the North Atlantic trade while, at the same time, developing trading connections with the rest of the world. This dominance was unsuccessfully challenged by new ports at Fleetwood and Barrow-in-Furness.

Coastal cargo vessels were key links of the distribution process, with large fleets of Mersey flats and canal-based boats to a similar design taking goods inland along the Mersey and the connecting canals, and coastal sloops and schooners carrying commodities such as iron ore from the booming iron ore mines of Cumbria, and coal to Ireland. Fishing was also stimulated by the growing demands of the inland urban centres and the establishment of railways made it possible to deliver fresh fish to many inland destinations. Besides the rich herring spawning grounds off Douglas, there were good catches for trawlers between north Lancashire and the Isle of Man, and in the deeper water to the southwest of the island. Major species included whiting, hake, coel, gurnard and 'Dublin Prawns'. As a result, Fleetwood grew to become the third biggest fishing station in the kingdom during the steam trawler era. Inshore fisheries such as those at Morecambe Bay and Southport depended more on the growing seaside resort of Blackpool to provide a market for fresh shrimps and day excursions. The dawn of the twentieth century saw Liverpool's position under increasing competition from other ports; for example, Manchester, which was now directly connected by sea by its own ship canal opened in 1894; and Southampton, for the express liner services. Other ports, such as those of Cumbria, declined because the resources of local iron ore and coal mines were exhausted. In the longer term, coastal traffic tended to lose out to railways and motor transport, and fisheries, particularly the inshore ones, were subject to over-fishing and industrial pollution. Most inshore fishing boats were motorised by the 1930s and a surprising number of Morecambe Bay prawners have survived and are now being converted back to sail. Most Mersey flats had all had their sails removed by about 1920 and were used as dumb flats until the 1950s. The last three were built between 1950 and 1953. The same applied to schooners, which plied to Runcorn in fairly large numbers until World War II. The last sail trader on the Mersey, and probably in the whole of the northwest, was the steel schooner *De Wadden*, which is now preserved in the Merseyside Maritime Museum. Today, most of the northwest coastal ports have little or no trade and are re-inventing themselves as yacht marinas and tourist attractions, including maritime museums at Ellesmere Port, Liverpool, Fleetwood, Lancaster, Barrow, Whitehaven and Maryport.

DEE JIGGER BOAT

The Dee Jigger boat operated from Heswall, Parkgate and Neston on the north bank of the Dee estuary. It was carvel built with a straight stem and transom stern with a yawl (jigger) rig of gaff mainsail, jackyard topsail, foresail and sprit mizzen. In bad weather, it could be shortened to foresail and mizzen. The last survivor, the *Capella*, now part of the Merseyside Maritime Museum's collection, was built by Winram & Son, Liverpool, for Reg Bushell of Parkgate. She measures 23ft 4in overall with a beam of 7ft 8in and a depth of 4ft 1in. She had an iron centreboard which was removed with the installation of her first engine in 1928. The jigger boat's main work was for trawling in the outer Dee and Liverpool Bay for shrimps. After World War II, the Dee estuary silted up and left Parkgate and Neston cut off; the few fishing boats that remained were moved to the Heswall moorings.

DEE SALMON BOAT

Clinker built, partly decked, rowing and sailing boat used for seine net fishing on the River Dee. The Dee was a noted salmon river, and salmon boats are to be seen in eighteenth-century prints and drawings of Chester. The centres for the salmon boats are: Handbridge, on the opposite bank to Chester, and Connah's Quay and Flint. A few still fish today, but pollution has reduced the catches substantially. They are clinker built boats, 17ft 6in long by 6ft 3in beam and 2ft 6in draft. They have a transom stern and are decked aft to carry a 200yd long seine net. This is rowed out from the river bank in a wide circle to capture the fish. The boat is propelled by a pair of oars and, in favourable winds, by a single sprit sail. They are strongly built of larch on steamed oak ribs to cope with frequent beaching. In the twentieth century, the majority were built at Taylor's yard at Chester, and the last three to be built between 1979 and 1981 were for the Merseyside Maritime Museum, the National Museum of Wales and Chester Museum.

Sources
M Tanner, *The Ship and Boat Collection of Merseyside Maritime Museum* (Liverpool 1995) has information on these boats.

MERSEY PILOT SCHOONER

Large, schooner rigged pilot vessel employed in the difficult approaches to Liverpool. The *Pioneer*, the first Mersey pilot schooner, was built by W Buckley Jones at Liverpool in 1852. She measured 68ft in length, 15.7ft beam and 7.8ft depth of hold. Her gross tonnage was 78 tons. Twenty to thirty pilots were carried and she served her turn at the two pilot stations off Point Lynas and the Mersey Bar, usually with another eleven boats.

The schooner replaced smaller cutters of about 50ft to 55ft length that carried only about seven pilots. The design seemed to owe a debt to contemporary yacht design and proved handy and seaworthy in the dangerous approaches to the Port of Liverpool. They were built by a large number of builders, including Thomas at Amlwch and Harvey at Ipswich. They had a straight stem, a counter stern and were rigged with two foresails on a sliding

The Morcambe Bay prawner – or shrimper or nobby as they were also termed – was the dominant fishing smack on the mainland side of the Irish sea, all the way from the Solway Firth to the coast of north Wales. One of the biggest fleets was at Fleetwood and some of that fleet are photographed here in about 1912. Shallow forward, with little forefoot, they are drawn up to the edge of the beach. Beam trawls can be seen lying on the decks. *(NMM, neg no G3256)*

bowsprit. The foremast carried a light signal topmast and there was a main topmast staysail. Sails carried the word 'pilot' and the number of the boat; the large pilot flag was flown from the main topmast. The pilots were ferried to their ships by a double ended, clink-

er built punt lashed on deck and launched through a sliding section of the bulwarks. Later motor punts in use to 1982 were of similar design. Collision with steamers became a major hazard and five schooners were sunk between 1882 and 1896. As a re-

sult, the first steam pilot cutter was placed on station in 1896. The *George Holt* (built at Dartmouth in 1892) was the last schooner to be sold in 1904. She was used as an island trader in the Falklands and her sunken hulk still lies in Stanley Harbour. Merseyside

Maritime Museum has a fine contemporary rigged model of the *Leader*, No 2, of 1856 and a half model of *Perseverance*, No 12, of 1861. The sail training schooner *Spirit of Merseyside* (now *Spirit of Scotland*), built in 1986, was loosely based on the pilot schooner design.

Sources
J S Rees, *History of the Liverpool Pilotage Service* (Liverpool 1949) and M K Stammers, *Sail on the Mersey* (Birkenhead 1984) both contain material on these vessels.

MERSEY FERRY

Before steam ferries (introduced in 1815), there were three sizes of ferry for crossing the Mersey: decked cutters for the three long routes to Runcorn, Ince and Eastham in the upper estuary; clinker built rowing and sailing boats not dissimilar to gig boats; and carvel built, schooner rigged 'shallops'. Both the latter were for the more direct crossings to Woodside and Rock

Left: A sketch of the Dee jigger boat boat *Capella* CH76, drawn by E W Paget-Tomlinson. This particular vessel was built in 1923 and is now part of the Merseyside Maritime Museum's collection. She is depicted here under gaff mainsail, sprit mizzen and foresail, but she would also have carried a jackyard topsail *(Trustees of the National Museums and Galleries, Merseyside)*

Lower left: The Dee Salmon boat *Joan*, built in 1946. Unlike the north Devon salmon boat *(qv)* the seine net is here stowed on a short deck aft. The thole pins are positioned for the forward thwart to leave room for handling the net aft. *(Mike Stammers Collection)*

Page opposite
Top right: This painting depicts the Liverpool pilot vessel No 2 leading ships into the Mersey in a heavy northwest gale on 8 February 1881, having been unable to put pilots aboard. This happened not infrequently and, rather than attempt to lower the pilot punt, a signal to follow the pilot schooner would be hoisted. *(NMM, neg no 6011)*

Bottom right: Lines plan of the Liverpool pilot boat No 11, taken off the original half model, and drawn by Bryan Hope. She was built by William Thomas of Amlwch in 1875 and was sunk by the SS *Landana* 10 years later. Deep and narrow she was only 19ft beam on an overall length of 80ft. She drew 10ft 8in. *(Bryan D Hope)*

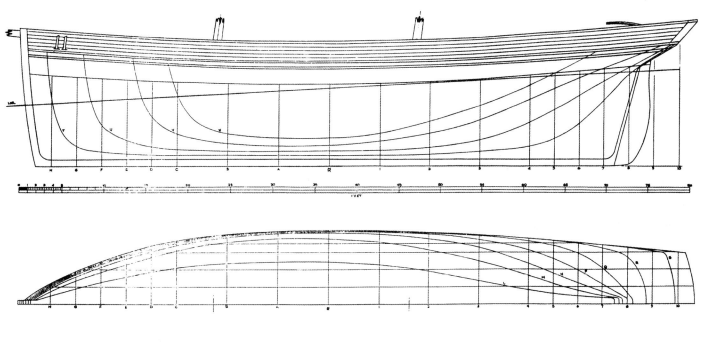

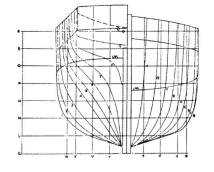

MERSEY N° 11

SCHOONER   79 GROSS TONS   L 80'7" B 19·0' D 10·8'
BUILT   WILLIAM THOMAS, AMLWCH 1875
SUNK BY S.S. LANDANA 1885

LINES DERIVED FROM THE ORIGINAL HALF MODEL (½" = 1FT)
IN THE POSSESSION OF MISS GERTRUDE THOMAS, GRANDAUGHTER
OF WILLIAM THOMAS

Lines plan and sail plan of a shallop built at Brocklebank's yard at Whithaven in 1806 for the West Indian sugar trade. Vessels similar to this, though smaller, were employed as ferries on the Mersey in the early part of the nineteenth century. *(David R MacGregor Collection)*

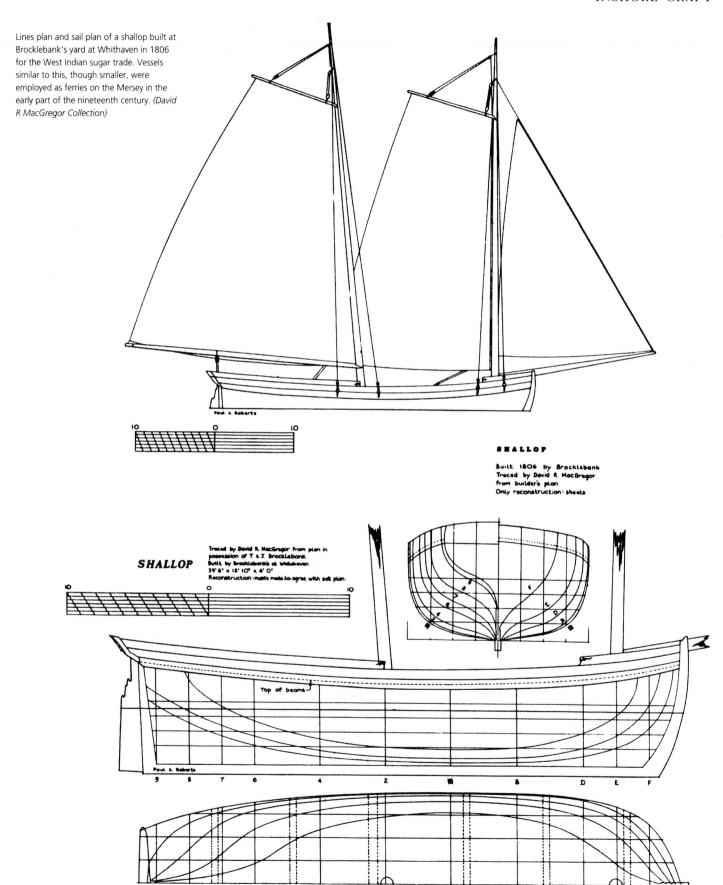

Paul A. Roberts

SHALLOP

Built 1806 by Brocklebank
Traced by David R. MacGregor
from builder's plan.
Only reconstruction: sheets

Traced by David R. MacGregor from plan in
possession of T. & J. Brocklebank.
Built by Brocklebank's at Whitehaven.
39' 6" x 12' 10" x 6' 0"
Reconstruction: masts made to agree with sail plan.

SHALLOP

Top of beams

Paul A. Roberts

Lines plan, constructional details and deck plans of the Mersey flat *Bedale* of Liverpool, measured and drawn by the late Frank Howard in 1971-72. The backbone of the flat consists of the keel and keelson with the frames sandwiched in between except at the bow and stern where the cant frames are let into the deadwoods. *(Trustees of the National Museums and Galleries, Merseyside)*

Ferry (Birkenhead) and Seacombe (Wallasey). Sailing ferries were probably extinct by about 1850, by which time steam paddle ferries were more reliable and indeed opened up the Wirral Peninsula to commuters.

S & N Buck's view of Liverpool of 1728 shows the Eastham and Rock Ferries with a flat's (*qv*) type of bow and a single square sail. Celia Fiennes, who crossed the Mersey with her horse in 1694, described the ferry as a type of hoy capable of carrying 100 people. Schooner rig was certainly in use by 1765 (as shown in a Lightoller's plan of the Liverpool docks) and in the late eighteenth and early nineteenth century, schooner rigged ferries appear in many views of Liverpool and in individual ship portraits. They were very much of the shallop type, with the foremast set well up in the bows, with or without a sliding bowsprit and foresail. Some had their ferry station painted on the mainsail. The *Mary Anne* of 1790, to take one typical example, measured 26ft 6in long, 8ft 10in on the

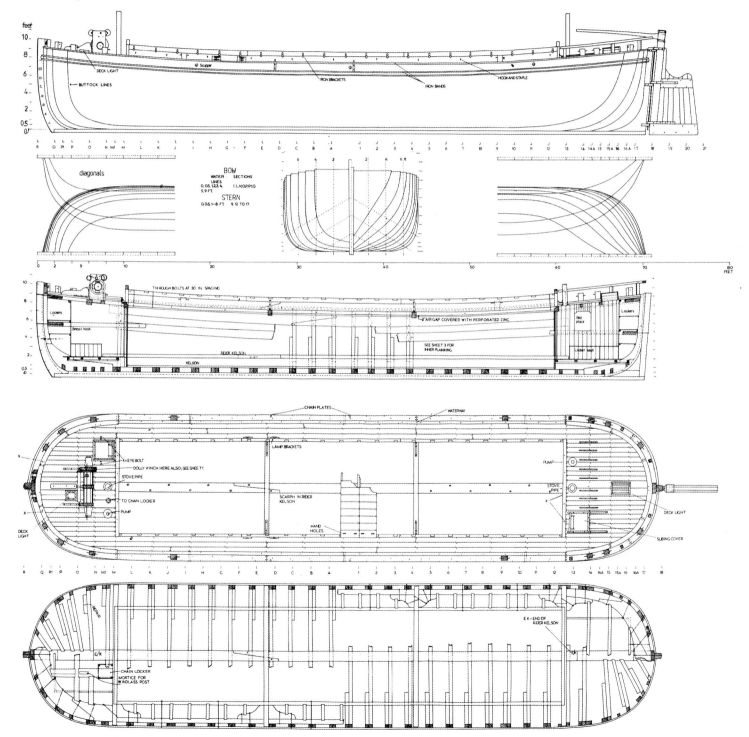

Above: A Mersey gig boat under sail in the Mersey. This craft is shown with sprit rigged main and mizzen but some of the larger boats carried three spritsails. There are no brails on the mainsail and the whole mast would simply have been unstepped when the crew wanted to take off sail. *(Trustees of the National Museums and Galleries, Merseyside)*

Kavanagh, 'Mersey Sailing Ferry Boats' in *Bulletin of Liverpool Nautical Research Society*, Vol 40 (1990) are the main sources.

FLAT
(Mersey flat, Weaver flat)

The flat was the inland and coastal barge of the northwest. It was built and operated from the Dee estuary to as far north as Whitehaven. The biggest concentration was on the Mersey and its linking navigable waterways: the River Weaver, opened 1732, the Rivers Mersey and Irwell, opened 1736, the Sankey Canal to St Helens, opened 1757, the Bridgewater Canal to Manchester, opened 1776, and the Leeds-Liverpool Canal, opened as far as north Lancashire in 1774. Although earlier texts have suggested that there were different types of distinct Mersey and Weaver flat, this was not the case.

The essentials of the flat, whether at sea or inland, were an apple cheeked bow, pointed or transom stern, very little sheer, especially in the case of canal boats, and a flat bottom. It was typically about 60ft to 65ft long and 15ft beam – the prevailing dimensions of

beam, and 4ft depth – the same length, but 1ft 2in wider than the Manx *Peggy* (*qv*). The largest, for example the *Vittoria*, were as much as 36ft long with a 12ft beam. Needless to say, none have survived.

The rowing and sailing ferries do survive in an accurate contemporary model of the Rock Ferry *Bless Us* of about 1820. Clinker built with a transom stern, a single lug sail and six rowing positions, she measured 24ft long and 7ft 2½in on the beam. She had a hollow bow with a fairly full body amidships, and a run from just aft of amidships. Contemporary paintings show a two masted sprit rig in use and there is also one of the Eastham ferry cutter. This has been used to construct a model for the Merseyside Maritime Museum collection.

Sources
M K Stammers, 'Mersey Sailing Ferries' in *A Second Merseyside Maritime History*, H Hignett (ed), (Liverpool 1990) and T

Right and page opposite: Lines plan, constructional details, deck layout and sail plan of a Morcambe Bay prawner. The cutaway forefoot and drag aft, the well raked sternpost and very hollow bottom sections, so similar to contemporary yacht design, made for a fast and handy vessel. The short luffed mainsail was set on a pole mast with a large, top heavy, jackyard topsail set above. *(Maxwell Blake Collection)*

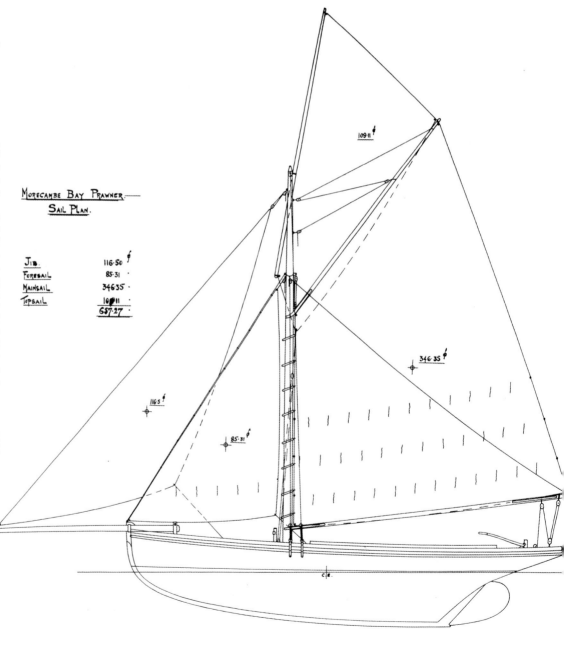

MORECAMBE BAY PRAWNER –
SAIL PLAN.

JIB.	116·50
FORESAIL	85·31
MAINSAIL	346·35
TOPSAIL	109·11
	657·27

the local locks. It was very strongly built, with a huge keelson to compensate for the wide hold openings, oak frames and planking up to 4in thick on the bilge. Some remained afloat for over a century. On the deck, there was a windlass forward, a fore hatch and a main hatch, and below, a store-cum-cabin under the fore deck and the main cabin aft. Steering was by a huge rudder with a long curved tiller controlled with the help of a tackle. The sailing version was sloop rigged, with tanned sails and massive spars. The boom could be as much as 40ft long

and 12in in diameter. There were large halyard blocks and winches at the foot of the mast to raise the sails. Wire shrouds and an iron bar forestay supported the mast. Some late eighteenth-century and early nineteenth-century flats carried a lifting bowsprit. Others were rigged as sloops with a topmast and square topsail for the coastal trade. Ketch rigged, jigger flats were built in some numbers at the end of the nineteenth century, and a few flats were converted into topsail schooners at Runcorn in the 1860s.

Steam towage was regularly used on

the Mersey from the 1830s and many of the inland flats lost their sails as a result. In 1863, a self propelled steam flat (the *Experiment*) was introduced on the Weaver. This was the first Weaver packet. It used the same shape as the traditional flats. Later examples were much enlarged, almost to the size of small steam coasters. The packets would usually tow a flat as well as carrying cargo. About twelve sailing flats survived after 1918 and the last was the sand flat *Keskadale*, which was still rigged in 1939. There was a wide variety of cargoes carried, including

coal, salt, timber, grain, sand and stone. In the eighteenth century, the flats also operated packet services inland and from Liverpool to various coastal destinations. The flat was usually manned by two people on inland trips and three or four on a coastal run. The crews were drawn from closely knit communities and there was a wide inherited knowledge of all the local currents, tides and sandbanks, and considerable expertise at manoeuvring these bulky craft in and out of dock. Three wooden dumb flats survive: the *Mossdale* of about 1870, at the

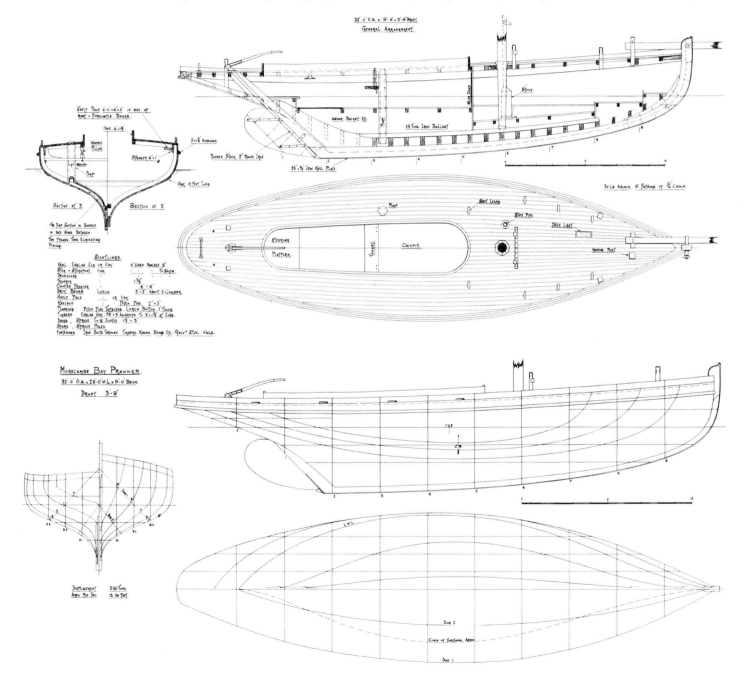

Ellesmere Port Boat Museum; the *Oakdale* of 1951, at Merseyside Maritime Museum; and the *Ruth Bate* of 1953, currently sunk at Widnes. The Boat Museum also has the flat-type canal barges, including the *Georgian Scorpio* from the Leeds-Liverpool Canal, and the two steel barges from the Bridgewater Canal, the *Barmere* and the *Bigmere*. The Merseyside

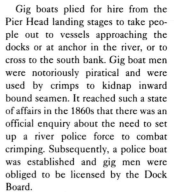

A Hoylake, or possibly Fleetwood, trawler leaving Canning half-tide dock, Liverpool, around 1900. A Mersey flat is in the background. She has a heavy, box shaped counter stern and very deep bulwarks. The beam trawl can be seen on the starboard side. These heavily built craft trawled for bottom fish all over the Irish Sea from Wales to Scotland and across to the Irish coast. *(Trustees of the National Museums and Galleries, Merseyside)*

Maritime Museum also houses a substantial archive of plans and documents relating to flats.

Sources
M K Stammers, *Mersey Flats and Flatmen* (Lavenham 1993).

MERSEY GIG BOAT

The Mersey gig boat was a clinker built, transom sterned, rowing and sailing boat, used from the eighteenth century onwards for transporting people on the Mersey and for handling mooring ropes. The name is still perpetuated in the steel motorboats used for handling mooring lines in the docks of today. They ranged between 18ft to 22ft in length and were equipped with two rowing positions and up to three spritsails. The mainsail was usually rigged in fair weather.

Gig boats plied for hire from the Pier Head landing stages to take people out to vessels approaching the docks or at anchor in the river, or to cross to the south bank. Gig boat men were notoriously piratical and were used by crimps to kidnap inward bound seamen. It reached such a state of affairs in the 1860s that there was an official enquiry about the need to set up a river police force to combat crimping. Subsequently, a police boat was established and gig men were obliged to be licensed by the Dock Board.

They were also used from time to time as excursion vessels from New Brighton Beach and their fast sailing and handiness attracted the interest of local yachtsmen, and a number were bought by the New Brighton Sailing Club, whose members later built modified boats for racing only. There was usually an annual race for gig boats, first of all in the Royal Mersey Yacht Club's regatta and later sponsored by Higsons, a local brewery. Sails seemed to have disappeared by the 1920s when reliable motors were available, at which point a larger carvel built motorboat took over. Unfortunately, no sailing gig boat survives but the Merseyside Maritime Museum owns a half model of the *Bear* of 1911, and two examples of the motor gig boats.

Sources
M K Stammers, 'The Mersey Boatmen and their Gigs', *The Mariner's Mirror*, 61 (1975), and M Tanner, *The Ship & Boat Collection of Merseyside Maritime Museum* (Liverpool 1995), describe these boats.

MORECAMBE BAY PRAWNER

Cutter rigged fishing smacks, employed in the shrimping fisheries along the northwest coast. This generic term is a misnomer (of unknown origin) because pink shrimps are the main catch. They are known by different names at different places, for example, 'smacks' at Maryport, 'half deckers' or 'shrimpers' at Fleetwood, and 'nobbies' on the Mersey. They were used mainly for trawling for shrimps and were widely distributed from the Solway Firth to North Wales. The biggest fleets were stationed at Morecambe, Fleetwood, Southport and the Mersey, where expanding seaside resorts provided a ready market. They were also used as trip boats in the summer.

The original model had a vertical stem and transom stern and could be either carvel or clinker. These were rapidly replaced in the late nineteenth century by a distinctive form with a

cutaway stern, rockered keel, broad beam, sharp bilges and a coaster, or tug, stern, a design that appears to owe something to contemporary yacht design. The standard length was 32ft overall, 9ft beam and a draught from about 3ft 8in to 6ft 6in according to their fishing ground. There were both smaller (down to about 23ft) and longer versions (up to 40ft). They were stable, fast and handy boats, capable of sailing to within four points off the wind in the many tortuous channels through offshore sand banks and, at the same time, weatherly enough to withstand the short vicious seas kicked up by the westerly gales. A few early boats were fitted with centreboards. They also had to be capable of lifting from moorings after going aground at low tide at places such as Morecambe, Southport and Hoylake. They were rigged as pole masted cutters, with about 500sq ft in the (normally tanned) mainsail and another 400sq ft in two headsails (the jib on a sliding bowsprit) and a jackyard topsail. The relatively short luff resulted in a mainsail liable to twist and create weather helm. When sailed hard, they could be wet boats. On the deck, they had a long centre cockpit with curved ends. In later boats and conversions, this was partially decked in to provide cover for an engine or accommodation. Older boats simply had a small 'cuddy' under the foredeck with two benches and small 'bogey' stove. The cockpit also housed a coal fired boiler for processing the catch while returning to harbour. Timber heads or knogs were fitted at the bow and stern for attaching the trawl warps.

They were usually crewed by a man and boy. The beam trawl was between 20ft and 25ft long and the net was made of ½in mesh and 1½ times the length of the beam. There was a ground rope fitted with wooden bobbins, and the manilla warp was about 60 fathoms long and shackled to two bridles, themselves shackled to the foreside of the irons. Trawling was usually in 6 to 15 fathoms with a haul about every hour. Occasionally, two nets were carried.

The main builders were Crossfields at Arnside, Hoylake (for a short period) and Conwy, Armour Brothers and Gibbons & Son at Fleetwood, Anderson at Millom, Wrights and Lathams at Crossens and Marshside (just north of Southport) and at Annan. They all produced differing versions of the basic form according to their own thoughts, the demands of their fisherman customers and the conditions of their particular fishing grounds. Crossfields,

A clinker built whammel boat with standing lugsail. These were shallow craft with a well curved stem and raking sternpost. *(Lancaster Maritime Museum)*

who were the most famous, usually took about six weeks to build one using oak or elm keel and frames and larch planking. In 1912, they cost £60 exclusive of sails and a trawl. Building ceased in the 1930s, but many survived with increasingly powerful engines. About thirty survive as yachts, with two more preserved in Merseyside and Lancaster Maritime Museums. There are two annual races on the Mersey and at Conwy, and an owner's association.

Sources
Edgar March, *Inshore Craft of Britain* is, as usual, a good source, while L Lloyd, *The Lancashire Nobby*, North West Model Shipwrights Archives Extracts series, No 15 (Birkdale 1994) contains material of considerable detail.

FLEETWOOD SMACK

Carvel built, ketch rigged vessel used for trawl fishing. Fleetwood was developed in the 1840s as a steam packet station, but found its true role as a fishing port. By 1876, seventy-six ketch rigged smacks were based there. Liverpool had similar trawlers, numbering forty-one in 1876. Most of these were owned and manned from the village of Hoylake. They used the Hoyle Lake anchorage until silting made it too shallow around 1900. The fishing grounds lay between Liverpool Bay and the Isle of Man and in Cardigan Bay, yielding sole, cod, haddock, plaice and roker. Many, but not all, were built at Fleetwood. They were carvel built, usually with oak keel and frames and pine planking of heavy scantling. The sole survivor (now a holiday home at Millom), the *Harriet*, FD III, was built by Hugh Singleton in 1893 at Fleetwood. She has a narrow entrance, a deep hull with a fine run aft and a counter stern. She measures 60.1ft registered length, 16.8ft beam and 9.5ft draft. The beam trawl was between 40ft and 50ft long and hauled by a steam capstan. The rig consisted of two headsails on a running bowsprit, main and mizzen with jackyard topsails and occasionally a mizzen staysail. Trips lasted for up to six days and the crew consisted of four men and a boy. Sailing trawlers disappeared rapidly after World War I and the *Harriet* was fitted with an auxiliary engine in 1929 but retained a cut down rig until after World War II.

Sources
Notes compiled by last owner of *Harriet*, George Fletcher, in Fleetwood Museum; Edgar March, *Sailing Trawlers*, and John Leather, *Gaff Rig* also cover them.

WHAMMEL BOAT

The whammel boat was used to fish for salmon in the swift flowing Lune estuary by the fishermen of Overton and Sunderland Point. 'Whammeling' was drift netting with a 320yd net working the tide. They were shallow draft, easily handled boats capable of being rowed and sailed. They were clinker built, 20ft long, 5ft in beam and drawing only 9in of water. They were lug rigged with a foresail (used mainly in regattas) and built by the Gardner and Woodhouse families at Overton. A few carvel built 'tank boats' were built to fish the stretch of dangerous shoal water at the mouth of the river, where good catches could be made. They were fitted with internal buoyancy for greater safety. A number of whammel boats (with engines) survive in their original villages and there are also GRP replicas. One tank boat, the *Lively*, was converted into a yacht in 1929 and is in the collection of the Dock Museum, Barrow-in-Furness.

Sources
Alan Lockett, *North Western Sail* (Brinscall 1978) and Cedric Robinson & W R Mitchell, *Life Around Morecambe Bay* (Clapham 1986) both describe these boats.

MUSSEL BOAT

Mussel boats were clinker built vessels, used to gather these shellfish from skears (rock outcrops) in Morecambe Bay and the Lune estuary. They had a transom stern and flat floors for taking the ground and carrying a heavy catch fitted with a centreboard. The Lune version had rather sharper lines, more keel and two or three 56lb weights for ballast. They were 20ft long with a 5ft beam. They were lug rigged with a foresail occa-

sionally set on a short metal bowsprit. Mussels were gathered with a long rake and a shovel. Silting, caused by the opening of Heysham Harbour in 1984, brought about the end of the fishery. One boat has been preserved at Fleetwood Museum.

Source
Alan Lockett, *North Western Sail* (Brinscall 1978).

MANX NICKEY

Very fast, straight keeled, two masted luggers employed in drift net fishing in the Irish Sea. Unlike the so-called Manx lugger (*qv*), the nickey was a lugger developed from the very successful Cornish type. In 1884, with the discovery of the route of mackerel from the Atlantic along the south Irish coast to the Isle of Man fishing grounds in the early summer, there was a major boom in fishing. This attracted Cornish and Manx boats to the Irish coast, particu-

A mussel boat racing at the Morecambe annual regatta in 1909. She carries a standing lug sail and a foresail set on a short bowsprit. *(NMM, neg no P75434)*

Manx nickeys under sail off the Old Pier at Douglas, Isle of Man. The nickeys came mostly from Peel and were fine sea boats, sometimes sailing as far afield as the Shetlands. Some nickies, as in the foreground here, were built with counter sterns. *(NMM, neg no P70072)*

larly around the Kinsale area. The fast Cornish luggers were shown to be markedly superior to the traditional Manx craft and such was the demand from Cornish builders that, in 1869, Paynter of St Ives set up a yard at Kilkeel to build luggers. They were subsequently copied and built extensively in the Isle of Man, particularly at Peel. There are various, but usually unsatisfactory, explanations for the origin of the name. The Manx nickey copied many of the features of the Cornish design. They tended to be slightly larger, typically 48ft in length,

15ft beam, and between 8ft and 10ft deep, with a long straight keel, with about 5ft 6in depth forward. They were rigged with a large dipping lug foresail and a dipping mizzen, which also carried a topsail and a staysail. They were very fast boats which could point high into the wind, and rather than reefing, they carried three suits of sails plus a set of storm sails which could be changed according to the strength of the wind. The foremast could be lowered while fishing and they carried a crew of seven men who, until the mid 1880s and the introduc-

tion of steam capstans, would man a hand capstan to haul in the nets.

MANX NOBBY

The nobby was essentially the same hull form as the nickey (*qv*) and it is said that the name derives from the Scottish fishing boat, a nabbie, but the rig is different, with two standing lugs and a bowsprit and jib. Local experts believe that the nobby was not such a good sailor as the nickey but was less dangerous in inexperienced hands. Typically, they were somewhat small-

er, on average about 35ft in length.

The Manx fisheries boomed between the early 1870s and 1900. In 1872, for example, there were 227 1st class, 82 2nd class and 66 3rd class boats registered at Castletown, Douglas, Ramsay and Peel. Decline was rapid in the twentieth century and by 1923, for example, only four 1st class vessels were registered as fishing out of Peel, the centre of the fishery. Unfortunately, no nickey or nobby has survived, although one nobby was converted into a yacht at Barrow in the 1970s. There are excellent models of both types in the Science Museum, the Nautical Museum, Castletown, and the Merseyside Maritime Museum, Liverpool.

Source
E J March, *The Sailing Drifters*, is the main source of published information on these vessels.

MANX WHERRY
(Irish Sea wherry)

The Manx wherry, or perhaps better called the Irish Sea wherry, was a clinker built, double ended craft used in the eighteenth century as a fish carrier, transporting the herring catches for sale and curing, principally to Liverpool. It was sailed as far north as the Shetlands in search of fish and was also used for smuggling and general cargo.

It had a distinctive deep hull with much sheer and was owned not only in the Isle of Man, but in Skerries (north of Dublin), Allonby, Whitehaven, Galloway, on the Mersey and in north Wales. The term 'wherry' was used to denote a schooner rigged vessel in the Isle of Man but, in fact, many were single masted cutters. There is a model of the *Athol* in the Manx Museum, which is a detailed contemporary model of about 1800. This gives a very good picture of the hull form and all the fixtures and fittings. At a scale of 1:16, it measures 54ft long. This is larger than a number of examples registered at Liverpool. For example, the *Betty*, registered in 1786 and built in 1775, measured 30.5ft long, 10.8ft in beam and 4ft depth. The hull had a fine entrance with fine bilges and a fuller rounded stern, giving plenty of buoyancy. There was a foredeck, below which there was crew accommodation, an open hold amidships massively framed, and a small well deck aft for the steering position.

Wherries seem to have died out in the mid-ninteenth century. Holdsworth noted that those at Skerries were the only ones of their type that he had come across in the kingdom, although a small number seem to have survived elsewhere somewhat later as cargo carriers. The hull configuration points to a design of some antiquity and was noted for being fast and weatherly, to the extent that the customs authorities at Whitehaven commissioned a wherry of their own in the late eighteenth century.

Sources
J Greton, 'The Athol of Douglas Trader', *Manx Journal*, Vol 6 (1957), E W H Holdsworth *British Fishing Boats*, and M K Stammers 'Irish Sea Wherries and Shallops', *Maritime Wales*, Vol 11 (1989), are the best sources.

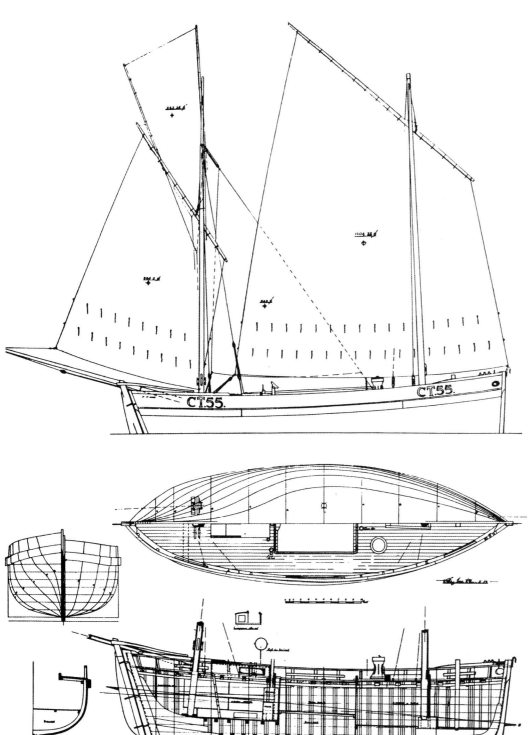

Lines plans, constructional details and sail plan of a Manx nickey. These craft regularly carried a mizzen staysail as well as a mizzen topsail. Though the lines are similar to the Cornish luggers *(qv)* the Manx boats were generally bigger. *(Philip Oke)*

MANX SCOWTE

A double ended, clinker built boat with a high bow and curved stem, straight stern and a good sheer. The Isle of Man was in the possession of the Norwegian kings until 1275 and the Viking influence persisted in the eighteenth-century fishing 'scowte'. By 1774, they ranged from 20ft to 24ft in length and were propelled by a single square sail and four oars. They had a crew of eight and were principally used for drift netting in the Manx herring fishery. They were superseded by larger half decked Manx wherries (qv). John Shewan, that superb modelmaker of Shetland boats, built a model of a scowte based on available evidence for the Manx Museum.

Sources

B & E Megaw, 'Early Manx Fishing Craft', *The Mariner's Mirror*, 27 (1991) is the main source, and they also feature in Edgar March, *Sailing Drifters*.

MANX BALC YAWL

Descendent of a Norwegian yawl (the Manx word 'balc' deriving from 'baak' meaning long line), the Manx balc yawl was used inshore between October and February, and in deep water for cod until April, filling in with catching conger eels until the start of the herring fishery in June. Clinker built and light enough for beaching, many were built with transom sterns from 1850 onwards. The average size was 17ft to 18ft long and 5ft 8in beam; they had a straight stem, a raked transom with fine lines aft and were not dissimilar to the Largs line skiff (qv) mea-

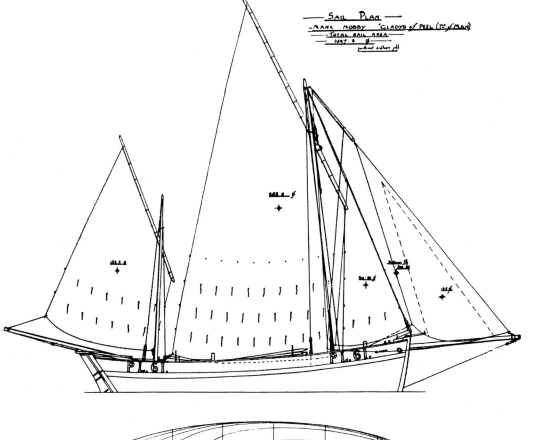

Lines plans, constructional details and sail plan of a Manx nobby. The hull form was similar to the nickey but the stem was more curved and the forefoot more rounded, and as a result she had a proportionally shorter keel. The main difference was in the sail plan. The dipping lug was replaced with a standing lug and a jib set on a bowsprit; inboard of this there was a small staysail. *(Philip Oke)*

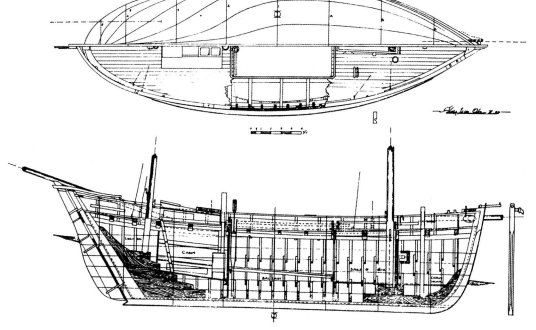

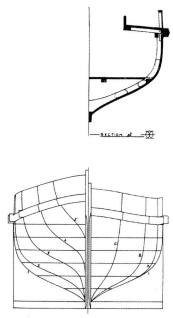

sured by the late P J Oke in 1936. They were propelled by a single broad lug sail (or in the case of the Ramsey 'cod yawl' variant, a standing lug with foresail and bowsprit) and two oars. The crew of seven baited (with whelks), shot and hauled the lines, and if the wind failed, rowed their yawl as far as Morecambe Bay in pursuit of cod. There is a fine contemporary model of the Ramsey cod yawl *King Orry* of 1883 in the Manx Museum.

Sources
Edgar March, *Inshore Craft of Britain*, and E W White, *British Fishing-Boats and Coastal Craft*, mention these vessels.

MANX LUGGER

The Manx lugger or dandy seems to have developed as an enlarged gaff rigged, decked version of the eighteenth-century Manx open fishing boats. By the time of the Washington Report of 1849, they were carvel built, as opposed to the original clinker version, 33ft 9in in length, 11ft 6in depth, with 7 tons of ballast, 23 tons old measurement, and carried a crew of six men. They were used in the herring fishery and for long lining at other times of the year. Around the 1860s, they were built to an increasing size, typically 50ft long by 16ft beam and 10.8ft depth of hold, and with a lug mizzen. They were fine lined with a straight stem and counter stern. There is a fine model of a lugger (dandy) in the Science Museum collection, which was built for the International Fisheries Exhibition of 1883.

Sources
E J March, *Sailing Drifters* and E W H Holdsworth, *British Fishing Boats*, cover the Manx luggers.

A contemporary model of the *Athol* of about 1800 displays the unique characteristics of the wherry hull form. The sharply raked stem and sternposts are typical, and though she is double ended she has a very well rounded stern. *(Manx National Heritage)*

Lines plans of a Manx lugger from the Washington Report of 1849. Though built with quite fine waterlines she has very curved upper strakes aft. They were dandy rigged with a gaff mainsail a a standing lug mizzen. *(NMM, Coastal Craft Collection)*

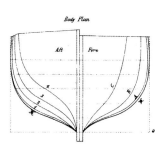

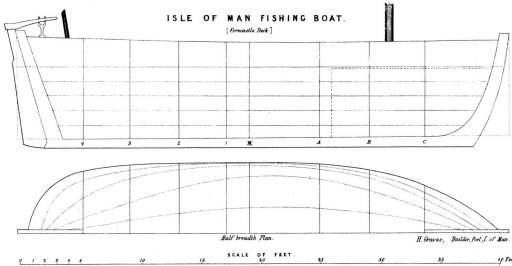

INSHORE CRAFT

The Peggy of Castletown

A boat built in 1791 for a partnership led by George Quayle of Castletown, Isle of Man, the head of an industrial, landowning and banking family, for use with other boats as a transport to and from the mainland, usually Liverpool, of goods and people connected with the family's business and private activities. These boats were expected to show a return on the capital invested in them.

The *Peggy* is similar in dimensions, hull form and rig, to the Chebacco boats in contemporary use for fishing from Essex County in Massachussetts. The type survived in use on the south shore of the Gaspé Peninsula in Quebec, Canada, into the 1960s. She is a clinker built, open boat, 26ft 5in overall, 24ft 4in on the waterline and 7ft 8in in maximum beam. She is full in the bow and fine in the run with a good rise of floor. She has a transom counter and was rigged as a schooner with a running bowsprit.

As a working, rowing and sailing boat the evidence of thwarts and oar ports shows the *Peggy* was rowed by six men. When she was sailing it has been commented that in her original form she would have been easy to swamp on

a wind unless carefully ballasted and handled. From evidence in the Quayle family papers it is apparent that her bulwarks were extended with side-cloths on the quarters, no doubt for this very reason.

To the annoyance of his partners it appears that George Quayle appropriated the *Peggy* for his personal use as a pleasure boat, and his first experiment was to install three drop keels. The fitting of these made the *Peggy* useless for working purposes and the family built a smaller *Peggy II* which remained in service as a working boat for at least 20 years. She appears to have been a great success and was described as 'the Dear Little Beauty' in family correspondence. In 1796 George Quayle sailed the old *Peggy* over to the mainland to race in an early Windermere regatta. On her return to the island she showed herself a wet boat, George Quayle wrote: 'The Quarter Clause were of the greatest protection, without them I believe we had gone to Davy Jones' Locker . . . and without the Slidg. Keels we cd. not have carried Sail enough'.

The boat as she lies in her boathouse at Castletown today shows evidence of considerable modification: an increase in her freeboard by a foot or

so; broadening her beam; and, in effect, turning a strong, relatively light, fast rowing and sailing boat into a rather heavy, purely sailing boat which was probably structurally weak.

There is considerable evidence, such as the complete absence of wear on the new mooring-bitts, and the absence of marks on the mast of the iron collar at the new mastfort level, to show that the mainmast was never used at all in the rebuilt *Peggy*. This evidence and much else suggests that in fact the *Peggy* may never have sailed in her modified form. In due course, she was sealed up in her cellar boathouse and there she remained until she was rediscovered in the 1930s. The cellar and the *Peggy* are now exhibits of the Manx Museum in Castletown. Unique, she is a vessel of great international importance.

Sources
In 1968 the Manx Museum and National Trust commissioned me to examine *Peggy* and all the Quayle family documentation associated with her. The result as published in a paper in *The Journal of the Manx Museum and National Trust* in 1968 replaces all earlier reports on her. To the best of my knowledge there has been nothing published since.

Lines, sheer and sail plans of the schooner *Peggy*. This authoritative drawing shows her as she now is in the Manx Museum, with her increased freeboard and broader beam (*D Jones and W Clarke*)

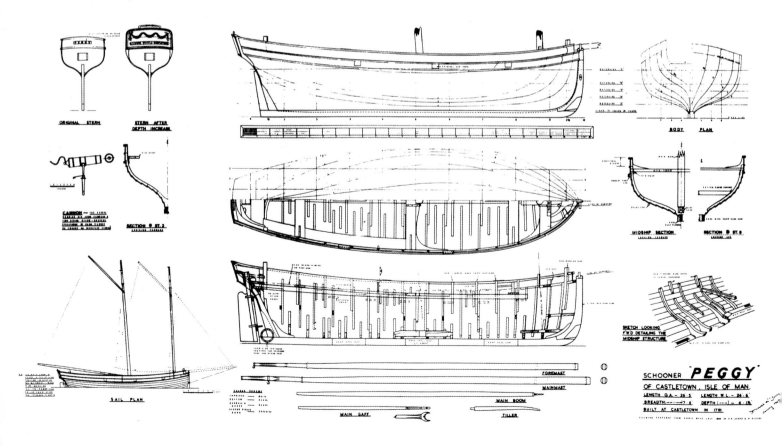

Ireland

THE ISLAND of Ireland lies on the edge of Atlantic Europe, west of Britain and midway between Scandinavia and the Iberian Peninsula. Geographically and historically Ireland is at a crossroads, or meeting place, on the western seaways of Europe. This has contributed to a rich vernacular culture and Irish traditional boats, with their local and regional identities, form part of this complex.

Like Britain, the island of Ireland rises from the undersea continental plateau. As can be seen on Admiralty charts, both islands are enclosed by the 100 fathom line. Running from Norway, beyond the Shetlands and the Outer Hebrides, the line keeps west of the Irish coast by 25 to 100 miles before running southward until it almost touches Spain. Beyond the line, out in the Atlantic, the depths increase rapidly as true oceanic waters are reached. Inside the line, the waters surrounding Ireland are rich in fish stocks and for centuries they have been exploited, not only by Irish fishermen, but also others from Britain and mainland Europe.

North and south of the Irish Sea, the eastern coasts of Ireland are separated from Britain by relatively narrow channels. The north

channel between Ireland and Scotland is, at its narrowest point, only 13 miles across and at Wexford, in the southeast, it is only 50 miles across to the coast of Wales. These enclosed waters, with strong tides, are characterised by choppy 'short seas' which are quite different to the long rolling swells and mountainous waves encountered on Ireland's Atlantic west coast.

Although the land mass of Ireland is only 30,000 square miles, the island has a total coastline of 2,250 miles. The general outline of the coast, particularly in the west, emphasises physical landscape connections between Ireland, Britain and the Atlantic ends of continental Europe. The heavily indented western coast, from Donegal to Cork, is characterised by large bays, numerous offshore islands and long fjord-like sea loughs. These features have their counterparts in Scotland, southwest Wales, southwest England, Norway, Brittany and Spain. In contrast, the east coast of Ireland is relatively smooth, with the exceptions of the major inlets of Belfast Lough, Strangford Lough and Carlingford Lough in the north and the natural harbours of Wexford, Waterford and Cork in the south.

The topography or general surface of Ireland has been described as saucer-shaped, with a highland rim surrounding central lowlands dominated by scattered loughs, bogland and the Shannon river system. Ireland's fragmented peripheral arrangement of mountain land is unique in Europe. It results in an often hilly and frequently mountainous coastline with dramatic cliffs, especially in the west. Only on a stretch of the east coast, centred on Dublin, is the highland rim broken by a 50-mile lowland gap. Since the earliest human habitation of Ireland this gap, lying between the Wicklow Mountains and the Carlingford Mountains, has given access to the interior of the island. Through many centuries, successive incomers – including Viking raiders and traders, Anglo-Normans and English kings – have established their main base on this part of the coast. However, if Dublin has always been the chief city of Ireland, it is no less significant that the other cities and main centres of population have important maritime dimensions and have developed at strategic locations on the coastal periphery of the island.

The earliest date for which there is consistent information on boats around the entire coastline of Ireland is 1836. In that year a Royal Commission on Irish Fisheries made its report and the minutes of evidence contain descriptions, not only of boats and fishing equipment, but also of the social and economic life of the coastal population in pre-famine Ireland.

In terms of a basic typology, analysis of statistics in the 1836 Report shows that open rowing boats represented 73 per cent of the total number of Irish fishing boats, open sailing boats 17 per cent, half decked sailing boats 8 per cent and decked sailing boats 2 per cent. Geographically, over 75 per cent of the boats in all coastal counties were open sailing rowing boats, with the exception of

The second half of the nineteenth century witnessed the importation into Ireland of types from Cornwall, the Isle of Man and Scotland. Many of the boats were secondhand, but the mackerel boats in this photograph, based on zulu and nobby types, were built in Connemara. *(Ulster Folk and Transport Museum)*

Counties Dublin and Wicklow where decked and half decked boats predominated. Various descriptive terms referred to boats of distinctive shape, rig, build and purpose. These included cutter, hooker, seine boat, smack, whale-boat, wherry, yawl and Norway yawl or skiff.

By plotting the distribution of clinker and carvel boats in Ireland, in 1836, a distinct pattern emerges. Clinker construction dominated on the northeast coasts, although the technique was also found on the Cork and Sligo coasts. Carvel built boats were found all around the coast, with the exception of the northeast. The 1836 minutes of evidence clearly reveal that on the west coast of Ireland carvel building was a well established tradition for boats of all types. At the Claddagh in Galway city, for example, shipwrights were said not to be acquainted with clinker building. In contrast, in Co Dublin on the east coast, the older tradition was clinker building, although carvel innovation was occurring chiefly as a result of the introduction of large decked, carvel built trawlers from southwest England. In north Co Dublin, the fishermen of Rush, Skerries and Balbriggan were famous for their decked, clinker built, schooner rigged wherries. They worked distant fishing grounds on the west coast of Ireland and the north of Scotland, as well as the Isle of Man. Many of them also employed their wherries in the carrying and smuggling

trades. These clinker wherries were the largest of all the Irish fishing boats, though by 1836 they were in decline and within 30 years had been largely replaced by boats of more efficient design and carvel construction.

The second half of the nineteenth century was a notable period of boat type innovation on the east coast of Ireland. Essentially it related to the increased importance of the Irish Sea summer herring fishery and to the development of the spring mackerel fishery of Kinsale in Co Cork. Boats from Ireland, Scotland, the Isle of Man and Cornwall fished together in large fleets, which provided the impetus for innovation and change. Increasingly, east coast Irish fishermen acquired large decked boats, new and secondhand, from the Isle of Man and Cornwall. These carvel built boats, with their dandy and later lug rigs, replaced the older clinker built smacks and wherries as the principal types of offshore herring and mackerel boats used by Irish fishermen.

Between 1836 and 1900, Donegal, in the northwest, changed from a mainly carvel zone to a predominantly clinker one due to the adoption of the Greencastle yawl or 'Drontheim', a local successor to the earlier Norway yawl. During the 1880s west Donegal fishermen began to replace their indigenous, heavy, carvel built, usually square-sterned rowing boats with the lighter, double ended, clinker built, sailing and pulling Greencastle yawl.

The diffusion of the Greencastle yawl in west Donegal in the 1880s was accelerated in the following two decades by the improving activities of the Congested Districts Board for Ireland. Established in 1891 and charged with ameliorating conditions of life in the poorest districts of the western coast of Ireland, the Board placed great emphasis on improving the infrastucture of fishing. Besides introducing Scottish zulus and Manx nobbys to Donegal and Galway fishermen, the Board made loans available to Donegal, Mayo and Galway fishermen for the purchase of Greencastle yawls. However the coastal population of Galway was so resistant to change, and the indigenous carvel building tradition so well established, that the implanted Greencastle yawls were not reproduced by local boatbuilders and there was no continuing demand for them by Galway fishermen. Today carvel built boats are still the characteristic vernacular craft of the coasts of Galway and west Mayo. The Galway hooker and the Achill yawl are the best known traditional wooden boats of this region.

An ancient boat type now unique to Ireland is the canvas-covered curragh found on the Atlantic seaboard. There are regional types of curraghs, but all are light, buoyant craft capable of carrying surprisingly heavy loads. Curraghs are relatively cheap to build and as they can be lifted by a few men, harbours and piers are not essential for their use. Today, many curraghs have been modified for propulsion by outboard motors. It is a boat type that has found its last European refuge in western Ireland, and it is with the curragh that we begin our survey of Irish craft.

IRISH CURRAGHS

Lightly built, close boarded or lath, canvas covered, open boats used for kelp gathering, fishing and the ferrying of goods and passengers along the wild wave swept Atlantic coastline of western Ireland. Their buoyancy and shallow draught permits them to ride safely over the rock strewn coastline, and their lightness of construction enables them to be beached and carried ashore above the waterline. Originally propelled by bladeless oars and classified as two-, four- or six-oared vessels, they now usually have outboard engines. The oars pivot on thole pins which protrude through a shaped piece of timber – a 'bull' or 'buicin' – which is fixed to the edge of the oar.

Historically such craft were commonplace along the entire coastline of Ireland; Irish mythology relates that the earliest inhabitants of Ireland, the Firbolgs, are reputed to have arrived in Ireland in their leather craft.

James Wellard hypothesises that the Irish in prehistory trafficked between Ireland and Saint Michael Mount, Cornwall, in their curraghs for cargoes of tin. According to tradition, in or about the year AD 222, the first Irish fleet of curraghs from the east coast made an expedition to raid the coasts of Wales, Cornwall and Gaul. Gildas wrote of the raiding curraghs as did the poet Claudian. His description, 'the sea foamed to their oars' related to the activities of Niall of the Nine Hostages who had his curragh fleet based in Strangford and Carlingford Loughs. Hornell records that 'the curragh was the favourite vessel of the hoards of plundering Irish who descended on the shores of Britain during Roman times and increasingly after . . . and were particular active during the fourth, fifth and sixth century.'

Saint Colmcille, also known as Columba, sailed his curragh from Derry to Iona in 563 to establish that islands' great monastery; *The Navigatio* recounts the voyage of Brendan the Navigator in a curragh from Dingle in Co Kerry to Newfoundland in the sixth century; this inspired Tim Severin to emulate this voyage in a

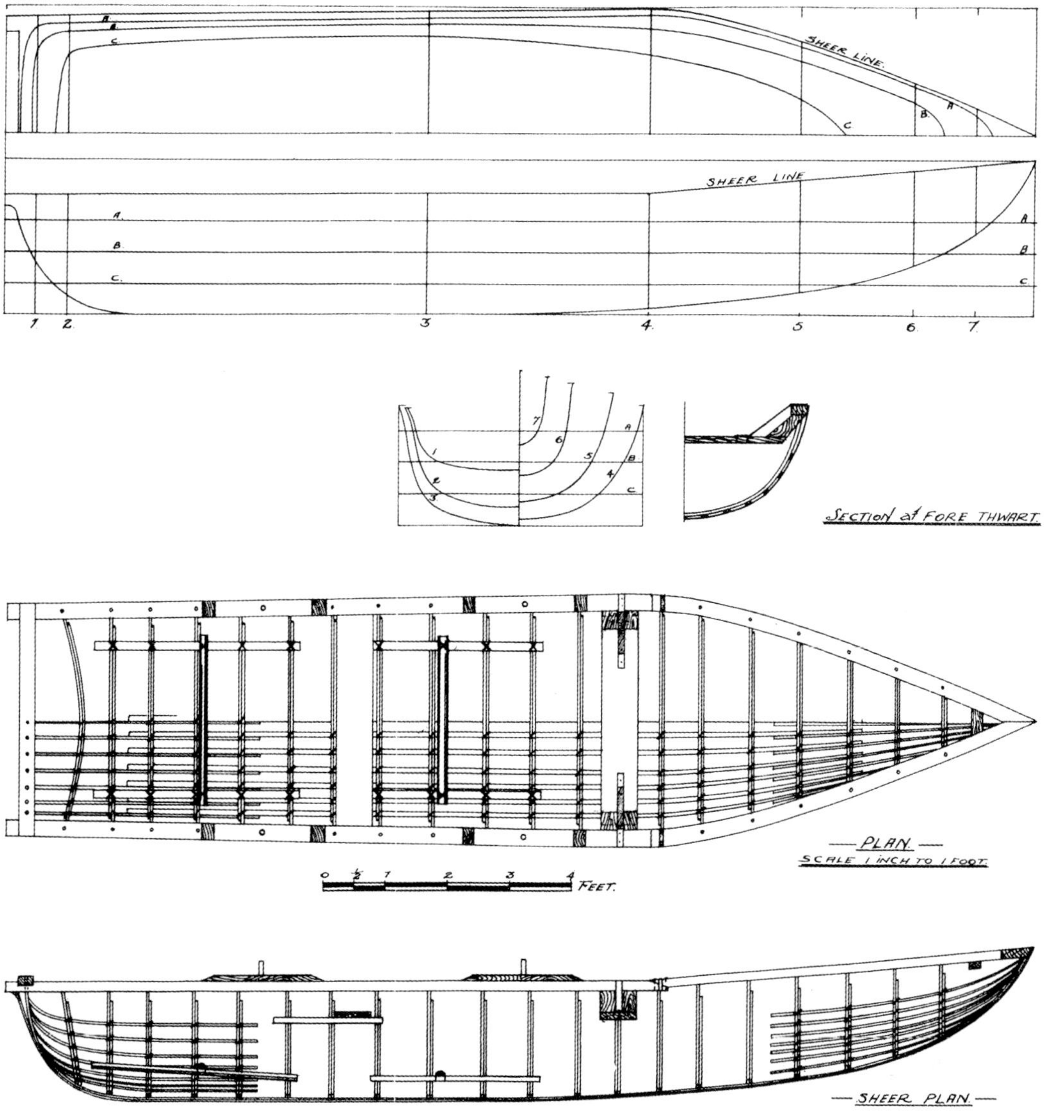

SHEER LINE

SHEER LINE

SECTION at FORE THWART

PLAN
SCALE 1 INCH TO 1 FOOT

0 ½ 1   2   3   4 FEET.

SHEER PLAN

Lines plans and constructional details of the small Dunfanaghy curragh from Co Donegal which has a single gunwale and is constructed of lattice work. She has single thole pins. She measures 16ft 8in overall and 4ft on the beam. (NMM, Coastal Craft Collection. All the plans of the curraghs illustrated here were drawn by Philip Oke from measurements taken off by James Hornell)

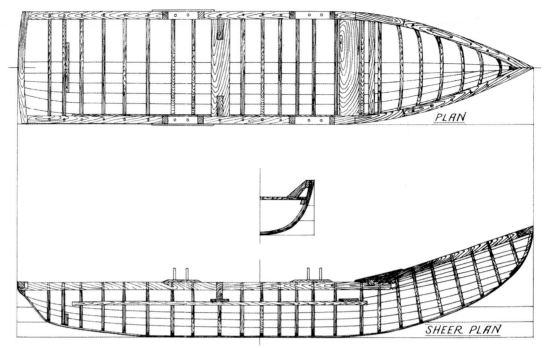

Top right: Lines plans and constructional details of an Iniskea Island curragh, from Co Mayo. She measured 17ft 7in overall with a beam of 3ft 10in. She was planked on her bottom and sides and, apart from the single gunwale, is similar to the Achill type. The crew used broad bladed feathering oars and the drawing shows double thole pins. *(NMM, Coastal Craft Collection)*

Lower right: Lines plans and constructional details of the Achill curragh. This curragh represented an advance on the Iniskea example in that it had a double gunwale. There is also a slight sheer at the after end. It measured 20ft 4in overall and was 3ft 11in on the beam, was planked on the bottom and sides and had a keelson. *(NMM, Coastal Craft Collection)*

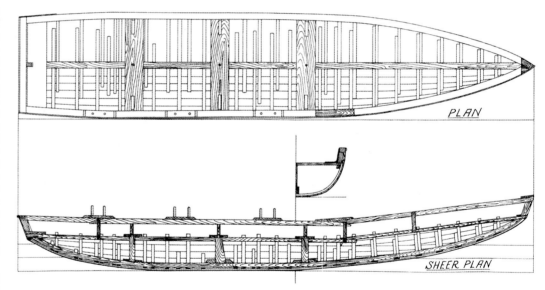

similar craft in 1976-77. By the nineteenth century the curragh was being superseded along the north, east and southern coasts with the introduction and use of other vessel types such as the Greencastle yawl (*qv*). The west coast of Ireland, however, remained true to tradition due, primarily, to the pertaining coastal conditions and the economics of crewing smaller vessels.

The curraghs were used for a variety of purposes including the towing of heavy livestock to offshore craft; the conveyance of smaller animals to grazing grounds on offshore islands; and the transport of turf from the mainland to the islands, as well as kelp gathering and fishing. Curraghs were also used on some inland lakes in the late 1940s and early '50s to carry turf from the upper region of Lough Dahybaun and Carrowmore Lake, Bangor Erris, Co Mayo, to roadside locations. Many authors testify to the innate seamanship of the rowers handling these craft which are capable of carrying in the region of 1½ to 2 tons in weight. The manner and style of rowing is akin to the action of the seabirds, the crew turning the craft to the breakers and riding to the crests of waves.

James Hornell undertook his survey of Irish curraghs during the 1930s. He recorded some ten distinct types ranging from the small paddling curraghs of Tory Island/Bunbeg, Co Donegal, to the naomhóg in Co Kerry. Each of the five counties, Donegal, Mayo, Galway, Clare and Kerry, together with some of their offshore islands had their own characteristic type. They ranged in length from the smallest paddling curragh of Tory Island/Bunbeg at 8ft 4in to the Kerry naomhóg at 25ft. The curraghs of Donegal, that is, the Sheephaven and Dunfanaghy, were 16ft 9in and up to 20ft respectively; the north

Mayo curraghs 23ft 6in; the Achill type 20ft 4in, with the Ross-a-Dilisk and Iniskea between 16ft to 18ft long. The offshore island of Aran produced a curragh of 25ft in length and the standard Kilkee curragh, Co Clare, was 17ft 8in.

The style and shape of curraghs differed depending on the sea conditions, from the relatively heavier, flatter Aran type to the graceful bird-like shape of the Kerry curragh. The Galway/Aran curragh with its straight bow gunwales, well-rounded cross section and wide stern which is rounded up to the tran-

som, is the ideal craft for the choppy conditions which pertain; the Kerry noamhóg with its nicely curved bows, steamed to obtain the necessary curvature, is swept back to the stern and rides lightly upon the water. It is eminently suited for the long rolling seas of this coastline. Evolution has also seen the curragh being lengthened to around 23-24ft and narrower in section. These are used as 'racing curraghs' in regattas along the western coastline. This is a continuation of a long tradition which saw rival villages

or counties competing one with each other. They are generally built in the style and manner of the Kerry curragh but without the pronounced upward sweeping sheer to the stern. Whilst there has been a decline in the numbers of hese craft in all areas as people drifted from the sea into industrialised settings and environments, the proven ability of this relict of the past, coupled with the existence of expert curragh builders, ensures the continuation, without foreseeable imperilment, of this inshore craft.

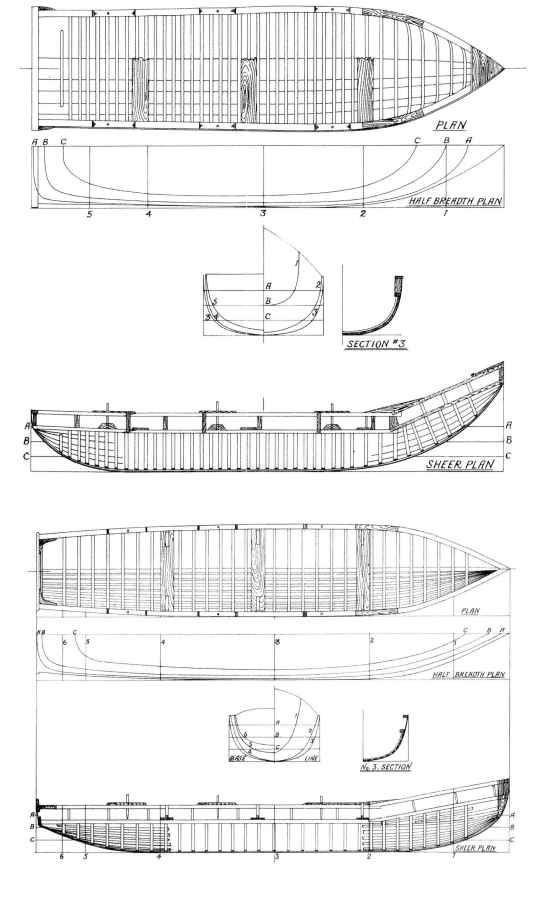

PLAN

A B C   C B A

HALF BREADTH PLAN

5   4   3   2   1

SECTION #3

A   A
B   B
C   C

SHEER PLAN

PLAN

A B   C   5   4   3   2   1   C B A

HALF BREADTH PLAN

BASE   LINE

No. 3. SECTION

A   A
B   B
C   C

6   5   4   3   2

SHEER PLAN

Top left: Lines plans and constructional details of a Ross-a-Dilisk curragh from mainland Connemara. These curraghs were usually of the three-thwart type and between 16ft and 18ft overall. The bottom and sides were fully planked; the oars were held on single tholes. *(NMM, Coastal Craft Collection)*

Lower left: Lines plans and constructional detail of the Aran Island curragh. It has a sharply sheered bow and a low transom stern. Curraghs were probably employed more by the Aran islanders than by any other coastal inhabitants. They were not planked but constructed of lattice work which was then covered with canvas. A two-man version was 15ft to 16ft: a four-man craft 22ft to 25ft. *(NMM, Coastal Craft Collection)*

The present curragh on the west coast of Ireland has evolved in outline, construction methodology, covering and length over the last century. The original coverings of horse and cow-hide were replaced sometime in the nineteenth century, in certain counties, by a covering made from flax; the normal cover at present in all counties is tarred canvas. Sawn uniform ribs of American oak have replaced the sally/osier material previously used; nails have replaced the leather lashings for securing the stringers to the ribs, and the double gunwale methodology of construction is now accepted practice as it gives greater strength to the craft. An increase in length was introduced, initially by the addition of a distinct and separate stern section which was 'added on' to the original craft. The period of evolution occurred between 1820 and 1940, when the first outboard engine was fitted to a Kerry curragh, or noamhog.

The number of classifications is now reduced, but separate types still remain. These tend to be concentrated in the western region of Galway/Mayo, their offshore islands and in the county of Kerry. These are the areas which have had an unbroken line of expert curragh makers over the years and the tradition remains, but the day has passed, however, when it was said of the fishing villages 'that all the houses here had a curragh'.

Sources
James Hornell, 'British Coracles and Irish Curraghs', *The Mariner's Mirror*, 22 (1937) and 24 (1938), is a particularly good source. Also of interest are Alan Anderson and Marjorie Ogilvy, *Adomnan's Life of Columba* (London 1961), and Tim Severin, *The Brendan Voyage* (London 1978).

Lines plans and constructional details of a Kilkee curragh from mainland Co Clare. Used on the same waters as the Aran Island vessels they are quite similar and, like the Aran versions, they employed lattice work rather than planking in their construction. Here and further south in Co Kerry the word 'currach' (Gaelic) was replaced by 'naomhóg', derived from old Irish. *(NMM, Coastal Craft Collection)*

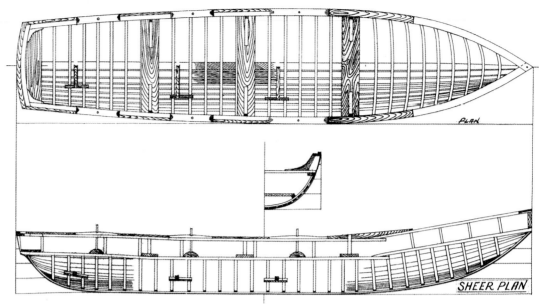

Lough Erne Cot

Cots are plank built, flat bottomed craft of various types, found on inland loughs and some coastal waters. The term cot derives from the Irish word 'coite' meaning dugout. Planked cots probably began replacing dugout cots during the seventeenth century because of increasing difficulty in obtaining suitable oak timber from which dugouts could be hewn.

In Co Fermanagh the Lough Erne cot clearly evolved from a dugout to a planked craft, as the vessel best adapted to carry people, animals and goods between the shores and islands of this lakeland region. Late sixteenth-century illustrations of dugout cots on the lough show remarkable similarity to later planked cots which continued in use until almost the present day. Cots varied in length from 12ft to 42ft and in beam from 3ft to 9ft. Their long hulls had no bow or stern in the usual sense, but were built with tapering squared off ends which were simply pitched extensions to the flat bottom construction. This characteristic feature of Lough Erne cots seems to have evolved largely as a response to the local need for a boat that combined the functions of transporter and landing craft.

One of the last working cot builders was Mr Paddy Gunn of Corratistune, Derrylin, on Upper Lough Erne. In 1969 he built a 22ft cot for the Ulster Folk and Transport Museum's collection of traditional boats. With a hull construction of battened flat floor planking, sawn oak frames and three overlapping larch strakes on each side, the completed cot was coated with tar and equipped with two 10ft oars, a steering paddle and a pushing out pole.

As well as working craft, cots were also used for recreation on the lough. In the past, cot racing was a highly competitive rowing sport and often valuable prizes could be won. Occasionally the cots competed with more conventional boats and a mid nineteenth-century traveller has left a graphic description of such a race: '. . .

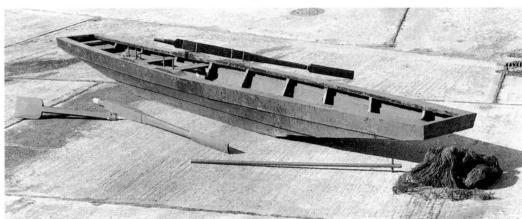

Above: A 22ft Lough Erne cot, which was built for the Ulster Folk and Transport Museum in 1969. Shown also in the photograph are the oars, the steering paddle, and pole. *(Ulster Folk and Transport Museum)*

Right: This drawing of a Wexford cot is taken from E W H Holdsworth's book on fishing boats published in 1874. It depicts a typical double ended cot, with raked stem and sternposts and a three masted spritsail rig with a jib set on a short bowsprit.

awkward and clumsy as it seems, if the day should happen to be perfectly still, it is the cot that invariably wins the race; their great, broad, shallow frames seem to slip over the surface without touching it. But the slightest breeze is fatal to them: they drop to leeward as unresistingly as a floating plant.'

Today the wooden cot, which for so long has been an important element in the lough economy, has virtually disappeared. Yet a need for this general type of craft still persists, if only to transport cattle to and from the islands, and this need has been met by the construction of one or two steel cots. Significantly, in these vessels, modern industrial materials and construction techniques have been combined with a shape that has continued more or less unchanged for at least four centuries. Thus the Lough Erne cot, in its various forms, is an apt illustration of continuity and change in local boatbuilding traditions.

Sources
Michael McCaughan, 'The Lough Erne Cot', *Ulster Folk and Transport Museum Year Book* (1969/70).

WEXFORD COT

Beach boats used by part time fishermen and distinctive as the only seagoing cots in Ireland. Today flat bottomed cots continue to be built at Rosslare Harbour on the coast of Co Wexford. In the 1980s, Mr Jack Wickham was the fifth generation of his family still building these traditional craft and there are other active cotbuilders in neighbouring localities. Varying in size from 20ft to 26ft, cots are now much smaller in size than formerly and with the advent of outboard motors, the old sharp stern generally has been modified to a narrow transom. Nevertheless, the style of construction and overall shape of modern cots has changed very little over many years. Traditionally, the Wexford cot is double ended, the stem and sternposts being slightly raked. The larch side planking is fastened clinker fashion to widely spaced sawn frames. Along the length of the carvel planked bottom of the cot, there is a sharp angle or chine between it and the topsides. No plans are used by cotbuilders, their skills being passed on from generation to generation.

At the end of the nineteenth century the biggest concentration of cots was at the mouth of the enclosed estuarine waters of the River Slaney at Wexford Harbour. Their usual length was about 30ft overall and with 7½ft or 8ft beam. They were sharp at both ends and flat bottomed, with the exception of a short length of keel at each end and a false keel or bilge piece extending some distance on both sides between the floor and the planking. At sea, cots were either rowed or sailed, being rigged with three spritsails and a jib. To reduce leeway, a centreboard, extending 5ft below the flat bottom, was lowered when sailing on the wind. Primarily used for herring drifting on inshore fishing grounds, shallow draughted cots were well suited to negotiating the shoals and sandbanks inside and outside the estuarine waters of Wexford Harbour. Each cot had a four-man crew and high standards of seamanship were required to work these treacherous tidal waters.

Sources
Holdsworth mentions the cots in *Deep Sea Fishing and Fishing Boats*. More recent is Owain Roberts, 'The Cots of Rosslare Harbour and Wexford', *The Mariner's Mirror*, 71 (1985).

LOUGH NEAGH DINGHY

The characteristic Lough Neagh fishing boat was the 16ft open 'dinghy', setting a simple spritsail and jib. It was also a pulling boat, with long oars pivoting on an iron pin or 'bolster' distinctively fitted as an outrigger on either

A Lough Neagh fishing boat, photographed at Cranfield, Co Antrim, around 1930. The wide expanse of the lake meant that considerable seas could build up down a long fetch and so these craft, with their full sections and fine entrance, were designed to meet quite rough conditions. The long oars, pivoted on iron tholes, are clearly shown here. *(Ulster Folk and Transport Museum)*

Greencastle yawls at Burtonport, Co Donegal, in about 1905. These double ended, clinker built boats in many ways resemble the Scottish sixerns *(qv)* and are very much part of the northern European tradition which spread from Scandinavia. The masts are unstepped here though the position for stepping the mainmast can be seen in the thwart. The usual rig was two spritsails and a jib set on a bowsprit. *(Ulster Folk and Transport Museum)*

side of the boat. The pins did not pass through the oars themselves but through a large wooden block or 'clog' fastened to the shaft of each oar. The practical advantage of this arrangement was that when the two-man crew was fishing, the oars could trail in the water clear of the boat. Dinghies had transom sterns and were clinker built, a type of construction consistent with general boatbuilding practice on Irish inland waters.

The last surviving example of a Lough Neagh dinghy was acquired by the Ulster Folk and Transport Museum in 1973. Built in 1932, her owner, the late Mr Joe Murray, had not fished with her for a number of years and in common with other fishing craft on the lough, the boat had not been given a name. Characterised by a broad beam of 6ft on a hull length of 16ft, she has a fine, slightly hollow entrance, full bilges amidships and a clean run aft. The boat is open, except for a short foredeck incorporating a 'mastboard' which supports the short unstayed mast. A thwart is fitted at the rowing position amidships, while a working platform aft is slightly raised above the bottom boards. The hull planking is a mixture of larch and spruce, while the stem, sternpost and keel are of oak. Interestingly, the transom or 'sternboard' is positioned forward of the sternpost rather than on its afterside.

Because of the poor condition of the dinghy, it was decided in 1982 that a replica boat should be built by the museum boatbuilder, Mr Alex Shaw. A year later the replica was completed and first launched in May 1983. Drawing 15in forward and 18in aft, the new boat sails quite well in a fresh breeze, although she is rather tender down to a certain point. Under oars she moves easily through the water and has excellent directional stability.

Sources
Michael McCaughan, 'A Lough Neagh Replica Fishing Boat', *Ulster Folklife*, 30 (1984).

Irish Yawls

Until boat type changes were brought about by the advent of engines in the early twentieth century, the common open fishing boat of the northwestern, northern and eastern coasts of Ireland was the sailing and pulling yawl. The term 'yawl' referred to boats which were double ended and clinker built, a notable exception being the carvel built Achill yawl on the west coast of Co Mayo. Essentially, yawls were identified by hull shape and not by rig. While 'yawl' was the most common descriptive name for Irish double ended, clinker built boats, in various localities they were also known as skiffs, shallops and drontheims. As with all boat types, yawls built and used in particular districts were often called after local place names, two of the most famous being the Greencastle yawl in Co Donegal and the Groomsport yawl in Co Down. However, despite regional variations in size, shape and rig, all of these yawls, skiffs, shallops and drontheims were essentially the same boat type within the broad parameters of double ended form and clinker construction. Characteristically, they were relatively cheap to build, had good seakeeping qualities, and were light enough to be hauled ashore on exposed coasts where

harbour accommodation was poor or non-existent. With their double ended shape and clinker construction, Irish yawls were in the same ancient northwest European boatbuilding tradition as the Viking ships of 1000 years earlier and which possibly first introduced clinker construction to Ireland.

GREENCASTLE YAWL
(Skerries yawl, Drontheim)

Although named after a village on the Inishowen Peninsula in east Donegal, the main centres for building Greencastle yawls, at the end of the nineteenth century, were at nearby Moville and at Portrush on the north coast of Co Antrim. In the latter district the preferred term was Skerries yawl, the name deriving from the rocky islets off Portrush and more acceptable to local pride than Greencastle yawl. Across Lough Foyle in Inishowen, and to some extent too in north Antrim, Greencastle yawls were also known as drontheims, a derivative of the Norwegian place name Trondheim which acknowledged the Scandinavian ancestry of these boats.

Generally, Greencastle yawls were about 24ft to 26ft in length, with a beam of 6ft to 7ft and a working rig of two spritsails and a jib. Each boat carried a crew of up seven men, four of whom were needed to pull on each of

the 18ft oars, when there was insufficient wind for sailing. Characteristically these clinker, double ended boats were easy to row and under sail they were fast on a reach. Before the wind they often ran goose-winged and in a following sea their sharp sterns kept them dry and safe. Donegal fishermen engaged in winter long lining and seasonal net fishing, often working long distances from land out in the open Atlantic. Despite the vulnerability of open boats in such waters, crews were skilled in handling their yawls in bad weather and heavy seas, which could set upon them with little warning.

From the 1880s onwards, Greencastle yawls were being sold to fishermen in west Donegal, as replacements for their older and heavier carvel built boats. By the turn of the century, yawls were also being exported to Scotland, notably to South Kintyre and the islands of Islay and Colonsay. The demand for Greencastle yawls was unprecedented and boatbuilding boomed in east Donegal and north Antrim. Boats were generally supplied at a charge of 10 shillings per foot length. The Portrush boatbuilders were James Kelly and James Hopkins and Co, while in Moville the builders were Hugh McDaid, Beattie and Son and James McDonald.

By World War I demand for Green-

The Groomsport yawl *Lissey* photographed around 1901 just prior to making a record passage to Port Patrick in Scotland in 2 hours and 40 minutes. The distinctive rig of two overlapping dipping lug sails was a powerful one, though oras were used when necessary. *(Ulster Folk and Transport Museum)*

castle yawls had declined. In 1928 the last yawl, or drontheim, was built in Moville by James McDonald. This boat continued fishing out of Port Ronan, near Malin Head, until the early 1980s and was the last working drontheim in Inishowen, albeit powered by an 8hp outboard motor. In 1983 her owner, Michael Doherty of Middletown, Ballygorman, sold the boat to the Ulster Folk and Transport Museum for preservation.

Today James McDonald and Sons (Boatbuilder) Ltd is the only surviving boatbuilding business in Inishowen. The firm enjoys a considerable reputation for its modern double ended, clinker built, half decked motorboats. In recent years, with a revival of interest in yawls and drontheims, McDonalds have also undertaken boat restoration work as well as new boatbuilding to their traditional design.

GROOMSPORT YAWL

Groomsport yawls were notable as the largest yawls around the Irish coast, being up to 32ft in length with a beam of 9ft. Groomsport is a small village at the mouth of Belfast Lough on the County Down shore. Its name suggests Viking origins and its small tidal harbour is of considerable age. At the beginning of this century, Groomsport was a close knit, fishing community in which long lining for cod was the main winter activity. As with all such fishing it was cold and arduous work, with crews sailing and rowing their yawls up to 10 miles to the fishing grounds. Incomes were augmented by offshore pilot work for the port of Belfast and in the summer months many fishermen worked as paid hands in local yachts.

These double ended, clinker built boats were distinctively rigged with two large and overlapping dipping lugsails set on a foremast and mainmast. Each sail could be held extended by the fitting of a light boom. Smaller 20ft yawls set only one lug on a mast stepped amidships. In both rigs, sails were cut high in the clew so that they would not touch the water in a seaway. Sometimes a bowline was used and set up to the towing bollard or 'Samson',

with which the yawls were fitted for their pilot work. Halyards consisted of a tye and single whip purchase, the tye running over half a sheave at the masthead. This fitting was strongly favoured by the Groomsport men, as there was little chance of a yard jamming in hoisting or lowering when going about. For reefing, the forelug was set on the mainmast. Groomsport yawls, like all Irish yawls, were essentially shallow draft, pulling boats with sails, and so frequent tacking was necessary when working to windward. Nevertheless, with a skillful crew of five men and ballasted with about 2 cwt of stones, they had a high reputation around Belfast Lough for speed and weatherliness.

Many Groomsport yawls were built

An Achill yawl at Curraun, Co Mayo. These double ended, carvel vessels with their large dipping lug sails were well suited to the big seas on the Atlantic shores. *(Ulster Folk and Transport Museum)*

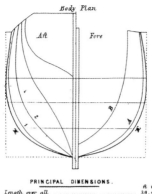

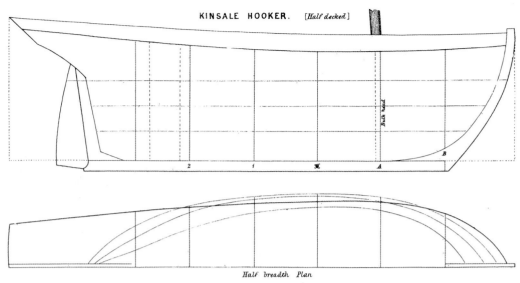

KINSALE HOOKER.   [Half decked]

Half breadth Plan

Cornelius Barrett, Builder Kinsale.

by James Emerson, who lived on the nearby Copeland Islands. When he died in 1914, the local tradition of yawl building came to an end. No Groomsport sailing and pulling yawl has survived the passage of years to the present day. However, at the time of his death, Emerson had started construction of a large motor/sailing yawl which was completed by a boatbuilder from another district. Named *Carpathia*, she was a developed model of the sailing and pulling yawls, built with more freeboard, greater length and with a sailing rig reduced to a single dipping lug. With an overall length of 34ft on a beam of 9ft, she was fitted with a 7/8hp petrol/paraffin single cylinder Kelvin engine. Of course *Carpathia* was not a fully powered motorboat, but rather a sailing yawl with an auxiliary engine, which also replaced the labour of rowing. Significantly, she represented the local transition from sail and oar to the modern dependence on engine power. In 1974 she was acquired by the Ulster Folk and Transport Museum and subsequently restored to her earliest form of a Groomsport motor/sailing yawl.

ACHILL YAWL

Achill is Ireland's largest island and forms part of the mountainous western seaboard of Co Mayo. Achill yawls were the local type of open workboat, chiefly used for long line and hand line fishing. They were also found on the adjacent Curraun peninsula and on neighbouring Clare Island, together with the more distant Inishturk. These boats were double ended, but differed from yawls elsewhere in that they were carvel built. This, of course, was the indigenous west coast construction method for building wooden planked boats. Although carvel built, Achill yawls were relatively light with fine lines fore and aft. Rigged with a dipping lug sail, each boat rowed four oars and carried stone ballast. With skilled crews, they were excellent sea boats and their double ended shape as well suited to running before a big sea, or landing on an open shore in a breaking sea. Overall length varied from 19ft to 25ft, but generally yawls were about 22ft long with a 6ft beam. The hulls were tarred black and the calico sails coated with a preservative known as 'cutch'. Following the introduction of outboard engines, transom stern yawls became more common and with the coming of inboard engines some yawls were modified and bigger motor yawls were also built. There were a number of yawl builders in Achill, together with a builder in Curraun on the other side of Achill Sound. Today the boat building craft is still being carried on in Achill by Pattern family and in Curraun by the O'Malley family. Although no longer used as work boats, Achill yawls are still sailed for recreation and competition in local regattas.

Sources
Material on Irish yawls appears in Michael McCaughan, 'Double-Ended and Clinker-Built: The Irish Dimension of a European Boatbuilding Tradition', *The Use of Tradition* (Ed Alan Gailey), (Cultra 1988), and also his *Sailing the Seaways* (Belfast 1991). The Greencastle yawl is dealt with in MacPolin, Donal, *The Drontheim, Forgotten Sailing Boat of the North Irish Coast* (Dublin 1992). The Groomsport yawl receives coverage in Dixon Kemp, *A Manual of Yacht and Boat Sailing* (Eighth edition, London, 1985) and

in Michael McCaughan, '*Carpathia*: An Early Motor Fishing Boat', *Ulster Folk and Transport Museum Year Book* (1977/78). Two pieces of research (unpublished) by Jarlath Cunnane and Denis Gallagher have dealt with the Achill yawl.

Irish Hookers

In the early nineteenth century the term 'hooker' was commonly used to describe heavily built, smack rigged boats, used for fishing and carrying on the western and southern coast of Ireland, from Donegal in the northwest to Wexford in the southeast. Characteristically, hookers were open or half decked and were carvel built with varying degrees of 'tumblehome' on their tarred black hulls. Essentially, they were eighteenth-century boats in their build and design. Nevertheless, while their shape and strength of construction gave hookers a bluff topside appearance, the underwater lines of Galway hookers in particular, were remarkably refined and graceful. The Kinsale hooker and the Galway hooker were the best known hooker variants, the latter type being the only one to have survived to the present day.

KINSALE HOOKER

Prior to the 1860s, Kinsale in Co Cork was famous for its offshore line fishermen and their seagoing hookers. After this date the old fishery was superseded by a new, highly profitable mackerel fishery, which attracted large fleets of boats from elsewhere. The local hookers were unable to compete successfully with purpose built, fast

Lines plans of a Kinsale hooker from the Washington Report of 1849. She was not as beamy as the Galway hooker and nor did she have quite such distinct tumblehome, but she was considerably deeper and the depth of hold on these lines is given as 10ft 9in. *(NMM, Coastal Craft Collection)*

sailing mackerel drifters from Cornwall, the Isle of Man and Scotland, as well as other parts of Ireland. As a result, demand for Kinsale hookers declined and eventually the boat type disappeared.

Earlier, in the 1830s and '40s, the Kinsale hooker was regarded as a very fine class of boat, manned by six to nine men fishing with nets, long lines and hand lines. Ranging from 15-25 tons, the building cost of a hooker was about £8 per ton, including materials. The Kinsale hooker was a distinctive vessel with a deep hull, slight tumblehome, a full bow, lean quarter and a transom counter stern. With the mast stepped forward, a gaff mainsail was set, together with a foresail and a jib on a long bowsprit. As safe and seakindly boats, hookers would often go to sea when nothing else would attempt it and they could ride out the heaviest of gales on their fishing grounds. In 1848 Cornelius Barrett of Kinsale built a 19-ton half decked hooker with an overall length of 39ft 4in, beam of 11ft and depth of 8ft. Fully laden it drew 5ft forward and 7ft 6in aft. When sailing light it carried 12 tons of ballast. Built for a crew of six men, the bare hull cost £120. The lines of this hooker were reproduced in Captain Washington's 1849 Parliamentary Report on British and Irish fishing vessels.

Above: A Galway hooker waiting for the breeze. The mast has a quite distinct rake and the luff of the mainsail is simply laced to the mast rather than attached with mast hoops. Note the sharp, hollow entry and the well raked stern. (NMM, neg no N47877)

Below: Lines plan of a Galway hooker from the Washington Report. This is an earlier example than in the photograph and she does not have quite such a refined entry. In addition, the maximum breadth is further forward. The body plan shows how the tumblehome reaches right back to the stern. (NMM, Coastal Craft Collection)

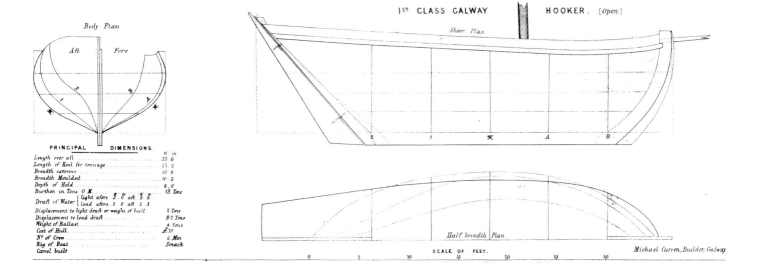

Body Plan

Aft   Fore

PRINCIPAL DIMENSIONS		
	ft	in
Length over all	33	6
Length of Keel for tonnage	27	2
Breadth extreme	10	6
Breadth Moulded	10	3
Depth of Hold	6	0
Burthen in Tons O.M.	13 Tons	
Draft of Water light afore 2 0 aft 3 6		
load afore 3 0 aft 5 8		
Displacement to light draft or weight of hull	2 Tons	
Displacement to load draft	8·7 Tons	
Weight of Ballast	4 Tons	
Cost of Hull	£30	
Nº of Crew	6 Men	
Rig of Boat	Smack	
Carvel built		

1ST CLASS GALWAY HOOKER. [Open]

Sheer Plan

Half breadth Plan

SCALE OF FEET.

Michael Curren, Builder, Galway

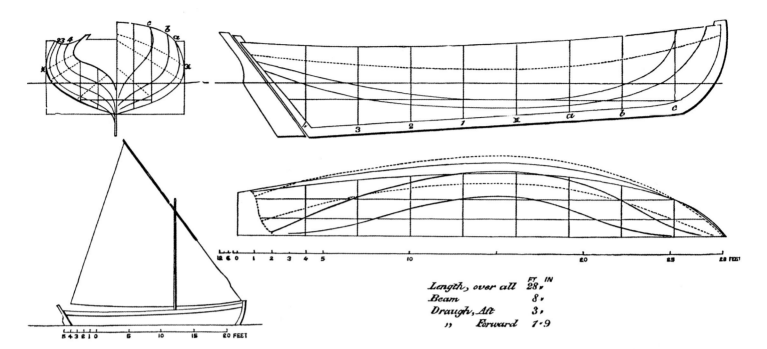

Length, over all   28. (FT IN)
Beam   8.
Draught, Aft   3.
     ,,   Forward 1·9

Lines plan and sail plan of a púcán. The hull form was very much that of her bigger sister, the hooker, but the sail plan is quite distinct. This plan shows the craft with only a dipping lug; more often a jib was set on a running bowsprit. There were no shrouds used and the jib halyard acted as a forestay. (Dixon Kemp)

GALWAY HOOKER

In the early nineteenth century, hookers were strongly identified with the Claddagh fishing community in the city of Galway, where the local fleet exceeded 100 boats. By the end of the century the fishing fleet had declined and hookers had become more significant as small carrying vessels in the local trade and rural economy of the Galway Bay region. Hookers, the largest up to 44ft in length, were engaged in transporting turf, limestone, seaweed and other cargoes around the rocky and heavily indented coast of Co Galway, and particularly between the mainland and the Aran Islands. Connemara in west Co Galway, with its sheltered bays, islands and channels, was a natural and economically viable environment for the Galway hooker. Here the necessity for hauling up did not exist and deep sailing craft could be berthed at tidal piers and inlets, convenient for local trade and close to the homes of their owners and their builders.

In 1874 Galway hookers were described as having long been famous and unlike other Irish fishing boats. At the time the large class of hookers,

about 15 tons, were half decked, from 30ft to 35ft overall and about 10ft beam. With a distinctive curved stem, raking transom stern and deep heeled keel, the Galway hooker was not so deep as the Kinsale hooker, but had a more pronounced tumblehome and was built with much finer underwater lines. Characteristically, the Galway hooker, with a larch on oak hull, was bluff above and fine below, with a hollow entry, rising floors and a long clean run aft. When afloat, the bows were high and the stern low, with marked upturn in the sheer forward. Setting a gaff mainsail, laced to the mast, together with a foresail and a jib, set on a long bowsprit, hookers carried a strong weather helm and were quick in stays. Sails were made from coarse calico, known as 'band linen', saturated with a mixture of Stockholm tar and butter, or more cheaply coal tar and pigs' lard. Although they could be lively in a seaway, hookers were weatherly boats and seldom shipped a sea, due not only to their remarkable hull shape, but also to the seamanship of their crews of three to six men.

The turf trade provided a livelihood for a dwindling fleet of hookers until the 1960s, with the last of them working into the early 1970s. However, in the 1970s a Galway hooker revival began, focusing on hookers as pleasure craft and as vibrant symbols of regional identity. Although initiated by east coast yachtsmen, Galwaymen themselves soon were restoring old hookers and building new ones for sailing in re-

gattas and festivals. Today this spirit of revival and renewal of tradition is so strong, that the unique Galway hooker has become the iconic Irish boat type.

GLEÓITEOG AND PÚCÁN

Pronounced 'glowchung' and 'pookaun', these craft were smaller versions of the large Galway hooker or 'bád mór' (big boat). The gleóiteog ranged from about 24ft to 28ft in length and was used as a general workboat for fishing or carrying small cargoes. Some were half decked while others were entirely open. Essentially, a gleóiteog had all the hull and rig features of a big hooker, albeit in reduced size.

The open púcán was similar in function, size and hull form to the gleóiteog, but differed in its rig. In contrast to the gaff rig, the púcán set a high peaked, dipping lug, with a peak halyard to support the upper end of the yard, and a small jib set on a running bowsprit.

With all these craft, from the bád mór to the gleóiteog and púcán, the skilled work of different builders was reflected in subtle variations of shape, style and sailing characteristics.

Sources
Holdsworth, *Deep Sea Fishing and Fishing Boats* and the Washington Report both contain material on Kinsale and Galway hookers. Richard J Scott, *The Galway Hookers* (Swords 1985) deals with the Galway hooker as well as the gleóiteog and the púcán. Dixon Kemp has details in *A Manual of Yacht and Boat Sailing*.

Luggers, and Nickeys, Nobbys and Zulus in Ireland

WEST CORNISH LUGGER OR NICKEY IN IRELAND

Although west Cornish fishermen had been coming to the Irish Sea herring fishery from 1818, it was their outstanding success at the Kinsale, Co Cork, mackerel fishery in the 1860s that stimulated an unprecedented demand for the superior west Cornish lugger. Penzance and St Ives boatbuilders were inundated with orders, especially from Manx fishermen, who called their new Cornish luggers 'nickeys' *(qv)*. In anticipation of a continuing demand for Cornish luggers, an entrepreneurial boatbuilder, William Paynter, left St Ives in 1875 to establish a boatyard in the Irish Sea fishing port of Kilkeel, Co Down. Despite a number of luggers being built for Kilkeel owners, which they referred to as 'nickeys', Paynter's enterprise was not wholly successful. Large orders from Isle of Man fishermen did not materialise, as Manx boatbuilders were now turning out their own 'nickey' version of the west Cornish lugger. As a fishery recession began to set in, Paynter sold his Kilkeel boatyard in 1883 and returned to St Ives. Nevertheless, in subsequent years there was a continuing demand by Irish fishermen, particularly in Co Down and west Cork, for secondhand luggers and nickeys being sold out of the Cornish and Manx fleets.

The last surviving Irish nickey, *Mary Joseph* N55 of Kilkeel, continued fishing until 1973, when she was aquired for preservation by the Ulster Folk and Transport Museum. Built in 1877 by William Paynter at his new Kilkeel boatyard, *Mary Joseph* underwent a number of modifications in a remarkably long working life of 96 years. She retains the distinctive lines and many of the constructional features of a nineteenth-century west Cornish lugger. Her double ended, carvel built hull, 52.5ft overall length and 14.5ft beam, is deep heeled, drawing 3.5ft of water forward and 6ft aft. With fine underwater lines, she has a sharp entrance, gently rising floors, well rounded bilge, a clean run aft, a straight, vertical stempost and rounded forefoot. The sternpost is also straight, but raked, and the large rudder is hung from the sternpost, from the head to the heel.

Nickeys were fine sea boats and sailed well to windward. One of *Mary*

Irish nobbys on the west coast, registered at Tralee. All the craft have their mizzens reefed and the second boat has lowered her mainmast. They have the distinct features of the Manx nobby hull (qv) – the curved and slightly raked stem and the well raked sternpost – as well as standing lug sails on both main and mizzen. *(NMM, neg no N47879)*

Joseph's former owners and skippers described her as 'wind greedy' when under sail. She was fast too, especially by the wind, which was generally regarded as the best sailing point of these boats. The nickey rig was a dipping lug foresail and a standing lug mizzen, with mizzen topsail and staysail and a big jib in light weather.

When fishing it generally took from three to four hours to haul the nets and in *Mary Joseph*, before 1903, this was done by hand capstan. In that year, however, it was replaced by a steam capstan which was installed when a new deck was laid and the accommodation moved from the forecastle to an after cabin. The boiler for the capstan was also accommodated in the cabin. Here the eight-man crew slept and ate their meals of broth, stew and fish, prepared on coal stove by the cook, who was usually the youngest hand.

Manx Nobby in Ireland

The Manx nobby (qv) evolved in the early 1880s as a smaller and more economical lug rigged drifter than the fast sailing nickey. Setting standing lug sails on both fore and mizzen masts, together with a jib on a long bowsprit, the nobby could be handled by a reduced crew and it was also cheaper to build. Nobbys were popular with Irish fishermen and many were bought new and secondhand from the Isle of Man. In addition, Irish versions of the Manx nobby were built, not only by boatyards in the east coast fishing stations of Portavogie and Arklow, to-

gether with Baltimore in west Cork, but also in the west coast counties of Galway and Donegal. While nobbys were favoured by many east coast fishermen, especially in Portavogie, large numbers of nobbys were built for and by the Congested Districts Board for Ireland as part of their improvement programme for the west coast fisheries. By 1906, the Board had purchased thirty-one nobbys from Manx boatyards and forty-seven from Irish boatyards. About half of the latter were built in Donegal and Galway under shipwright instructors provided by the CDB, while the majority of all of the Board-purchased nobbys were for use by fishermen in Co Galway.

By the mid 1880s, the developing Co Down fishing village of Portavogie, about 40 miles from the Isle of Man, had a fleet of over fifty Manx built herring and mackerel boats, mainly nobbys. However, in 1885 a local boatbuilder, William Mahood, began to build nobbys in Portavogie to meet the growing demand for this type of boat. Mahood continued to build nobbys until the First World War, his last boat of this type being the 41.5ft *Family Friend*, completed in June 1914 for Samuel Adair of Portavogie.

Scottish Zulu in Ireland

Although herring fleets of Scottish zulus (qv) were well known in Irish waters and some second hand zulus were bought by Irish fishermen, their main impact was on the western fisheries of Donegal and Galway, through the im-

proving activities of the Congested Districts Board for Ireland. The first boats were bought by the Board in 1896 in Frazerburgh, Scotland, at a cost of £80 each. By the following year the first Irish built zulu was under construction in Co Galway. By 1906, forty-six zulus had been built in Scotland for the Board and twenty-four in counties Galway and Donegal, most of the Irish zulus being built under the guidance of shipwright instructors provided by the Board. Although all the Board zulus built in Ireland and Scotland had the conventional rig of a dipping lug foresail and standing lug mizzen, they werre built to smaller dimensions than was usual in Scottish zulus, as the Irish boats were intended for both inshore and offshore fishing. With a maximum overall length of about 50ft, Board zulus were mainly supplied to fishermen in Co Donegal for the western herring and mackerel fisheries.

Sources
The nickeys in Ireland are covered in Michael McCaughan, 'Dandys, Luggers, Herring and Mackerel: A Local Study in the Context of the Irish Seas Fisheries in the Nineteenth Century', *The Irish Sea*, (Eds Michael McCaughan and John Appleby), (Belfast 1989), and also in his '*Mary Joseph* N55: A Nineteenth-Century Fishing Boat', *Ulster Folk and Transport Museum Year Book*, (1973/74). The nobby and the zulu in Ireland are dealt with by William P Coyne (Ed), *Ireland, Industrial and Agricultural* (Dublin 1902), and also in *Reports and Returns relating to the work of the Congested Districts Board for Ireland*, British Parliamentary Papers (various).

General Sources

Illustrations

The majority of the photographic illustration used in the book is held by the National Maritime Museum, Greenwich (credited NMM in the photo credits), and the majority of that from the Oliver Hill Collection. Commander Henry Oliver Hill RN gifted some 12,000 negatives to the Museum, most of which are of small sailing vessels and fishing boats. The MacPherson Collection contains Scottish material.

The Coastal Craft Collection of drawings at the Museum consists mainly of the work of Philip Oke. A number of his sail plans have not been included in this book for reasons of space but these are available through the Museum. They also hold a number of Oke's sketchbooks. The Maxwell Blake drawings are held privately.

Apart from photographs provided by the contributors and a number of individuals, most of the remaining illustration comes from local maritime museums and county libraries, and, as a general rule, these are good sources for images of local craft.

Unpublished material

The National Maritime Museum holds the thirty-two notebooks of Oliver Hill which contain a wealth of detail on small coastal craft and larger coastal trading vessels as well as information on seafaring generally. These were a useful source for some dimensions and some anecdotal information but they warrant closer study at some date in the future. Notebooks and albums of Eric McKee are also at the Museum

Published sources

The publications listed below are those which are referred to regularly in the 'Sources' throughout the book, simply by title and author, and their full bibliogrpahic details are given here. Where a book is a source for only one or two craft it is given its full details in the main run of the book and is not listed here at all. Thus the list below represents the best general works on the subject.

ANSON, PETER F, *Fishing Boats and Fisher Folk on the East Coast of Scotland* (London 1930)

CHRISTENSEN, ARNE EMIL (Ed), *Inshore Craft of Norway* (London 1979)

COOK, E W, *Shipping and Craft* (London 1829)

GREENHILL, BASIL, *Westcountry Boats* (London 1964)

HARRIS, KEITH, *Hevva: Cornish Fishing in the Days of Sail* (Redruth 1983)

HOLDSWORTH, E W H, *Deep-Sea Fishing and Fishing Boats* (London 1874)

HORNELL, JAMES, *Water Transport* (Cambridge 1946)

KEMP, DIXON, *A Manual of Yacht and Boat Sailing* (Seventh edition, London 1891)

LEATHER, JOHN, *Gaff Rig* (London 1989)
——, *Spritsails and Lugsails* (London 1978)

LETHBRIDGE, T C, *Boats and Boatmen* (London 1952)

MARCH, EDGAR J, *Sailing Drifters* (London 1952)
——, *Sailing Trawlers* (London 1953)
——, *Inshore Craft of Britain in the Days of Oar and Sail*, 2 volumes (Newton Abbott 1970)

MCKEE, ERIC, *Working Boats of Britain* (London 1983)

MOORE, SIR ALAN, *Last days of Mast and Sail – An Essay in Nautical Comparative Anatomy* (Oxford 1925)

OLIVER, A S, *Boats and Boatbuilding in West Cornwall* (Truro 1971)

REYNOLDS, STEPHEN, *Alongshore: Where Man and the Sea Face one Another* (London 1910)
——, *A Poor Man's House* (London 1911)

SANDERSON, MICHAEL, *The Development of the Boat: A Select Bibliography* (London, date unknown)

SIMPER, ROBERT, *Beach Boats of Britain* (Woodbridge 1984)

THURSTON HOPKINS, J, *Small Sailing Craft* (London 1931)

WARRINGTON-SMYTHE, H, *Mast and sail in Europe and Asia* (Edinburgh 1929)

WASHINGTON, CAPTAIN JOHN RN, *Report on the Loss of Life and Damage to Fishing Boats on the East Coast of Scotland* (Parliamentary Reports 1849)

WHITE, E M, *British Fishing-Boats and Coastal Craft* (London, 2-volume edition 1950, 1-volume edition reprinted 1973)

PAGE OPPOSITE   Ketch rigged fifie boat. *(NMM Philip Oke, neg no PAI7530)*

Index